THE NEW MILTON CRI

The New Milton Criticism seeks to emphasize ambivalence and discontinuity in Milton's work and to interrogate the assumptions and certainties in previous Milton scholarship. Contributors to the volume move Milton's open-ended poetics to the center of Milton studies by showing how analyzing irresolvable questions – religious, philosophical, and literary critical – transforms interpretation and enriches appreciation of his work. *The New Milton Criticism* encourages scholars to embrace uncertainties in his writings, rather than attempt to explain them away. Twelve critics from a range of countries, approaches, and methodologies explore these questions in new readings of *Paradise Lost* and other works. Sure to become a focus of debate and controversy in the field, this volume is a truly original contribution to early modern studies.

PETER C. HERMAN is Professor of English and Comparative Literature at San Diego State University.

ELIZABETH SAUER is Professor of English at Brock University, Canada.

THE NEW MILTON CRITICISM

EDITED BY
PETER C. HERMAN
AND
ELIZABETH SAUER

CAMBRIDGE UNIVERSITY PRESS

CAMBRIDGE UNIVERSITY PRESS
Cambridge, New York, Melbourne, Madrid, Cape Town,
Singapore, São Paulo, Delhi, Mexico City

Cambridge University Press
The Edinburgh Building, Cambridge CB2 8RU, UK

Published in the United States of America by Cambridge University Press, New York

www.cambridge.org
Information on this title: www.cambridge.org/9781107603950

© Cambridge University Press 2012

This publication is in copyright. Subject to statutory exception
and to the provisions of relevant collective licensing agreements,
no reproduction of any part may take place without the written
permission of Cambridge University Press.

First published 2012

Printed in the United Kingdom at the University Press, Cambridge

A catalog record for this publication is available from the British Library

Library of Congress Cataloging in Publication data
The new Milton criticism / [edited by] Peter C. Herman, Elizabeth Sauer.
p. cm.
Includes index.
ISBN 978-1-107-01922-5 (hardback) – ISBN 978-1-107-60395-0 (paperback)
1. Milton, John, 1608–1674–Criticism and interpretation.   I. Herman, Peter C., 1958–
II. Sauer, Elizabeth, 1964–
PR3588.N48   2012
821'.4–dc23
2011049970

ISBN 978-1-107-01922-5 Hardback
ISBN 978-1-107-60395-0 Paperback

Cambridge University Press has no responsibility for the persistence or
accuracy of URLs for external or third-party internet websites referred to in
this publication, and does not guarantee that any content on such websites is,
or will remain, accurate or appropriate.

Contents

Notes on contributors	*page* vii
Acknowledgments	xi
Note on editions	xii

	Introduction: Paradigms lost, paradigms found: the New Milton Criticism *Peter C. Herman and Elizabeth Sauer*	1

PART I THEODICIES

1.	Milton's fetters, or, why Eden is better than Heaven *Richard Strier*	25
2.	"Whose fault, whose but his own?": *Paradise Lost*, contributory negligence, and the problem of cause *Peter C. Herman*	49
3.	The political theology of Milton's Heaven *John Rogers*	68
4.	Meanwhile: (un)making time in *Paradise Lost* *Judith Scherer Herz*	85
5.	The Gnostic Milton: salvation and divine similitude in *Paradise Regained* *Michael Bryson*	102
6.	Discontents with the drama of regeneration *Elizabeth Sauer*	120

PART II   CRITICAL RECEPTIONS

7. Against fescues and ferulas: personal affront and the path to individual liberty in Milton's early prose   139
   Christopher D'Addario

8. Disruptive partners: Milton and seventeenth-century women writers   156
   Shannon Miller

9. Eve and the ironic theodicy of the New Milton Criticism   175
   Thomas Festa

10. Man and Thinker: Denis Saurat, and the old new Milton criticism   194
    Jeffrey Shoulson

11. The poverty of context: Cambridge School History and the New Milton Criticism   212
    William Kolbrener

12. Afterword   231
    Joseph A. Wittreich

Index   249

Notes on contributors

MICHAEL BRYSON is Associate Professor of English at California State University, Northridge. He is the author of *The Tyranny of Heaven: Milton's Rejection of God as King* (2004). He has also written on the relationship between sacrifice, death, and community formation in the book of Judges (in Religion and Literature), and has recently finished the manuscript for a new book on "The Atheist Milton."

CHRISTOPHER D'ADDARIO, Assistant Professor of English at Towson University, is author of *Exile and Journey in Seventeenth-Century Literature* (Cambridge, 2007). He has also written articles on John Donne, Abraham Cowley, and John Manningham's Diary that have been published or are forthcoming in *The Huntington Library Quarterly*, *English Literary Renaissance*, and various essay collections. His current book project is on perceptions of the everyday in early modern England.

THOMAS FESTA is Associate Professor at the State University of New York at New Paltz. He is author of *The End of Learning: Milton and Education* (2006) and editor, with Michelle M. Dowd, of *Early Modern Women on the Fall: An Anthology* (forthcoming). His articles on Milton, Donne, Browne, Shakespeare, Spenser, and Wordsworth have appeared, or are forthcoming, in *Milton Studies*, *Studies in Philology*, *English Language Notes*, and elsewhere. His essay "Milton's 'Christian *Talmud*'" (*Reformation* 8) won the 2004 William Tyndale Prize, awarded by the Stationers' Company of London.

PETER C. HERMAN is Professor of English and Comparative Literature at San Diego State University. He is the author of *Royal Poetrie: Monarchic Verse and the Political Imaginary of Early Modern England* (2010), *Destabilizing Milton: "Paradise Lost" and the Poetics of Incertitude* (2005), and *A Short History of Early Modern England: British Literature in Context* (2011). He is also the editor of *Approaches to Teaching Milton's Shorter Poetry and Prose* (2007), and the forthcoming *Approaches to Teaching Milton's "Paradise Lost"*, 2nd edition.

JUDITH SCHERER HERZ is Professor of English at Concordia University in Montreal. She works on both early modern and early twentieth-century writing. She has published two books on E. M. Forster and numerous articles and essays on, among others, Leonard Woolf, Donne, and Milton. She is a former President of the Association of Canadian College and University Teachers of English and of the John Donne Society.

WILLIAM KOLBRENER, Professor of English at Bar-Ilan University, is author of *Milton's Warring Angels* (Cambridge, 1997) and co-editor of *Mary Astell: Reason, Gender, Faith* (2007). His essays on early modern writing have appeared in journals such as *English Literary History*, *Common Knowledge*, *The Eighteenth Century*, and *Milton Studies*. His book on Jewish hermeneutics and epistemology, *Open Minded Torah: Of Irony, Fundamentalism and Love* was published in 2011.

SHANNON MILLER is Professor and Chair of the English Department at Temple University. She has authored *Invested in Meaning: The Raleigh Circle in the New World* (1998) and *Engendering the Fall: John Milton and Seventeenth-Century Women Writers* (2008). She has also published articles on women writers of the early modern period, including Mary Wroth, Mary Sidney, Margaret Cavendish, and Aphra Behn. Her current book project is titled "On the Margins of History: Studies in Seventeenth-Century Pamphlet Collections."

JOHN ROGERS, Professor of English at Yale University, authored *Matter of Revolution: Science, Poetry, and Politics in the Age of Milton* (1996), winner of the MLA Prize for a First Book, the James Holly Hanford Award (Milton Society of America), *Choice* magazine's award for an Outstanding Academic Book in 1996, and the Samuel and Ronnie Heyman Prize for Outstanding Scholarly Publication by a Yale Junior Faculty Member in the Humanities. He has also published articles on Milton, Marvell, early modern gender relations, and women's literary history in *English Literary History*, *Milton Studies*, the *Huntington Library Quarterly*, and in multiple essay collections. He has twice received awards from the Milton Society of America. *Milton's Passion* is forthcoming.

ELIZABETH SAUER, Professor of English at Brock University, has authored two books, *"Paper-Contestations" and Textual Communities in England* (2005) and *Barbarous Dissonance and Images of Voice in Milton's Epics* (1996). She has also edited twelve volumes, including *Milton and Toleration* with Sharon Achinstein (2007), *Milton and the Climates of Reading* (2006), *Reading Early Modern Women* with Helen Ostovich (2004), and *Books and Readers in Early Modern England* with Jennifer Andersen (2002). She is the recipient of awards from the Milton Society of America; *Choice*; The Society for the Study of Early Modern Women; and the Canada Council for the Arts (Killam Research Fellowship).

JEFFREY SHOULSON, Associate Professor of English and Judaic Studies at the University of Miami, is author of *Milton and the Rabbis: Hebraism, Hellenism, and Christianity* (2001), winner, American Academy of Jewish Research Salo Baron Prize for First Book in Judaic Studies, and co-editor, with Allison P. Coudert, of *Hebraica Veritas? Christian Hebraists and the Study of Judaism in Early Modern Europe* (2004). He is on the editorial board of *Milton Quarterly* and has served on the board of the Milton Society of America. His articles have appeared in *English Literary History*, *Journal of English and German Philology*, *Milton Studies*, and *Essays in Literature*. He is completing a book on "Fictions of Conversion: Jews, Christians, and Cultures of Change in Early Modern England."

RICHARD STRIER, Frank L. Sulzberger Professor at the University of Chicago, is author of *Unrepentant Renaissance From Petrarch to Shakespeare to Milton* (2011), *Resistant Structures: Particularity, Radicalism, and Renaissance Texts* (1995; pbk., 1997), and *Love Known: Theology and Experience in George Herbert's Poetry* (1983; pbk., 1986). He has edited *Writing and Political Engagement in Seventeenth-Century England* with Derek Hirst (Cambridge, 1999), *Religion, Literature and Politics in Post-Reformation England, 1540–1688* with Donna B. Hamilton (Cambridge, 1996), and *The Theatrical City: Culture, Theatre and Politics in London, 1576–1649* with David L. Smith and David Bevington (Cambridge, 1995; pbk. 2002).

JOSEPH A. WITTREICH is Distinguished Professor in the Ph.D. Program in English at the CUNY Graduate Center and Honored Scholar of the Milton Society of America. His books include *Why Milton Matters: A New Preface to His Writings* (2006); *Shifting Contexts: Reinterpreting "Samson Agonistes"* (2003); *Feminist Milton* (1987); *Interpreting "Samson*

Agonistes" (1986), winner of the James Holly Hanford Award; "*Image of that Horror*"*: History, Prophecy, and Apocalypse in* "*King Lear*" (1984); *Visionary Poetics: Milton's Tradition and His Legacy* (1979), *Angel of Apocalypse: Blake's Idea of Milton* (1975). He is also the author of dozens of articles, chapters, and reviews.

Acknowledgments

First and foremost, the editors want to thank Ray Ryan for his patience, wise guidance, and his confidence in this project, and we likewise extend our gratitude to the contributors for their diligence and collegiality, and for sharing their expertise with us. This volume also benefited tremendously from the constructive and incisive reports of the anonymous readers, which helped strengthen and sharpen our argument.

Peter C. Herman: I want to thank Joseph A. Wittreich for his work and for his example. Feisal Mohamed has been a worthy interlocutor, and John Rumrich consistently provided sage advice and much-needed encouragement. I owe my interest in law and literature to Constance Jordan, and I am privileged to have been, and continue to be, her student. I am also grateful to the Modern Language Association and the Renaissance Society of America for sponsoring panels on the New Milton Criticism, where some of these articles had their first public outing, and to the Milton and the Law Symposium at the University of London for inviting me to participate.

Elizabeth Sauer: I gratefully acknowledge the support of the Canada Council and Killam Trusts for a Killam Research Fellowship that provided invaluable release time. Additionally, I would like to thank the Social Sciences Humanities Research Council of Canada for its generous research funding, and my colleagues and students at Brock University for their counsel and community. Christopher Stampone served as a tremendously efficient, rigorous, and conscientious research and editorial assistant for this project. Particularly influential for me has been the Milton scholarship by Joseph A. Wittreich, Balachandra Rajan, Paul Stevens, Sharon Achinstein, Nigel Smith, and Barbara Lewalski.

While the naming of debts in the acknowledgments is a pleasure, we also take this opportunity to remember four people who are no longer with us: Douglas A. Brooks, John T. Shawcross, Marshall Grossman, and James Paxson. All were stellar scholars, colleagues, and friends. All are deeply missed.

Note on editions

Unless otherwise stated, all references to Milton's *Paradise Lost* are from Barbara K. Lewalski (ed.), John Milton, *Paradise Lost* (Oxford: Blackwell, 2007), and all references to Milton's prose works are from Don M. Wolfe (ed.), *Complete Prose Works of John Milton*, 8 vols. in 10 (New Haven: Yale University Press, 1953–82).

Introduction: Paradigms lost, paradigms found: the New Milton Criticism

Peter C. Herman and Elizabeth Sauer

"Conflict, ambivalence, and open-endedness" occupy a contested place in Milton studies.[1] While discontinuities in Milton's works have long been noted, Miltonists have traditionally regarded them as anomalies, and the critics who opted to explore, without resolving, them were often designated as marginal, or outliers in the field. The predilection for coherence and resolution in Milton studies has led Nigel Smith to observe that "the nature and complexity of [Milton's] contradictory energy is not appreciated, even by Milton specialists."[2] *The New Milton Criticism* seeks to provide and encourage the appreciation Smith calls for. The chapters assembled here interrogate various paradigms of certainty that have characterized many contributions to the field. This book also intends to show through a variety of approaches how analyses of Milton's irresolvable complexities can enrich our understanding of his writings. To be sure, as Paul Stevens recognizes, "there is a degree to which almost all Milton criticism tends to imagine itself, at some point, as the New Milton Criticism."[3] We hope, however, to earn this label by showcasing a Milton criticism resistant to reading Milton into coherence, a criticism that treats his work – *Paradise Lost* especially but not exclusively – as conflicted rather than serene, and that explicitly highlights the spirit of critical inquiry in Milton's writing.[4]

Interpretations of the Pilot metaphor in the first epic simile demonstrate how paradigms of certitude and a will to order have traditionally shaped criticism on *Paradise Lost*. In attempting to describe Satan's size to the reader, the Muse declares that the fallen angel is as huge as:

Some material in this Introduction first appeared in Peter C. Herman, "Paradigms Lost, Paradigms Found: The New Milton Criticism," *Literature Compass* 2 (2005). Article first published online December 21, 2005, DOI: 10.1111/j.1741–4113.2005.00176.x. We are greatly indebted to Richard Strier for his astute, corrective, and supportive remarks on the present chapter.

>   that Sea-beast
> *Leviathan*, which God of all his works
> Created hugest that swim th' Ocean stream:
> Him haply slumbring on the *Norway* foam
> The Pilot of some small night-founder'd Skiff,
> Deeming some Island, oft, as Sea-men tell,
> With fixed Anchor in his skaly rind
> Moors by his side under the Lee, while Night
> Invests the Sea, and wished Morn delayes:
> So stretcht out huge in length the Arch-fiend lay.
>   (1.200–9)

Crucially, Milton defies expectation and his various sources by *not* supplying the anticipated or traditional conclusion.[5] In fact, he leaves the episode unresolved, with the Pilot stranded on the whale "while Night / Invests the Sea, and wished Morn delayes" (1.207–8). Most readers assume that the whale dives and takes the Pilot with him, even though Milton's verses provide no such evidence. According to Roland M. Frye, "Just as Leviathan lured seamen to anchor on the seeming security of his great bulk, only then to plunge to the bottom of the sea and destroy them, so Satan had already lured his angelic followers to Hell and would so lure many deceived men and women in future ages."[6] Roy Flannagan notes that "'Leviathan' became synonymous with Satan, and the story of mariners anchoring on his back only to be swept under to their death was as popular as the similar Will-o'-the-Wisp or *ignis fatuus* story."[7] Bryan Adams Hampton predicts that the mariner "has unwittingly abandoned hope for returning home, finding rest, or simply surviving – a terrifying realization *he will have all too soon* when he finds himself lurching and plunging at the whims of the great creature" (emphasis added).[8]

Even when critics recognize that the story is not finished, they incline toward providing an expected ending. Christopher Grose, for example, concedes that "Milton omits the conclusion – at least it is not rehearsed," but then adds, "the ending, like the meaning of the simile, is hardly in doubt."[9] Linda Gregerson likewise decides that the morning "will presumably disclose to the pilot his doom."[10] Though Milton leaves the Pilot's fate unclear, critics almost uniformly impose a closure that the passage itself resists, and thus miss opportunities afforded by Milton's invitation to a multivalent and open-ended reading. By deliberately withholding the conventional ending, is Milton creating a moment when the reader, suddenly faced with a passage that defies expectation, must re-assess the possible significances of the passage? What might be the relations between this simile and the other epic figures and devices that end in a similarly suspended fashion, such as the Plowman who "doubting stands" (4.983), unsure of how his harvest will turn out? William Kerrigan, who is among the few who are sensitive to the open-endedness of the Pilot simile, suggests that the "ominous lack of closure in this story" represents the "excess and uncertainty" of poetry, which allows Milton "to outwit as well as absorb philosophy."[11] Others will arrive at their own conclusions, but our point is that by not supplying the ending Milton leaves out, we invite a richer set of interpretations in much the same way that Shakespeareans now approach *Measure for Measure*:

> Critical efforts to exorcise the play's demons, to disregard Shakespeare's illumination of the darker regions of the soul, in effect deny the play one of its boldest claims to truth. And to impose any external ... solutions ... is, in fact, to deny this play its rightful claims to greatness. Finally, it seems impertinent to consider it the duty of criticism to solve the problems that Shakespeare himself refused to solve. What remains pertinent are the problems posed.[12]

Similarly, the New Milton Criticism encourages criticism that does not solve the problems that Milton himself resists solving.

I: EARLY MILTON CRITICISM

The paradigm of imposing certainty on an unruly Miltonic text could be said to have started with the addition of Andrew Marvell's poem, "On *Paradise Lost*," to the second edition of *Paradise Lost* (1674). Faced with the vastness of the subject and the poet's nerve ("I behold the Poet blind, yet bold" [1]), Marvell, like another early reader of the poem, Sir John Hobart,"[13] feared that Milton, embittered by the loss of his sight and likely also by the failure of his revolutionary hopes, would do something terrible:

> ... the Argument
> Held me a while misdoubting his Intent,
> That he would ruine (for I saw him strong)
> The sacred Truths to Fable and old Song
> (So *Sampson* groap'd the Temples Posts in spight)
> The World o'rewhelming to revenge his sight.
> (ll. 5–10)

In the opening stanza of this encomium, Marvell registers uncertainty about the poet's intentions and perhaps also his overreaching: "the Argument / Held me *a while* misdoubting his Intent" (ll. 5–6; emphasis added). Would Milton's overweening strength "ruine … / The sacred Truths to Fable and old Song" (ll. 7–8)? The Samson image that follows remains deeply resonant and deeply troubling – "(So *Sampson* groap'd the Temples Posts in spight) / The World o'erwhelming to revenge his sight" (ll. 9–10). Is the poem a hymn of resentment? Initially unsettled by what David Norbrook aptly characterizes as "the aggressive, iconoclastic aims of Milton's epic, which run counter to the patriotic harmony the conservative reader might ask for," Marvell's speaker realizes that his worries over the poem's impulses are unfounded, for they are "more creative than destructive."[14] Moreover, nothing in this poem violates decorum, as Marvell later determines: "Thou hast not miss'd one thought that could be fit, / *And all that was improper dost omit*" (ll. 27–8; emphasis added). Though Marvell's fears about the ruining of "sacred Truths" are allegedly allayed, assurance does not overwrite his earlier anxieties. Late in Marvell's poem, *Paradise Lost* still seems to present a sense of real danger to "sacred Truths" and a sacred inner core. At line 34, one notes the strange and strong word "inviolate" set off by stops. The threat of Milton's "strength" lingers. The very fact that Marvell rehearsed such concerns suggests, along with his endorsement of Milton's versification as a vehicle for liberty and rebellion, that this poem will not necessarily repeat or endorse pieties. At the end of the century, in 1699, Milton's biographer John Toland felt compelled to defend his subject against the proliferating charges of "Heresy and Impiety."[15] Faced with a poem that challenges convention and defies a definitive interpretation, some of Milton's Restoration readers and editors would do some fitting or omitting of their own.

In *The State of Innocence and Fall of Man: An Opera Written in Heroique Verse* (1677), for example, John Dryden openly rewrites Milton's epic.[16] As he states in prefatory remarks, "The Authors Apology for Heroique Poetry; and Poetique Licence," "I cannot without injury to the deceas'd Author of *Paradice Lost*, but acknowledge that this POEM has receiv'd its entire Foundation, part of the Design, and many of the Ornaments, from him" (sig. B1r). Despite Marvell's assurances of the poem's observance of decorum, *Paradise Lost* evidently did not sit well with a Restoration audience, and Nathaniel Lee, in his prefatory poem, "To Mr. DRYDEN, on his POEM of PARADICE," suggests some of the reasons why John Dryden would feel compelled to revise Milton's masterwork: "For *Milton* did the Wealthy Mine disclose, / And rudely cast what you could well dispose: / He roughly drew, on an old fashion'd ground, / A Chaos, for no perfect World was found, / Till through the heap, your mighty Genius shin'd; / His was the Golden Ore which you refin'd" (sig. A4r).

But in refining, as it were, the ore, Dryden highlights those parts of Milton's text that he finds unsettling. For example, at the end of Book 3, Milton has Satan transform himself into a cherub, and in this disguise, he suborns Uriel, "The sharpest sighted Spirit of all in Heav'n" (3.691), into revealing the location of Eden: "So spake the false dissembler unperceiv'd; / For neither Man nor Angel can discern / Hypocrisie …" (3.681–3). This passage creates all sorts of problems, not the least being: if Satan can so easily delude the "sharpest sighted Spirit," what chance do Adam and Eve have? Dryden, however, rewrites *Paradise Lost* so as to restore certainty and resolve the problem. In his version, Uriel tells Satan the location, but the angel immediately suspects that something is amiss:

> Not unobserv'd thou goest, who e'r thou art;
> Whether some Spirit, on Holy purpose bent,
> Or some fall'n Angel from below broke loose,
> Who com'st with envious eyes, and curst intent,
> To view this World, and its created Lord:
> (sig. C3v)

Dryden deals similarly with the problem of Milton's God, a character who has disturbed many readers and continues to do so to this day, as the essays in Part 1 of this volume discuss in some detail. In the eighteenth century, Alexander Pope complained that "God the Father turns a school-divine,"[17] and the controversy continues, the most famous example being William Empson's *Milton's God*, in which he accuses the Christian deity in *Paradise Lost* and elsewhere of resembling Stalin.[18] Dryden proceeds to eliminate God entirely from his rhymed rewriting of Milton's epic, thus stabilizing potentially subversive aspects of the text. Dryden's strategy throughout this poem, as Joseph A. Wittreich writes, is "to cancel out Miltonic ambiguity,"[19] to restore the poem to certainty.

Related efforts to address misgivings about the poem mark eighteenth-century criticism. John Dennis's defense in the 1720s of Milton against the aspersions of George Sewell exemplifies the desire for aesthetic integrity or "justness" in his reading of *Paradise Lost*, and specifically in the depiction of the epic machinery and the ontology of the angels. "Most of the Machines … have the appearance of something that is inconsistent and contradictory, for in them the Poet seems to confound Body and Mind, Spirit and Matter," is Sewell's objection. Dennis judges the human, corporeal nature of the angels and demons as more "delightful" and as enabling "more clear and distinct Ideas of them." Milton's own rendering of the angels,

Dennis maintains, follows that of Cowley and Tasso, whose "Descriptions of those fall'n Angels [are devoid of] any real Contradiction," and further, they have taken "the trouble of shewing, that what is thought to be a real Contradiction, has but the false Appearance of one."[20]

The seeming debate between Richard Bentley and Zachary Pearce in the 1730s offers more telling examples of the compulsion to stabilize the poem. The debate, however, is "seeming" because the two are not as opposed as they initially might appear. As William Empson first noted,[21] the impetus to make *Paradise Lost* conform to preconceived notions of religious orthodoxy underlies Richard Bentley's infamous theory that, "Some acquaintance of our Poet's, entrusted with his Copy, took strange Liberties with it, unknown to the blind Author …" (sig. B1r),[22] and Bentley's edition occasioned furious opposition, the most famous example being Pearce's thorough *Review of the Text of Milton's "Paradise Lost"* (1732–3). Pearce's *modus operandi* is instructive, for he always explains how the moments Bentley objects to as unconventional or contradictory are, if only "properly" understood, perfectly traditional. Thus, the two agree on what *Paradise Lost* should be, but whereas Bentley judges that Milton's poem needs to be purged of supposedly interpolated passages that compromise its integrity, Pearce concludes that *Paradise Lost* is for the most part intact and already perfectly acceptable. Both maintain that the poem should be absolutely consistent and contain no contradictions.

For example, Bentley mightily objected to the metaphors in *Paradise Lost* on the grounds of incongruity. At the end of Book 4, Milton uses an epic simile to illustrate the confrontation between Satan and his enemies, namely Gabriel, Ithuriel, Zephon, and the remainder of the angelic squadron:

> While thus he spake, th' Angelic Squadron bright
> Turnd fierie red, sharpning in mooned hornes
> Thir Phalanx, and began to hemm him round
> With ported Spears, as thick as when a field
> Of Ceres ripe for harvest waving bends
> Her bearded Grove of ears, which way the wind
> Swayes them; the careful Plowman doubting stands
> Least on the threshing floore his hopeful sheaves
> Prove chaff.
>
> (4.977–85)

Bentley senses two problems here. First, the simile troubles him by portending the defeat of the angels, since Milton compares their spears to wheat ripe for the harvest. Second, the plowman who "doubting stands," wondering whether he has wheat or chaff, introduces incertitude. Both are anathema to Bentley. In order to eliminate the introduction of doubt, Bentley brackets "the Careful Plowman ..." in the text of his edition, and suggests that this phrase be eliminated: "Join the two pieces of Verse together: *Which way the Wind / Sways them. On the other side* Satan *alarmed*" (sig. T4r). Because the Plowman clause introduces doubt, the lines could not, in Bentley's view, have been written by Milton: "The pragmatical Editor inserted the Two between; which clearly betray whose Manufacture they are" (sig. T4r). As for the rest of the simile, Bentley huffs: "What are sheaves bound up in a Barn to the Phalanx, that hem'd Satan? Where's the least Similitude? Besides to suppose a *Storm* in the Field of Corn, implies that the Angels were in a ruffle and hurry about *Satan*, not in regular and military Order" (sig. T4r). But Pearce counters that Milton's similes and epic comparisons only *seem* problematic: "that here is no Contradiction at all; for *Milton* in his similitudes (as is the practice of *Homer* and *Virgil* too), after he has shew'd the common resemblance, often takes the liberty of wandring into some unresembling Circumstances" (sig. F2v–r). Pearce rebuts Bentley's accusation of impropriety in two ways. First, he emphasizes how Milton's technique is not novel, but entirely traditional ("as is the practice of *Homer* and *Vergil*"). Second, Pearce defuses the problem of doubt by dismissing these lines as a mere flight of fancy, of no thematic import whatsoever: Milton "often takes the liberty of wandring into some unresembling Circumstances: which have no other relation to the Comparison." Pearce preserves orthodoxy by refusing to grant that these lines carry any weight at all.

In his edition of *Paradise Lost,* Bentley frequently highlighted instances where he decided that Milton contradicted himself, and as Empson pointed out, thus became an invaluable guide to the many problems in *Paradise Lost*. The fact that he regarded these problems as corruptions is less important "than the fact that he saw them at all."[23] In a sense, it is Pearce who establishes the paradigm for later criticism by continuously resolving the contradiction, as he does in the quotation above ("here is no Contradiction at all"). When Bentley objected to the famous oxymoron, "darkness visible" (1.63) because the phrase constitutes "a flat Contradiction" (sig. B3v), Pearce responds: "I cannot agree with him: *M.* seems to have us'd these words to signify *Gloom*: Absolute darkness is strictly speaking invisible; but where there is a Gloom only, there is so much Light remaining as serves to shew that there are objects, and yet that those Objects cannot be distinctly seen" (sig. B5r). Note that both deny the possibility of contradiction in Milton.

II: CONTEMPORARY MILTON CRITICISM

One could attribute these interpretive gyrations to the influence of neo-classicism, dismissing Dryden, Bentley, and Pearce as representatives of the same literary culture that embraced Nahum Tate's revival "with alterations" of Shakespeare's *King Lear* (1681), except that one finds similar assumptions governing some of the best Milton criticism throughout later centuries. Christopher Ricks's study of Milton's similes in his remarkable and still deeply influential *Milton's Grand Style* provides a case in point.[24] Generally, Ricks successfully demonstrates that Milton composed verse as subtle as any New Critic could wish, despite the attacks of F. R. Leavis and T. S. Eliot, but when he comes to Milton's troublesome similes, Ricks draws the same conclusions as Pearce. Faced with the Plowman simile, Ricks notes that Bentley left out these lines, and he has the benefit, as obviously Bentley did not, of Empson's brilliantly iconoclastic reading of this simile as demonstrating that the poem constitutes an attack on God and a celebration of Satan's rebellion. Ricks grants that Empson has a point: "[The simile] certainly makes the angels look weak. If God the sower is the ploughman, then he is anxious; another hint that he is not omnipotent. If the laboring Satan is the ploughman he is only anxious for a moment, and he is the natural ruler or owner of the good angels."[25] Consequently, Ricks is faced with a doubly difficult task, as he must defend Milton's verse against the combined forces of the anti-Miltonists, who charge Milton with writing bad verse, and Empson, who reveals Milton's religious and poetic unorthodoxy. Ricks responds by neatly rehearsing Pearce's rebuttal of Bentley. Just as the earlier critic defended Milton's conventionality by aestheticizing the similes and evacuating them of all meaning – Milton "often takes the liberty of wandring into some unresembling Circumstances: which have no other relation to the Comparison, than that it gave him the Hint, and (as it were) set fire to the train of his Imagination" (sig. F2r–v) – so does Ricks determine that "Mr. Empson is jubilant, since this allows him either way to make the poem pro-Satan and anti-God. But it seems more likely that here we do have one of the epic similes, beautiful but digressive."[26] Both Pearce and Ricks defuse the problem by emptying the simile of any thematic significance.[27]

For other twentieth-century Miltonists, the problem of the narrator, or narrators, poses similar difficulties. In her influential study on narrative voice, which she distinguishes from the poet himself, Anne D. Ferry argues that "[t]hroughout *Paradise Lost* we find statements by the narrator which at least in part contradict the impression made immediately upon us by the actions or speeches of the characters. These apparent contradictions must of course be explained, if we are to be satisfied with our reading of the poem." Ferry judges that a satisfying reading experience demands the presence of a univocal, ubiquitous narrator who successfully conveys an "impression of conscious control, deliberate artistry, and carefully articulated method."[28] Louis Martz, and, in the following decades, William Riggs, Arnold Stein, and John Guillory subscribe to a view of the narrator as authoritative, or as Stanley Fish later puts it, "a natural ally against the difficulties of the poem."[29] J. Martin Evans opts for Riggs's identification of the narrator with Milton as author by eliding the distinctions between them while also announcing that the narrator is "not a single euphonious instrument but a chorus of individual and sometimes discordant voices."[30] The criticism we are advancing here invites the interrogation of questions like narrative authority by, as Joseph A. Wittreich states in his Afterword, "reach[ing] beyond the narrator's voice to narrative voices, and then to the questions of whether some are privileged and, more challengingly, to an assessment of the relative reliability of those often competing voices." In the case of *Paradise Lost*, the multiple, often irreconcilable, narrative perspectives are among the features that prevent the poem from adding up to one monumental whole.

Balachandra Rajan identified the commitment to coherence made by various Milton scholars, initially including himself, as a "unifying imperative."[31] Among the examples thereof that appear in seminal works of Milton scholarship is Diane Kelsey McColley's integrationist, regenerationist defense of Eve, a character she rescues from "a reductive critical tradition," as Milton himself is said to have redeemed Eve "from a reductive literary and iconographic tradition."[32] In the same year in which *Milton's Eve* appeared, Barbara Lewalski published the results of her pioneering analysis of the multiple genres of *Paradise Lost* as exemplifying the poem's capacity to blend multiplicity into unity.[33] The synthesis of the heterogeneous becomes the order of the day. In a later essay, Lewalski again reminded us that the "generic paradigms" of the poem are multiple, consisting of the heroic genres, the epic-of-wrath, the quest epic, the romance, tragedy, and others. The successful assimilation of the genres into a unified whole constitutes the multi-genre epic, which, she points out, is not marked by "the indeterminacy and inconclusiveness" that Russian genre-theorist Mikhail Bakhtin associates with early modern and later prose narratives.[34] One also sees some evidence of a "unifying imperative" in Gordon Teskey's prize-winning *Delirious Milton* (2006). At first, Teskey argues that "Milton's creative power is drawn from a rift at the center of his consciousness over the question of Creation itself, forcing him to oscillate between two incompatible perspectives, at once affirming and denying the presence of spirit in what he creates."[35] But later in the book, instances of the predilection for certainty appear in the form of Teskey's proposition that "dissonances become harmonies," and in the statement that "[t]he very difficulty of imagining such diverse works as Milton wrote composing a unity *impels us to seek that unity on a higher plane*" (emphasis added).[36]

In various cases, the gravitational pull toward unification in Milton studies is complemented by a methodological prudence in the scholarship, partly evident in the limited impact theoretical developments have had on the field. Post-structuralism, for example, did not gain many adherents among Miltonists, though it did produce Nyquist and Ferguson's landmark anthology, *Re-membering Milton*, which explicitly criticized Milton scholarship "for its comparative indifference to the theoretical literature and debates" of the 1970s and 1980s.[37] A few critics, including Herman Rapaport, Catherine Belsey, and Jonathan Goldberg applied their understanding of deconstruction to Milton, but this approach did not gain many followers.[38] The New Milton Criticism follows in the wake of the deconstructionist concern to explore textual moments of contradiction and ambivalence. The central difference is that the New Milton Criticism tends not to take its inspiration from French theory or philosophy, but from close readings of Milton's texts and from critical and theoretical evaluations of the interpretive histories of those texts.

Locating Milton in relation to historical, religious, and political contexts came naturally for many Miltonists after and even during the reign of the New Criticism, if one considers, for example, A. S. P. Woodhouse and Arthur Barker. The New Historicist movement, however, failed to make a significant impression on Milton studies.[39] Stanley Fish dismissed what he called "the New or Newer Historicism" on the grounds of its supposed incoherence: "Historicism ... is embarrassed because it refuses to do the work and indeed doesn't even know what its work *is*," and gleefully announced that the failure of post-structuralism and New Historicism does not matter because "the layered richness of Milton criticism ... continues to propel it forward no matter what the deficiencies of various new methods and nonmethods."[40] Needless to say, we disagree with Fish's blanket dismissal, though it is apparent that New Historicist theories of power, authorship, and theories about the effect of literature on historical change have not been enthusiastically embraced.[41] Miltonists' discontents with the movement gave rise instead to a Milton liberated from Foucauldian-inflected interpretations, a "self-representing" figure whose self-division leaves his authority intact and virtually uncontested.[42]

Arguably the most forceful and uncompromising articulation of the will-to-order in Milton is Fish's *How Milton Works*. Echoing perhaps Lewalski's dismissal of "indeterminacy and inconclusiveness," Fish asserts toward the start of the first chapter, "The Miltonic Paradigm," that "conflict, ambivalence, and open-endedness – the watchwords of a criticism that would make Milton into the Romantic liberal some of his readers want him to be – are not constitutive features of the poetry but products of a systematic misreading of it."[43] Slightly later, he banishes the problem of doubt: "In Milton's world, however, there are no moral ambiguities, because there are no equally compelling values. There is only one value – the value of obedience – and not only is it a mistake to grant independence to values other than the value of obedience, it is a temptation."[44] To think otherwise, Fish maintains, is to be not just mistaken but irreverent, even heretical.

To be clear, in calling attention to a preference for certainty and stability in statements by various major critics, we do not dismiss or denigrate their work, but rather attempt to present some examples of a dominant paradigm and trajectory in this field of criticism. Further, we recognize that the examples of Milton criticism surveyed in the Introduction and throughout the volume represent merely a fraction of the voluminous scholarship on Milton. Even so, the treatment of the Pilot episode by critics and editors alike and the examples from the brief history of Milton criticism sketched out here suggest a degree to which Milton studies is inclined toward a unifying imperative and the reining in of contrary energies.

Indisputably, evidence of the recognition and appreciation of Miltonic contradiction and irresolution appears throughout the centuries, while surfacing most noticeably in the Romantic period and later in the work of John Peter, A. J. A. Waldock, and, among others, Denis Saurat, as Jeffrey Shoulson cogently argues in his contribution to this volume.[45] But in the mid 1980s, the lineaments of a new Milton criticism became more readily apparent in the scholarship of such critics as Mary Nyquist, Balachandra Rajan, Paul Stevens, Thomas N. Corns, and John P. Rumrich, all of whom sought to recast uncertainty as a constituent element in Milton's writings, thereby opening up opportunities to identify and work through new problems.[46] And throughout the 1990s, Joseph A. Wittreich published a powerful series of articles that expressly called for a new Milton criticism, a desire "to nudge Milton criticism into the future tense,"[47] in response to his observation that Milton studies "has been paralyzed, indeed impoverished, by the suppression of … conflicts or just plain avoidance of them" (1997), which he reiterated at the start of *Shifting Contexts: Reinterpreting "Samson Agonistes"* (2002) and in *Why Milton Matters* (2006).[48] Among the critics who anticipated or accepted Wittreich's challenge are William Kolbrener, Jeffrey Shoulson, Michael Bryson, and Peter C. Herman.[49] Yet these scholars wrote largely in isolation from each other, as have subsequent critics who studied Milton's discontinuities.[50] Nobody realized they were part of a larger group.

That is now changing because, as J. Martin Evans recently attested, something fundamental is happening to Milton criticism: "Milton's works are now beginning to be seen as sites of contention and conflict rather than unified verbal and intellectual structures or syntheses of heterogeneous ideas and values."[51] Given the resistance to the imposition of unity or coherence on Milton's work, it is appropriate that the New Milton Criticism not speak with one voice. Herman and Strier, for example, disagree about the matter of intentionality in *Paradise Lost*.[52] What unites these essays, however, is the commitment to interpretations that expose, as Stephen Greenblatt writes in a different context, "the half-hidden stress points …, the tensions, ideological negotiations and rifts that are often plastered over."[53] This anthology gives the New Milton Criticism a local habitation and a name by seeking first of all to make explicit a tendency in Milton studies to rein in the parts of Milton's writings that go in surprising and unexpected directions. Secondly, we attempt to demonstrate the advantages of embracing "conflict, ambivalence, and open-endedness" by providing both a genealogy for the New Milton Criticism and illustrations of what happens when critics resist pressure to resolve ambivalences in Milton's key works.

III: THEODICIES

The question of Milton's relationship to normative Christianities has a long history and has never been further from being definitively answered.[54] Martin Larson concluded in the 1920s that Milton "had much more of the rational, the ethical, the pagan, the modern, the one-world point of view" than his Protestant counterparts,[55] but this view was not about to take root. Orthodox readings of Milton's poetics and Christianity, supported in part by the influential and formidable Anglo-American school of E. M. W. Tillyard, Douglas Bush, C. S. Lewis, and others, would – as Jeffrey Shoulson and Elizabeth Sauer point out in their contributions to this volume – bestow a long life on the "neo-Christian" Milton, despite efforts by Christopher Hill and William Empson to investigate different sides of the poet's relationship to religion.[56] Miltonists scrutinized the evidence available in a poem that set out to justify God's ways. From the aforementioned John Peter, who complained about the irritating and poetically unsound practice of anthropomorphizing God, which left readers with no choice but to denounce God's ways as "vindictive and devious,"[57] to Dennis Danielson who claimed two decades later that the aesthetic success of *Paradise Lost* depended on the depiction of God's goodness, critics have sought to settle the lingering issue of Milton's religious commitments. Related questions on Milton's theodicy, on free will versus determinism, on the justness or tyranny of God's ways, and on the politics of Milton's Heaven have vexed critics and commentators for three centuries, since controversies over Milton's Christianity and his literary representations of God first erupted. The following six chapters on Milton's great poems join with scholarship on Milton's religious and literary unorthodoxies[58] by exemplifying ways of gauging the above-mentioned issues through examinations of the "discordant" elements in the verse.

We begin with an essay that connects the New Milton Criticism and the literary criticism of key Romantic poets attentive to the fault-lines – and fetters – in Milton's poetry, notably in the representation of his theodicy. Richard Strier's interpretation in Chapter 1 of the poem's Great Argument is comparable to Dennis Danielson's influential reading thereof: *Paradise Lost* sets out to justify and reinforce God's goodness. However, whereas Danielson and others maintain that the poem's aesthetic and religious success was tied to the success of its theodicy, Strier demonstrates that Milton's effort to represent his theodicy produces aesthetic and religious failures or what William Blake called "fetters." Milton writes without "fetters" in depicting prelapsarian life, which was not, however, part of the project of theodicy.

Peter C. Herman frames questions of theodicy in the terms of early modern developments in litigation and the nascent legal doctrine of contributory negligence that are applied in his chapter to a compelling investigation of the issue of blame in *Paradise Lost*. Using the paradigm of the New Milton Criticism, which does not insist on Milton's certainty or orthodoxy, Herman shows that Milton provides several answers to the question, "Whose fault?" thus establishing a vital context for an unsettling reading of the poem as indicting, rather than exonerating, God.

John Rogers reminds us that Milton criticism has consistently reinforced the stability of Miltonic belief, the standard of which is generally taken to be a consistent articulation of identifiable theological, political, or social positions. Milton indeed is largely responsible for this situation, having produced innumerable instances of the literary affect of conviction, most obviously in his representation of the political theology of Milton's Heaven. His surprisingly unsympathetic representation of arbitrary authority in Heaven works, argues Rogers, to provide a mythological point of origin for the principles of human liberty and "the most radical form of creaturely freedom he could imagine." The result is a more compelling account of the tensions at play in the poem's portrayal of God than those previously articulated.

"Eternalist" critics, Rogers recently argued,[59] tend to present a Milton whose beliefs are certain and stable, while the "temporalist" critics are more inclined to affiliate Milton with the post-structuralist ideals of open-endedness and ambiguity. Applying this distinction, Judith Scherer Herz complicates notions of linearity, temporality, and chronology in Milton, thus challenging the claims to narrative stability founded on these features. The recurrent term "meanwhile" becomes the perfect temporal marker for a text whose undecidability is a function of its endlessly recursive structure. Herz traces the word's movement through *Paradise Lost*, with particularly close attention to Book 10, examining its spatialization of time, its questions about theodicy, its unsettling of narrative coherence, and its relation to other markers of undecidability.

The penultimate chapter in this section deals with a different set of epistemological issues while returning to the questions on theodicy raised by Strier, Herman, and Rogers. Michael Bryson revisits his pronouncement in *The Tyranny of Heaven* about Milton's antithetical relationship to Gnosticism, showing instead that the Son of *Paradise Regained* embodies a form of Miltonic Gnosticism, a poetic attempt to leave an external concept of God for a concept of God found within.

The second of the two companion poems in the 1671 volume is the subject of the final essay in Part 1. Elizabeth Sauer examines *Samson Agonistes*, a poem whose received tradition has been underwritten by the "neo-Christian" perspectives and regenerationist readings. In a text for which "there seems to be a counterstatement for every statement,"[60] efforts to settle on a definitive reading of Samson's catastrophic final act entail a suppression of *Samson Agonistes*' counterstatements, including Dalila's apologia, which, in conjunction with the dramatic poem's contentious reception history, defy the containment of its "fifth act."

IV: CRITICAL RECEPTIONS

The essays in the second part of this book study Milton's self-portrayal and his writings in terms of literary critical readings generated in Milton's own time through to the present day. The received tradition of Milton's works is marked by acts of suppression, but also reassessment and rewriting throughout the more than three centuries of Milton criticism. In the following six chapters, the recasting of Milton as poet and polemicist sheds light on the fraught nature of the critical endeavors and methodologies of Miltonists, while exhibiting what William Kolbrener describes as "a Milton whose complex and sometimes multiple intentions elude the singularity of the simplistic contextualist grasp."

Less attention has generally been devoted to the rhetorical function of uncertainty in Milton's prose than in his poetry. When the prose has been considered in this regard, as in the provocative work of Stanley Fish, it is typically with a sense that Milton intentionally contrived ambiguities with a pedagogical objective. In the opening chapter of Part II, Christopher D'Addario examines Milton's pamphlets defending domestic liberty, in order to trace the extent to which Milton transforms personal affront and doubts over the response to his writing into principled political and religious stances on liberty. Rather than exploring the personal origins of Milton's theories to elucidate the author's psychology, D'Addario probes the inherent inconsistencies that arise in a theory of individual liberty originating in distrust and assumed misunderstanding.

Shannon Miller broadens the early modern context from which Milton's work derives its significance and which it informs. One of the key developments in the field has been the contextualization of Milton's work in terms of non-canonical, extra-literary, and popular writings that resituate and compel a reassessment thereof.[61] The conversation Miller develops between Milton's major epic and earlier narratives of the Garden and the Fall, particularly those in writings of Rachel Speght and Aemilia Lanyer, challenges established readings of Milton's representations of gender and structures of governance. The "traces" of the gender-inflected "influences" on *Paradise Lost* also prompt such later writers as Mary Chudleigh and Aphra Behn to respond. *Paradise Lost* thereby becomes an incitement to later reconfigurations of the gender hierarchy in Eden. Investigating the question of gender while advancing the study of Milton's theodicy discussed in Part I of this volume, Thomas Festa reads *Paradise Lost* through Eve's narrative of her birth as Edward Young appropriates it in his *Conjectures on Original Composition* (1759). Contrary to more orthodox interpreters from the first and last centuries of the epic's reception, Young valorizes Eve's self-discovery in ways that predict the afterlife of the epic in the later centuries.

Turning to the more recent antecedents of the New Milton Criticism and the theological positions articulated in Milton's work, Jeffrey Shoulson deftly argues that Denis Saurat's 1925 *Milton: Man and Thinker* was the underlying trigger for the Milton Controversy and played a particularly important role in the development of Empson's antithetical readings of *Paradise Lost*. Many of the most provocative and controversial claims associated with the New Milton Criticism can in fact be traced back to Saurat's sustained and comprehensive analysis of Milton's poetry and thought.

The twentieth-century critical tradition analyzed by William Kolbrener in the penultimate chapter of Part II concentrates on the contextualist methodology of the Cambridge School Historians such as Quentin Skinner and J. G. A. Pocock. The Skinnerian paradigm of "language-games" and the desire to situate texts as performative utterances within specific rhetorical contexts contributed to re-historicizing political philosophy and moving it away from considerations of "universal truths" and "perennial problems." Yet the rigors of Skinnerian methodology, which, as conceived in the late sixties, demanded "consistency of expression and perspective," may not always serve in elucidating the complexity of Miltonic texts. The development of a methodology aware of the potentially reductive tendencies of the contextualizing gesture is among the practices of the New Milton Criticism.

The final essay in "Critical Receptions" is Wittreich's Afterword, which expertly weaves the volume's contributions into a map of reading. This denouement advances the critical methodology outlined in the Introduction and offers an exemplum of the New Milton Criticism and its applications. Wittreich anticipates new directions and orientations in Milton studies and in literary history more broadly, which the New Milton Criticism opens up for the twenty-first-century reader, one who is "less taken with certainties than with new opportunities." Rather than assuming that Milton's problems are puzzles to be solved and that if "properly understood," all conflicts resolve into reassuring certitude, the essays in this volume demonstrate that we gain much more by allowing the ambiguities and ambivalences to stand and transform our interpretive experiences. In conclusion, by moving Milton's sites of contention into the center of Milton studies, we hope to establish the parameters of a vital, resonant, and destabilizing approach: the New Milton Criticism.

NOTES

1 Stanley Fish, *How Milton Works* (Cambridge, MA: Harvard University Press, 2001), p. 14.
2 Nigel Smith, *Is Milton Better than Shakespeare?* (Cambridge, MA: Harvard University Press, 2008), p. 7.
3 Paul Stevens, "Introduction: Milton in America," in Paul Stevens and Patricia Simmons (eds.), "Milton in America," special issue of *The University of Toronto Quarterly* 77, 3 (2008), 790 n. 1.
4 In *Re-membering Milton*, editors Mary Nyquist and Margaret W. Ferguson expressed their discontents with the monumentalizing of Milton. See "Introduction," in Mary Nyquist and Margaret W. Ferguson (eds.), *Re-membering Milton: Essays on the Texts and Traditions* (New York: Methuen, 1987), pp. xvi–xvii.
5 See for example, Matteo Maria Boiardo, *Orlando Innamorato* ii.xiv.3 and Ariosto, *Orlando Furioso* vi.37–43.
6 Roland M. Frye, *Milton's Imagery and the Visual Arts: Iconographic Tradition in the Epic Poems* (Princeton University Press, 1978), p. 93.
7 Roy Flannagan (ed.), *The Riverside Milton* (Boston: Houghton Mifflin, 1998), p. 360 n. 80.
8 Bryan Adams Hampton, "Milton's Parable of Misreading: Navigating the Contextual Waters of the 'Night-Founder'd Skiff in *Paradise Lost*, 1.192–200," *Milton Studies* 43 (2004), 95.
9 Christopher Grose, *Milton's Epic Process: "Paradise Lost" and its Miltonic Background* (New Haven: Yale University Press, 1973), p. 152.
10 Linda Gregerson, "The Limbs of Truth: Milton's Use of Simile in *Paradise Lost*," *Milton Studies* 14 (1980), 142.
11 William Kerrigan, "Milton's Place in Intellectual History," in Dennis Danielson (ed.), *The Cambridge Companion to Milton,* 2nd edn. (Cambridge University Press, 1999), p. 264.
12 Harriett Hawkins, "'The Devil's Party': Virtues and Vices in *Measure for Measure*" (1978), in Catherine M. S. Alexander (ed.), *The Cambridge Shakespeare Library, Vol. 2: Shakespeare Criticism* (Cambridge University Press, 2003), p. 44. See also A. D. Nuttall's analysis of Shakespeare's *A Midsummer Night's Dream* as a play whose "suppression of dark forces is not only incomplete at the beginning ... [but] ... remains incomplete throughout": "*A Midsummer Night's Dream*: Comedy as *Apotrope* of Myth," *Shakespeare Survey* 53 (2000), 51, 52.
13 James M. Rosenheim, "An Early Appreciation of *Paradise Lost*," *Modern Philology* 75, 3 (1978), 281.
14 David Norbrook, *Writing the English Republic: Poetry, Rhetoric and Politics 1627–1660* (Cambridge University Press, 1999), p. 491.
15 John Toland, *The Life of John Milton* (London, 1699), sig. I1v.
16 John Dryden, *The State of Innocence and the Fall of Man: An Opera Written in Heroique Verse* (London, 1677). Critical treatments of Dryden's "opera" assume that it remained unperformed. Elizabeth Bobo, however, has discovered that

The State of Innocence was indeed performed – by *puppets*! ("Advertising in *The Spectator* and the Early 18th Century Promotion of *Paradise Lost*," unpublished paper delivered at the Pacific Coast British Studies Conference, 2010.) We are grateful to Professor Bobo for allowing us to read and cite her work in advance of publication.

17 Quoted in Michael Bryson, *The Tyranny of Heaven: Milton's Rejection of God as King* (Newark, DE: University of Delaware Press, 2004), p. 24.

18 William Empson, *Milton's God* (London: Chatto & Windus, 1961), p. 146. See also Bryson, *The Tyranny of Heaven*, pp. 24–6, and Peter C. Herman, *Destabilizing Milton: "Paradise Lost" and the Poetics of Incertitude* (New York: Palgrave Macmillan, 2005), pp. 107–11.

19 Joseph A. Wittreich, "Milton's Transgressive Maneuvers: Receptions (Then and Now) and the Sexual Politics of *Paradise Lost*," in Stephen B. Dobranski and John P. Rumrich (eds.), *Milton and Heresy* (Cambridge University Press, 1998), p. 249.

20 John Dennis, "Letters on Milton and Wycherley," *The Proposals for Printing By Subscription … Miscellaneous Tracts (1721–1722)*, in E. N. Hooker (ed.), *The Critical Works of John Dennis* (1939), quoted in John T. Shawcross (ed.), *Milton: The Critical Heritage: 1628–1731* (London: Routledge and Kegan Paul, 1970), pp. 240, 242.

21 William Empson, "Milton and Bentley," in *Some Versions of Pastoral* (New York: New Directions, 1960), pp. 141–84.

22 Richard Bentley, *Milton's Paradise Lost: A New Edition* (London, 1732). Subsequent citations are parenthetical.

23 Empson, "Milton and Bentley," p. 141; Strier, private correspondence (e-mail dated 17 August 2011).

24 For example, Annabel Patterson begins *Milton's Words* (Oxford University Press, 2009) with a discussion of Ricks's book and how it essentially rescued Milton from the negative evaluations of T. S. Eliot and F. R. Leavis (pp. 1–3).

25 Empson, "Milton and Bentley," p. 164. Christopher Ricks quotes Empson in *Milton's Grand Style* (Oxford: Clarendon Press, 1963), pp. 129–30.

26 Ricks, *Milton's Grand Style*, p. 130.

27 Gordon Teskey adopts a similar strategy to nullify the problems of Milton's classical allusions when he proposes that we should ignore the resonances of Satan's resemblance to Virgil's Turnus or the Son to Hector: "the similarity is largely irrelevant because Milton is not alluding to the spirit of the earlier context" (Gordon Teskey, *Delirious Milton: The Fate of the Poet in Modernity* [Cambridge, MA: Harvard University Press, 2006], p. 126). Nor is this approach limited to Milton. Rosamond Tuve, for example, proposed that "the aim of criticism is to eliminate strangeness," and therefore, William Empson's views on Herbert must be rejected because of his "'illegal' critical practices" resulting in "'illegitimate' readings [that] must be detected and rebuked" (see Richard Strier, "Tradition," *Resistant Structures: Particularity, Radicalism, and Renaissance Texts* [Berkeley: University of California Press, 1995], pp. 24, 17).

28 Anne D. Ferry, *Milton's Epic Voice: The Narrator in "Paradise Lost"* (Cambridge, MA: Harvard University Press, 1963), p. 17.
29 Louis Martz, *The Paradise Within; Studies in Vaughan, Traherne, and Milton* (New Haven: Yale University Press, 1964), p. 107; William Riggs, *The Christian Poet in "Paradise Lost"* (Berkeley: University of California Press, 1972); Arnold Stein, *The Art of Presence: The Poet and "Paradise Lost"* (Berkeley: University of California Press, 1977); John Guillory, *Poetic Authority: Spenser, Milton, and Literary History* (New York: Columbia University Press, 1983), p. 104; Stanley Fish, *Surprised By Sin: The Reader in "Paradise Lost,"* 2nd edn. (Cambridge, MA: Harvard University Press, 1997), p. 47.
30 J. Martin Evans, *Milton's Imperial Epic: "Paradise Lost" and the Discourse of Colonialism* (Ithaca: Cornell University Press, 1996), pp. 170 n.1, 113; see also Stephen M. Fallon, *Milton's Peculiar Grace: Self-Representation and Authority* (Ithaca: Cornell University Press, 2007), pp. 2–3.
31 Balachandra Rajan, "Surprised by a Strange Language: Defamiliarizing *Paradise Lost*" [1985], in Elizabeth Sauer (ed.), *Milton and the Climates of Reading: Essays by Balachandra Rajan* (University of Toronto Press, 2006), pp. 46–63.
32 Diane Kelsey McColley, *Milton's Eve* (Urbana: University of Illinois Press, 1983), p. 4.
33 Barbara Lewalski, "The Genres of *Paradise Lost*: Literary Genre as a Means of Accommodation," in Richard S. Ide and Joseph A. Wittreich (eds.), "Composite Orders: The Genres of Milton's Last Poems," *Milton Studies* 17 (1983), 75–103. See Balachandra Rajan's critique in *Form of the Unfinished: English Poetics from Spenser to Pound* (Princeton University Press, 1985), p. 111.
34 Barbara Lewalski, "The Genres of *Paradise Lost*," in Dennis Danielson (ed.), *The Cambridge Companion to Milton* (Cambridge University Press, 1989), pp. 84, 81–2. Balachandra Rajan argues in contrast that *Paradise Lost*, "is not simply a mixed-genre poem but a poem of which generic uncertainty may be a keynote. Critics may be understandably reluctant to admit uncertainty at the heart of a poem. A work of art thus divided is considered to be in a state of civil war. But creative indeterminacy can also be read as a sign of the authentic rather than the chaotic" (Balachandra Rajan, "*Paradise Lost*: The Uncertain Epic," *Milton Studies* 17 [1983], 105–19).
35 Teskey, *Delirious Milton*, p. 5.
36 Ibid., pp. 150, 149. See Joseph A. Wittreich's review of Teskey's *Delirious Milton* in *Renaissance Quarterly* 59, 4 (2006), 1332; and Herman, *Destabilizing Milton*, p. 7. More emphatically and recently than Teskey, Feisal G. Mohamed, in his trenchant study of Milton's pre-secular thought and current post-secular political theory and ethics, maintains that Milton "makes us keenly aware of the limits of an emphasis on ambiguity, for his writings continually subsume contrary energies." Feisal G. Mohamed, *Milton and the Post-Secular Present: Ethics, Politics, Terrorism* (Stanford University Press, 2011), p. 2.
37 Nyquist and Ferguson, "Preface," *Re-membering Milton*, p. xvi.

38 Herman Rapaport, *Milton and the Postmodern* (Lincoln: University of Nebraska Press, 1983); Catherine Belsey, *John Milton: Language, Gender and Power* (New York: Blackwell, 1988); Jonathan Goldberg, "Dating Milton," in Elizabeth D. Harvey and Katharine Eisaman Maus (eds.), *Soliciting Interpretation: Literary Theory and Seventeenth-Century English Poetry* (University of Chicago Press, 1990), pp. 199–220.

39 The New Historicism's adoption of deconstruction's emphasis on textual aporias is what distinguishes this movement from the "Old Historicism."

40 Stanley Fish, "Milton's Career and the Career of Theory," in Stanley Fish, *There's No Such Thing as Free Speech: And It's a Good Thing, Too* (Oxford University Press, 1994), p. 266. See also Stanley Fish, "Why Milton Matters; Or, Against Historicism," *Milton Studies* 44 (2005), 1–12.

41 Even so, the New Historicism's cousin, the "New Bibliography," which takes its cue from Michel Foucault's essay, "What is an Author?" ([tr. Donald F. Bouchard and Sherry Simon], in Donald F. Bouchard [ed.], *Language, Counter-Memory, Practice* [Ithaca, NY: Cornell University Press, 1977], pp. 124–7) has made significant inroads in Milton criticism; see in particular Stephen B. Dobranski's groundbreaking work on Milton and the book trade [Stephen B. Dobranksi, *Milton, Authorship, and the Book Trade* (Cambridge University Press, 1999)].

42 Fallon, *Milton's Peculiar Grace,* p. 12. Blair Worden observed that Milton's own self-representations "invite us to situate him in lonely eminence above the collaborative world of civil war polemic" (Blair Worden, *Literature and Politics in Cromwellian England: John Milton, Andrew Marvell, Marchamont Nedham* [Oxford University Press, 2007], p. 208), but the political historical criticism of Worden, Laura Knoppers, Nigel Smith, Sharon Achinstein, and David Loewenstein, among others, has complicated that unified self-portrayal by putting him squarely in the midst of the turbulence and barbarous dissonance from which he sought to sequester himself.

43 Fish, *How Milton Works*, p. 14.

44 Ibid., p. 53.

45 On the reception of Milton by the Romantics, see Lucy Newlyn, *"Paradise Lost" and the Romantic Reader* (Oxford: Clarendon Press, 1993); Leslie Brisman, *Milton's Poetry of Choice and Its Romantic Heirs* (Ithaca: Cornell University Press, 1973). See Balachandra Rajan's survey of Milton criticism in the 1930s and 1940s in *"Paradise Lost" and the Seventeenth Century Reader* (London: Chatto & Windus, 1947; reissued 1962), p. 11. See also Sharon Achinstein's penetrating analysis of the academic climate and literary critical wars of the mid-twentieth century in "Cold War Milton," *University of Toronto Quarterly* 77, 3 (2008), 801–26.

46 Nyquist and Ferguson (eds.), *Re-membering Milton* (1987); Rajan, "Surprised by a Strange Language," *Milton and the Climates of Reading*, pp. 46–63; Paul Stevens, "Discontinuities in Milton's Early Public Self-Representation," *The Huntington Library Quarterly* 51, 4 (1988), 260–80; Thomas N. Corns, "'Some Rousing Motions': The Plurality of Miltonic Ideology," in Thomas Healy and Jonathan

Sawday (eds.), *Literature and the English Civil War* (Cambridge University Press, 1990), pp. 110–26; Goldberg, "Dating Milton", pp. 199–220; John P. Rumrich, "Uninventing Milton," *Modern Philology* 87, 3 (1990), 249–65.

47 Wittreich, "Milton's Transgressive Maneuvers," p. 246; Wittreich, "'Inspir'd with Contradiction': Mapping Gender Discourses in *Paradise Lost*," in Diana T. Benet and Michael Lieb (eds.), *Literary Milton: Text, Pretext, Context* (Pittsburgh: Duquesne University Press, 1994), pp. 10–60; Wittreich, "'He Ever was a Dissenter': Milton's Transgressive Maneuvers in *Paradise Lost*," in Kristin Pruitt McColgan and Charles W. Durham (eds.), *Arenas of Conflict: Milton and the Unfettered Mind* (Selinsgrove: Susquehanna University Press, 1997), pp. 21–40; Wittreich, "Why Milton Matters," 22–39.

48 Joseph A. Wittreich, "'He Ever was a Dissenter,'" p. 36; *Shifting Contexts: Reinterpreting "Samson Agonistes"* (Pittsburgh: Duquesne University Press, 2002), pp. xiii ff.; Wittreich, *Why Milton Matters* (New York: Palgrave Macmillan, 2006), p. xxii.

49 Bryson's and Herman's books, along with John T. Shawcross's *Rethinking Milton Studies: Time Present and Time Past* (Newark: University of Delaware Press, 2005), led to Wittreich's observation that Milton studies is "switching to a revised paradigm" (*Why Milton Matters*, p. xxii).

50 See, for example, Yaakov Mascetti, "Satan and the 'Incompos'd' Visage of Chaos: Milton's Hermeneutic Indeterminacy," *Milton Studies* 50 (2010), 40, 62 n.18.

51 J. Martin Evans, "Critical Responses: Recent," in Stephen B. Dobranski (ed.), *Milton in Context* (Cambridge University Press, 2010), p. 152.

52 Perhaps because Milton, unlike, say, Shakespeare, oversaw the publication and revision of his works, Milton criticism is largely committed to intentionalism. Stanley Fish, for example, in the early 1990s rejected his earlier belief in meaning as a creation of interpretive communities (see the last four essays in *Is There a Text in this Class? The Authority of Interpretive Communities* [Cambridge, MA: Harvard University Press, 1980]) in favor of arguing that "meaning, intention, and biography are inextricable" (Stanley Fish, "Biography and Intention," in William H. Epstein [ed.], *Contesting the Subject: Essays in the Postmodern Theory and Practice of Biography and Biographical Criticism* [West Lafayette: Purdue University Press, 1991], p. 15). Having presented a valuable survey of the treatment (chiefly, the suppression) of intention in literary criticism, Stephen Fallon reads Milton with intention in mind while simultaneously acknowledging the "unresolved tensions in the author" that surface unintentionally (Fallon, *Milton's Peculiar Grace,* p. 12). Even so, some Miltonists, such as Strier but also Sharon Achinstein, have maintained that a more skeptical approach toward intentionalism "could open up Milton studies to new ideas and new resources of creativity" (Sharon Achinstein, "Cloudless Thunder: Milton in History," *Milton Studies* 48 [2008], 10).

53 Stephen Greenblatt, "Introduction: New World Encounters," in Stephen Greenblatt (ed.), *New World Encounters* (Berkeley: University of California Press, 1993), p. xvi.

54 Cf. Patrick Murray, *Milton: The Modern Phase* (London: Longman, 1967), p. 96.
55 Martin Larson, *The Modernity of Milton: A Theological and Philosophical Interpretation* (University of Chicago Press, 1927), p. 168.
56 C. S. Lewis, *A Preface to "Paradise Lost"* [1942] (London: Oxford University Press, 1963); Empson, *Milton's God*, Christopher Hill, *Milton and the English Revolution* (New York: Viking, 1978).
57 John Peter, *A Critique of "Paradise Lost"* (New York: Columbia University Press, 1960), p. 17; Dennis Richard Danielson, *Milton's Good God: A Study in Literary Theodicy* (Cambridge University Press, 1982, reprinted 2009), p. ix.
58 For example, Dayton Haskin's *Milton's Burden of Interpretation* (University of Pennsylvania Press, 1994), William Poole's *Milton and the Idea of the Fall* (Cambridge University Press, 2005), and Catherine Gimelli Martin's rigorous reassessment of Milton's Puritanism, *Milton among the Puritans: The Case for Historical Revisionism* (Aldershot: Ashgate, 2010).
59 John Rogers, "Time and Eternity and the Fiction of Miltonic Belief," The New Milton Criticism, Modern Language Association Convention, Philadelphia, PA, 2006.
60 Joseph A. Wittreich, *Feminist Milton* (Ithaca: Cornell University Press, 1987), p. 134.
61 Laura Knoppers and Gregory M. Colon Semenza (eds.), *Milton in Popular Culture* (New York: Palgrave Macmillan, 2006).

PART I

Theodicies

CHAPTER 1

Milton's fetters, or, why Eden is better than Heaven

Richard Strier

This essay joins the chorus of those from Blake to Tillyard and beyond who have seen *Paradise Lost* as a poem deeply divided against itself.[1] The essay is not a "Satanist" reading, although it does adopt a number of premises of the "Satanist" view. It adopts Blake's idea that Milton wrote "in fetters" of God and the good angels, and it will adopt Shelley's view of Heaven and Hell in the poem as, in a sense, morally equivalent.[2] It will try to address Empson's feeling that even though the Shelleyan view is true, it "leaves the mind unsatisfied" because, in holding it, one "becomes so baffled in trying to imagine how Milton came to write as he did."[3] The most problematic and unsatisfactory aspects of the poem will be seen as flowing directly from Milton's conscious and articulated intentions: to show God to be good, or at least, not to be wicked. Where I differ from many other critics is that while they think that the aesthetic (and religious) success of the poem depends on the success of its theodicy,[4] I think that the attempt at theodicy – whether one regards it as successful or not – produces most of the aesthetic and religious failures of the poem. I see the great aesthetic and religious success of the poem, where Milton wrote without fetters, as being in an area free of the Great Argument: the presentation of Eden and of unfallen human life within it.

RATIONALISM (AND ON CHRISTIAN DOCTRINE)

It is important to be clear from the outset about the implications of theodicy. It is essentially a rationalistic project. Although many critics are confused about this, it is not a project that an *echt* Calvinist would

---

Portions of this essay appeared as "Milton's Fetters, or, Why Eden is Better than Heaven," in Michael Lieb and Albert Labriola (eds.), "John Milton: the Author in His Works," *Milton Studies* 38 (2000), 169–97, and are here reproduced with permission from Duquesne University Press. The current version is updated and revised.

attempt. As John Rumrich has rightly noted, the context represented by the shared beliefs of Luther and Calvin was "deeply inimical to the very notion of theodicy."[5] The idea of showing God to be "good" – of showing divine actions to correspond to some humanly intelligible conception of fairness – verged upon blasphemy for Luther and Calvin. Luther mocked Erasmus for wanting God to be "good."[6] The author of *Paradise Lost* stands squarely with Erasmus. The desire to "*assert* Eternal Providence" is not necessarily rationalistic – something can be asserted, after all, in the face of evidence and common sense – but the intention to "justifie the wayes of God to men" is indeed a rationalistic project (1.25–6). There is, moreover, a slight but telling ambiguity in this famous formulation. Line 26 may be read as stating either that what the poet is going to justify is "the ways of God to men," meaning how God behaves toward mankind, or as stating that the poet is going to justify "the ways of God" in general, and is promising to do so in terms that will be humanly intelligible. The difference, in other words, is (roughly) between stating a subject-matter ("the ways of God to men") and stating a philosophical-rhetorical project ("to justifie … to men"). We cannot initially choose between the readings. The prominent "Man" in line 1 would probably favor the former, but as soon as the action gets underway, we recognize that Milton's topic is larger than "the wayes of God *to men*." We come to realize that the second meaning, "justifie … to men," must be the intended one. The goal is rational explanation.

This is where *On Christian Doctrine* is helpful. Whatever its authorship, it can help us understand Renaissance theological rationalism. Even if the evidence is strong that the treatise probably is by Milton, W. B. Hunter has done a service not only in reopening the authorship issue, but in pointing to the intellectual lineage of the treatise.[7] It belongs, as Maurice Kelley had earlier argued, squarely in the line of the rationalist and biblicist critics of Reformation theology, the line of Servetus and Arminius.[8] Anti-Trinitarianism is a good place to begin. The major argument in the treatise against the orthodox doctrine of the Trinity is not that the doctrine is unbiblical (though the treatise does dispute the biblical sources); the main argument is that the doctrine is unreasonable. God's oneness must be understood "in the numerical sense, *in which human reason always understands it*" (*CPW* 6:216; italics mine). The argument by which this author is most troubled is that while Scripture "does not say in so many words that the Father and the Son are essentially one," this conclusion can be logically deduced from various passages (*CPW* 6:222). In the face of this, the author retreats, momentarily, from "mere reason."

But he is not happy with this strategy. He poses the question, "I ask you, what can reason do here?" (*CPW* 6:222). The author's answer is not, as one might expect, "nothing," but "everything." But formally correct inferences are not enough to constitute reason. "The product of reason must be reason" – that is, "reasonable." "Reason" cannot produce "absurd notions which are utterly alien to all human ways of thinking." Reasonableness trumps reasoning.

If, for this author, anti-Trinitarianism protects Christianity from being intellectually unintelligible, anti-Calvinism protects it from being morally so. Nothing is more important to *On Christian Doctrine* than the assertion of free will. Only this doctrine can prevent God from being seen as wicked.[9] The author does, in fact, conceive of Luthero-Calvinism as a form of devil-worship. For Luther, as I have suggested, it was the essence of Christianity to outrage "natural reason" in just this way. For the author of *On Christian Doctrine*, Christianity never offended natural reason. Of those who "do not hesitate to assert that God is, in himself, the cause and author of sin," he writes: "If I did not believe that they said such a thing from error rather than wickedness, I should consider them of all blasphemers the most utterly damned" (*CPW* 6:166). He cannot even conceive of their view. The doctrine of double predestination is "repulsive and unreasonable" and therefore must be false (*CPW* 6:180). Moral autonomy is an absolute premise: "everyone is provided with sufficient innate reason … to resist evil desires by his own efforts" (*CPW* 6:186); sufficient grace is necessary, but God considers all persons "worthy of sufficient grace" (*CPW* 6:193). This view does not, as the Luthero-Calvinists say, swell man with pride, but rather allows "divine wisdom and justice" to become apparent (*CPW* 6:190).

Christian Doctrine tends to see all conceptions of necessity as negative. "From the concept of human freedom," it says, "all idea of necessity must be removed" (*CPW* 6:161). This is a conception of freedom as entirely a matter of deliberation and choice. But it is important to see that in the religious and the philosophical traditions, there are alternative conceptions of freedom. Luther asserted "the bondage of the will," yet the core of his system was the idea of "Christian freedom."[10] Freedom was his great watchword, and what "Christian freedom" meant was precisely the opposite of deliberation. Freedom was freedom from calculation, from weighing of options, from attempting to live up to demands. It was freedom from self-conscious selfhood, a spontaneous outpouring of gratitude toward God that expresses itself in love for and happy service of one's neighbor.[11] Freedom and necessity are not in opposition. The "free" person, for Luther, acts out of an inner necessity, a necessity to express his joy and sense of liberation. This is a conception of "freedom" entirely different from the deliberative one of *On Christian Doctrine*.

In many respects, Luther is an anti-Platonist, but the conception of goodness as involving non-ratiocinative spontaneity, abundance, and overflowing has its origin and home in the Platonic tradition; it is part of what A. O. Lovejoy has called "the principle of plenitude." Lovejoy brilliantly traced out how, in Plato, "the concept of Self-Sufficing Perfection, by a bold logical inversion, was – without losing any of its original implications – converted into the concept of Self-Transcending Fecundity."[12] Plotinus contributed to both sides of this dialectic, but he was especially important in developing the latter. Without "communication" – not of meaning, but of being – he explained, "the Good would not be Good."[13] That "all that is fully achieved engenders" is a fundamental premise for Plotinus.[14] This "higher Kind of engendering" is "a natural process" – which means, as Plotinus quite explicitly holds, that the cosmos is "a product of Necessity, not of deliberate purpose."[15] And it is better that this should be so since, he argues, the cosmos would be worse if it were the product of deliberation.[16] As Ernst Cassirer puts it, emanation stands "not in the sign of freedom, but in that of necessity."[17] This tradition came close to Milton. Arminius insisted that "God is good by a natural internal necessity, not freely"; and the English Platonist George Rust, Milton's contemporary, noted that "If you pitch upon the Platonick way," you must "assign the production of all things to that exuberant fullness of life in the Deity" – that is, to "the blessed necessity of his most communicative nature."[18]

The author of *On Christian Doctrine* is aware of this conception. At one point he acknowledges that it may be said that in God there is "a certain immutable internal necessity to do good," but he insists that this "can be consistent with absolute freedom of action" (*CPW* 6:159). He does not, however, stick to this "compatibilist" position. He ends the discussion by withdrawing his initial tentative assent to it – "Nor, incidentally, do I concede the point that there is in God any necessity to act" (*CPW* 6:159). He prefers to believe, as he said earlier, that God is "not impelled by any necessity" (*CPW* 6:154). As part of his anti-Trinitarianism, he asserts that "this particular Father begot his Son not from any natural necessity but of his own free will" – a method, the author assures us, "more excellent and more in keeping with paternal dignity" (*CPW* 6:209). Similarly, this author argues that the Holy Spirit was "created, that is, produced, from the substance of God, not by natural necessity but, by the free-will of the agent" (*CPW* 6:298). Finally, in a remarkable passage on Creation, this author attempts to reconcile a vision of diffusion with a vision of will: "It is, I say, a demonstration of God's supreme power and goodness that he should not shut up this heterogeneous and substantial virtue within himself, but should disperse, propagate and extend it as far as, and in whatever way, he wills" (*CPW* 6:308). This passage attempts to bring the vision of plenitude, of propagation, and of "substance" all under the aegis of will. As to the coherence of this attempt, opinions differ. As to the motive of the attempt, there is no doubt: to make deliberative choice cosmically central.

REASON OR FORCE? POLITICS EVERYWHERE

In embarking on the Great Argument, Milton asks the Muse/Spirit to "say first … / … what cause" (1.27–8). He is proceeding in what we know he considers the most rational manner, since in the *Art of Logic*, he characterizes providing a cause as "the source of all knowledge" (*CPW* 8:222). We do not yet know, however, what sort of rational–causal explanation we are going to be given. It turns out that we are going to be given an explanation through an account of a malicious agent – "Who first seduc'd them to that foul revolt?" (1.33). The focus has already shifted from the Fall of Man, the announced subject of the poem, to the agent who was the "cause" of this Fall. Understanding this agent is presented as the necessary context for understanding the Fall. The way in which this agent is initially described is our first indication of the terms in which Milton will attempt to carry out the rational explanation that he has promised. Out of the poet's loathing for the event and the malicious agent of it ("foul revolt … infernal Serpent"), a larger story, with more specific terms of description, begins to emerge:

>   he it was, whose guile
> Stird up with Envy and Revenge, deceiv'd
> The Mother of Mankind, what time his Pride
> Had cast him out from Heav'n, with all his Host
> Of Rebel Angels, by whose aid aspiring
> To set himself in Glory above his Peers,
> He trusted to have equal'd the most High,
> If he oppos'd; and with ambitious aim
> Against the Throne and Monarchy of God
> Rais'd impious War in Heav'n and Battel proud[.]
>   (1.34–43)

What is striking about this description is the way in which it moves from using moral terms as explanatory – "Envy and Revenge ... Pride" – to telling its story in political terms – "aspiring ... above his Peers"; "ambitious aim / Against the ... Monarchy." As Empson says, "it is all weirdly political."[19] When, in a wonderful moment, Milton first shifts from describing Satan to having him speak, Satan turns out to view his story in military and political terms as well. He acknowledges God's superior weaponry ("the stronger prov'd / He with his Thunder" [1.92–3]), and asserts that neither for thunder nor:

> what the Potent Victor in his rage
> Can else inflict, do I repent or change,
> Though chang'd in outward lustre, that fixt mind
> And high disdain, from sence of injur'd merit,
> That with the mightiest rais'd me to contend,
> And to the fierce contention brought along
> Innumerable force of Spirits arm'd
> That durst dislike his reign, and me preferring,
> His utmost power with adverse power oppos'd[.]
> (1.95–103)

Satan seems to have a clear and recognizable sense of himself. The discontented courtier, servant, or military figure suffering from "sense of injur'd merit" was a familiar figure in Elizabethan and Jacobean drama – think of Bosola, Iago, or Coriolanus. We know how complex these figures can be. We do (or should) immediately recognize that we are witnessing here one of these complex portrayals. The challenge the poem is setting for itself is not in Satan's self-description but in his portrayal of God.

For Satan, God is "the Potent Victor"; he sees God's only attribute (aside from wrath) as power.[20] For this, God desires to be worshipped (that others "bow ... / ... and deifie his power" [1.111–12]). This characterization continues throughout Book 1. In Satan's third speech, he presents a completely Nominalist view of God: through power, God "can dispose and bid / What shall be right" (1.246–7). The whole situation is entirely a product of power – "Whom reason hath equald, force hath made supream" (1.248). Satan's insistence on his unchanged mind is part of his recognition of the limits of physical coercion. The picture of God that the fallen angels consistently present is of a sadistic, vindictive, and implacable conqueror who takes pleasure in their suffering. They see God's consciousness as exactly parallel to their own: "tearms of peace" have been neither "Voutsaf't or sought" (2.331–2). The key point, again, is not "none ... sought" but "none / Voutsaf't." The challenge that Milton has set for himself by having both his narrator and the fallen angels talk in political terms is to distinguish Heaven from Hell *in these terms*.

One of the problems involved in doing this is the difficulty of keeping political life in Hell demonic rather than merely, well, political. A spectacular example occurs in the narrator's comment on Belial's speech in the demonic council: "Thus *Belial* … / Counsell'd ignoble ease, and peaceful sloath, / Not peace" (2.226–8). This is perhaps an apt comment on the speech in general political terms, but it makes no sense in the narrative context. Apart from the dubious paradoxes of *felix culpa,* wouldn't it be better for the cosmos if the fallen angels had adopted a policy of "ease" and sloth, however "ignoble" from some neutral strategic–political point of view? A case that might seem easier is that of the unanimity of the fallen angels. Satan claims this as a positive and distinguishing feature of Hell – "a safe unenvied Throne / Yielded with full consent" (2.23–4). This is echoed in the "full assent" (2.388) of the fallen angels to the Beelzebub–Satan plan. Such agreement might seem merely to confirm how "diabolical" they all are. Yet Milton is quite struck by this unanimity, and finds himself in the anomalous position of admiring the fallen angels. He attempts to untangle the situation by turning his admiration for the political life of fallen angels into an attack on the political life of fallen humans:

> O shame to men! Devil with Devil damn'd
> Firm concord holds, men onely disagree
> Of Creatures rational, though under hope
> Of heavenly Grace: and God proclaiming peace,
> Yet live in hatred, enmity, and strife[.]
> (2.496–500)

Yet this is clearly a desperate move. The "devilishness" of the devils is bracketed. In a similar moment a few lines earlier Milton (or "the narrator") was forced to acknowledge that "neither do the Spirits damn'd / Loose all thir vertue" (2.482–3).

So, if Milton has a hard time keeping politics in Hell diabolical, we must now ask whether he is any more successful in keeping heavenly politics heavenly. The challenge is to counter the view of God as He whom "force hath made supream" (1.248). This means that mockery of Satan for being weaker than God or for fighting against an overwhelmingly more powerful force is irrelevant (not to say, with Shelley, morally contemptible). The key texts for examining Satan's claims about God are in Books 5 and 6, since the War in Heaven is the immediate "historical" context for all the actions and speeches in Books 1 and 2. Virtually all attentive readers of *Paradise Lost* have noted that the "history" that the poem includes begins with the Exaltation of the Son before the angels dramatized toward the end of Book 5.[21] This Exaltation is a pure fiat:

> Hear my Decree, which unrevok't shall stand.
> This day I have begot whom I declare
> My onely Son, and on this holy Hill
> Him have anointed, whom ye now behold
> At my right hand; your Head I him appoint;
> And by my Self have sworn to him shall bow
> All knees in Heav'n, and shall confess him Lord[.]
> (5.603–9)

All the major verbs here denote divine action – "begot … declare … anointed … appoint." The responses of the angels are commanded – "shall bow / All knees … and shall confess." The next lines attempt to present this event as beneficent toward the angels – "Under his great Vice-gerent Reign abide / United as one individual Soule / For ever happie" (5.609–11) – but this vision is still governed (not just grammatically) by an imperative ("abide"), and is, in any case, quite obscure. Rather than explicating this benevolent command, God immediately turns to a warning in which only Milton's Latinate treatment of English keeps the focus on the Son rather than on the wicked ("Him who disobeyes / Mee disobeyes" [5.611–12]), and then to a detailed, terrifying threat: "Cast out … / Into utter darkness … / without end" (5.613–15). I do not mean to suggest that Satan's response to this speech, "envie against the Son of God, that day / Honour" (5.662–3), is an admirable one. But I do mean to suggest that his specific claim, "new Laws thou seest impos'd" (5.679), is true; and that the lie he tells – "I am to haste / … Homeward … / … there to prepare / Fit entertainment to receive our King" (5.686–90) – is plausible.

The only answer to Lucifer/Satan's account in Book 5 is Abdiel's. He accuses Satan of ingratitude – given Satan's high and favored position in Heaven – and then asks the great Job-like Nominalist–Reformation question, "Shalt thou give Law to God …?" (5.822). Luther or Calvin could leave the matter there, but Milton cannot. Abdiel then argues that the angels have abundant evidence of God's beneficence, and notes that God in fact proclaimed beneficence to them in the "Under his … Vice-gerent … abide / United" lines. After producing another argument from power – the Son was the instrument of God's Creation of "All things, ev'n thee [Satan]"(5.837) – Abdiel finally attempts to make sense of the claim that the Exaltation of the Son somehow benefits the angels:

> nor by his Reign obscur'd,
> But more illustrious made, since he the Head
> One of our number thus reduc't becomes,
> His Laws our Laws, all honour to him done
> Returns our own.
>
> (5.841–5)

This argument is clearly hard going, since the key line – "One of our number thus reduc't becomes" – is, even by Miltonic standards, contorted. The idea seems to be that the Son, by becoming the "Head" of angels, is "reduced" to being one of them, which in turn raises the status of the angels. This is tricky, and the next lines sound like a sophistical argument for how special treatment of one member of a group is not special treatment ("all honour to him done / Returns our own").

What is central, however, is not the claim that the Son's exaltation benefits the angels but the claim that the exaltation is rational. Satan and his followers must be seen as refusing not an arbitrary decree but reason. God implies this in asserting that the Son "by right of merit Reigns" (6.43). In perhaps the most important speech in Book 6, Abdiel explains that there is a difference between service and servitude, and that it cannot be servitude to serve one who is objectively worthier (6.174–8). Much in Greek philosophy supports this view,[22] but the question remains as to in what the Son's objective worth ("merit") consists. This was putatively demonstrated in Book 3 – though there is a specious quality to the Son's unnecessary heroism (a "heavenly" parallel to Satan's heroism in Book 2) – but it is important to recognize that the events of Books 2 and 3 follow those narrated in Books 5 and 6, so an event dramatized in Book 3, whatever its status, cannot be used in relation to Satan's earlier actions.[23] The issue of merit, moreover, was not even mentioned in the key passage in Book 5, the Exaltation quoted above.

God, in Book 5, speaks of Satan intending "to try / In battel, what our Power is, or our right" (5.727–8), a line that leaves the two abstractions uneasily related, with "right" appearing almost as an afterthought.[24] In Book 6, after the (I do not believe intentionally grotesque) *Sturm und Drang* of the war between the angels,[25] God decides "To honour his Anointed Son" (6.676) by having him end the war:

> that the Glorie may be thine
> Of ending this great Warr, since none but Thou

> Can end it. Into thee such Vertue and Grace
> Immense I have transfus'd, that all may know
> In Heav'n and Hell thy Power above compare,
> And this perverse Commotion governd thus,
> To manifest thee worthiest to be Heir[.]
> (6.701–7)

It is hard to see how "Vertue" can be functioning here to mean anything but potency, and it is hard to see what "Grace" means at all. The speech is a paean to Power. It is not clear what "worthiest" can mean here except most powerful. In the next lines, the assertion of the Son's "deserved right" is followed immediately by the description of him as "Mightiest in thy Fathers might" (6.710). The Son suggests, very briefly and abstractly, a rational basis for his actions through an espousal of Abdiel's view (6.741), but the whole emphasis of this section of the poem is on the Chariot of Paternal Deity as an immense war machine.[26]

Milton recognizes the problem at this point. Before presenting the scene of military terror, he does have the Son restore Heaven's beauty (6.781–4), and he does present Satan's legions unmoved by this and "hard'nd more by what might most reclame" (6.791). This latter line, however, is very opaque. It is not at all clear how a demonstration of Power is supposed to "reclame" the rebels in any moral sense. But Milton's major attempt to get out of the problem is through acknowledging it. He has the Son inform the good angels that the Father has "assign'd" the suppression of the revolt to the Son in order that the rebel angels,

> may have thir wish, to trie with mee
> In Battel which the stronger proves, they all,
> Or I alone against them, since by strength
> They measure all, of other excellence
> Not emulous, nor care who them excells.
> (6.818–22)

This is another brilliant but desperate maneuver. The "might equals right" perspective that has dominated this entire section of the poem is presented, retroactively, as a kind of accommodation to the diabolical perspective – which it does not, in any case, accurately capture, since the fallen angels seem, in fact, to appreciate many kinds of "excellence" (as in the account of their music-making, athletic contests, and philosophical discussions in Book 2 [528ff.]). In the final lines of Raphael's narrative, moreover, the "Saints," meaning the good angels, are presented as seeing the Son's military triumph as what proves him to be "Worthiest to Reign" (6.882, 888).[27] Milton cannot keep this framework demonic.

HEAVENLY MINDS? CHOICE EVERYWHERE

We have now seen how the political framework in which Milton presented his theodicy creates the continuity between Heaven and Hell that Shelley thought was the deepest meaning of the poem. But what of Milton's presentation of life in Heaven apart from the great rebellion? C. S. Lewis has acknowledged (along with many other critics from the eighteenth century on) that there are problems with this presentation, but Lewis has classified these problems as merely matters of "poetical prudence" into which, he warns, "it is easy to look too deep."[28] But surely the presentation of heavenly life in the poem is something into which we should "look deep." When we do, we find that the peculiarities of Milton's presentation flow from his most fundamental and consciously held values – his commitment, as we have already seen, to rational moral explanation. The problems with Milton's Heaven can be seen as flowing directly from how Milton understands this bed-rock commitment. Here a contemporary (with us) moral philosopher can help. Bernard Williams has argued that it is a mistake to assume "that the moral point of view must be ubiquitous" – that all actions are to be evaluated from a moral point of view.[29] Williams has also argued that it is a mistake (of a similar sort) to maintain "a rationalistic conception of rationality," a view that holds, for instance, that only acts done out of rational deliberation are reasonable.[30] Milton holds both these views. They determine the limits of his Heaven – of his ability, that is, to present a distinctively heavenly consciousness.

Let me begin, as seems proper, with God. Milton's decision to have God speak, and to have Him speak as He does here, has troubled a multitude of critics. The most successful defense of the speech has assured us that this speech is meant to trouble us, that we are meant to see this trouble as a sign of our depravity, and that, properly seen, the speech is a totally toneless and affectless "unfolding" of a state of affairs.[31] Apart from whether these claims are true, or even plausible, there is something fundamentally wrong with this approach. It is purely formal. In the (first) *Defence of the People of England*, Milton noted that "it is the custom of poets to place their own opinions in the mouths of their great characters" (*CPW* 4.1:446). Milton gives this speech to God. He puts it where he does because of what it says.

The speech falls into three major parts and a coda. The third part of the speech is where it becomes directly theological.[32] To say that God does not anticipate objections here seems absurd, since it is precisely in response to an anticipated (or foreseen) accusation that Milton's God, like Homer's Zeus, and with the same distinctive tone of mock-bemusement, makes His point about human responsibility.[33] What is characteristically Miltonic in God's speech is the extraordinary value it places on free will. The longest section of the speech (3.96–111) is devoted to justification of this valuation. The progress to this section is not straightforwardly logical, since one could easily imagine a narrative continuation of what precedes it. The topic of moral responsibility ("whose fault?") enters the speech not inevitably but rather with a jolt, after a strong caesura, and as a new topic (3.96). While it is true that "ingrate" in the following line ("Whose but his own? ingrate, he had of mee" [3.97]) is not an insult – especially if the foot is iambic and the word an adjective – nonetheless the tone here is unquestionably defensive. God is working, as the prose Argument to Book 3 says, to clear "his own Justice and Wisdom from all imputation" (p. 67). The point that God develops is the parallel between the moral condition that will be granted to man – "Sufficient to have stood, though free to fall" – and that of the angels (3.99–102). The argument for the special importance of this follows, in a series of rhetorical questions that progressively lose their status as questions:

> Not free, what proof could they have givn sincere
> Of true allegiance, constant Faith or Love,
> Where onely what they needs must do, appeard,
> Not what they would? what praise could they receive?
> What pleasure I from such obedience paid,
> When Will and Reason (Reason also is choice)
> Useless and vain, of freedom both despoild,
> Made passive both, had servd necessitie,
> Not mee.
>
> (3.103–11)

This is perfectly intelligible. It is what Aristotle said a legislator concerned with assigning honors and punishments needs to consider.[34] In explaining the same point in *Areopagitica*, Milton appealed to what "We our selves esteem" (*CPW* 2:527). But this is also very odd. Shelley's point clicks in. This passage makes God *exactly* like us. Yet why should He be concerned with "proof" of sincerity, and with the proper assignment of praise? Why must His "pleasure" derive only from the kind of sincerity that arises from deliberation? And, the most theologically and philosophically interesting question (as we saw in regard to *Christian Doctrine*), why must "necessity" and acting out of necessity be only negatively conceived?

This is the point at which Milton's insistence on the ubiquity of the moral starts to seem odd, and can be seen as having eliminated possibilities – especially heavenly ones. As a number of critics have noted, the presentation of God's speech is immediately followed by an aggressively sensuous and lyrical narrative moment:

> Thus while God spake, ambrosial fragrance fill'd
> All Heav'n, and in the blessed Spirits elect
> Sense of new joy ineffable diffus'd[.]
> (3.135–7)

As the impersonal syntax here suggests, this does not seem to be a moment of choice or will on anyone's part. It seems merely to happen – "while God spake … fragrance fill'd" – and the agent of the "Sense of new joy" in the "Spirits elect" is the fragrance itself.[35]

The angels simply respond to what is "diffus'd" into them. Milton knows the importance of such moments, but his ideological framework does not allow him to give them much value. As in *On Christian Doctrine*, this is true even in high metaphysical and ontological moments. In speaking of creating the cosmos, God explains (as Raphael reports):

> Boundless the Deep, because I am who fill
> Infinitude, nor vacuous the space.
> Though I uncircumscrib'd my self retire,
> And put not forth my goodness, which is free
> To act or not, Necessitie and Chance
> Approach not mee, and what I will is Fate.
> (7.168–73)

This passage is remarkable for its mixture of ontological and voluntaristic terms; "fill" hovers between the realms, though Pleroma, "fullness," is a term from the realm of emanation. God's substance is not equivalent to his "goodness," which is (somehow) "free / To act or not." This "goodness" is conceived not only as independent of God's being, but also as if it were intelligible for goodness to withhold itself. This is exactly what the "diffusion principle," which sees generativity as intrinsic to, analytic to, goodness, means to deny.

Interestingly, the character in *Paradise Lost* who most clearly enunciates the principle of diffusion, and who has the clearest experience of being moved to goodness, is Satan. It is he who states that "good, the more / Communicated, more abundant growes" (5.71–2). This gives the principle a sinister cast, since it is not stated elsewhere. The experience of "sweet / Compulsion" is not valued. The phrase occurs when Satan is psychologically, almost physically, struck by Eve's beauty (9.463–7). Milton describes him as having been momentarily rendered "Stupidly good" (9.465). With regard to a similar moment in Book 4, Milton had commented (also with regard to Satan) on the "awful" power of beauty and goodness (4.845–8). But this kind of instinctive awe is not the characteristic experience of Milton's Heaven; it is an experience of necessity, not of deliberative choice. Milton knows that there are morally positive states that are non-deliberative – "a grateful mind / By owing owes not, but still pays, at once / Indebted and dischargd" (4.55–7) – but his presentation of heavenly life is not based on these. It is based on tests.

Only a positive conception of necessity (or a conception of positive necessity) can keep Heaven from being a realm of ordinary psychology and politics. Dante recognized this. Early in the *Paradiso*, Dante the pilgrim initially fails to recognize a Florentine woman he knew named Piccarda. Finally recognizing her, and being impressed by her "wondrous looks" ("*mirabili aspetti*"), Dante asks her whether she can be happy with her lowly status in Heaven. She explains to him that "to be in charity is here *necesse* … if thou consider well its nature."[36] There is no question of deliberation. That is what blessedness means for Dante. The beatified Piccarda is not free "To love or not" or to "forget to love" (*PL,* 5.540, 550). It is not clear, moreover, that it is in anyone's will to do these things; it is not clear that "to love" is the kind of thing that can be chosen (or forgotten) – another point on which Platonism and Reformation theology agreed. Milton, with his insistence that all praiseworthy action had to spring from choice, could not.

Raphael describes the angels who later fell as "perfet while they stood" (5.568), but while this claim may be physically or ontologically true, it is not morally or spiritually so. Toward the end of Book 1, Mammon is characterized by the epic voice as the "least erected Spirit that fell / From Heav'n" (1.679–80) because:

> *ev'n in heav'n* his looks and thoughts
> Were always downward bent, admiring more
> The riches of Heav'ns pavement, trod'n Gold,
> Then aught divine or holy else enjoy'd
> In vision beatific[.]
>
> (1.680–4; emphasis mine)

This is an admirable evocation of a degraded spirit, but an odd account of a heavenly one. Similarly, the description of Belial in Book 2 as one who "could make the worse appear / The better reason" and whose "thoughts were low" (2.113–15) is an account of a long-standing character, not of one newly destroyed. The parallel between the "muteness" of the fallen angels in response to Satan's challenge in Book 2 (420) and that of the unfallen angels in response to the Son's in Book 3 (217) is a lovely structural feature of the poem, but it has the effect of establishing a moral equivalence.

Milton is extremely interested in the Virgilian question about what sorts of negative emotion can dwell in heavenly minds – "*tantaene animis caelestibus irae*" ("Can there be so much anger in celestial spirits?" [*Aeneid*, 1.11]). This line is paraphrased or directly alluded to four times in *Paradise Lost*. In Book 4, the narrator tells us that "heavenly minds" are free of the kinds of passion that "disfigur'd" Satan on Mount Niphates (4.127), though later in the passage the difference seems to be merely one of degree – "more then could befall / Spirit of happie sort" (4.127–8). In the second (most distant) allusion, Satan states that he had thought that "Libertie and Heav'n / To heav'nly Soules had bin all one" – exactly Piccarda's position – but that he had learned this to be false (6.164–5). Later in Book 6, the line is almost directly translated – "In heav'nly Spirits could such perverseness dwell?" (788). The answer, as in Virgil, is "yes." The final allusion to the line again almost directly translates it. In tempting Eve, Satan asks with mock-ingenuousness, "Can envy dwell / In heav'nly breasts?" (9.729–30). The rhetorical situation requires that the implied answer be negative, and Satan can rely on Eve's innocence to provide this answer. Yet in the context of the poem as a whole the answer is less clear. Satan claims that one of the features that distinguishes Hell from Heaven is precisely that in Hell, envy is incoherent, whereas in Heaven "the happier state / … which follows dignity, might draw / Envy from each inferior" (2.24–6). This is phrased in an oddly hypothetical way – "might draw" – but we know that in at least one case (his own), this occurred. Satan's pre-fallen eminence "In favour" as well as "in Power" (5.661, 660) is never made morally intelligible.

The fallen angels present a view of devotion in Heaven as merely a matter of "Knee-tribute" (5.782). Mammon gives a full picture of what forced devotion would be like; it would:

> celebrate his Throne
> With warbl'd Hymns, and to his Godhead sing
> Forc't Halleluiah's; while he Lordly sits
> Our envied Sovran, and his Altar breathes
> Ambrosial Odours and Ambrosial Flowers,
> Our servile offerings.
>   (2.241–6)

Surely this should be impossible, and the imagination of it the product (and symptom) of a fallen nature. Yet one of the strangest episodes in the poem is that in which Uriel, "held / The sharpest sighted Spirit of all in Heav'n," is shown to be unable to detect hypocrisy, "the onely evil that walks / Invisible, except to God alone, / By his permissive will, *through Heav'n* and Earth" (3.690–1, 683–5; emphasis mine). So hypocrisy in Heaven is treated not just as a possibility but as a fact. And it is dramatized in the poem. After the Exaltation of the Son and the explicit demand for "Knee-tribute" to Him, Milton provides a wonderful picture of the angels dancing "about the sacred Hill" in "Mystical dance" and eating and drinking "in communion sweet" (5.619, 637). This is the sort of picture on which the defenders of Milton's Heaven rely. But it is all merely external. The fact of the matter is that "All seemd well pleas'd, all seem'd, but were not all" (5.617). *At least* one of the highest angels – Satan – was, at that moment, participating in the "Mystical" dances and festivities in exactly the hypocritical mode that Mammon describes. At the end of Book 3, Satan was presented as "bowing low" to Uriel "As to superior Spirits is wont in Heaven, / Where honour due and reverence none neglects" (3.736–8). Satan's punctiliousness to the outer signs of reverence exactly mirrors his long-standing behavior in Heaven. A presumably authoritative speaker (Gabriel) describes Satan as having "Once fawn'd, and cring'd, and servilly ador'd / Heav'ns awful Monarch" (4.959–60). Satan was the chief of the hypocritical adorers. No wonder this Monarch is concerned with proof "Of true allegiance" (3.104) and sends his servants on pointless errands to test and "enure" their "prompt obedience" (8.237–40).[37]

DIFFUSION AND SPONTANEITY

Thus far, I have concentrated on the problems and limitations that are created in *Paradise Lost* by Milton's commitment to rational explanation and to what Bernard Williams calls "a rationalistic conception of rationality." A whole set of religious and ethical possibilities are precluded by this commitment. Yet there are stretches in *Paradise Lost* in which Milton escapes from his preoccupation with deliberation and choice. To find Milton writing without "fetters," in my view, is not to turn to his treatment of Satan but to turn primarily to his treatment of two other topics, nature and innocence.[38] In relation to these, Milton escapes – or at least provides the material for escaping – the framework of choice, deliberation, and anxious duty.

The sun is one of the great images, in Christian as in neo-Platonic contexts, of overflowing, non-deliberative, and diffusive bounty.[39] In the magnificent passage describing the sun in Book 3, Milton is (almost) freed from his obsession with freedom. The "great Luminarie" is at first a great lord, "Alooff," dispensing "Light from farr" (3.576, 577, 579), but, as the description continues, a sense of happy natural process supervenes; we hear of:

> his Magnetic beam, that gently warms
> The Univers, and to each inward part
> With gentle penetration, though unseen,
> Shoots invisible vertue even to the deep[.]
> (3.583–6)

In this context, the fact that this "vertue" is of the power rather than the moral sort makes it more, rather than less, benign. The account in Book 7 of the Creation of the non-human cosmos happily celebrates "vital vertue" and benign natural processes like fermentation and generation (7.236, 281, 387).[40] Genesis and Lucretius happily mix. This presentation allows Milton to evoke a sense of divine goodness independent of the (for him) tense realm of freedom. The sense in which the Creation is seen as "good," here and in Genesis, has little to do with passing a test. But even more than the account of the Creation, it is the presentation of nature in Eden that is Milton's great success in the evocation of benign process independent of moral categories. Edenic nature is notably un-rule bound:

> Flours worthy of Paradise which not nice Art
> In Beds and curious Knots, but Nature boon
> Powrd forth profuse on Hill and Dale and Plaine.
> (4.241–3)

In Book 5, Milton repeats the theme, making the rejection of any kind of regulation or inhibition even more emphatic; Eden is:

> A Wilderness of sweets; for Nature here
> Wantond as in her prime, and plaid at will
> Her Virgin Fancies, pouring forth more sweet,
> Wilde above Rule or Art, enormous bliss.
> (5.294–7)

"Wantond" is here a positive term – without, I think, any "testing" of the reader – and it is notable that this vision allows for a positive sense of play. "Will" here is a term for happy spontaneity, not for deliberation. Diffusion ("pouring forth") is unchecked.

Perhaps the most successful metaphysical passage in *Paradise Lost* is the vision Raphael presents of what seems to be a natural movement of matter up the scale of being to spirit. Various sorts of matter are "Each in thir several active Sphears assignd, / Till body up to spirit work" (5.477–8). This cosmic process of sublimation (5.483) is illustrated by two purely natural processes: the way in which a flower produces fragrance, and the way in which, in Galenic physiology, the human blood system produces "animal" (intellectual) out of "vital" spirits (5.479–87). The culmination of this process would be that human bodies would "at last turn all to Spirit," and allow the resulting "Ethereal" creatures to exercise choice in a purely preferential, non-moral manner – they "may at choice / Here [in Eden] or in Heav'nly Paradises dwell" (5.497–500). But this whole cosmic process turns out to have an ethical basis – "If ye be found obedient" (5.501). This is perhaps Milton's most successful mingling of the ontological and the ethical – here ethical behavior allows a cosmic *entelechia* to be realized – but the question remains as to whether it makes sense, in terms of the vision of Edenic life that Milton gives us, for the "obedience" necessary to this cosmic process to be conceived in a narrow, specific, and negative way: "not to taste that onely Tree" (4.423). Why couldn't Adam and Eve be "obedient" by following the "dictates" of their unfallen natures?

It is a measure of the profound difference between Milton's Heaven and his Eden that when in Heaven Satan protests against the superfluity of "Law and Edict" to those who "without law / Erre not" (5.798–9), his claim seems merely rhetorical. In Eden, it seems pertinent. Joseph E. Duncan points out how extraordinary it was for Milton not to have presented Adam and Eve in Eden as following a "Covenant of Works."[41] They are not following prescriptions in order to obtain a reward. They do not have to be constantly instructed in virtue. Their impulses are trustworthy. With "instinctive motion," Adam stood upright (8.259). Eve, "With unexperienc't thought," falls victim to an illusion but responds immediately and spontaneously to a correcting "voice" and quickly responds to Adam's words and gestures by recognizing in her experience a complex moral lesson (4.456–92).[42] Adam and Eve do not have to be told to be grateful to "the Power / That made us ... / and plac't us here / In all this happiness" (4.412, 416–17). They do not have to be told how to worship, and do not have to deliberate about how to do so (5.144–9). They do not have to be told to be willing. They learn moral lessons directly from their environment, from Eden where "Nature multiplies / Her fertil growth, and by disburd'ning grows / More fruitful, *which instructs us not to spare*" (5.318–20; emphasis mine). It is not even clear that they needed to have had work "Appointed" to them (4.619), since they seem to have an aesthetic aversion to the messiness of Eden (4.630–1) as well as an intuitive sense of how to intervene usefully in it (5.212–16).

The moment when Milton first has evil enter (in some sense) the mind of these creatures who truly are "perfect" in their unfallen state bears close attention. As epic narrator, Milton comments on this moment in a way that is completely appropriate, even admirable, within his rational–moral scheme. Yet it is strikingly inappropriate to the lives of the morally perfect beings that he has imagined. Satan is described as having a difficult task when, squatting at the ear of the sleeping Eve, he seeks to "taint / Th' animal Spirits that from pure blood arise / Like gentle breaths from Rivers pure" (4.804–6). This is an image of benign natural process that has, as we have seen, potentially cosmic reach for Milton. Satan does succeed in giving Eve a vision of "high exaltation" (5.90), but Eve, instead of being disappointed to wake up and find her vision of flying false, immediately characterizes the dream as a nightmare (5.92–3).[43] Adam gives Eve a lecture on the psychological mechanisms by which dreams are produced (5.100–13), and reassures her with a moral point: "Evil into the mind of God or Man / May come and go, so unapprov'd, and leave / No spot or blame behind" (5.117–19).

This is, as I suggested, an admirable assertion of the juridical independence of mere thoughts from actions – a major issue in Milton's period, both before and after the Civil War and Interregnum – but it is strikingly inappropriate to Eve's situation. Evil did not spontaneously "come into" her mind; it was put there by an outside agent. Adam should have stopped at "evil whence?" ("Yet evil whence? In thee can harbour none, / Created pure" [5.99–100]). His moral generalization is no more relevant to Eve's situation than his lecture on dreams (she has had, as she says, dreams before, and this experience was nothing like those [5.30–4]). My point is that while what Adam says is fully appropriate to the consciousness of angels (called "Gods" elsewhere in the poem), and to that of fallen men, it is not appropriate to Milton's presentation of unfallen persons. Evil would not spontaneously have come into their minds.[44] They do not need injunctions, promises, or threats in order to be good; they are good because they are creatures of a certain kind. They do not need constantly to choose to be good. Tillyard's declaration that "no human being can conceive or represent evil entering into a mind quite alien to it" eliminates one of Milton's greatest achievements by denying that it could have occurred.[45]

I hope that I have now given a sense of how extraordinary it is that the apostle of moral deliberation, of reason as choice, should have given one of the most compelling pictures ever created of an alternative vision of the ethical life. Perhaps it is worth ending with a bit more argument that what Milton has presented in his Eden really is a vision of the ethical life, and not something inferior and less truly, rigorously desirable. Aristotle's *Ethics* seeks to encourage the development of creatures of a certain kind rather than of perfect rational calculators. The goal of the ethical life, for Aristotle, is not simply to make correct choices but to become, through training, education, and moral experience, the sort of creature who does not have to be constantly making moral choices – sudden reactions best reveal character (*NE* 1117ª20). For Aristotle, the ease with which good acts are done, precisely the absence of moral effort, is what defines virtue. Williams's attack on "the moral" in the name of the ethical is getting at this same idea. In discussing the importance for any conception of social life for people to be able to rely on certain things not happening (not being killed, etc.), Williams notes that one way of assuring this is to instill into persons a disposition to give the considerations against such actions a very high deliberative priority. But he goes on to note that, alternatively, "an effective way for actions to be ruled out is that they never come into thought at all." And he claims that "this is often the best way." Lest this seem mere dogmatizing, he gives an example: "One does not feel easy with the man who in the course of a discussion of how to deal with political or business rivals says, 'Of course, we could have them killed, but we should lay that aside right from the beginning.'" Williams comments, "It should never have come into his hands to be laid aside" (recall Adam's inability to understand ingratitude).[46] Williams's large conclusion is that "it is characteristic of morality that it tends to overlook the possibility that some concerns are best embodied in this way, in deliberative silence."[47]

So how was it possible for Milton to present the picture of life in Eden that he did? The answer might be that unfallen life was not part of the project of theodicy. In Eden, there was no problem of evil; there was no pressure on God's goodness. By contrast, we never see Heaven as solely a place of bliss. It is always the place where the rebellion has happened. Milton does not have to moralize prelapsarian life – except, of course, the propriety of the single prohibition, which need not be focused on until the actual moment of the Fall. Finally, I should say that I am not sure that the "counter-currents" to deliberative moralism were truly unconscious to Milton. His most unfettered imaginings of happiness always involved a vision of relying on "the faultles proprieties of nature" (*CPW* 2:237).

NOTES

1 "The Marriage of Heaven and Hell," in David V. Erdman (ed.), *The Poetry and Prose of William Blake* (New York: Doubleday, 1965), p. 35; E. M. W.

Tillyard, *Milton,* [1930] rev. edn. (New York: Collier, 1967), part 3, ch. 4 ("The Unconscious Meaning").
2 "Milton has so far violated the popular creed (if this shall be judged to be a violation) as to have alleged no superiority of moral virtue to his God over his Devil," *A Defence of Poetry,* in Carlos Baker (ed.), *The Selected Poetry and Prose of Percy Bysshe Shelley* (New York: Modern Library, 1951), p. 512.
3 William Empson, *Milton's God* (London: Chatto & Windus, 1961), p. 35.
4 See, *inter alia,* Dennis Richard Danielson, *Milton's Good God: A Study in Literary Theodicy* (Cambridge University Press, 1982).
5 John Peter Rumrich, *Matter of Glory: A New Preface to "Paradise Lost"* (University of Pittsburgh Press, 1987), p. 10.
6 Martin Luther, *The Bondage of the Will,* J. I. Packer and A. R. Johnston (trans.) (New Jersey: Revell, 1957), p. 282. For Calvin, see John T. McNeill (ed.), Ford Lewis Battles (trans.), John Calvin, *Institutes of the Christian Religion* (Philadelphia: Westminster Press, 1960), I:xiv:1.
7 See Gordon Campbell, Thomas N. Corns, John K. Hale, David I. Holmes, and Fiona J. Tweedie, *Milton and the Manuscript of "De Doctrina Christiana"* (Oxford University Press, 2007).
8 See William B. Hunter, *Visitation Unimplor'd: Milton and the Authorship of "De Doctrina Christiana"* (University of Pittsburgh Press, 1998), ch. 5; and Kelley's "Introduction" to *Christian Doctrine, CPW* 6:54–8 (on Servetus), and pp. 74–86 (on Arminianism).
9 For the importance of the free-will argument, see D. P. Walker, *The Decline of Hell: Seventeenth-Century Discussions of Eternal Torment* (University of Chicago Press, 1964), pp. 42–8; and Danielson, *Milton's Good God,* ch. 4.
10 Luther saw his little book on *The Freedom of a Christian* as containing "the whole of Christian life" (John Dillenberger [ed.], *Martin Luther: Selections from his Writings* [Garden City, New York: Doubleday Anchor, 1961], p. 52). Hereafter *Luther: Selections.*
11 See "The Freedom of a Christian," in *Luther: Selections,* p. 74.
12 Arthur O. Lovejoy, *The Great Chain of Being: A Study of the History of an Idea* (Cambridge, MA: Harvard University Press 1936), p. 49.
13 Plotinus, *The Enneads,* Stephen MacKenna (trans.), abridged and with an intro. by John Dillon (London: Penguin, 1991), II.ix.3, p. 111.
14 Plotinus, *Enneads,* v.i.6, p. 354. One scholar states that the importance of this passage "cannot be overestimated" (Lloyd Gerson, *Plotinus* [London: Routledge, 1994], p. 23).
15 Plotinus, *Enneads,* III.ii.3, p. 138.
16 Plotinus, *Enneads,* IV.iv.10–12, pp. 294–7.
17 Ernst Cassirer, "Giovanni Pico della Mirandola," in Paul O. Kristeller and Philip Wiener (eds.), *Renaissance Essays* (New York: Harper & Row, 1968), p. 22.
18 "Certain Articles to be Diligently Examined" in James Nichols (trans.), *The Works of James Arminius* (London: Longman, 1853), vol. II, p. 480; George Rust, *Letter of Resolution Concerning Origen* (1661), p. 25. I owe my awareness

of the importance of this theme in Arminius and Rust (and others) to Stephen M. Fallon, "'To Act or Not': Milton's Conception of Divine Freedom," *Journal of the History of Ideas* 49 (1988), 425–49.

19 *Milton's God*, p. 138 (see also pp. 123–4), and see Stella Purce Revard, *The War in Heaven: Paradise Lost and the Tradition of Satan's Revolt* (Ithaca: Cornell University Press, 1980), p. 204.

20 Compare Michael Bryson, *The Tyranny of Heaven: Milton's God as King* (Newark: University of Delaware Press, 2004), who argues that Milton intended for the reader to see God in this way. My own view is that Milton intended this conception to be "Satanic," but was unable to defuse it successfully.

21 See, for instance, Northrop Frye, *The Return of Eden: Five Essays on Milton's Epics* (University of Toronto Press, 1965), p. 15.

22 See, for instance, Aristotle, *Politics*, Ernest Barker (trans.) (New York: Oxford University Press, 1958), 1254^{b}24, p. 15. Aristotle carefully distinguishes such a "natural" relationship from one based merely on a differential in power (1255b10).

23 God's initial speech in Book 3 ended by asserting and explaining, on purely moral grounds, why Man (but not the fallen angels) "therefore shall find grace" (3.129–34). So the Son's account (150–67) of the undesirability of the destruction of man describes a possibility that has already been forestalled. Irene Samuel's contrast between the genuineness of the dialogue in Heaven in Book 3 and the falseness of the dialogue in Hell in Book 2 ("The Dialogue in Heaven: A Reconsideration of *Paradise Lost*, III, 1–417," in Arthur E. Barker [ed.], *Milton: Modern Essays* [Oxford University Press, 1968], pp. 233–45) has the matter exactly reversed.

24 This is the sort of moment that leads Peter C. Herman to see "or" as a crucial word in *Paradise Lost*. See Peter C. Herman, *Destabilizing Milton: "Paradise Lost" and the Poetics of Incertitude* (New York: Palgrave Macmillan, 2005), ch. 2.

25 For the claims that the "farce" in the War is intentional, and that the military trappings in the poem are meant to undercut themselves and thereby conduce to a pacifist message, see Arnold Stein, *Answerable Style: Essays on "Paradise Lost"* (Minneapolis: University of Minnesota Press, 1953), pp. 22ff. and 196ff. On the unlikeliness of this, see Robert Thomas Fallon, *Captain or Colonel: The Soldier in Milton's Life and Art* (Columbia, MO: University of Missouri Press, 1984), pp. 204–5, and Revard, *The War in Heaven*, pp. 154–5.

26 See Michael Lieb, *Children of Ezekiel: Aliens, UFOs, the Crisis of Race, and the Advent of the End of Time* (Durham: Duke University Press, 1998).

27 In *The War in Heaven*, Revard (p. 262) notes that the Son's return "at first suggests a martial victor," but then goes on to explain how we have to discount this impression. Similarly, in *Images of Kingship in "Paradise Lost": Milton's Politics and Christian Liberty* (Columbia: University of Missouri Press, 1983), Stevie Davis has a difficult time rationalizing the imperial Roman association of Christ's triumph (pp. 121–4).

28 C. S. Lewis, *A Preface to "Paradise Lost"* (Oxford University Press, 1942), p. 130.
29 Bernard Williams, *Morality: An Introduction to Ethics* (New York: Harper & Row, 1972), p. 75.
30 Bernard Williams, *Ethics and the Limits of Philosophy* (Cambridge, MA: Harvard University Press, 1985), p. 18.
31 Stanley Fish in *Surprised by Sin: The Reader in Paradise Lost* (New York: St. Martin's, 1967), ch. 2.
32 This is the sort of moment that leads Stephen Fallon to say that "while Milton is a theological poet, he is not a religious one." See Stephen Fallon, *Milton's Peculiar Grace: Self-Representation and Authority* (Ithaca: Cornell University Press, 2007), pp. x and passim.
33 *The Odyssey of Homer*, Robert Fitzgerald (trans.) (New York: Doubleday, 1963), 1:32–4, p. 2.
34 See Aristotle, *Nicomachean Ethics* (hereafter *NE*), Terence Irwin (trans.) (Indianapolis, 1985), 1109^b, pp. 30–5, 53.
35 "Spirits elect" here, and throughout Book 3, does not imply Calvinist predestination. As in "Decree / Unchangeable," Milton uses the terminology of Calvinism in an anti-Calvinist sense. On this, see Fallon, *Milton's Peculiar Grace*, ch. 7.
36 *Dante's "Paradiso," Italian Text with English Translation* by John D. Sinclair (New York: Oxford University Press, 1961), pp. 50–3 (3.64–84).
37 See Empson, *Milton's God*, p. 111.
38 John Rogers, *The Matter of Revolution: Science, Poetry, and Politics in the Age of Milton* (Ithaca: Cornell University Press, 1996) also sees Milton's treatment of nature as escaping from some of his more explicit views. My treatment differs from that of Rogers in that for Rogers rationalism and "vitalism" (what I call "the diffusion principle") stand together against authoritarianism, whereas I see a major tension between rationalism and "vitalism."
39 See, for instance, Dionysius, *The Divine Names*, ch. 4, in C. E. Rolt (trans.) *The Divine Names and the Mystical Theology* (New York: Macmillan, 1940), pp. 86–7.
40 This is what Empson had in mind in suggesting that it was not unintelligible or despicable for Satan to imagine being self-begotten through "our own quick'ning power" (5.860–1; *Milton's God*, pp. 88–9). Compare Rogers's treatment of "the principle of the ferment" (*The Matter of Revolution*, pp. 121ff.).
41 Joseph E. Duncan, *Milton's Earthly Paradise: A Historical Study of Eden* (Minneapolis: University of Minnesota Press, 1972), pp. 134ff.
42 I am in sharp disagreement with critics who see Milton as "faking" with regard to pre-fallen life (see E. M. W. Tillyard, "The Crisis of *Paradise Lost*," in *Studies in Milton* [London: Chatto & Windus, 1951], p. 11). I am opposed to all versions of the "fall before the Fall" view. The view that this scene dramatizes Eve's "successful" internalization of a patriarchalist system is less easily answered, and perhaps unanswerable.

43 Compare Diane Kelsey McColley, *Milton's Eve* (Urbana: University of Illinois Press, 1983), p. 99.
44 I do not think that anything in the dialogue about division of labor in Book 9 contravenes this. As Joseph Addison said, "It is such a Dispute as we may suppose might have happened in *Paradise*" (*The Spectator* # 351, in Gregory Smith [ed.], *The Spectator* [London: J. M. Dent, 1907], vol. III, page 98).
45 Tillyard, "Crisis," 11. See also A. J. A. Waldock, "*Paradise Lost*" *and its Critics* (Cambridge University Press, 1947), p. 61.
46 See Adam's puzzled response to the conditionality of Raphael's "*If ye be found / Obedient*" at 5.513ff. ("What meant that caution …?").
47 *Ethics and the Limits of Philosophy*, p. 185.

CHAPTER 2

"*Whose fault, whose but his own?*": Paradise Lost, contributory negligence, and the problem of cause

Peter C. Herman

Paradise Lost is much concerned with the question of blame. The poem begins with the initial speaker, usually identified with John Milton, asking the Muse "what cause / Mov'd our Grand Parents ... / ... to fall off / From thir Creator ... ? / Who first seduc'd them to that foul revolt?" (1.28–30; 1.33). Whose fault, in other words, is the Fall? Who bears responsibility? And in what degree?[1] In answer, the Muse identifies both culprit and motivation: "Th'infernal Serpent; he it was, whose guile / Stird up with Envy and Revenge, deceiv'd / The Mother of Mankind" (1.34–6). Satan caused the Fall because of envy and a desire for revenge (envy of what and why he wants revenge will be answered later in the poem). Yet God views the matter differently. In Book 3, after He predicts that despite all warnings, all His due care, "man" will listen to Satan's "glozing lyes" and "transgress the sole Command" (3.93–4), God asks the same question that Milton asks: "whose fault?" (3.96), but provides an alternative answer: "Whose but his own? ingrate" (3.97). According to God, "man" is primarily responsible, not Satan.[2]

The poem thus presents the reader with two answers to the same question from two ostensibly unimpeachable sources. Certainly, the question of blame follows Milton's habit of providing different versions of the same event (e.g., two Creation stories, two versions of Adam and Eve's first meeting, two Elevations of the Son, etc.).[3] While the impossibility of deciding between the two answers constitutes yet another example of Milton's poetics of incertitude, the different responses also show how Milton deeply complicates the question of blame in *Paradise Lost*. The developing case law on negligence helps illuminate what Milton is doing.

Would Milton have known about such details? Given his proximity to the law (he once thought about becoming a lawyer;[4] his father, John Milton Sr. was a scrivener; his brother, Christopher did become a lawyer), and Milton's involvement in various suits (mainly concerning real estate), it would not be surprising if he did.[5] Furthermore, J. Milton French reminds us that despite Milton's stated distaste for the legal profession, he was "at least a dilettante in legal matters," and that he owned eleven lawbooks at the time of his death.[6] Even so, I would not argue that Milton had first-hand knowledge of the cases I will discuss below, although neither would I rule out such a possibility. Rather, I base my argument on the proposition that developments in the law generally follow developments in the culture, that the "horizon of expectation," to invoke Jauss's phrase, very much included a model for thinking about fault and blame in ways more complex than the simple one adopted by the Muse at the poem's start and God in Book 3.

As we will see, the case law on negligence underwent a very significant expansion at nearly the same time that Milton published *Paradise Lost*, and Milton does something very similar in his poem. Both God and the Muse assume that only one agent is to blame and that "strict" liability applies, meaning, the defendant is responsible regardless of negligence or fault, and that the plaintiff – in this case, God – has no obligations beyond those He sets for Himself. Furthermore, both speakers limit the actors involved with the Fall to a very small group: Satan, Adam, and Eve. The poem, however, puts all of these assumptions into question by demonstrating that the story of the Fall has many more junctures where key choices are made and many more participants making those choices. The poem, in other words, spreads blame both wider and deeper than either God or the Muse allow. But before we move into *Paradise Lost*, we need to first understand how the early modern period understood negligence and the developing concept of contributory negligence.

I: THE LEGAL BACKGROUND

As numerous legal historians have pointed out, a specific action based on negligence remained unknown until the eighteenth century. None of the digests prior to Comyns (1762–7) use the term for a separate pleading or refer to negligence as a cause of action.[7] Yet while the recognition of negligence as a defined tort would have to wait, the meaning, if not the name, of both negligence and contributory negligence figures significantly in case law from the fourteenth century onward. In Stapleton's Case (1354), the court found for the plaintiff for the water damage done by the defendant's negligence in keeping up a restraining wall, and in an anonymous 1388 case, the judge enunciated this principle: "If one who is bound to fence against my land fails to do so, whereby the beasts of his tenants enter my fields and do damage to me, I may have an action on the case."[8] In another case from the early fifteenth century, over flooding due to a breach in a restraining wall, the liability was "founded upon the negligent keeping of the wall" rather than the flooding itself,[9] and in a case dating from 1401, a defendant successfully charged that his neighbor "so negligently [kept his fire] that for want of due keeping of the aforesaid fire [his goods and chattels were] burned by the fire …"[10] While these cases were filed under trespass on the perhaps overly technical grounds that the water, fire, or the beast entered the plaintiff's property without permission, the liability itself arose from the defendant's failure to fulfill the duty of care imposed "'by the common custom of the realm' – that is, they were liable because their conduct was regarded by the law as wrongful."[11] The general principle, enunciated during the reign of Edward IV, is that "When a man does a thing he is bound to do it in such a way that by his acts he causes no damage to others."[12] Or as an Elizabethan judge puts it: "I have never known an action to lie for negligence *save where one is retained to do something for someone and does it negligently*; and the reason why it lies in that case is because *he has undertaken to do it*" (my emphasis).[13]

Even so, medieval and early modern judges implicitly set different thresholds for liability for different occupations. Those who professed competence in certain callings were held to a higher standard. As Sir Anthony Fitzherbert put it in *La Novel Natura Brevium* (1534), "It is the duty of every artificer to exercise his art rightly and truly as he ought."[14] Thus, in 1347, the court found against a ferryman who negligently overloaded his boat and caused the drowning of the plaintiff's horse, and a 1371 case held a surgeon liable "who 'unskillfully' hurt the wounded arm he was supposed to heal."[15] In 1441, Justice Ascoghe said "If a carpenter promises to build a house and does not, I shall not have a writ of trespass, but only covenant if I have a specialty; but if he builds the house negligently, then I shall have an action of trespass on the case."[16]

In particular, medieval and early modern courts implicitly developed "what may be termed an implied duty arising out of public calling."[17] While slightly later than our period, Lord Holt, in the 1701 case Lane *v.* Cotton, would state: "When a man takes upon himself a public employment he is bound to serve the public as far as his employment goes, or an action lies against him."[18] Thus a sheriff can be liable if he fails to return a writ or execute a summons, whereby a party was put into default.[19] But liability also extended beyond law enforcement. Innkeepers and carriers were also held liable if they did not do their jobs appropriately because these occupations were considered "public callings." Innkeepers were held liable if their guests suffered a loss through theft even when the innkeeper had no part in the robbery because, as a fourteenth-century case plaintiff's lawyer puts it, the plaintiff "was lodged with him; and so long as that is so, he comes under your protection and safeguard."[20] The court agreed, and according to Chief Justice Knyvet, "a similar case had previously been adjudged in the Council, and the cause of the judgment was that an innkeeper should answer for himself and his household in respect of the rooms and stables ..."[21] And in 1348, a ferryman who overloaded his boat was judged liable for violating "his duty of care in discharging this quasi-public function."[22]

All of the above cases involve a previous relationship, usually contractual, between the plaintiff and defendant. The late seventeenth century, however, witnessed an expansion of the realm of responsibility: "negligence was so extended as to make one liable, in an action on the case, for damage flowing from the negligent performance of his own projects and undertakings unconnected with duty arising from statute, public calling, bailment, or prescription ..."[23] For example, in a case brought before the King's Bench *c.*1675, one "E.R." complained that "J.P.," a carrier, had allowed his horses to run wild and trample E.R.'s pig, and the court decided for the plaintiff on the grounds that "the aforesaid J., little regarding the same laudable laws and customs, but wholly neglecting and thinking little of them, on etc. at etc., so negligently, improvidently and inadvisedly drove and governed three horses" ("adeo negligenter improvide & inconsulte fugavit & gubernavit quod equi praedicti") that the horses ran over E.R.'s sow.[24] In another case decided by the King's Bench with a similar set of facts, Mitchell *v.* Allestry (1676), the defendant brought two untamed horses into a public place, Little Lincoln's Inn Field. But because "of their wild nature," the horse ran over James Mitchell's wife, Mary, causing her to become "lame and mutilated and cannot now be restored to perfect health."[25] The plaintiff alleged that the defendant should be held liable because he acted "improvidently, rashly and without due consideration of the unsuitability of the place for the purpose," [26] and the judge agreed, because "it is at the peril of the owner to take strength enough to order them [the horses]," and cited as precedent another case in which "Smith of Westminster [was held liable] for not penning an ox but setting a dog on him, whereby he ran into the Palace Yard and hurt him."[27] Similarly, in a case brought in 1680, a plaintiff brought an action against a master of a ship who steered it "so negligently and improvidently" that it sank the plaintiff's vessel.[28] While, again, the precise cause of action was trespass, the principle lying behind the court's finding for the plaintiff is the same: the defendant acted negligently, and by failing in the care required, he is liable for damages.

Judges and juries, however, also focused their attention on the plaintiff's behavior, and while the full articulation of contributory negligence, defined in a contemporary legal handbook as "conduct on the part of the plaintiff, contributing as a legal cause to his damage, which falls below the standard to which he is required to conform to his own protection,"[29] would not occur until the beginning of the nineteenth century in the case of Butterfield *v.* Forrester,[30] the concept that the plaintiff in an action may have caused his own harm is clearly present in medieval and early modern law. The distinguished legal historian, John H. Baker, notes that by the early Tudor era, "'Fault' by reason of causation could be negatived by act of God, or of a stranger, or of a servant exceeding his authority, or of an animal behaving unpredictably, *or by the negligence of the plaintiff himself*" (my emphasis).[31]

The case Baker has in mind for the last item is Terry *v.* White. In 1528, a dispute arose over who was responsible for breaking a barrel of wine, leading to the loss of the container, and, even worse, the wine. The plaintiff alleged that the defendant "had so carelessly loaded [the barrel] on the wagon that the wagon overturned and the hoops of the butt were broken, and that on arrival he had so carelessly unloaded the damaged butt that one hundred gallons of malmsey gushed out and were lost."[32] The defendant, on the other hand, counter-claimed that the loss was as much the plaintiff's fault as his, since the plaintiff had directed the defendant to unload the butt in stormy weather, and even more, did not deliver on the promised help:[33]

the agent had then urged him to unload at the plaintiff's own risk, promising to support the tail of the wagon while he did so; then, while the butt was being unloaded, the agent had carelessly let go of the tail of the wagon so that the butt had fallen on the ground; and, finally, apparently in an attempt to hammer the hoops back into position, the agent had smashed the butt with an axe and the wine had been spilt.

The same issues arise in the cases concerning shooting accidents. In 1534, for example, a man wandered onto a field commonly used for archery practice, where the defendant "fired an arrow at the target, and … while the arrow was in flight *the plaintiff negligently* ran across the butts and was struck…" (my emphasis).[34] In the 1616 case of Weaver *v.* Ward, the defendant, who had shot the plaintiff while both were taking part in military exercises, pled that the shooting was accidental and against his will. While this case was decided on technical grounds, "the court intimated in passing that liability was not absolute: the defendant could excuse himself if he showed that the plaintiff ran across the musket when it was discharging":[35]

no man shall be excused of a trespass ... except it may be judged utterly without his fault. As if a man by force take my hand and strike you. Or if heere the defendant had said that the Plaintiff ran cross his Peece when it was discharging, or had set forth the case with the circumstances, so as it had appeared to the Court that it had been inevitable, and that the Defendant had committed no Negligence to give occasion to the hurt.[36]

In a Jacobean case also reported in *The Second Part of the Reports of Sir George Crok*e (1669), Fowler *v.* Sanders, the plaintiff alleged that the defendant had obstructed the highway with logs upon which his horse stumbled and injured itself. The defendant countered that there was an "ancient" custom to lay the logs thus, and that everyone carefully left "sufficient [room] for passage of chariots, horsemen, and footmen, etc." More importantly, the injury to the horse was caused, so the defendant argued, by the plaintiff's carelessness: "the Plaintiff riding by the highway *improvidè* turned his horse upon the blocks and fell."[37] The defendant's plea was rejected, and "the action well lay for the Plaintiff" since he suffered "Special damage."[38] But my point is that the defense of what today is called contributory negligence was *thinkable*, that acting in an improvident manner could "negative" fault, not that the defense was always successful. But in another case included in the same volume, Bayley *v.* Merrel, the judges found for the defendant. Although everyone agreed that he had committed fraud (the defendant tricked the plaintiff into transporting a load much heavier than he alleged, resulting in the exhaustion and collapse of the plaintiff's horses), yet the judges agreed that the fraud was easily discoverable: "and if he doubted of the weight thereof, he might have weighed it; and was not bound to give Credence to anothers speech: and being his own negligence, he is without remedye ... For the lawe gives no remedy for voluntary negligence."[39]

In sum, medieval and early modern law, like *Paradise Lost*, was "much concerned with causation – indeed it was probably through the development of the concept of causation that the modern notion of negligence emerged."[40] Judges and juries looked to whether the defendant had fulfilled the duty of care required of him, and they looked to whether the plaintiff had also failed in the duty of care required of him. The reports used the same vocabulary to talk about fault: one keeps seeing the terms "negligent," "improvident," and "inadvised." The question I want to turn to now is how this background helps inform Milton's treatment of cause and the question of blame in *Paradise Lost*. Did all the parties fulfill their duty of care? We are used to assuming that Adam, Eve, and Satan are exclusively to blame for the Fall. But as we will see, Milton constructs his narrative so as to invite precisely the sort of questions raised by early modern judges when dealing with cases involving negligence.

II: *PARADISE LOST*

At the start of his speech to the Son in Book 3, God very quickly glosses over the precise mechanisms of Satan's escape from Hell:

> Only begotten Son, seest thou what rage
> Transports our adversarie, whom no bounds
> Prescrib'd, no bars of Hell, nor all the chains
> Heapt on him there, nor yet the main Abyss
> Wide interrupt can hold
>
> (3.80–4)

As I have argued elsewhere, this speech deserves close attention because nearly every statement God makes is questionable.[41] Right now, I want to focus on how God's narrative carefully elides certain events crucial for the unfolding of the story of the Fall because they show God or another divine agent contributing, either by omission or commission, to these events, and by implication, sharing responsibility for the results. As He will do later in this speech, God disclaims all responsibility for Satan's act, placing all the blame on the fallen angel, who, despite all the care that God claims to have taken, the bounds prescribed, the bars, and the chains heaped on him there, has managed to escape. Yet the narrative provided by the Muse suggests that the answer to God's question – "Whose fault?" – needs to be more expansive than the one God provides.

First, the chains. The Muse twice reiterates that Satan is supposed to be locked to the Lake of Fire: God hurls him "down / To bottomless perdition, there to dwell / In Adamantine Chains and penal Fire" (1.46–8); and "So stretcht out huge in length the Arch-fiend lay / Chain'd on the burning Lake" (1.209–10). These chains, however, seem to disappear the moment Satan decides to get up: "Forthwith upright he rears from off the Pool / His mighty Stature; ... / Then with expanded wings he stears his flight / Aloft" (1. 221–2, 225–6). How effective, one must ask, are these

"Adamantine" chains? The discussions of liability in early modern legal culture suggest that if these chains are so ineffective that Satan and the other fallen angels can get up and fly away without even noticing their existence, then God, like the innkeepers and carriers who were liable for damages if they did not do their jobs appropriately, shares some responsibility for the results of doing a poor job of confining Satan.

Understandably, God spends little time on the chains, perhaps not wanting to draw attention to the matter. The Muse, on the other hand, clearly feels the need to offer an explanation for why Satan bound suddenly becomes Satan unbound, but her efforts only raise more questions of liability:

> So stretcht out huge in length the Arch-fiend lay
> Chain'd on the burning Lake, nor ever thence
> Had ris'n or heav'd his head, but that the will
> And high permission of all-ruling Heaven
> Left him at large to his own dark designs,
> That with reiterated crimes he might
> Heap on himself damnation, while he sought
> Evil to others[.]
>
> (1.209–16)

The Muse seeks to defuse the problem by asserting that Satan has God's *permission* to get up in order for Satan to deserve the "Treble confusion, wrath and vengeance" (1.220) that will pour upon him for seducing "Man" (1.219), thus introducing the question of free will. God, according to this view, frees Satan so that the fallen angel could *choose* to do evil, thus damning himself, just as God allowed the rest of the angels to choose whether to stand or fall. So God says in Book 3 (3.98–105). "Reason," as God says, "also is choice" (3.108). Clearly, God has a point here. Satan makes his choice (the "Address to the Sun" at the start of Book 4 follows the process of his reasoning); Eve, faced with eating or not eating the fruit, makes hers, and Adam, confronted with the same option, makes his.

One could certainly argue (many have) that these passages represent the difficult and dangerous freedom that comes with free will: all that God guarantees is that humankind will make choices, and indeed, God ensures that they will *have to* make choices. God assures opportunity, not outcome. But the ineffective chaining of Satan (as well as the other incidents discussed below) casts a shadow over the question of free will because once God acts to restrain Satan, then another element enters the interpretive mix. It is one thing to allow for free will, to allow or even encourage temptation and let the consequences fall where they may; it is quite another to act first to *prevent* Satan's escape, but do so in a way that fails, thus allowing Satan free movement. Allowing another party free will does not obviate even God's responsibility to act in a responsible, prudent manner. As the judgment in a 1700 case puts it, a man is "answerable for all mischief proceeding from his neglect or his actions,"[42] a description that disturbingly fits the scenario described by the Muse. Once God takes it upon Himself to confine Satan, early modern legal thinking suggests that God then has a duty to do so successfully. Alternatively, if one privileges the Muse's version – God allowed Satan to get up and commit his "dark deeds" – then the plaintiff (God) gave occasion to his own hurt, and as the judges in Bayley *v.* Merrel write, "the lawe gives no remedy for voluntary negligence."[43] Either way, the simple has become complex, and the penumbra of blame has just gotten wider.

Nor are the chains the only such example. The next juncture at which divine choices contribute to the story of the Fall arrives when Satan confronts Sin and Death at the gates of Hell. Critics of this sequence differ as to whether Sin and Death are strictly allegorical figures or whether they are as physically "real" as Satan, Raphael, or the human couple. Yet assuming that Sin (whom I will be focusing on) is fundamentally insubstantial not only contradicts key passages in the narrative, but allows one to sidestep a key passage in the story of the Fall.[44]

When Satan reaches the limits of Hell, he finds himself confronted with what appears to be an insurmountable barrier:

> at last appeer
> Hell bounds high reaching to the horrid Roof,
> And thrice threefold the Gates; three folds were Brass,
> Three Iron, three of Adamantine Rock,
> Impenetrable, impal'd with circling fire,
> Yet unconsum'd.
> (2.643–8)

Doubtless, these are the "barrs of Hell" that God spoke of earlier, and they are so formidable that it certainly seems as though God has fulfilled his duty to adequately protect the created universe from Satan. Breaking out, it would seem, is impossible, which makes even more terrible God's description of Satan to the Son:

> seest thou what rage
> Transports our adversarie, whom no bounds
> Prescrib'd, no bars of Hell, nor all the chains
> Heapt on him there, nor yet the main Abyss
> Wide interrupt can hold[.]
> (3.80–4)

But God omits a key detail. Sin tells her father and paramour that she fell along with the other rebel angels, and she clearly identifies herself as part of Satan's forces: "wherein remain / (For what could else) to our Almighty Foe / Cleer Victory, to our part loss and rout" (2.768–70). At this point, however, God makes a fateful choice: "at which time this powerful Key / Into my hand was giv'n, with charge to keep / These Gates for ever shut" (2.774–6). As I have previously argued, the fact that God leaves this detail out of His narrative significantly impacts His credibility as a narrator.[45] My present point is that giving the key to Sin is exactly the kind of *improvidè* act that early modern lawyers would use to demonstrate that the negligence of the plaintiff at least partly caused his damage. That is to say, God devolves the key to a being He despises and therefore cannot reasonably be expected to obey His commands:

> The key of this infernal Pit by due,
> And by command of Heav'ns all-powerful King
> I keep, by him forbidden to unlock
> These Adamantine Gates; against all force
> Death ready stands to interpose his dart,
> Fearless to be o'rmatcht by living might.
> But what ow I to his commands above
> Who hates me, and hath hither thrust me down
> Into this gloom of *Tartarus* profound[?]
> (2.850–8)

One cannot overestimate the importance of "the fatal Key / Sad instrument of all our woe" (2.871–2).[46] Once placed in the lock, "the key-hole turns / Th'intricate wards, and every Bolt and Bar / Of massie Iron or sollid Rock with ease / Unfast'ns" (2.876–9)], and the Fall eventually results. Without the key, and without God's devolving the key to Sin, the Fall would not, could not, have occurred. Because God decided to create a key and then deliberately give it to someone whose loyalty, He knows, lies elsewhere, it seems that God, to appropriate Weaver v. Ward, gives "occasion to the hurt,"[47] and therefore, the principle enunciated in Bayley v. Merrel should obtain – that "the lawe gives no remedy for voluntary negligence."[48] While not absolving Satan, Adam, and Eve – the principle of free will remains – God's choices also enable the events that will ensue after Sin takes "the fatal Key, / Sad instrument of all our woe" (2.871–2), puts it in the lock, and opens the Gate of Hell.

The next fork occurs before Satan makes his way across Chaos. Satan has just crossed through Limbo when "farr distant he descries / Ascending by degree magnificent / Up to the wall of Heaven a Structure high" (3.501–3).

Satan sees stairs leading up to Heaven, but at this moment, these stairs remain inaccessible. This is another crucial moment in the chain of events leading to the Fall, as climbing these stairs gives Satan his first glimpse of the created universe.[49] To be sure, the stairs are not strictly necessary. Satan can fly, and so he may have gained his first view with a few flaps of his wings. That would have made Satan completely responsible for what follows afterward, but that is not what Milton wrote and so, presumably, not the thematic result Milton desired. Instead, Milton credits Satan's first view of the universe to his taking advantage of someone else's actions: "*The Stairs were then let down*, whether to dare / The Fiend by easie ascent, or aggravate / His sad exclusion from the dores of Bliss" (3.532–6; my emphasis).

This description offers a fascinating puzzle. On the one hand, it is remarkable that the Muse suddenly lapses into the passive voice, thus rendering opaque the question of agency. While most assume that God is the responsible party, we just do not know. Yet at the same time, the Muse provides alternative motivations for letting down the stairs. This unknown agent acts either to dangle before Satan the possibility of re-entering the place from which he was expelled ("to dare / The Fiend by easie ascent") or to further enrage him ("aggravate / His sad exclusion"). Neither possibility reflects well upon whoever let down the stairs. The former seems almost jejune, daring Satan to just try to get back into Heaven, while the latter is breathtakingly irresponsible, the cosmic equivalent of President George W. Bush in 2003 daring the insurgents in Iraq to "bring it on." Whichever motivation one chooses (and as is so frequently the case with the Miltonic "Or," we have no way of deciding between them), the agent who let down the stairs contributes materially to the events leading up to the Fall, and therefore shares responsibility because these stairs, however mysteriously meant, become the instrument by which Satan gains his first view of the universe and this world. Taking advantage of this opportunity to re-enter Heaven, Satan climbs up a few of the stairs (he does not fly), and this crucial act unexpectedly provides him a view of the created universe and Earth:

> [Satan] from hence *now on the lower stair*
> That scal'd by steps of Gold to Heav'n Gate
> *Looks down with wonder at the sudden view*
> *Of all this World at once.*
> (3.540–3; my emphasis)

Seized with envy "At sight of all this World" (3.554), Satan suddenly decides to change direction. No longer interested in re-entering Heaven,

Satan "without longer pause / Down right into the Worlds first Region throws / His flight precipitant" (3.561–3). Crucially, Satan gains his initial view of "this World" by climbing, albeit partway, the stairway to Heaven, and so, this passage necessarily raises three questions: *who let down the stairs? Why? And doesn't this party bear some responsibility for the results of this act?*

Up until now, I have dealt exclusively with instances in which the choices made by Milton's God (and the unknown agent presumed to be God) contribute significantly to the Fall. But God is not the only actor who does not do his job, as Sir Antony Fitzherbert put it, as "rightly and truly as he ought."[50] Angels were popularly known as "perfect, pure intelligences,"[51] but Milton's treatment of them, as Feisal Mohamed argues, "is audacious, original, and still unique."[52] Part of Milton's audaciousness lies in his portraying how the collective failure of Milton's angels to perform competently also contributes to the story of the Fall. Uriel, supposedly "The sharpest sighted Spirit of all in Heav'n" (3.691), does not see through Satan's disguise as a cherub and thus reveals Eden's location to Satan. The Muse excuses the angel on the grounds that "neither Man nor Angel can discern / Hypocrisie, the onely evil that walks / Invisible, except to God alone" (3.682–4), but she errs. After successfully tricking Eve into eating the fruit, Satan returns to Hell "in likeness of an Angel bright" (10.327), yet Sin and Death – unlike Uriel – have no trouble recognizing their father: "Disguis'd he came, but those his Children dear / Thir Parent soon discern'd, though in disguise" (10.330–1).[53] Nor do Gabriel and his troop perform much better. After discovering Satan squatting "like a Toad" by Eve's ear (4.800), they mistake his purpose ("Imploi'd it seems to violate sleep" [4.883]) and they allow him to get away. After Gabriel points to the heavenly scales, Satan understands their meaning, and decides to flee: "The Fiend lookt up and knew / His mounted scale aloft: nor more; but fled / Murmuring, and with him fled the shades of night" (4.1013–15). By making no effort to impede his escape, Gabriel and his troop allow Satan's return to Eden.

Given this track record, one has to ask how well Raphael fulfills God's charge to advise Adam:

> of his happie state,
> Happiness in his power left free to will,
> Left to his own free Will, his Will though free,
> Yet mutable; whence warne him to beware
> He swerve not too secure: tell him withall
> His danger, and from whom, what enemie

> Late falln himself from Heav'n, is plotting now
> The fall of others from like state of bliss;
> By violence, no, for that shall be withstood,
> But by deceit and lies; this let him know,
> Least willfully transgressing he pretend
> Surprisal, unadmonisht, unforewarnd.
> (5.234–45)

Michael J. Allen observes that the angel "is a pedagogical failure if judged pragmatically, for Adam ends up doing exactly what Raphael warns him against,"[54] at least partly because of Raphael's overreaction to Adam's confession of passion leads Adam to resent "Raphael's injustice and spleen" and – more importantly – to discount Raphael's warning.[55] While I agree in the main with Allen's critique, there are two further details I want to explore.

First, the poem provides mixed evidence on how effectively Raphael follows God's instructions. Raphael certainly does not begin auspiciously. His first attempt at fulfilling his mission consists of an oblique hint dropped in the middle of a larger discussion about the relationship between angels and humans. People may, says Raphael, in the process of time become more like angels:

> Or may at choice
> Here or in Heav'nly Paradises dwell;
> If ye be found obedient, and retain
> Unalterably firm his love entire
> Whose progenie you are. Mean while enjoy
> Your fill what happiness this happie state
> Can comprehend, incapable of more.
> (5.499–505)

Raphael, it seems, would have rested here had not Adam picked up on this hint and asked for a clarification: "But say, / What meant that caution joind, *if ye be found / Obedient?*" (5.512–14; emphasis in the original). Raphael responds with a long, elliptical speech that does not directly answer Adam's question or fulfill God's commandment because Raphael omits the most important point: Satan's plot against Adam and Eve:

> Attend: That thou art happie, owe to God;
> That thou continu'st such, owe to thy self,
> That is, to thy obedience; therein stand
> This was that caution giv'n thee; be advis'd.
> God made thee perfet, not immutable;
> And good he made thee, but to persevere

> He left it in thy power, ordaind thy will
> By nature free, not over-rul'd by Fate
> Inextricable, or strict necessity;
> ...
>   ... [F]reely we serve,
> Because we freely love, as in our will
> To love or not; in this we stand or fall:
> And som are fall'n, to disobedience fall'n,
> And so from Heav'n to deepest Hell; O fall
> From what high state of bliss into what woe!
>   (5.520–8, 538–43)

Again, it is up to Adam to draw out the implications. In response to Adam's request for the "full relation" (5.556), Raphael finally launches into the story of Satan's rebellion and the War in Heaven that concludes with his firm warning to Adam. But had Adam not asked for more information, Raphael would never have told Adam about "His danger, and from whom" (5.239).

Even so, at the end of his narrative about the war in Heaven, Raphael (at last) fulfills God's charge by delivering an explicit warning:

> Thus measuring things in Heav'n by things on Earth
> At thy request, and that thou maist beware
> By what is past, to thee I have reveal'd
> What might have else to human Race bin hid;
> The discord which befel, and Warr in Heav'n
> Among th'Angelic powers, and the deep fall
> Of those too high aspiring, who rebelld
> With *Satan*, hee who envies now thy state,
> Who now is plotting how he may seduce
> Thee also from obedience, that with him
> Bereavd of happiness thou maist partake
> His punishment, Eternal miserie[.]
>   (6.893–904)

But Raphael dilutes the force of this passage by delivering (at Adam's request) another lengthy speech about the story of Creation so charming that when Raphael ends, Adam "Thought him still speaking, still stood fixt to hear" (8.3). The warning gets buried even deeper as Raphael allows Adam to seduce him into staying longer ("Desire with thee still longer to converse" [8.252]) by telling his origin story, which leads directly to Adam's confession of how passion undoes him and his question about angelic sex. The topic so embarrasses Raphael that he blushes ("a smile that glow'd / Celestial rosie red" [8.618–19]), lapses into euphemisms ("Let it suffice thee that thou know'st / Us happie" [8.620–1]), and rushes off the moment he senses an opportunity ("But I can now no more; the parting Sun / … / sets, my Signal to depart" [8.630, 632]). This ending might be comic, were it not for how Raphael's evident discomfort leads to this "peremptory"[56] summation:

> Be strong, live happie, and love, but first of all
> Him whom to love is to obey, and keep
> His great command; take heed lest Passion sway
> Thy Judgement to do aught, which else free Will
> Would not admit[.]
>
> (8.633–7)

In his rush to depart, Raphael once more omits Satan and his plot to destroy the human pair. The angel leaves Adam thinking that passion might be the issue, not a supernatural being who waged war on God and now has Adam and Eve in his sights. While Raphael does not completely fail to fulfill God's charge, neither does the angel deliver the warning as effectively as the stakes required.

Finally, there is Raphael's treatment of Eve. God directs Raphael to "Converse with *Adam*" (5.230), and that is exactly what he does. Certainly, Raphael greets Eve when he first arrives (5.385–91), but afterward, he acts as if she were not present. At the end of Book 6, Raphael enjoins Adam to: "warne / Thy weaker; let it profit thee to have heard / By terrible Example the reward / Of disobedience" (6.908–11), implying that Eve is not present to hear the warning herself. But the poem suggests otherwise.[57] The Muse unequivocally states at the start of Book 7 that Adam "with his consorted *Eve* / The storie heard attentive" (50–1), and in Book 8, she more ambiguously states that Eve "sat retir'd in sight" (8.41). Whether or not Eve sits next to Adam or "retir'd," it is clear that Raphael directs his speech to Adam alone, as also evidenced by how Eve can slip out to visit her flowers without either Adam or Raphael noticing (or caring).

God's and Raphael's indifference to Eve's presence shocks because it is Eve, not Adam, who will face Satan, yet both God and Raphael direct their warnings to Adam alone. While it is true that Eve (according to the Muse, at least) would rather hear things from Adam than Raphael ("Her Husband the Relater she preferr'd / Before the Angel" [8.52–3]) because Adam "would intermix / Grateful digressions, and solve high dispute / With conjugal Caresses" (8.54–6), there are two problems here. First, it is not clear how solving high dispute with caresses comports with Adam's confession that "All higher knowledge in her presence falls / Degraded, Wisdom in discourse with her / Looses discount'nanc't, and like folly shewes" (8.551–3). It is not clear, in other words, that Adam would be capable of repeating the warning.

Second, Raphael and God's willingness to ignore Eve, or to rely on Adam to convey the warning, reveals especially poor judgment because Eve, not Adam, has already been the object of Satan's machinations. But Raphael omits that fact. The angel does not tell Eve (or Adam) that her dream was in fact Satan's first try at seducing Eve.[58] The crucial debate between Adam and Eve on whether to separate thus takes place without this vital piece of information. Consequently, both parties proceed on the assumption that an assault *may* happen in the future, not that one has *already* happened in the recent past. Thus Eve tells Adam that she knows "we have a foe / [Who] *may tempt*" her "firmness" (9.280–1, 279; my emphasis), and Adam seeks "to avoid / Th' attempt it self, *intended* by our Foe" (9.294–5; my emphasis). Neither realizes that Satan has already tried Eve's "firmness," and that one "attempt" has already occurred. By leaving out this essential piece of information, Raphael makes the Fall more, not less, likely, and consequently shares some responsibility for the event.

God of course absolves the angels of any complicity in the Fall: "be not dismaid, / Nor troubl'd at these tidings from the Earth, / Which your sincerest care could not prevent" (10.35–7). Yet the narrative Milton devises for *Paradise Lost* suggests that if "sincerest care" could not have prevented the Fall, God and others made the Fall much more likely through their various choices. Fascinatingly, none of the incidents examined in this essay – the weak chains on the fiery lake, God's devolving the key to Hell to Sin, lowering the stairs to Heaven, Uriel's inability to penetrate Satan's disguise, Gabriel's allowing Satan to escape, Raphael's poorly executed warning to Adam – are not strictly speaking necessary. They are not in Genesis, nor in any of the analogues to *Paradise Lost*. Milton was therefore free to construct these episodes any way he wanted, and in each case he chose to have his characters act in ways that are highly problematic. Michael Lieb once noted that "the idea of contending with one's God is part of the fabric of Old Testament theology. God's faithful are forever engaged in controversy with him, whether in the form of Job, who wishes to arraign God in a court of law (Job 13:5; 40:2), or Jeremiah, who is prompted to dispute with God concerning the nature of God's ways (Jer. 12:1)."[59] What the pattern I have outlined above shows, I suggest, is that even as he sets out to "justifie the wayes of God to men," Milton creates a narrative in which blame keeps spreading outward until it seems that nearly everyone in the poem – obviously Satan, but also Adam, Eve, the angels, and even

God, "give occasion to the hurt" by acting "negligently, improvidently and inadvisedly."[60]

NOTES

1 While the question of blame has been treated before, earlier critics have focused exclusively on Adam and Eve. See A. J. A. Waldock, *"Paradise Lost" and its Critics* [1947] (Cambridge University Press, 1964), pp. 30–8; Millicent Bell, "The Fallacy of the Fall in *Paradise Lost*," *PMLA* 68, 4 (1953), 863–83; and Stella P. Revard, "Eve and the Doctrine of Responsibility in *Paradise Lost*," *PMLA* 88, 1 (1973), 69–78.
2 It should not escape notice that while the Muse, who is female, focuses on Eve, God concentrates on Adam – "man."
3 See Peter C. Herman, *Destabilizing Milton: "Paradise Lost" and the Poetics of Incertitude* (New York: Palgrave Macmillan, 2005), pp. 42–59.
4 Gordon Campbell and Thomas Corns, *John Milton: Life, Work, and Thought* (Oxford University Press, 2008), p. 101.
5 See J. Milton French, *Milton in Chancery: New Chapters in the Lives of the Poet and his Father* (New York: MLA, 1939), *passim*.
6 French, *Milton in Chancery*, p. 4.
7 Thomas Atkins Street, *The Foundations of Legal Liability* (Northport, NY: Edward Thompson, 1906), vol. I, p. 182; P. H. Winfield, "The History of Negligence in the Law of Torts," *The Law Quarterly Review* 42 (1926), 195; James Fleming, "Contributory Negligence," *The Yale Law Journal* 62 (1953), 692; J. H. Baker, *An Introduction to English Legal History*, 3rd. edn. (London: Butterworths, 1990), pp. 455, 468. W. S. Holdsworth, *A History of English Law* (London: Methuen, 1923), vol. VIII, p. 449.
8 Quoted in Street, *Legal Liability*, p. 183.
9 Ibid., p. 183.
10 "Beaulieu *v.* Finglam," in J. H. Baker and S. F. C. Milsom (eds.), *Sources of English Legal History: Private Law* (London: Butterworth, 1986), p. 557.
11 Holdsworth, *A History of English Law*, vol. VIII, p. 450.
12 Ibid., vol. III, p. 375.
13 Bradshaw *v.* Nicholson (1601), quoted in Baker and Milsom, *Sources of English Legal History*, p. 463.
14 Quoted in Winfield, "The History of Negligence," 185. This work remained the principal reference work on writs until the nineteenth century. See J. H. Baker, "Fitzherbert, Sir Anthony (*c.*1470–1538)," *Oxford Dictionary of National Biography*, Oxford University Press, Sept. 2004; online edn., Jan. 2008 [http://www.oxforddnb.com/view/article/9602, accessed Aug. 5, 2008].
15 Winfield, "The History of Negligence," 187.
16 Ibid., 188 n.9.
17 Street, *Legal Liability*, p. 184.
18 Ibid., p. 185.
19 Ibid., p. 184.

20 Nevenby v. Lassells (1368), Baker and Milsom, *Sources of English Legal History*, p. 553.
21 Ibid., p. 554.
22 A. K. Kiralfy, *The Action on the Case* (London: Sweet & Maxwell, 1951), p. 11.
23 Street, *Legal Liability*, p. 189.
24 E.R. v. J.P., Baker and Milsom, *Sources of English Legal History*, pp. 562–3; *The Clerk's Manual* (London, 1678), sig. F4.
25 Mitchell v. Allestry, Baker and Milsom, *Sources of English Legal History*, p. 572.
26 Ibid., p. 572.
27 Ibid., p. 573.
28 Mustard v. Harnden (1680), quoted in M. J. Prichard, "Trespass, Caw and the Rule in Williams v. Holland," *The Cambridge Law Journal* 22 (1964), 284–5.
29 William L. Prosser, *Handbook of the Law of Torts*, 2nd edn. (St. Paul, MN: West Publishing, 1955), p. 283.
30 Ibid., n.1.
31 Baker, "Introduction," in J. H. Baker (ed.), *The Reports of Sir John Spelman*, vol. II (London: Selden Society, 1978), p. 223. Holdsworth also holds that "the doctrine, if the plaintiff's act was the proximate cause of the damage, the plaintiff could not recover, was well-established mediaeval doctrine" (*A History of English Law*, vol. VIII, p. 459).
32 Baker, "Introduction," p. 226.
33 Ibid., p. 227.
34 Ibid., p. 224.
35 Ibid., p. 458.
36 "Weaver against Ward," *The Reports of the Reverend and Learned Judge the Right Honorable Sir Henry Hobart*, 3rd edn. (London: 1671), sig. Q3r.
37 *The Second Part of the Reports of Sir George Croke ... As Were Adjudged in the said Courts, During the Whole Reign of the Late King James* (London, 1669), sig. Lll4v.
38 Ibid., sig. Lll4v.
39 Ibid., sig. Ddd2.
40 Fleming, "Contributory Negligence," p. 693.
41 Herman, *Destabilizing Milton*, pp. 120–5.
42 Baker, "Introduction," p. 466.
43 *The Second Part of the Reports of Sir George Croke*, sig. Ddd2.
44 Stephen Fallon holds that Sin is insubstantial, as do Maureen Quilligan and Philip Gallagher. See Stephen Fallon, "Milton's Sin and Death: The Ontology of Allegory in *Paradise Lost*," *English Literary Renaissance* 17 (1987), 346; Maureen Quilligan, *Spenser's Milton: The Politics of Reading* (Ithaca: Cornell University Press, 1983), p. 126, and Philip J. Gallagher, "'Real or Allegoric': The Ontology of Sin and Death in *Paradise Lost*," *English Literary Renaissance* 6 (1976), 317, 322–3.

45 Herman, *Destabilizing Milton*, pp. 120–1. See also J. Allan Mitchell, "Reading God Reading 'Man': Hereditary Sin and the Narrativization of Deity in *Paradise Lost* Book III," *Milton Quarterly* 35, 2 (2001), 72–86.
46 Very few critics or editors draw attention to this passage (there are no annotations for the key incident in editions by Merritt Y. Hughes, Roy Flannagan, Scott Elledge, Gordon Teskey, David Kastan, and Barbara Lewalski). The exception is Judith Anderson, who argues that the entire incident reflects Satan's solipsism: "Sin, as Satan's sin projected directly from his head, holds the key to hell and therefore he is self-confined, albeit evidently with God's active co-operation." (*Reading the Allegorical Intertext: Chaucer, Spenser, Shakespeare, Milton* [New York: Fordham University Press, 2008], p. 305).
47 "Weaver against Ward," sig. Q3r.
48 Ibid., sig. Ddd2.
49 Cf. Victoria Silver, *Imperfect Sense: The Predicament of Milton's Irony* (Princeton University Press, 2001), pp. 262–3.
50 Quoted in Winfield, "The History of Negligence," 185.
51 Lucy Hutchinson, *Order and Disorder*, David Norbrook (ed.), (Oxford: Blackwell, 2001), I. 253.
52 Feisal Mohamed, *In the Anteroom of Divinity: The Reformation of the Angels from Colet to Milton* (University of Toronto Press, 2008), p. 108.
53 I owe this point to my student, Diana Ferrell.
54 Michael J. Allen, "Divine Instruction: *Of Education* and the Pedagogy of Raphael, Michael, and the Father," *Milton Quarterly* 26 (1992), 115. For a more positive evaluation of Raphael, see Margaret Thickstun, *Milton's "Paradise Lost": Moral Education* (New York: Palgrave, 2007), pp. 105–18, and Mohamed, *In the Anteroom of Divinity*, pp. 115–40.
55 Allen, "Divine Instruction," p. 116.
56 Ibid.
57 I owe this point to my student, Jenni Liu.
58 I am grateful to John Rumrich for suggesting this point.
59 "Milton's 'Dramatick Constitution': The Celestial Dialogue in *Paradise Lost*, Book III," *Milton Studies* 23 (1987), 231.
60 "Weaver against Ward," sig. Q3r; E.R. *v.* J.P., quoted in Baker and Milsom, *Sources of English Legal History*, pp. 562–3.

CHAPTER 3

The political theology of Milton's Heaven

John Rogers

Readers of *Paradise Lost* have long struggled to understand the apparent tension between Milton's uncompromising commitment to a non-monarchic politics, as evidenced in the regicide tracts, and the decidedly monarchic structure of what seems to be the exemplary polity of the poem's Heaven. The God of *Paradise Lost* is not just a father, but a king, a king, in fact, who may share an awkward affinity with the absolutist sovereigns against whom Milton had inveighed so passionately in such treatises as *The Tenure of Kings and Magistrates* and *Eikonoklastes* at mid century. The interpretive problem that Milton's representation of God as king has posed to critics is a familiar one, and is felt almost immediately by the epic's readers. Might the unquestionably monarchic structure of Milton's Heaven work to elevate kingship – *earthly* kingship – in spite of the anti-monarchic commitments proclaimed so eloquently in those treatises composed from 1649 to 1652?[1] Or might the divine monarchism of the epic function, as William Empson argued so provocatively, to derogate the poem's God, to force an oblique questioning of the "ways of God" that *Paradise Lost*, at least at an explicit level, claimed at its opening that it would labor to justify?[2]

Two of the liveliest and most acute critics of Milton's poem have recently taken up these central questions concerning the critical interpretation of the politics of Heaven. Michael Bryson and Peter C. Herman both point out that the dominant critical tendency among scholars of Milton has been to avoid the notorious conclusions of Empson's interpretation: critics of the last forty-five years have tended rather to argue for the sheer incommensurability between earthly and heavenly sovereignty.[3] As Herman notes, "the most common strategy for imposing political stability onto *Paradise Lost* is the assertion, in [Barbara] Lewalski's formulation, that 'there can be no possible parallel between earthly kings and divine kingship'" (p. 84).[4] The king of Heaven, and only the king of Heaven, is thus entitled to displays of arbitrary monarchic authority. Any comparison of Milton's God with a similarly absolutist Charles, or even Cromwell, here on earth, it has further been argued, far from diminishing the sanctity or the authority of deity, can only shine an unflattering light on the presumptive Satanic arrogance of the earthly imitator of Heaven's monarch.

Bryson and Herman have written passionately and articulately in rejection of those (and other) post-Empsonian attempts to explain, or explain away, what can often seem to be the almost irredeemably tyrannical nature of the God of *Paradise Lost*. Bryson's is a systematically ironic reading of the republican Milton's Heaven, a space whose representation as a kingdom in *Paradise Lost* is seen to serve the ultimately didactic function of mirroring, and thus exposing, the culture's own misbegotten projections of a monarchic deity. Bryson rejects, rightly, any simple-minded interpretation of *Paradise Lost* whereby Milton is viewed to "highlight … good and evil by giving the reader a God who is totally good and a Satan who is totally evil" (p. 16). But the solution he proposes as a counter to this simplistic interpretive strategy may well threaten merely to reverse the conventional reading's identification of the monarchic God with good, proposing in its place a new identification of Milton's monarchic God with evil. For Bryson, *Paradise Lost* and *Paradise Regained* function as "an indictment and rejection of a God imagined in terms of military and monarchical power"; the demonically monarchic Father, therefore, serves as Milton's "sublime artistic rendering of the execrable tendency to conceive of God in Satanic terms. The Father of *Paradise Lost* is not Milton's illustration of how God *is*, but Milton's scathing critique of how, all too often, God is *imagined*" (p. 12). What Milton's God really *is*, suggests Bryson, is a deity who inspires not fear and resentment, but love, loyalty, and admiration (p. 12).

It is a different interpretive solvent that Peter Herman applies to the heavenly politics of *Paradise Lost*. For Herman it's not one particular image of the heavenly polity that's at stake, but the co-existence, rather, of multiple, contradictory images. The contradiction can for Herman present itself in the form either of competing representations within the poem itself, or the conceptual tension that arises when we consider Milton's documented detestation of Stuart absolutism on the one hand, and, on the other, Milton's lavish representation of heavenly absolutism in *Paradise Lost*. The complex effect that Milton achieves by means of these oppositions is what Herman calls the "poetics of incertitude," a literary strategy Milton developed in the aftermath of a failed revolution, a period in which Milton subjected himself to a "wholesale questioning of just about everything he had argued for in his earlier prose works" (p. 21). Herman is right to suggest that Milton's epic offers its readers innumerable instances of representational and conceptual contradiction; and it may well be the case that many of those instances correlate with contradictions and uncertainties confronted, or inhabited, by Milton himself. But his argument for the poet's deliberate cultivation of a "poetics of incertitude" might also be construed at times to argue for a new, almost monolithic, Miltonic absolute: the poet's commitment to, or perhaps even his faith in, a paradoxically *certain* form of "incertitude," one that is unwavering not merely in its multiple investments in competing positions or ideas, but in its singular investment in the value of incertitude in and of itself.

What these recent responses to Milton's monarchic Heaven share with an earlier generation's more critically conservative defense of Milton's heavenly king in *Paradise Lost* is the assumption that the significance of the relation of Milton's poetic representation of the heavenly polity to his intimately held religious ideals is founded on the rhetorical principle of analogy: for Herman the contradictory or conflicted representation of heavenly kingship is analogous to the mature Milton's contradictory or conflicted relation to the political sphere in general, while for Bryson, the uncompromisingly absolutist representation of heavenly kingship functions by means of negative analogy to figure forth the positive vision Milton really held of God. These critics are unquestionably right to argue that the contours of the political authority Milton has ascribed to God are in some way intimately tied to the theology or political philosophy he is committed to elaborate in the space of his epic poem, and right to reject any assertion of the incommensurability of Milton's heavenly and earthly representations. But the political theology of Milton's Heaven does not, I hope to argue in this essay, function analogically, his heavenly polity serving simply as a positive or negative example of, or a contrasting foil for, an ideal political structure or religious vision on earth. Milton's shockingly unsympathetic representation of arbitrary authority in Heaven works, rather, as I will argue, to provide a radical mythological point of origin for the principles of human liberty he had long idealized as the foundation for successful political institutions on earth. Heavenly absolutism is neither incommensurate with nor analogous to the ideal Milton held up for terrestrial politics; it bears rather, perhaps troublingly, an intimate, logical tie to the highest form of human liberty Milton was able to imagine.

Let us begin by looking at the passage in *Paradise Lost* that readers of Milton have no choice but to confront when considering the enormously complex problem of the politics of Milton's Heaven: the Father's proclamation before the assembled angels of the ceremonial unction, or messianic anointing, of the Son:

> Hear all ye Angels, Progenie of Light,
> Thrones, Dominations, Princedoms, Vertues, Powers,
> Hear my Decree, which unrevok't shall stand.
> This day I have begot whom I declare
> My onely Son, and on this holy Hill
> Him have anointed, whom ye now behold
> At my right hand; your Head I him appoint;
> And by my Self have sworn to him shall bow
> All knees in Heav'n, and shall confess him Lord:
> Under his great Vice-gerent Reign abide
> United as one individual Soule
> For ever happie.
>
> (5.600–11)

Sealing the connection of the poem's *empyrean* with the politics of *empire*, Milton, by means of Raphael's narration of divine history in Book 5, had introduced this royal proclamation of the Father's by sketching a scene of political assembly that far outshone in its portrayal of absolute dominion any previous image of a tyrannical Satan, "High on a Throne of Royal State" (2.1) in Hell: "th'Empyreal Host / Of Angels by Imperial summons call'd, / Innumerable before th'Almighties Throne / Forthwith from all the ends of Heav'n appeerd" (5.583–6). Here more than anywhere else in *Paradise Lost*, Milton insists that we consider the authority of God as monarchic, and the nature of that monarchy as uncompromisingly absolutist.

In order to explore the possibility of the *non*-analogical, indeed paradoxical, tie the Miltonic ideal of human freedom might have to such uncompromising representations of divine absolutism, I propose in this essay that we augment our investigation of the political lineaments of Milton's portrayal of God to include a consideration of that portrait's theological contours. The political absolutism that distinguishes God's role as heavenly king in *Paradise Lost* is inseparable from the power attributed to him by virtue of the poem's theology. It is in fact just this scene of the Father's elevation of the Son, maybe more than any other in *Paradise Lost*, which has long encouraged readers to assume the poem's engagement with one of Christianity's most notorious heresies.[5] Denying the equality and essential identity of the three persons of the Trinity, Milton, we know from the theological treatise *Christian Doctrine* he wrote in the years before the composition of *Paradise Lost*, came to embrace many aspects of the ancient heresy of Arianism, the fourth-century theology of the Father and the Son universally acknowledged to be the archetypal Christian heresy.[6] Like the implicit theology that dominates *Paradise Lost*, Arianism insisted that the Son was a creature, inferior to the Father, generated, or "begot," in Heaven at a specific point in time before the Son's incarnation as the Messiah; that the Father alone was omnipotent, omniscient, and ubiquitous; that in creating the Son the Father shared or communicated none of his essential substance, or what theologians call his *hypostasis*, with him; and that the Father's will and consciousness were entirely distinct and separate from the Son's. This is the theology of the Father and Son as stated explicitly in Milton's *Christian Doctrine* and implicitly in *Paradise Lost* and *Paradise Regained*, all works written within the last two decades of Milton's life.[7]

That the scene in *Paradise Lost* of the Father's proclamation of his anointing of the Son is an explicitly Arian fiction is made clear by a reading of the fourth-century Athanasius, Arius's great confuter and the founder of the Church's orthodox position on the equality and co-essentiality of the Father and Son. The great Church Father knew that the representations of the Son's ceremonial exaltation in Scripture were all scenes from the life of the incarnate Christ (his baptism, for example); or, as in Hebrews, if it wasn't actually the Messiah *on earth* who was exalted, it was the resurrected Christ who received his exaltation in Heaven after the Ascension. But the early Arians, whose Christology, like Milton's, rested on a belief in the Son's actual generation at a point in time well before the Creation of the universe, consistently placed the scene of exaltation in the life of the pre-existent Son, a fact that Athanasius rightly pointed out could not be supported by any of the scriptural references to exaltation.[8]

A brief consideration of early modern Reformation Trinitarianism, and of the dominant religious culture's positive articulation of the doctrine of the Trinity whose existence Milton so passionately denied, might at this point be useful. At the bottom of many of the official Reformation defenses of the existence of the Trinity (all of which are heavily indebted to the Church Fathers) is the principle of necessity. It is a commonplace to say that, with respect to man, the Reformation deity assumed an extraordinary degree of freedom and power: the God of Calvin was alone free and capable of determining the path to salvation. But with respect to the inner workings of the godhead itself, the three persons of the Trinity, even for Calvin, enjoy nothing like freedom; they are inescapably bound to the relations and actions in a divine drama founded strictly on a principle of unswerving necessity.[9] The Father and the Son are of course, for Trinitarians, co-eternal; but the Father nonetheless "generated" the Son, mysteriously outside of any temporal framework, in an act that was necessary and inevitable. This necessary and inevitable generation of the Son merely establishes the paradigm for all of the actions, or functions, of the Trinitarian godhead, none of which, it is endlessly repeated in the theological literature, could have occurred otherwise. Just as the Father had no choice but to create the Son, the Father has no choice but to demand judicial satisfaction for the crime of Adam's fall, and the Son has no choice but to be sacrificed on the cross: a perfect and sufficient sacrifice, adequate to atoning for Adam's crime because the Son is himself, of course, God. The Father in the Trinitarian scheme does not voluntarily *accept* the sacrifice he had no choice but to demand: he can't be afforded the liberty of accepting or doing anything of his own arbitrary volition. The necessary action of Christ's sacrifice in and of itself automatically, necessarily, effects the atonement, the consequence of which is the necessary and inevitable salvation and damnation (in the Calvinist scheme) of the elect and the reprobate. The three persons of the Trinity, with respect certainly to their role as actors in the divine drama of Creation and redemption, endure a bondage of the will easily as constrictive as that suffered by the sinful man of Reformation Protestantism. And it was, I propose, the seeming implications *for man* of the iron determinism by which the persons of the Trinity were themselves gripped that as much as anything else moved some of the most radical early modern Protestants, Milton included, to articulate or adopt a *critique* of the orthodox doctrine of the Trinity.

Critics of Milton have mused for a long time now on the meaning of the scene in *Paradise Lost* of the Father's decree of the Son's begetting: "This day I have begot whom I declare / My onely Son" (5.602–4).[10] They have largely attempted to justify the ways of Milton's God by supplying a more or less rational interpretation of the Father's mysterious declaration of the Son's kingship. And in this respect, the scholars of *Paradise Lost* are only reproducing the efforts of the poem itself to rationalize this first event of Milton's story, which had presented itself at the time of the Father's decree as one of perfect reasonlessness. In a related scene of exaltation, occurring after this event in the chronology of the story (but appearing earlier in the poem), the Son is rewarded for his atoning offer to be "accounted" man himself by a second exaltation, an elevation not merely over the angels in Heaven, but over newly created man as well (3.305–22).[11] Asserting with great emphasis, at this second occasion of elevation, the Son's *right* to this new position as "Head Supreme," the Father makes as perspicuous as possible the rationale behind this second, yet more glorious, promotion: the Son has "been found / By Merit more than Birthright Son of God, / Found worthiest to be so by being Good" (3.308–10).[12] A "multitude of Angels," too, gathered for a psalm of praise (3.345), will join the work of explaining the justice of the Son's promotion as head, celebrating not just the Son's late victory over the "warring angels" in the recently completed war in Heaven, but the event, now belatedly established as historical truth, that the Father "created" "Heav'n of Heavens and all the Powers therein" "by" the Son (3.390–1).

Shortly after the chronologically first event of elevation, in the scene from Book 5 cited above, in which the Father had initially commanded the angels to obey the Son, Milton's poem will pressure us again to credit a supposition, articulated by the loyal angel Abdiel (5.831–45), that the original elevation of the Son was not the announcement of the Father's inscrutable and arbitrary act of unction, begetting, or creation, but merely a long-belated acknowledgment of a creative act at once prior and superior to any subsequent creation. In an elaborate defense of the justice of the Father's decree of the Son's new headship over the angels, Abdiel will first remind Satan, rightly, that the source of the Father's authority over the angels derives from his creation of them: God is he "who made / Thee what thou art, and formd the Pow'rs of Heav'n / Such as he pleasd, and circumscribd thir being" (5.823–5). But, as Abdiel knows, an appeal to God's authority as creator is not in itself a justification of the particular action of the Son's elevation. Abdiel will thus continue his defense of the Father's decree by means of the poem's chronologically first conjecture concerning the Son's *right* to his new elevated status as head. "[B]y experience taught," Abdiel claims, the angels "know" of the Father's goodness and his concern for angelic dignity (5.826–8); and it is this "knowledge," acquired not by divine revelation but by "experience," that authorizes Abdiel's bold justification of the Father's elevation of the Son: the Son is he "by whom / As by his Word the mighty Father made / All things, ev'n thee, and all the Spirits of Heav'n / By him created in thir bright degrees" (5.835–8).

How Abdiel makes the leap from his experiential knowledge of divine goodness to this extraordinary Christological conjecture of the Son's ancient role as the vehicle by which the Father created Heaven and the angels is never divulged; we know that his supposition precedes in time the Father's pronouncement of the Son's "merit," and the angelic choir's celebration of the Son's Creation of Heaven, both of which will not be uttered until *after* the war in Heaven. It can come as no surprise that the source of Abdiel's apparent knowledge of the Son's role in the creation of the angels is a matter of considerable interest to Satan, who bases his subsequent argument with Abdiel on what he takes to be the unstable foundation for that angel's claim, improbably grounded in "experience," of the Son's *right* to headship: "strange point and new!" Satan will exclaim, "Doctrin which we would know whence learnt" (5. 855–6). It will soon be the case that this strange and new doctrine of the Son's role in the creation of the angels is to be treated as truth, as the Father will later presumably intimate when he tells Abdiel, in Book 6, that "*Messiah* ... by right of merit Reigns" (6.43), a formula, as we have seen, the Father will repeat later in the chronology of the story in 3.309. But the imprimatur that the poem appears later to place on Abdiel's improbable theological conjecture, whether by means of the voice of the Father in Book 6 or the voice of the Father and then of the angelic choir in Book 3, in no way countermands our, or Satan's, experience of the Father's actual decree as one whose basis in justice or reason in no way manifests itself at the time.

At the very least we are obliged to join William Empson in acknowledging the fact that the Father, in the scene of the original elevation represented in Book 5, has gone out of his way to make it difficult to interpret his declaration of the Son's headship over the angels as an action founded in reason or justice.[13] The Father seems if anything to exult in the sheer reasonlessness of the act, appealing in this public proclamation to no other source of justification than his own authority as God ("And by my Self have sworn" [5.607]). He takes pains to blur any distinction between the ceremonial unction performed earlier "this day," which he is announcing at the present moment, and what we have to assume were the more ancient acts of his originary creation of the Son and of his later use of the Son as vehicle through which he created very Heaven and the angels themselves. In fact, it would have to be said of that initial scene of elevation that the Father has shrouded the rationale for his decree in such mystery for the express purpose of making this announcement of the long-completed event of his initial creation of the Son construable as an arbitrary, even whimsical, act of begetting, or adoption, only recently accomplished.

Why, we are entitled to ask, would God so flagrantly present himself in the guise of a tyrannical emperor? Why, especially in light of what appears now to be the *fact* of God's justice in decreeing the Son's headship over the angels, would the Father so carefully withhold from the assembled angels the information necessary to understand that decree's rationale? The Father, I suggest, is doing more than what Empson characterizes as an attempt to provoke Satan into rebelling (although it is nearly impossible to deny that that is one of the consequences of the scene of the Father's decree). The Father has presented his presumably justifiable elevation of his first begot as an egregiously unjustifiable one for an important reason. The tie between Son and Father, as that between any creature and creator, can only achieve the intellectually pure ideal Milton sets for it if the creator and creature in question act *as if* their relation were founded not on natural necessity or instinctive obligation, but on free, voluntary election. The seeming fiction of the Father's whimsical adoption of the Son, of the arbitrary election of a randomly elected being to serve henceforth in the privileged role as the beloved "only son," functions not merely, as Peter Herman might argue, as a way to insert a disorienting incertitude into this crucial moment in the poem, or, as Michael Bryson might argue, as a way to distance Milton's readers from a cripplingly conventional way of imagining divine sovereignty. The Father's strategic, and exasperating, obfuscation of the Son's birthright as heir of the Father's sovereignty, serves the strange but crucial role of introducing choice and contingency into what could otherwise be thought the determinative, perhaps necessary, tie that connects Father to Son, creator to creature, or superior to inferior being. With sublime counterintuitiveness, Milton, as we will see, exploits a fiction of tyrannical absolutism in order to inscribe within his universe a liberal ethos of elective affinities.

The evidence supplied in Milton's theological treatise, and in several other scenes of *Paradise Lost*, suggests that the most meaningful aspect of this monarchic scene of exaltative anointing rests in what strikes everybody – Satan of course included – as the sheer arbitrariness of the Father's imperial decree. It is certainly the case that Milton goes as far as any anti-Trinitarian in isolating omnipotence and omniscience in the Father. But Milton presses the matter further by appropriating some key features of Socinianism – the early modern anti-Trinitarian heresy that updated the ancient Arianism with a rigorously logical and juridical method of scriptural interpretation – and depicting thereby a Father who punctuates Christian history with a series of arbitrary, voluntary, temporally specific, decrees. There was, for Milton, first, the generation of the Son, who was begotten, as Maurice Kelley rightly noted, "in consequence of a decree" made "within the limits of time," a first-order creation implied, though never represented, in *Paradise Lost*, and one that, in the *Christian Doctrine*, is seen to establish the crucial pattern of divine decrees, which share the singular feature of being unprompted and unnecessary. The Son, for Milton, is not tied to the Father, as the orthodox insisted, out of a natural necessity; he was created rather out of a perfectly voluntary act of the Father's arbitrary will. The generation of the Son was merely the first event to issue from the Father's arbitrary decree, but it would be followed, Milton tells us in the *Christian Doctrine*, by the institution of the Son's kingship (Book 5), the Son's priesthood (Book 3), and his resurrection from the dead, all events that follow subsequent, similarly arbitrary, monarchic decrees.[14] To this list of the Father's decrees, we could also add one not directly involving the Son, the prohibition of the fruit from the tree of the knowledge of good and evil in the garden of Eden.

Why Milton so consistently presses the heretical view that God's decree to create the Son, and in fact all of the decrees issued by God, are not necessary acts, but contingent, arbitrary, fundamentally unnecessary, acts, is not a question that scholars have addressed. In fact, as noted above, critics attempting to unfold the "politics" of Milton's poetry and theology have traditionally turned to the rhetorical principle of analogy as the means by which they interpret the awkward tension between Milton's radical, indeed heretical, insistence, in the *Christian Doctrine* and *Paradise Lost*, on the Father's arbitrary kingship in Heaven and historical Milton's equally radical insistence on the subjection of any earthly polity to the decidedly non-arbitrary, rational standards of natural law. But what has never been fully appreciated is the extent to which the radical contingency that underlies each of the actions of the Miltonic deity works not to counterpoise or undermine, but actually to bolster, the work that both the theological treatise and the epic poem are performing in the service of a liberatory politics.

When writing as a political philosopher, Milton, as is well known, had no patience for arbitrary sovereignty or any kind of civil law that had its origin in an earthly sovereign's positive, arbitrary decree. Milton would always turn to the realms of contract law, covenantal law, and the law of nature when imagining the readiest ways to establish a true commonwealth. For Milton the political philosopher, only civil laws founded in the law of nature, which is inscribed on the hearts of men, could be seen as binding.[15] Freedom in the civic realm, for Milton, was always freedom from arbitrary law decreed from the outside. And this civic freedom found its compass and stability in man's gentle subjection to a law of nature already dwelling within. In a state ideally structured by rational laws written in accordance with the law of nature, the individual, whose faculty of reason was also tuned to the law of nature, could almost be thought to govern himself: his minimal obligation to the laws of the state could be viewed as little more than a self-determined obligation to obey the internal dictates of his own heart.

The type of reason the ideally self-sufficient Miltonic subject exercised was often known as "right reason," a concept that establishes itself in the early modern period as a morally informed guide for rational behavior potentially distinct from simple reason, which was always construable as a canny, self-interested rational calculation (as "reason" seems often to function, for example, in the writing of Hobbes). Right reason, though, is the exercise of one's rational faculty in accordance with an internalized sense of the law of nature, or what early modern philosophers often call the moral law. An act of the will performed in conjunction with "right reason," then, is an act that conforms to a set of laws and principles objectively inscribed into the Creation – the natural world – but which also conforms to an internalized moral law to which every individual, theoretically at least, has some type of subjective access. To perform, then, a morally good act, one need merely subject oneself to a natural principle of reason divinely implanted within the self.

That was the political philosophy that marked the central theory of obligation in the majority of Milton's political writings. But when writing as a theologian, and imagining the exercise of the human will in a context outside the historical framework of the political state, Milton held the ideal of freedom to a higher standard. He could not permit himself to ascribe the ultimate governance of the universe to anything like a rationally accessible law of nature, and for precisely the reason that the law of nature *had* to be the governing principle of the state. A law of nature as viewed from the perspective of right reason is naturally binding: one would have to counter one's own morally tuned rational instincts to violate a natural law. And in the political sphere it was precisely this sense of obligation to the natural law that justified Milton's assertion of its priority over any of the positive, civic, laws decreed from outside the individual by the arbitrary powers of Church or state. But Milton was never unmindful of the fact that the free Christian's moral obligation to obey the internally inscribed natural law rather than the externally imposed positive civil law was still an *obligation*. In the oxymoronic account of the Will's freedom within the context of "right reason" Adam presents to Eve on the morning of the Fall, "God left free the will, *for what obeyes / Reason, is free*, and Reason he made right" (9.351–2; my emphasis). The Miltonic subject, both in *Paradise Lost* and in the prose, written ten years earlier, expressive of Milton's most idealistic political philosophy, may have been liberated from the arbitrary dicta issued by Church or state, but he could not in any ultimate sense experience himself as fully liberated, bound and obliged as he was to obey the divinely endowed predisposition to virtue and goodness that subtended "right reason."[16] It is the obligation, therefore, of Milton's theology, as it is worked out both in *Christian Doctrine* and in *Paradise Lost*, to carve out for the will a liberatory space from which the will is freed of its obligation not only to the external powers of arbitrary magistracy in the state, but freed as well from its obligation to the internally experienced dictates of the law of nature, those rationally intuitable moral laws that subtend the individual's exercise of right reason.

Milton argues in *Christian Doctrine* that an arbitrary divine decree, to which one's adherence can be motivated by neither nature nor reason nor any internalized propensity toward goodness, is the only law that one can obey, or disobey, with perfect, unfettered freedom.[17] The decree proscribing the fruit is, crucially, *not* the product of a natural or a moral law, discoverable by the inward power of human reason. Milton insists that the commandment had to be an arbitrary, positive, one, because man's obedience could not have been made evident if the prohibition of the fruit had been a simple consequence of the law of nature, or an innately discernible moral law: "For man was by nature good and holy, and was naturally disposed to do right, so it was certainly not necessary to bind him by the requirements of any covenant to something which he would do of his own accord. And he would not have shown obedience at all by performing good works, since he was in fact drawn to these by his own natural impulses, without being commanded" (*CPW* 6:352).[18] Had man shown even the slightest *natural* inclination to obey the decree against the fruit, his act of obedience, which would have been determined or swayed by an internalized moral instinct, would not have been willed with perfect freedom; and man would never thereby have been able freely to demonstrate his obedience to God. Therefore, Milton argues, only a prohibition fundamentally meaningless could properly create the conditions for the ultimate form of human liberty, which is a "liberty of indifference."[19]

In this respect, Milton makes a radical departure from the Calvinist William Ames, to whose *Marrow of Theology* he is otherwise indebted for the structure of his chapter in *Christian Doctrine* on the "Special Government of Man before the Fall," which discusses the prohibition against the fruit. For Ames, the Fall was a transgression not just against God but against the faculty of reason God implanted in man, as the prohibition was a moral law perfectly in tune with the law of nature: "First, the law prescribed to men and angels has the same moral essence summed up in the decalogue. Second, it is written in the heart in the form of disposition [*habitus*], where the first foundation of conscience called συντήρησις, *synteresis*, is located, Rom. 2:15."[20] Countering Ames's natural moralization of the prohibition, Milton turns for argumentative support to some of the late sixteenth-century Counter-Reformation moral philosophies of the radically free will, especially those of the Spanish philosophers Luis de Molina and Francis Suarez (Suarez's philosophy, we know, Milton had been obliged to study at Cambridge, and in fact one of his academic exercises, the fourth *Prolusion*, explicitly takes up some arguments from Suarez's *Disputationes Metaphysicae* [1597]). These moral philosophers had, in explicit opposition to the binding of the will espoused by Luther, Calvin, and the other magisterial Reformers, argued for a radically free human will that was bound or swayed by nothing, not even the rational pressures applied by an internalized law of nature. Man has a faculty of *reason*, sometimes called intellect, and that faculty is attuned to a divinely implanted moral compass or law of nature; but man also has a distinct faculty of the *will*, which is completely free to choose objects and actions and ideas that are in no way bound by, or guided by, or responsive to, the faculty of reason. And this radically free human will exists in a universe governed by a radically free, arbitrary God, whose commandments can only be obeyed freely, by a human will unbound or untethered by reason or any other faculty naturally predisposing the subject to the good. In the universe of radical contingency sketched by these Counter-Reformation philosophers, the very arbitrariness of divine will, far from trampling or dismantling human freedom, provides the necessary conditions under which this radical freedom – a perfect freedom of indifference to any internalized sense of the morality of good or bad – can be exercised.

Surely it was Milton's conviction that perfect freedom in this ultimate sense can only play itself out on a field of perfect arbitrariness that drew him to the celebrated philosophies of Molina and Suarez, and, further back, to the ancient heresy of Arianism. The arch-heretic Arius had stripped the founding social relation of the universe, that of the Father to the Son, of anything that smacked of nature, or necessity, or any fundamental or essential form of binding connectivity. Milton followed Arius in radically distinguishing the Father from the Son, with whom the Father has shared none of his unique essence, or *hypostasis*, and whom he created, and later exalted at distinct moments in time, entirely at his pleasure. All human beings after Adam and Eve are begotten, begotten, as Adam reminds us after the Fall in Book 10, not by "election," but by "Natural necessity" (10.764–5). Human offspring are the inevitable products of the determinative dynamics of desire and reproduction, one of whose consequences is the natural, instinctive obligation that children feel toward their parents. (It is as if the "Natural necessity" of sexual desire that conditioned the child's conception were reproduced in the natural tie that binds him to the parent, and vice versa.)

The heavenly Father's absolutely voluntary, perhaps even whimsical, creation of the Son of God (and by extension, we have to assume, his fundamentally *un*necessary creation of each of the angels as well), offers each of his creatures a perfect liberation from a binding *habitus* or any instinctive, or natural, obligation to the Father. Freed from the genetic bind of shared essence and the ethical or political bind of inescapable obligation, or the obliging constraint that Satan will characterize as the "debt immense of endless gratitude" (4.52), the Son (like all his fellow angels) enjoys a relation to the Father that is essentially synthetic rather than natural, elective rather than appointed. As Machiavelli and Hobbes would before him, in their radical reconceptualization of the link that connects a sovereign to the state, Milton takes a tie that had always and everywhere been seen as natural and necessary and decrees it artificial and contingent. It is fundamentally a free, *political* relation, and not an obligatory, *filial* relation that the Son of God has with the Heavenly Father. And it is likewise a fundamentally political and not a filial relation that each of the Father's angelic and human creatures should assume to have with the Father's decrees. It is, finally, this radically anti-Trinitarian independence from the Father that guarantees the uniqueness and freedom of the Son's will, and which lays the foundation for the uniqueness and freedom of each of God's other creatures.

What, then, is the nature of the relation between the political structure of Milton's Heaven and the ideal political structure on earth? It is not, as I have already suggested, one simply of positive or negative analogy. Milton attempts in *Paradise Lost*, and at many points in *Christian Doctrine,* to reach beyond the obligation of the rule of reason and the law of nature that had served so nobly as the cornerstones of his political vision. He pushes himself in *Paradise Lost* to conjure states of being in existence *before* the onset of modern political institutions (virtuous or not), which Milton had always identified as postlapsarian phenomena. With a counterintuitive, and likely even perverse, zeal, Milton finds in the divine absolutism of his heretical Arian deity not a model for, but an enabling point of origin for, the most radical form of creaturely freedom he could imagine. The radically free prelapsarian will whose existence is dependent solely on the unencumbered absolutism of the Father can be seen in turn to subtend the more circumscribed but nonetheless potent liberties available to man after the Fall, the political, social, and religious freedoms for which Milton would continue to argue so passionately in the late polemical prose and the final books of *Paradise Lost*. The potential for a radical creaturely freedom, underlying what literary tradition has rightly deemed the most liberal strands of Milton's thought, emerges not in spite of, but because of, the dread phenomenon that Satan labels, provocatively, and on some level justly, the "Tyranny of Heav'n" (1.124).

NOTES

1 Such is essentially the position assumed by Malcolm Mackenzie Ross in *Milton's Royalism: A Study of the Conflict of Symbol and Idea in the Poems* (Ithaca: Cornell University Press, 1943).
2 William Empson, *Milton's God* (Cambridge University Press, 1981), pp. 36–42.
3 Michael Bryson, *Milton's Rejection of God as King* (Newark: University of Delaware Press, 2004), and Peter C. Herman, *Destabilizing Milton: "Paradise Lost" and the Poetics of Incertitude* (New York: Palgrave Macmillan, 2005). Citations from these two books will be noted by page number parenthetically in the text.
4 Herman is quoting Barbara K. Lewalski, *The Life of John Milton: A Critical Biography* (Oxford: Blackwell, 2000), p. 466.
5 The best account of the early identification of the heretical theologies of *Paradise Lost* is in Michael Bauman, *Milton's Arianism* (Frankfurt am Main: Verlag Peter Lang, 1987), pp. 276–89.
6 Milton's once-disputed authorship of the theological treatise, *De Doctrina Christiana*, has been authoritatively established by Gordon Campbell, Thomas N. Corns, and John K. Hale in *Milton and the Manuscript of "De Doctrina Christiana"* (Oxford University Press, 2007).
7 See Chapter 5 of Book 1 of the treatise, edited by Maurice Kelley and translated by John Carey, in Don M. Wolfe (ed.), *Complete Prose Works of John Milton*, 8 vols. (New Haven: Yale University Press, 1953–82), 6:203–80. Citations from the English translation of Milton's *De Doctrina Christiana* will be taken from this edition, noted as *CPW*, and cited parenthetically by volume and page number in the text.
8 See Athanasius on Arius's reading of Philippians 2:5–11: "These things were not said before, only when the Word became flesh, that it might become clear that 'he was humbled' and 'he will be exalted' are said about the human nature." *Trinitarian Controversy*, William G. Rusch (trans.) (Philadelphia: Fortress Press, 1980), p. 104.
9 Milton's contemporary, the Congregational divine John Owen, is probably mid-century England's fiercest critic of anti-Trinitarianism, and the noisiest proponent, as in *De Divina Justitia* (1653) and *A Brief Declaration and Vindication of the Trinity* (1669), of the absolute necessity of the Trinity's

actions, especially that of the Son's satisfaction of the Father's demand for justice after the Fall.
10 Critical interpretations of this scene of Exaltation include: Edmund Creeth, "The 'Begetting' and the Exaltation of the Son," *Modern Language Notes* 76 (1961), 696–700; William B. Hunter, Jr., "Milton on the Exaltation of the Son: The War in Heaven in *Paradise Lost*," *English Literary History* 36 (1969), 215–31; Richard S. Ide, "On the Begetting of the Son in *Paradise Lost*," *Studies in English Literature* 24 (1984), 141–55; and, most useful, Maurice Kelley, *This Great Argument: A Study of Milton's "De Doctrina Christiana" as a Gloss upon "Paradise Lost"* (Princeton University Press, 1941), pp. 94–106.
11 For discussions of the distinct acts of exaltation narrated in Books 5 and 3 of *Paradise Lost*, see John S. Diekhoff, *Milton's "Paradise Lost", A Commentary on the Argument* (New York: Columbia University Press, 1946), pp. 78–80; and Michael E. Bauman, *Milton's Arianism* (Frankfurt: Peter Lang, 1987), p. 238. Herman, in *Destabilizing Milton*, pp. 193–4, usefully digests some of the competing critical claims about the relation of the poem's exaltation scenes.
12 Marvin P. Hoogland describes Calvin's opposition to any notion that "Christ merited His Exaltation," in *Calvin's Perspective on the Exaltation of Christ* (Kampen: J. H. Kok, 1966), p. 149.
13 Empson, *Milton's God*, p. 102, writes: "If the Son had inherently held this position from before the creation of all angels, why has it been officially withheld from him till this day, and still more, why have the angels not previously been told that he was the agent of their creation? … to give no reason at all for the Exaltation makes it appear a challenge, intended to outrage a growing intellectual dissatisfaction among the angels with the claims of God."
14 See Milton's argument for the scriptural proof of the arbitrariness of the Father's begetting of the Son, and of the arbitrariness of the Father's other decrees regarding the Son: "When all the above passages, and especially the second Psalm, have been compared and digested carefully, it will be apparent that, however the Son was begotten, it did not arise from natural necessity, as is usually maintained, but was just as much a result of the father's decree and will as the Son's priesthood, kingship, and resurrection from the dead. The fact that he is called 'begotten,' whatever that means, and God's own Son, Rom. viii.32, does not stand in the way of this at all" (*CPW* 6:208).
15 In *The Tenure of Kings and Magistrates* (1649), Milton writes that "God put it into mans heart to find out that way at first for common peace and preservation, approving the exercise thereof" (*CPW* 3:209). See, too, Martin Dzelzainis's remarks on Milton and the law of nature, in John Milton, Martin Dzelzainis (ed.), *Political Writings* (Cambridge University Press, 1991), p. xxii.
16 This argument is indebted to the reading of the divorce tracts by Victoria Kahn, in *Wayward Contracts: The Crisis of Political Obligation in England, 1640–1674* (Princeton University Press, 2004), pp. 198–207. Kahn argues that what "Milton discovers in his own inward being – or what Milton's prose discovers – is not simply the autonomous subject but a subject who is at once

voluntary and involuntary, for whom consent to contract is not always so readily distinguished from voluntary servitude to one's passions" (p. 207).

17 Milton's thinking is aligned with that of the influential "Molinist account of freedom," named after the seventeenth-century Jesuit theologian Luis de Molina, whose closely related position on the freedom of the will is valuably characterized by Sean Greenberg, "Leibniz Against Molinism: Freedom, Indifference, and the Nature of the Will," in Donald Rutherford (ed.), *Leibniz: Nature and Freedom* (Oxford University Press, 2005), p. 218: "A man is free, given that with all the requisites for action having been posited, he is able to act or not act. On this account, agents are said to be 'indifferent' with respect to their choices, because they determine themselves to choose as they do on the basis of perceptions, desires, and so on, the 'requisites for action': in other words, the requisites for action do not determine the agent's choice."

18 The implicit philosophy of the will that emerges in this section of Milton's theological treatise has affinities with the earlier seventeenth-century philosophy of Francis Suarez, in particular the argument laid out in the nineteenth of Suarez's *Metaphysical Disputations*. Describing Suarez's celebrated theory of the will's relation to the intellect (the "intellect" serving as the philosopher's equivalent of the faculty of "reason"), Greenberg, "Leibniz Against Molinism," p. 225, writes: "The intellect is naturally necessitated to assent to what is true and dissent from what is false, and because it is determined by its objects, it cannot determine itself. By contrast, the will is not naturally necessitated to any particular good or any particular end, and therefore the will must determine itself to some particular good or end. Suarez's point is that the nature of the will is such that it must determine itself, while the intellect cannot do so."

19 I take this phrase, "liberty of indifference," from James A. Harris, *Of Liberty and Necessity: The Free Will Debate in Eighteenth-Century British Philosophy* (Oxford University Press, 2005).

20 William Ames, *The Marrow of Theology*, John D. Eusden (ed.) (Grand Rapids, Michigan: Baker Books, 1968), p. 112.

CHAPTER 4

Meanwhile: (un)making time in Paradise Lost

Judith Scherer Herz

> Ring the bells that still can ring
> Forget your perfect offering
> There is a crack, a crack in everything.
> That's how the light gets in.
>   Leonard Cohen, "Anthem"

What does it mean to count the days in *Paradise Lost*, to plot its chronology? Indeed, can one count out the poem's time and by such counting account for time, and what is at stake in this arithmetic? Why do we need to be assured that thirty-three days pass? Or maybe only twenty-eight or twenty-nine plus four, those four being days of a different *durée*, not days as we know them (as if the others were, although Raphael says that he has "measure[ed] things in Heav'n by things on Earth" [6.893] – but what "things"?). Accounting for time – so many days for fighting, falling, weltering, circling, traversing each colure, destroying, creating – assumes (and is then offered as proof of) a narrative coherence and an epistemological certainty, which may be more illusory than not. Of course, the materials are all there and as readers suspended in our own time, we are busy counting; arithmeticians all, we sum those thirty-three days to make them (Eureka!) equal the life span of Christ and we know with numeric certainty that the absolute center of the original ten-book text is the word "ascended," as the Son, "the copious matter" of the poet's song as he had promised in Book 3, caesura to follow, steps up into the chariot of paternal deity. No doubt Milton liked to play numerological games (one might pity the amanuenses who had to do the counting and the adjusting to make it work out), but even as the text asks us to count, it baffles our certainties. Indeed as reader-accountants we are rather like Satan, the ultimate literalist, time's accountant. Surveying the Eden he has returned to undo in Book 9, Satan glories how:

> in *one* day [he had] marr'd
> What he *Almightie* styl'd, *six* Nights and Days
> Continu'd making, and who knows how long
> Before had bin contriving, though perhaps
> Not longer then since I in *one* Night freed
> From servitude inglorious welnigh *half*
> Th'Angelic Name.
>
> (136–42; emphasis added)

Of course all readers are not chronologists who, like Grant McColley, Alastair Fowler, Gunnar Qvarnström, and more recently, Sherry Lutz Zively,[1] work with the assumption that a definitive number can be arrived at. (Zively, for example, asserts that her essay, "The 33 Days of *Paradise Lost*," will "determine the exact number of days in the plot of the poem and what the major characters did on each day." Amy Boesky, Blair Hoxby, James Dougal Fleming, and Anthony Welch, for example, each in relation to different arguments probe time's gaps and contradictions in the text's narrative.[2] Anthony Welch, attentive to what he calls "the series of fissures in time," argues that Milton "parries our efforts to exploit … chronological clues," so as to suggest the difference between our fallen time and the time of the poem's events. Thus, instead of a single overarching time, there are in his words "local timelines that correspond … to the poem's several settings."[3] Boesky, in an essay that emphasizes the multiplicity of the poem's time, shows how Milton both enables and impedes chronological time, how "narration is continually linked … to the temptation of sequence and its impossibility."[4]

But that chronological impasse acknowledged, baffling questions remain: when do things happen? Trying to answer that question begins to reveal the stresses in the poem's attempt to "assert Eternal Providence," bringing to the surface the contradictions inherent in showing the justice of "the wayes of God to men" (1.25–6). Certainly, we are instructed to count so many days for this, for that, but whatever the day, whatever local time line we are that moment within, there is always another time. It is always *meanwhile*. This adverb is indeed the perfect temporal marker for a text whose uncertainties are in part a function of its endlessly recursive structure (the reader has always to catch up to a moment that has happened / will happen) that is always present as past and as future in the text and in the reader's experience. *Meanwhile* both makes and unmakes time, advances and holds it back, pointing to a then which is at once before and after, to a now that is unmoored either in space or time. It sets up equivalences (*a* occurs while *b* is/was happening) and then disperses the temporal points of contact. Of course, it is hardly an unusual narrative device; how else keep track of multiple narrative strands? It is modern insofar as the novel naturalizes it, but older as medieval iconography positions multiple befores and afters as a frame to a central event. In *Paradise Lost*, however, it does more than keep story and back story moving. As a temporal marker, it occurs far less frequently than *now* and *then*, but its usages are salient. For in its blurring of now and then, in its multi-directionality, and in its potential for deferral and delay, it creates disturbances that betray an unease in the declared project of theodicy, an undertaking that might better be described as about theodicy rather than an example of it. In this sense the poem is less a justification of God's ways than an exploration of what justification implies, especially as poetry rather than theology can probe it in the meanwhile space of the poem's shifting temporalities.[5]

Before locating the space of meanwhile, however, one might ask when is now. It is a question made problematic, however, when the *now* as present moment is cast as past as in "… now, / While time was," for here time is simultaneously present and past: now/while/was). Thus the narrator attempts to conflate apocalypse with the first moment in/before time, as if there still could have been time. The enjambment (now/while…was) drops the narrative present *now* into time already past, but this *now* does not designate the present moment, for if time has already happened, there never was enough time:

> O for that warning voice, which he who saw
> Th' *Apocalyps*, heard cry in Heaven aloud,
> Then when the Dragon, put to second rout,
> Came furious down to be reveng'd on men,
> *Wo to the inhabitants on Earth!* that now,
> While time was, our first-Parents had bin warnd
> The coming of thir secret foe, and scap'd
> Haply so scap'd his mortal snare.
>
> (4.1–8)

This entrapment between times not only locates Satan in the narrative as it runs backward and then forward to the end of time, it also places the poet within the text, enabled, he claims, by the Muse to imagine a before as if it were present, and as a result, by force of desire, that is to say, poetry, to attempt to hold back the present.

As *now* loses location, tenses shift: the apocalyptic moment is yet to come, but it is past in the narration; indeed throughout the passage and the lines that follow, the tenses slip from past to past perfect to present. Yet the word *now*, once located in that passage, repeats and repeats. It places Satan in a time he is initiating ("now / *Satan*, now first inflam'd" [4.9–10]), indeed a time that has already begun ("nigh the birth / Now rowling" [15–16]) even as Satan's *now* goes back into "bitter memory" and then forward as it collides with the high noon of an Eden "now in his view" (27). Indeed, Satan first enters the poem in Book 1 on just such a *now*, the deicitic marking the first moment of narrative time, but simultaneous with that present is the past, the time that was: "for now the thought / Both of lost happiness and lasting pain / Torments him" (1.54–6). If Satan is trapped in a *now* that is always already past, Adam and Eve inhabit a densely layered present, where time is nearly at a standstill, indeed is easily forgotten. "With thee conversing I forget all time" (4.639), Eve tells Adam, even as she disturbs the enclosed perfection of her speech with a question, "[b]ut wherfore all night long shine these […]?" (4.657), which troubles that perfection, indeed almost breaks the mirror that has structured the passage's syntax of reflection. Adam's answer, however, at least momentarily, restores that stasis. But Adam and Eve inhabit time whether they know it or not. Eve's speech follows from Adam's detailing the cycle of day to night to morn within the Edenic work time of their pleasant labors, where he notes that the overgrown branches mock their scant manuring and observes that more hands than theirs will be needed to lop the wanton growth, concluding with "[m]ean while, as Nature wills, Night bids us rest" (4.633). Adam's *meanwhile* is to the night's rest before the day's labors, and is echoed in Eve's reply, where even these small shifts in time disappear as all times and seasons please alike, although she, too, like the narrator, like Adam, details each stage in the cycle. Forgetting time acknowledges time; time is marked in the language of its suspension. But we know that that night's rest is going to be singular rather than eternally repeatable. Fewer than a hundred lines earlier, another *meanwhile* ("Mean while in utmost Longitude … the setting Sun / Slowly descended" [4.539–41]) had marked the transition from Satan silently addressing the embracing Adam and Eve ("Live while ye may, / Yet happie pair" [4.533–4]) as he "began … his roam" (4.537–8) through Eden, to Uriel's entry with his warning to Gabriel. That conversation between angels occurs while Satan roams, while night falls, while Eve replays Adam's words and then echoes back her own. For Adam and Eve, time is almost at a standstill, although around them it is building hurriedly. Adam's glimpse of the future (those needed hands) is to the future as present. Time is stasis; for Adam and Eve, *meanwhile* is always *now*.

However, as God enters the poem he identifies a *now* that carries with it the *meanwhile* of all human time from a present that is not yet in time to the end of time. "Now had the Almighty Father from above, / … bent down his eye" (3.56–8), seeing Adam and Eve "[r]eaping immortal fruits of joy and love, / … In blissful solitude" (5.67–9), static in an eternal participial present, then seeing Satan "ready now" to step onto the outside of our world, which *now*, as it moves in time, is in an entirely separate time zone and tense from the one Adam and Eve are at that moment inhabiting. But what God sees, what the narrative points to (but in an essential sense, what the poet cannot see, blindness troping blindness here) is not the present but the future – the fall, the call for sacrifice, the elevation of the Son, who in accounting himself man, opens time until its end, when "long absent" (3.261) he will return with the multitude of his redeemed. Collapsing the first temporal event (the Fall) into the messianic event, Milton, following Paul, opens what Giorgio Agamben calls "the time of the now" in his working through Paul's understanding of the relation of the messianic moment to the eschaton.[6] The now is the space in which "time … contracts itself and begins to end." Messianic time, Agamben argues, "is that time [that] time takes to come to an end" (p. 67). Another word for that space/time would be "meanwhile". Yet as a narrative marker it offers no Pauline assurance of a then when all will be clarified since meanwhile time in narrative is backward moving, nostalgic, recursive rather than end directed; it delays what theodicy would bring to conclusion.

However, narrative delay can also be read as millenarian expectation. In response to the Son's proving himself "by merit more than birthright son of God," the Father looks through and past all human time to "the general doom" when Hell "shall be forever shut":

> Mean while
> The World shall burn, and from her ashes spring
> New Heav'n and Earth, …
> …
> Then thou thy regal Scepter shalt lay by,
> For regal Scepter then no more shall need,
> God shall be All in All.
> (3.333–41)

This account of the Son eventually returning to the Father has already been presented even though we have not yet read it, at the poem's midpoint of ascent, as God acknowledges that he will resign sceptre and power "when in the end / Thou shalt be All in All" (6.731–2). When is this *meanwhile* that is, at once, all history and God's *now*? (The numerologists might ask if its location in Book 3.333 is a coincidence.) It is outside of narrative time, even if, as readers, we try to fold it in, the begetting of the Son in Book 5 yet to come in our experience of the poem.[7] Further, how does the Son's *not long* ("Under his gloomie power I shall not long / Lie vanquisht" [3.242–3]) line up with God's *meanwhile*? How long is that *long*? Arguing from Milton's mortalism, one might underline the Son's acknowledgment that it will not be until the end of time that he will "enter Heaven *long* absent" (3.261): indeed how does this "long" line up with the earlier "not long"? This, of course, opens the problem of Christ's thousand years' reign in Milton's eschatology and thus the question of when and where this "new heaven and earth" will be. There have been multiple and varying responses to this question and while I entirely agree with Stella Revard's argument that the millenarian subtexts in both *Paradise Lost* and *Paradise Regained* "speak[s] eloquently of the hopes Milton yet cherished" in the 1660s and 70s,[8] *meanwhile* as it deconstructs time opens gaps in narrative linearity disturbing those hopes, as indeed the millenarian expectations evoked by the speech in Book 3 are uneasily recalled from the retrospect of the first elevation in Book 5.

God's second *meanwhile* occurs at the start of Book 7, "after *Lucifer* from Heav'n / ... fell" (131–4) and both before and simultaneous with the Son's becoming God's word in the act of Creation, an act that is both within time (it took six plus one days) and outside, for "Immediate are the Acts of God, more swift / Then time or motion, but to human ears / Cannot without process of speech be told, / So told as earthly notion can receave" (7.176–9). "Meanwhile," God tells the remaining angels as they are asked to fill Heaven's newly emptied spaces, "mean while inhabit laxe, ye Powers of Heav'n" (7.162) until "Earth be chang'd to Heav'n, & Heav'n to Earth, / One Kingdom, Joy and Union without end" (160–1). If Adam and Eve's *meanwhile* is an eternal present before time, God's is an eternal present through, after and beyond time that stands in disturbing juxtaposition to theirs, indeed, from the Empsonian point of view, even mocks it.[9] For their *now*, full of the plenitude and freedom of what seems to them a perfect world (or nearly perfect, for their labor cannot quite keep up with the plenitude), is already foreclosed by God's knowingness. Their resultant vulnerability is also compounded by their ignorance of the crucial word in the contract that has offered them this plenitude. That word, "death," in what is, perhaps, the most chilling line in the poem ("what ere Death is / Som dreadful thing no doubt" [4.425–6]), is entirely without reference for Adam and Eve, and marks the pathos of their situation as it measures time in a way they have no means to understand.

The problems here are multiple and have been often restated, but one problem in the old "if God foreknew [as, indeed, he says he did], then why ..." paradox is visible in the narrator's role in that earlier scene in Book 3 of the Son's second elevation.[10] There the narrator elides his voice with the song of the heavenly choir as he hails the Son, whose name "[s]hall be the copious matter of *my* Song/ Henceforth" (413–14; emphasis added). But time troubles that moment, too, for simultaneous with it is the *meanwhile* of line 418, which happens as those happy hours are spent hymning and Satan is alighting on the outside of this round world. Time rushes forward here in Satan's meanwhile space, the fall already having happened in the similes that track his movements: "as when a Vultur on *Imaus* bred" or "where *Chineses* drive / ... thir canie Waggons light" (3.431, 438–9) as he "[w]alk'd up and down alone bent on his prey" (3.441). It is as if heavenly happiness depends on, even requires, the Fall; without the Fall there would be no need to place as the end words of lines 212 and 213, *death/love*.[11] The move from God to Son in the scene in Heaven may obscure the problem of God's earlier "if I foreknew"; it does not make it go away. For despite the narrator's presence among the hymning angels, his poem is constructed on a split imperative: to make the moral complexities of human life paramount *and* to hymn the "greater Man / [who will] [r]estore us" (1.4–5). He gives neither priority in practice, whatever priority there may have been in intention, and because both are nearly overwhelmed by the imagination invested in the figure between, the Satanic double (human and angelic), *Paradise Lost* is, as Richard Strier argues, "deeply divided against itself";[12] one might even say trifurcated. Exacerbating the reader's uncertainty about where her sympathies should lie, and where the ethical center can be found, is a narrative structure that never allows for a resting place that is always meanwhile.

Although there are several relatively simple *meanwhile*s in the narration, many trouble and disturb the narrative line. Book 5 offers a simple example when the word leads Adam to Raphael while Eve is choosing and mixing her delicacies and tempering dulcet creams, and some lines later it has her crowning flowing cups while Adam and Raphael discuss angelic digestion. However, that discussion leads to a more complex, far more dangerous *meanwhile* as Raphael links divine timelessness with the impermanent *meanwhile* of human time, indeed opens a narrative space with that word into which the entire text plummets. "Time may come," says Raphael,

> when men
> With Angels may participate, and find
> No inconvenient Diet, nor too light Fare:
> And from these corporal nutriments perhaps
> Your bodies may at last turn all to Spirit,
> Improv'd by tract of time, and wingd ascend
> Ethereal, as wee, or may at choice
> Here or in Heav'nly Paradises dwell;
> *If* ye be found obedient, and retain
> Unalterably firm his love entire
> Whose progenie you are. *Mean while* enjoy
> Your fill what happiness this happie state
> Can comprehend, incapable of more.
> (493–505; emphasis added)

Raphael's *meanwhile* follows a description of time without Fall, where man "[i]mprov'd by tract of time" can eat as angels eat and then, all spirit, enter Heaven. But the adverb is not comforting, for before that participation with angels, there is the time of the present, hinged on an "if," intimating quite other possibilities, indeed foreclosing such expectations, suggesting the point where obedience will fail, as if Raphael knew the poem's first line, as indeed he does since he and all the angels heard God say that "man will hark'n to his glozing lyes" (3.93). "Mean while enjoy" also echoes Satan's "[l]ive while ye may, / Yet happie pair" (4.533–4) and the narrator's equally uneasy, "Sleep on / Blest pair; and O yet happiest *if* ye seek / No happier state, and know to know no more" (4.773–6; emphasis added). *Yet* (filling several columns in the *Concordance*) is another radioactive and omnipresent word in time's vocabulary and its use by both Satan and the narrator plays off *meanwhile* and also suspends time in its sense of "still," of "as yet," "not yet," but possibly too soon.[13]

 The lining up of *if* and *knowledge* in the narrator's words to the sleeping pair also recalls God's evasive "if I foreknew / Foreknowledge had no influence on their fault" (3.117–18),[14] the narrator here seeming to offer them the chance that God has already foreclosed. Mean time in Eden is conditional time, and the space opened and then collapsed between "if" and "meanwhile" in Raphael's speech intimates failure, as does God's. Adam's response (how could there be an "if") requires narration and the undoing begins. Raphael's "if" does not only entirely realign the Edenic situation for Adam and Eve, it puts his own narration into jeopardy, pointing to the larger problem of narrative for the poem. For if Raphael cannot keep his narrative under control, how can Milton?[15] The story that Adam receives as it unfolds in the meanwhile space of Satan's encircling is not simply a holding action: as long as this conversation continues, nothing need happen. For even that is an illusion, since natural time structures the supernatural dialogue – they have only an afternoon. It also offers in its retrospect a prospect at odds with its exemplary message to "stand fast."

Sin's narrative of origins, which she offers Satan, provides a further perplexing instance of this destabilizing of time. As has often been pointed out, there is no time for the events she narrates to have occurred. She springs out of Satan's head at the conclave in the north (presumably the same narrative time/space when Abdiel stands firm against those "Seraphim […] combin'd / In bold conspiracy" [2.750–1]), but then time distends, enough for her to win over those averse and for Satan in secret to take his pleasure with her and for her womb to conceive the growing burden of death. "Mean while," she continues, "Warr arose, / And fields were fought" (767–8). Meanwhile to what time? Or is *meanwhile* here less a marker of time than of narrative modes, as if to imply that there is another way of recounting this: first allegory, then romance, then epic? Thus meanwhile is the same while but in a different kind of story, a different genre. In the romance version there is seduction, in the epic version there is clear victory on one side, rout on the other. But in the meanwhile version of her story, she is not a goddess armed, rather a hapless victim, as she disclaims agency. "[D]own they fell," she says, but she has no verb ("in the general fall / I also"), even as she still marks time in her next words: "at which time" she continues, "this powerful Key / Into my hand was giv'n" (2.771–5).

This Satan/Sin/Death encounter also begins on a *meanwhile*, which has Satan beginning his move toward the Gates of Hell. It is a particularly baffling *meanwhile* as it at once refers to the various activities from Olympic games to poetry to philosophy to mining that the other angels undertake at the conclave's end and to a geography and mythography of a Hell that will only come to be once that journey out of Hell is accomplished and Hell becomes the place (but in the present narrative, as in the reader's experience, it already is) where "[a]t certain revolutions all the damn'd / Are brought" (2.597–8). As James Dougal Fleming reads this passage, Satan in some sense never leaves. He is last seen "midst the infernal peers," and the description of Hell that follows constitutes "an interim space … marked off explicitly as a separate narrative segment," as "Satan leaps across the gap from midst to meanwhile." On the level of story, however, Satan does leave, indeed must leave, or "story" could not happen, even if his steps are not followed from council chamber to the scouring of "the right hand coast." But because *meanwhile*, in its displacement of time, suggests that there is always an alternative time then there is an alternative story such as the one Fleming offers that subtends and troubles the one we are reading.[16] Thus as a narrative marker the word signals the difficulty of fixing a narrative moment and, as a consequence, of fixing meaning in a poem that is at once transparent and opaque, seemingly absolute in its assertions, yet rendering them resistant to resolution.

The ways in which the narrative builds and unbuilds itself as *meanwhile* constructs a Rubik's cube of time–space is best seen in Book 10, which opens on that word as the narrative of 9 is replayed in Heaven. What happened there had not escaped "the Eye / Of God All-seeing" (10.5–6), even as the angelic guard now brings the unwelcome news. God knows, God knew and the narrator seems to have no doubts as to God's justice as he emphasizes not only Satan's heinous and despiteful act, but also Adam and Eve's weakness, who "ought to have still remember'd / The high Injunction not to taste that Fruit" (10.12–13). Yet the story he tells challenges that certitude. After the Son enacts his double function of judge and savior he returns to the Father, but both before and simultaneous with that scene, another *meanwhile* returns the narrative to Sin and Death in what is perhaps its most baffling and time-unsettling usage in the poem. Following the scene of judgment, the narrator continues, "Meanwhile ere thus was sin'd and judg'd on Earth, / Within the Gates of Hell sate *Sin* and *Death*, / In counterview within the Gates, that now / Stood open wide, belching outrageous flame" (229–32), ready to begin their bridge building. This *meanwhile* takes us back not to another point in the present narrative, but to a time before ("ere thus"), located simultaneously in Books 9 and 2. As the Fall is about to happen within Book 9 time, Sin begins to feel new strength within her rise and, "drawn by this new felt attraction," she suggests they "found a path / Over this Maine from Hell to that new World / Where *Satan* now [but now has not yet happened] prevailes" (10.256–8). However, the reader has been here before; in Book 2, as Satan passes through the gates, the construction of the "broad and beat'n way" (2.1026) to come is anticipated, with the difference that the bridge is to be built "soon after when man fell" (2.1023) and not, as in 10, preceding or possibly simultaneous with that act. Sin's *meanwhile* is never present; it is always at once before and after. Thus rather than assenting to Welch's observation that "the mystically layered time zone that sin and death inhabit is never grafted onto that of sublunar paradise, and they can make their way to our universe only after the Fall has unsettled the firm foundations of prelapsarian time,"[17] I suggest that their time is already intertwined with human time, that in the recursive loop of narrative the one is always catching up with the other, that something else is always happening in the meanwhile moment.

The most complex instance of this, and the passage that first generated the questions I'm meditating here, occurs soon after, in the metamorphic episode that enacts both crime and punishment and transforms the applause Satan expected for his glorious and so easy conquest into a universal hiss:

> Thus were they plagu'd
> And worn with Famin, long and ceasless hiss,
> Till thir lost shape, permitted, they resum'd,
> Yearly enjoynd, some say, to undergo
> This annual humbling certain number'd days,
> To dash thir pride, and joy for Man seduc't.
> However some tradition they dispers'd
> Among the Heathen of thir purchase got,
> And Fabl'd how the Serpent, whom they calld
> Ophion with Eurynome, the wide-
> Encroaching Eve perhaps, had first the rule
> Of high *Olympus*, thence by *Saturn* driv'n
> And Ops, ere yet *Dictæan Jove* was born.
> *Mean while* in Paradise the hellish pair
> Too soon arriv'd, *Sin* there in power before,
> Once actual, now in body, and to dwell
> Habitual habitant.
>
> (10.572–88; emphasis added)

This *meanwhile* parallels the events in Hell with the arrival on earth of Sin and Death, but the metamorphic moment extends in time and space. Thus even as *meanwhile* points to that moment, the moment disperses to become first an annual humbling in some undefined future time that is as much ours as theirs and then mythological time, which then merges with historical time in the deformed fables of pagan worship, as the serpent is there called Ophion, and Eve, Eurynome.

And where is Sin in this *meanwhile*? She is now in Paradise in body but she was there before in *power*, suggesting at once sin's potential (potency, power), her allegorical actualization (*actual* suggesting actively chosen, acted on), and her realization in narrative, *in body*. As in the previous example, Sin's *now* is always before as well as after, where she will remain "Habitual habitant," "in Man residing through the Race" (10.588, 607). Indeed, much the same can be said of God, especially in the person of the Son. Sin's *meanwhile* in this passage crosses all time zones: before, once, now and to come, which is perhaps why she can have no verb in her statement of her fall. In an attempt to contain the moment within God's time, the narrator makes a familiar move, positioning the lines within "the almighty seeing" from the vantage of the end of time as the poison becomes the potion and the Hell hounds, sin and death, lick up the "taint [that sin] hath shed," merging this *meanwhile* with the finality of "Heav'n and Earth renewd" (10.631, 638). But *meanwhile* offers textual resistance to this containment. As a measure of "this transient World, the Race of time (perhaps punning on Sin's earlier usage) / Till time stand fixt" (12.554–5), it offers little assurance (although Adam as he speaks these words at the poem's end tries to find comfort in them), and for the reader, who still strives after sequence (when did this happen? what caused what?), who tries to locate herself within a narrative space, the ground shifts and trembles and the clock has no hands. But for all the apocalyptic foreshadowing, the repeated "when time shall be" in its anticipation of a final time when "time [will] stand fixt," the strongest pull within the text is backward moving ("now / While time was" [4.5–6]). The narrator's voice is an odd compound of urgency, anticipation, and nostalgia, and *meanwhile* in its blurring of now and then, offers a resonant emblem of this.

The final *meanwhile* in the text illustrates this perfectly as it connects the meanwhile time of epic theodicy with history both sacred and profane.

> Meanwhile they in thir earthly *Canaan* plac't
> Long time shall dwell and prosper, but when sins
> National interrupt thir public peace,
> Provoking God to raise them enemies:
> From whom as oft he saves them penitent
> By Judges first then under Kings; of whom
> The second, both for pietie renownd
> And puissant deeds, a promise shall receive
> Irrevocable, that his Regal Throne
> For ever shall endure.

The roll call continues as Michael moves next to Solomon and then describes those who follow as:

> Part good, part bad, of bad the longer scrowle,
> Whose foul Idolatries, and other faults
> Heapt to the popular summe, will so incense
> God, as to leave them, and expose thir Land.
>   (12.315–39)

Beginning with a sequence that moves "[f]rom shadowie Types to Truth" (12.303), Michael unfolds a history that lapses backwards despite the occasional appearance of the pious and wise, and opens a space in history that proleptically identifies the poem's moment. For as much as the phrase in Book 7, "bounds; beyond" (120) can be read as a synecdoche for the difficulties of the intellectual, ethical enterprise of the entire text (the semicolon a wistful marker of the impossibility of knowing where or even how to make that demarcation), it can also serve to identify the place of the poem itself.

For *Paradise Lost* was composed over that boundary time when a free commonwealth seemed at first faintly possible, but then was finally lost when the nation "besottedly [ran] their necks again into the yoke" (*CPW* 7:428) (one is tempted to say into *bounds*, into bonds, afraid to venture *beyond*). Indeed, *The Readie and Easie Way to Establish a Free Commonwealth* could almost have been sub-titled *meanwhile*, as Milton there looks for a warning voice sufficiently powerful, "[n]ot so much to convince these [that is, those who "past reason and recoverie are devoted to kingship"] … as to confirm them who yield not" (*CPW* 7:455) as indeed he "yield[ed] not" to his extreme peril in the months that followed. It was a more perilous meantime than the one he wrote from nearly two decades earlier when in *Areopagitica* he invoked "the mean while … [of] the slow-moving Reformation which we labour under," for "differences, or rather indifferences … need not interrupt the *unity of Spirit*, if we could but find among us *the bond of peace*" (*CPW* 2:565). But in 1660, meanwhile turned into an urgent and rapidly shrinking *now*. Indeed, meanwhile to its writing was its rewriting, its opening paragraph rewritten even before its first February publication, and then again rewritten in the expanded early April version, by which time what remained of the Long Parliament had been dissolved and those "[w]rits … sent out for elections" (*CPW* 7:430) were certain to return a Parliament ready to return a king. Milton offers schemes to forestall this return of a monarch however near it may be (weeks, days) until a structure be put in place, "[t]ill the Commonwealth be throughly setl'd," "till this be done," even as he allows the reality "if ther be a king" (*CPW* 7:441, 444, 446). But this attempt to halt time, to imagine in the language of "*the good Old Cause*" (*CPW* 7:462) some structure, some stay against the imminent restoration – say, perpetual senates, offered, he hopes practically, possibly refreshed in part every two or three years, some plan, some means to resist the inevitable, even if these be only the "words of our expiring libertie" (*CPW* 7:463) – this is the meanwhile of Milton's time and text. As the 1660s advance and Milton brings *Paradise Lost* to its close (the series of printings of the original ten-book version from 1667 to the fifth iteration in 1669 with different title pages and opening matter offering a material figuring of its textual meanwhiles),[18] warning voices, his included, availed little. Although the final *meanwhile* of the poem moves, in its full unfolding, into redemptive time with the birth of Christ, it is still shadowed by "sins / National interrupt[ing] thir public peace" (12.316–17) by God's leaving, by the land exposed – then, now .... meanwhile.

Thus whatever Milton believed about God, about the Son, about goodness and salvation from, say, 1657 to 1665, it is important to emphasize that the poem does not necessarily express those beliefs in any straightforward or consistent way. And to the degree that it attempts to do so, it struggles with them; it certainly becomes its own master, or, perhaps more accurately, its own master interpreter. For *Paradise Lost* is a *poem*, wayward and inconsistent as all good poems are. It is a truism, but one that bears repeating, that poems know, indeed can reveal, far more than their poets know. *Paradise Lost* as text is often far less certain, far less located in a describable space/time than is its author/narrator.[19] Gordon Teskey's *Delirious Milton* speaks to this issue as a problem of creation both for maker and reader: "the being of the poem as a thing made ... actively interferes with the interpreter's need to make the poem into a text that can be disseminatively read," and elsewhere: "something in Milton's spirit cannot accept this subordination of creativity to Creation, hard as he works to affirm it."[20] Giorgio Agamben in an earlier study, *The End of the Poem*, offers another way of formulating this problem: "poetry lives in the tension between the semiotic and the semantic";[21] that is, what the poem's words point to and what that means are often at (productive) odds. None of this is to suggest that Milton is not deeply engaged with understanding human motivation, human reason, human freedom or, for that matter, with trying to understand the ways of God and possibly believing, or at the least hoping, that they can be justified and, crucially, that there is justice in them. Indeed, there have been numerous studies that attempt to work through these problems, most recently Gregory Chaplin's argument that "Milton was more enthralled by human possibility than human limitation," and that his Arian theology "brings man closer to Christ as it distances the Son from the Father."[22] The poem is certainly homiletic and didactic in intention, even if the results are, at the very least, cross-grained, both light and darkness coming in through the cracks. One might profitably apply another line from Leonard Cohen in which one can take David the psalmist, "the baffled king composing hallelujah," as figuring Milton in his poem.[23] The poet joins his voice in hallelujah to the heavenly choir, but the poem obstinately says other things.

As poem it resists what is set forth as argument, for its imaginative as well as its ethical mode is to think through the very propositions it sets forth, to offer alternatives even to the point of contradiction, hence the crucial role of *or*, as Peter C. Herman has argued, as that conjunction offers "a series of suspended choices," leaving "key moments unresolved."[24] *Meanwhile* performs much the same function; its destabilizing of time destabilizes meaning as well. It is not just that there are separate narratives happening meanwhile to each other, so much as the unfolding of one puts the others in jeopardy. This narrative instability in turn unsettles the project of theodicy. However, the failure of the theodicy, or at the very least its incompleteness, is, in fact, the triumph of the poem. Thus the time accountants or the "God is good, therefore" literary theologians are not so much finding the poem out as finding the poem they assume to be there and then forensically marshalling the evidence. Meanwhile, less certain readers take pleasure in the multiple bafflements it copiously offers.

NOTES

1 Grant McColley, *Paradise Lost: An Account of its Growth and Major Origins* (University of Chicago Press, 1940), pp. 16–17; Alastair Fowler (ed.), *Paradise Lost*, 2nd edn. (London: Longman, 1998), pp. 29–33; Gunnar Qvarnström, *The Enchanted Palace: Some Structural Aspects of Paradise Lost* (Stockholm: Almquist & Wiksell, 1967), pp. 10–54; Sherry Lutz Zivley, "The Thirty Three Days of *Paradise Lost*," *Milton Quarterly* 34 (2000), 116–26.
2 Amy Boesky, "*Paradise Lost* and the Multiplicity of Time," in Thomas Corns (ed.), *A Companion to Milton* (London: Blackwell, 2001), p. 383; Blair Hoxby, "Milton's Steps in Time," *SEL Studies in English Literature* 38 (1998), 149–72; James Dougal Fleming, "Meanwhile: Medusa in *Paradise Lost*," *English Literary History* 69, 4 (2002), 1009–28; Anthony Welch, "Reconsidering Chronology in *Paradise Lost*," *Milton Studies* 41 (2002), 1–17.
3 Welch, "Reconsidering Chronology," 15, 5, 15.
4 Boesky argues that Eve's "desire is experienced … as delay. Her hesitation opens up a space in the epic … that confounds the linearity of time, doubling experience and making it circular rather than moving it forward" ("*Paradise Lost* and the Multiplicity of Time," p. 387).
5 Michael Bryson explores the varied meanings, modes, and theological traditions behind "to justify," to make an important distinction between representation and that which is represented, arguing that "what the narrator wishes to 'justify' is not God, but 'the ways of God'" ("'That far be from thee:' Divine Evil and Justification in *Paradise Lost*," *Milton Quarterly* 36 [2001], 94). "Milton *accuses* God in the image of the Father so that he may then *acquit* him in the image of the Son" (99).

6 Giorgio Agamben, *The Time that Remains: A Commentary on the Letter to the Romans*, Patricia Dailey (trans.) (Stanford University Press, 2005), p. 62.
7 In an essay that probes the temporal ambiguity of the begetting in Book 5, David Mikics argues that the poem's energy "eludes messianic rest." "The Begetting of the Son: Curiosity, Politics, Trial in *Paradise Lost*," *Literary Imagination* 10 (2008), 286.
8 Stella Revard, "Milton and Millenarianism: from the Nativity Ode to *Paradise Regained*," in Juliet Cummins (ed.), *Milton and the Ends of Time* (Cambridge University Press, 2003), p. 71. Among the other useful essays in this collection, see, especially, Juliet Cummins, "Matter and Apocalyptic Transformations in *Paradise Lost*," pp. 169–83 and Claude N. Stulting, Jr., "'New Heav'ns, New Earth': Apocalypse and the Loss of Sacramentality in the Postlapsarian Books of *Paradise Lost*," pp. 184–201.
9 William Empson's *Milton's God* (London: Chatto & Windus, 1961) has (in) formed my reading of many passages. Although I may resist or dispute some of his arguments, they remain invigorating and necessary.
10 See Peter C. Herman's discussion of the difficulty/impossibility of determining when the elevations occur in "*Paradise Lost*, the Miltonic 'OR,' and the Poetics of Incertitude," *SEL Studies in English Literature* 43 (2003), 197–9. Also chapter 5 with the same title in his *Destabilizing Milton: "Paradise Lost" and the Poetics of Incertitude* (New York: Palgrave Macmillan, 2005). His discussion in that study of God as unreliable narrator is very helpful in identifying some of the problems of theodicy which I discuss here.
11 Richard Strier's point that "Heaven … is always the place where the rebellion has happened" offers another version of my argument here. See "Milton's Fetters, or, Why Eden is Better than Heaven," in this volume, p. 44).
12 Strier, "Milton's Fetters," p. 25.
13 The *OED* lists multiple divisions and subdivisions for "the senses related to time." The definition for the usage here would be "now as until now … often also implying contrast to a future or subsequent state."
14 John Leonard observes in a footnote to this line in his edition of *Paradise Lost* (Harmondsworth: Penguin Books, 2000) that "this statement can only damage God's and Milton's theodicy, for it inadvertently concedes that the certainty (not just the possibility) of the Fall is grounded in something other than God's foreknowledge" (p. 326).
15 In "Uncertainty and 'the Sociable Spirit,'" Kent Lenhof makes the case for Raphael's partial responsibility for the Fall, suggesting that his role is "sinister, perhaps even satanic." Kent Lenhof, "Uncertainty and 'the Sociable Spirit,'" in Kristin A. Pruitt and Charles W. Durham (eds.), *Milton's Legacy* (Selinsgrove: Susquehanna University Press, 2005), p. 33. He locates his reading in the line of Empson, A. J. A. Waldock, Donald Bouchard, Russell Smith Jr., and John Tanner. However, by turning the issue into an illustration of the *Areopagitica* argument with "Milton's God … refus[ing] to pursue a program of textual suppression," thereby illustrating "the Father's commitment to the kind of virtue that arises only in an environment of choice" (p. 47), Lenhof ultimately gives both Raphael and God a free pass.

16 Fleming, "Meanwhile: Medusa in *Paradise Lost*," 1024.
17 Welch, "Reconsidering Chronology," 7.
18 I follow Stephen B. Dobranski here in referring to five issues. See "Simmons Shell Game: The Six Title Pages of *Paradise Lost*," in Michael Lieb and John Shawcross (eds.), *Paradise Lost: A Poem Written in Ten Books: Essays on the 1667 First Edition* (Pittsburgh: Duquesne University Press, 2007). Meanwhile, of course, the final version will not appear until 1674.
19 Balachandra Rajan in "The Poetics of Heresy" speaks to this issue in a richly nuanced discussion of the "negotiations between the author and the autonomy progressively claimed by his own poem," which is grounded on the premise that "the poet writes the poem but major poems sometimes rewrite their authors." The first printing of this paper, which I had the good fortune to hear delivered in 1981, is in a collection of his essays and papers: Elizabeth Sauer (ed.), *Milton and the Climates of Reading* (University of Toronto Press, 2006), pp. 33–45.
20 Gordon Teskey, *Delirious Milton: The Fate of the Poet in Modernity* (Cambridge, MA: Harvard University Press, 2006), pp. 18, 50.
21 Giorgio Agamben, *The End of the Poem*, Daniel Heller-Roazen (trans.) (Stanford University Press, 1999), p. 114.
22 Gregory Chaplin, "Beyond Sacrifice: Milton and the Atonement," *PMLA* 125 (2010), 359, 367.
23 Leonard Cohen, "Hallelujah" from *Various Positions*, 1984 (at one point David changes places with Samson in that song, offering another resonant figure for the Milton speaker). The lines from "Anthem," which I used as my epigraph, come from the album *The Future* (1992).
24 Herman, *Destabilizing Milton*, pp. 183, 186.

CHAPTER 5

The Gnostic Milton: salvation and divine similitude in Paradise Regained

Michael Bryson

The temptations of Milton's work are powerful. Rare is the reader who is not seduced, at least initially, by the power of Satan's speeches in the first two books of *Paradise Lost*. Professional "Miltonists" may have moved beyond this reaction – or at least may claim to have done so – but other temptations abound. The famous reading of Stanley Fish, in *Surprised by Sin*, takes the idea of readerly temptation quite seriously, making it the backbone of a powerful interpretive paradigm that is still with us approximately forty years later. However, it is not the temptation to identify with "Sin" or with "Evil" that has long been most powerfully present in contemporary (twentieth- and twenty-first-century) Milton studies, but instead, the temptation to identify with Milton's portrayals of the divine. From C. S. Lewis's claim that "Many of those who say they dislike Milton's God only mean that they dislike God,"[1] to Dennis Danielson's famous titular claim in *Milton's Good God* (as well as his argument that the success of the poem and the success of its theodicy are in a direct relationship),[2] Milton scholars have often been concerned to defend Milton's literary character the Father with all of the energy of an actual defense of an actual deity in which they actually believe (or, at the very least, a deity in which they argue *Milton* actually believed).[3] In short, Milton studies have long flirted with a curious kind of critical idolatry. In the terms of this odd critical veneration, Milton's Father is God, or is at least Milton's overt idea of God, and as such he had best be defended with all of the intellectual might a sympathetic critic can bring to bear.

Milton's own works, however, contain eloquent refutations of this kind of equation between representation and that which is represented, especially at the level of the divine. Milton declares, in *De Doctrina Christiana*, that "God, as he really is, is far beyond man's imagination, let alone his understanding" (*CPW* 6:133). If God is beyond imagination, let alone understanding, how can he be represented in literary form? The answer lies in Milton's depiction of the human Jesus (more often referred to as the Son), in *Paradise Regained*.

In order to understand what Milton is doing with his portrayal of this character, I maintain that we need to put aside any attempt to defend the Father and instead explore a reading of the Son as embodying a form of Miltonic Gnosticism, a poetic attempt to leave an external concept of God for an internal concept of God, a God found without for a God found within. The emphatic interiority of Milton's Jesus has previously been explained as the result of Quaker influence. For David Loewenstein, the "meek, calm yet sharply polemical Jesus of *Paradise Regained*" is a figure for whom "interiority and politics are realigned."[4] In Loewenstein's view, *Paradise Regained* portrays Jesus in the manner of "Quaker writing," as an "inward-looking saint enduring great opposition and trials and yet remaining, almost in a superhuman fashion, firm and unmoved."[5] This explanation accounts for much of the emphasis on interiority in Jesus's character. My argument is that Milton goes further than Fox or Pennington or other Quaker contemporaries in portraying a Jesus who specifically refuses to play the traditional role of savior. See, for example, the attitude expressed by George Fox:

[T]his Jesus is the Foundation of the Prophets and Apostles, and our Foundation; so that there is no other Foundation to be laid, but what is laid, even Christ Jesus: and that he tasted Death for every man, and shed his Blood for all men: that he is the Propitiation for our Sins, and not for our Sins only, but for the Sins of the whole World [...] And we do believe, That he is our Alone Redeemer and Saviour, even the Captain of our Salvation; who saves us from Sin[.] [6]

Milton never portrays a Jesus who sheds his blood, or tastes death for *any* man (much less "every man"); rather, he portrays a Jesus, who, like the Gnostic conceptions of Christ dealt with in this essay, refuses to save anyone from sin.

Now, in making this argument, I am not suggesting that Milton was directly influenced by the Gnostic texts, most of which were unavailable to him in anything other than the form of lengthy quotations by such heresiologists as Iraeneus and Hyppolytus (whose *Adversus Haereses* and *Refutatio Omnium Haereseum*, respectively, were among the primary resources on the groups called by the name of *gnostikoi* before the Nag Hammadi discoveries in the mid-twentieth century). My argument is one of parallel development, not historical influence. Milton, like Blake over a century later, is thinking in ways that align him, at certain crucial points, with an old "heretical" tradition – the details and texts of which he was not, and could not be fully aware of – that sought to leave what it regarded as dangerously errant ideas of God for something closer to the divine truth. Milton's project in *Paradise Regained* is much the same, and seen in this light, his character Jesus is a remarkably Gnostic creation.

I

In earlier work, I proposed that "John Milton was not a Gnostic," following Regina Schwartz's argument that "an intimation of an evil creative act [in *Paradise Lost*] would soon plunge Milton into the mire of Gnostic thinking so antithetical to his own cosmology that it suggests Blake's radical revision instead."[7] John Rumrich also argued this point particularly cogently, claiming that "Milton ... describes the confused, disordered first matter as good in itself and the necessary basis of a good creation,"[8] citing this passage from *De Doctrina Christiana*:

> original matter was not an evil thing, nor to be thought of as worthless: it was good, and it contained the seeds of all subsequent good. It was a substance, and could only have been derived from the source of all substance. It was in a confused and disordered state at first, but afterwards God made it ordered and beautiful. (*CPW* 6:308)

On this basis, it would seem that Milton would find Gnostic thinking "antithetical to his own cosmology." But the various groups referred to by the term "Gnostic" were large and contained multitudes (to borrow shamelessly from Walt Whitman). So too was Milton. Dismissing a cosmological connection between Miltonic thought and Gnostic thought is not enough to support the rather bald assertion with which I started this section of my essay. What of epistemology, or soteriology (knowledge and salvation, respectively)? It is here, not in cosmology, where I would suggest that the interesting questions reside.

For the Gnostics, true knowledge – not the memorized facts that comprise much of what often gets called "education," or the "everyone knows *that*" level of prejudged, and predigested orthodoxies that Milton would come to call "custom" – always already resides entirely within the individual. In a variation of Platonic *anamnesis* (or unforgetting), the gaining of true knowledge is not a matter of what the Greeks called *pistis* or faith – a word that gained currency among the Valentinians as the quality found among those who merely accept that what they are told is true – but of insight or *gnosis*, what Elaine Pagels has described as "an intuitive process of knowing oneself" which "at the deepest level is simultaneously to know God."[9]

This process of knowing God is described in the *Gospel of Thomas* as becoming like the divine: "He who will drink from my mouth will become like me. I myself shall become he, and the things that are hidden will be revealed to him."[10] And what is primary among those hidden things? The idea that the kingdom of God is *here now*, though unseen except by the few: "the kingdom of the father is spread out upon the earth, and men do not see it."[11] Those few, those "fit [...] though few" who saw, were referred to as *gnostikoi* – those who knew, or Gnostics.

In matters of salvation, the Valentinians drew a distinction between *pistis* and *gnosis* that is remarkably like Milton's own distinction between custom and knowledge. The Valentinians regarded *pistis* as a beginning point, a limited path, one leading – at best – to the Demiurge, a lower "deity" that insisted on itself as the Alpha and Omega, when in fact it was no such thing. Though, according to *The Gospel of Philip*, "No one will be able to receive without faith [*pistis*],"[12] it was *gnosis* through which salvation could finally be achieved: "Faith is our earth, that in which we take root [....] Knowledge then is the light through which we ripen."[13]

For Milton in *The Reason of Church-Government*, famously it is "custome" that is "the creator of Prelaty" (*CPW* 1:778), and it is "Custom" once again, in *The Tenure of Kings and Magistrates*, that enables tyranny in a nation:

If men within themselves would be govern'd by reason, and not generally give up thir understanding to a double tyrannie, of Custom from without and blind affections within, they would discerne better, what it is to favour and uphold the Tyrant of a Nation. (*CPW* 3:190)

But it is knowledge – true knowledge – that makes a man like God. In *Of Education*, Milton argues that "The end then of learning is to repair the ruins of our first parents by regaining to know God aright, and out of that knowledge to love him, to imitate him, to be like him, as we may the neerest by possessing our souls of true vertue, which being united to the heavenly grace of faith makes up the highest perfection" (*CPW* 2:366–7). Custom, like faith, may be where we begin our journey toward "the highest perfection," but knowledge and learning are absolutely necessary, like the "light through which we ripen" of the *Gospel of Philip* if one is to "be like [God]."

This dynamic, this interplay of earth and light, of *pistis* and *gnosis*, of custom and learning, operates within each individual mind and heart. In the terms of *The Gospel of Thomas*, "the kingdom is inside of you."[14] In Milton's poetry, this is illustrated most effectively by the character of the Son in *Paradise Regained*. In the Son, Milton portrays something very much like a Gnostic image of Jesus. As Andrew Philip Smith argues:

> Conventional Christianity emphasizes faith in Christ, in his crucifixion and resurrection and his status as the son of God, the saviour and redeemer of humanity, at the centre of its religion. The Gnostics also saw Jesus as a savior and redeemer, but their Jesus saved and redeemed by bringing knowledge of the universe and man's true place within it. The knowledge that he brought could teach mankind how to liberate the seed of spiritual light that was hidden within, and enable humanity to know the true God.[15]

In *The Passion*, which would presumably have been a poem "emphasiz[ing] faith in Christ, in his crucifixion and resurrection and his status as the son of God, the saviour and redeemer of humanity," Milton refused to narrate the crucifixion and resurrection, never getting beyond an increasingly overwrought stage-setting, as if trying to work himself up to a topic for which he had no true enthusiasm or interest – and "nothing satisfied with what was begun, left it unfinisht." Decades later, in *Paradise Regained*, Milton creates a Son who emphasizes *gnosis* over *pistis*, the internal over the external, seeking an inner light experienced as a sense of divine similitude, an intimate and experiential knowledge as opposed to the formal, book-learned knowledge Satan offers, and he displays a manifest lack of interest in inhabiting the traditional savior role. The Son does this in two ways: (1) by refusing to "save" either the Jews or the Gentiles when Satan tempts him with power, and (2) by disparaging book knowledge in favor of inner illumination when Satan tempts him with learning. This then leads to the crucial revelation of *Paradise Regained*, the insistence on the ultimately salvific knowledge of divine similitude reflected in the final words of the emphatically human Jesus: "Tempt not the Lord thy God" (4.561). Milton's poetic Jesus, like the figure imagined by the *gnostikoi*, saves not through a sacrifice of blood, but by bringing knowledge of divine similitude, the oneness of the human and divine nature.

II

The Son's rejections of Satan's temptations in *Paradise Regained* powerfully illustrate the movement from *pistis* to *gnosis*, from faith to knowledge, a dynamic often portrayed as a movement from external to internal values and motivations. This becomes especially clear when we consider the role of temptation in both *Paradise Lost* and *Paradise Regained*. Each work features a temptation by Satan. In *Paradise Lost*, that temptation is successful, first with Eve, then soon afterward with Adam. In *Paradise Regained*, the temptation is a failure, as the Son scornfully rejects everything Satan offers. But despite their different targets and circumstances, each temptation is the same. At the core of each is an appeal to identify oneself with power, with knowledge, and even with divinity itself, but each of these things is considered, and offered, as a thing external to the one tempted – as if the tempted were *required* to look outside the self in order to acquire power, knowledge, and divinity. In Eve's case, she is told that she will acquire all these things as a direct result of eating the fruit of the tree of knowledge:

> … he knows that in the day
> Ye Eate thereof, your Eyes that seem so cleere,
> Yet are but dim, shall perfetly be then
> Op'nd and cleerd, and ye shall be as Gods,
> Knowing both Good and Evil as they know.
> (9.705–9)[16]

Satan portrays this knowledge – and the power that comes with it – along with divine similitude (being as "Gods") as an effect of the fruit itself; he even implies that "the Gods" themselves get their knowledge and power and divinity from their food: "And what are Gods that Man may not become / As they, participating God-like food?" (9.716–17). In doing so, Satan is cleverly trying to cultivate the seeds of the same idea earlier planted by Raphael, when he tells Adam and Eve that "from these corporal nutriments perhaps / Your bodies may at last turn all to Spirit, / Improv'd by tract of time, and wingd ascend / Ethereal, as wee" (5.496–9). Raphael ties this suggestion of physical transformation and attainment of "Ethereal" status to obedience ("If ye be found obedient" [5.501]), an idea that Satan quietly elides in his version. His elision highlights, however, the *external* nature of the idea Raphael introduces. Raphael conceives of the effect of both the "corporal nutriments" and being "found obedient" as physical, external transformations. Food is ingested from outside the self. Obedience is offered to a figure outside the self. Ethereal status (as near as Raphael comes to the idea of divine similitude) is something to be achieved, grasped for, taken into oneself from outside, and/or conferred on oneself from outside. It is these external mechanics that Satan highlights in his temptations of both Eve in *Paradise Lost* and Jesus in *Paradise Regained*. What is lost, then, in *Paradise Lost* is the inner focus on divine similitude, a connection to the divine source of all things that is always already there in Eve and Adam. Satan is able to focus both Eve and Adam on externals – for Eve, knowledge as a means to gain a greater place in a hierarchy of two, and for Adam, the potential loss of Eve – and, in so doing, manages to pluck Paradise, the "paradise within" (12.587), right out of the human pair's hearts. Paradise had always been within. Eden was merely a place, a marvelous and beautiful place, but it was not, in and of itself, "paradise." *Paradise Lost* is not a narrative of the loss of Eden, but of the loss of the "paradise within," the sense of divine similitude, the realization of connection to all things and to the source of all things. *Paradise Regained* is a corresponding narrative of a reclamation of the "paradise within," of a restoration of the focus on internals through a successful rejection of the temptations to focus on externals.

Satan's temptations in *Paradise Regained*, modeled on the temptation sequence from Luke 4:1–13 and Matthew 4:1–11, are designed in the same way as the temptation of Eve; thus their goal is to trick the Son into identifying himself with, and through, externals. In rejecting temptation, what the Son rejects are not the things (bread, gourmet food, wealth, knowledge, even power) in themselves, but the external focus that results in regarding such things as ends in themselves. The Son's rejections of each temptation relentlessly return the focus back to the internal sense of divine similitude.[17]

The first temptation sets the pattern. "But if thou be the Son of God, Command / That out of these hard stones be made thee bread" (1.342–3). What could be simpler than the need to eat? And what could be more basic to that need than bread? But it is not the bread that is the point of the temptation; rather, it is the *means of attaining* that bread. *If* thou be *the Son of God* – the test, and the temptation, is an attempt to get the Son to show off. Satan is taunting the Son in a way that might throw a lesser man off balance and trick him into identifying his primary strength as an *external* strength: the ability to transform – through power of some kind – *external* objects.

The Son rejects – as he will throughout – Satan's external focus, and instead refocuses the issue as one of internals, in this case, Man's true sustenance by "each Word / Proceeding from the mouth of God" (1.349–50). He also gives evidence of his true focus through his ability to see past external appearances to the true nature of his tempter. The Son easily sees through Satan's disguise as "an aged man in Rural weeds" (1.314): "I discern thee other than thou seem'st" (1.348). In addition to seeing through Satan's *physical* disguise – something Uriel was unable to do in *Paradise Lost*, since such "Hypocrisie … walks / Invisible, except to God alone" (3.683–4) – the Son also sees through Satan's *mental* disguise as someone who does not know whether or not the man Jesus is the particular Son of God known only as "the Son" in *Paradise Lost*. Jesus cuts through this latter disguise – one which Satan may not be admitting to himself that he is donning until he is "smitten with amazement" (4.562) much later – by confronting Satan directly: "Why dost thou then suggest to me distrust, / Knowing who I am, as I know who thou art?" (1.355–6). The implications of this line are radical: if only God can see through hypocrisy's guise, and Jesus knows who this "aged man in Rural weeds" really is, then in some sense the Jesus of *Paradise Regained* is God. But in what sense?

Here is where the temptation of *Paradise Regained* itself – and its corresponding modeling of how to resist that temptation – comes into play. Look past the external, the surface, and focus on the internal, the substance. What this means for the Son is a focus on connection to the divine, through a constant remembrance and realization of divine similitude.[18] Where a focus on identity and power will be the thread that runs through all of Satan's temptations, it will be this focus on divine similitude that runs through all of the Son's rejections of temptation. Even when Satan is tempting the Son to identify himself with the glory and power of the Father, he is missing the point. It is not the trappings of glory and power through which divinity can be found; those things, in fact, are distractions, accidents, *externals*. The key to divine similitude, and thus to the Son's rejections of temptation, is to be found in the "inward Oracle" (1.403), the "Spirit of Truth" (1.462) that dwells within, as does "the Spirit, which is *internal, and the individual possession of each man*" (*CPW* 6:587, emphasis added).

It is this "inward oracle," this "spirit of truth" from which the Son draws his strength to fight off Satan's temptations. Even after having given considerable thought, in 2.245–53, to the fact that he is *hungry after forty days with no food*, the Son rejects Satan's offer of "A Table richly spread, in regal mode, / With dishes pil'd, and meats of noblest sort / And savor, Beasts of chase, or Fowl of game, / In pastry built, or from the spit, or boil'd" (2.340–3). He refuses even the smallest nibble, much less the opulence of the feast that has been spread before him "at a stately sideboard by the wine" (2.350). The food is not the point; rather, it is the focus that Satan is trying to tempt the Son into adopting, a focus on the physical, the palpable, the external. Satan is trying, in each of his temptations, to get the Son to look outside of himself for the Good, and to focus on such external things as if they were ends in themselves.

In rejecting Satan's bounty, the Son declares that he could himself "Command a Table in this Wilderness" (2.384), but has not. Why? Earlier, in his private meditation on his hunger, he established a hierarchy of value that placed physical food beneath his "hung'ring more to do [his] Father's will" (2.259). The "will" the Father has expressed in *Paradise Regained* is that the Son "drive [Satan] back to Hell" (1.153), and "conquer Sin and Death" (1.159). This is part of an effort by the Father to show Satan that he "can produce a man / Of female Seed, far abler to resist" (1.150–1) than Adam turned out to have been, and to show future generations of mankind "From what consummate virtue I have chose / This perfect Man, by merit call'd my Son, / To earn Salvation for the Sons of men" (1.165–7). The rest of the statement is couched in metaphors of war and combat, as the Father imagines the Son "Winning by Conquest what the first man lost," but first, the Father means to "exercise him in the Wilderness," where the Son will "lay down the rudiments / Of his great warfare" (1.154, 156–8).

However, the Son rejects this martial model of external conquest (a model with which both Satan and the Father seem obsessed), easily saying no to the temptations of political and military power that Satan offers through the Parthian and Roman realms. But to fully appreciate both the power and perceptiveness of the Son's stance, consider the subtlety of Satan's lead-in to this temptation, the appeal to duty:

> If Kingdom move thee not, let move thee Zeal
> And Duty ...
> ...
> Zeal of thy Father's house, Duty to free
> Thy Country from her Heathen servitude;
> So shalt thou best fulfil, best verify
> The Prophets old, who sung thy endless reign[.]
> (3.171–2, 175–8)

This is some of Satan's best work, a fiendishly clever appeal that plays on the Son's own youthful desires. At 12 years old, the Son already felt that his "Spirit aspir'd; to victorious deeds" and "heroic acts" to "subdue and quell o'er all the earth / Brute violence and proud Tyrannic pow'r" (1.215–19). Satan is precisely targeting these sentiments with appeals to duty and zeal. But in the Son's case, these feelings are presented, not as the noble thoughts of a hero, but as a remembrance of the fantasies of a child, fantasies which were quickly rejected in favor of higher, and more reasoned thoughts, as the Son "held it ... more heavenly," even as a child, to "make persuasion do the work of fear" (1.221, 223), though a trace of the fantasy of force survives in the line "the stubborn only to subdue" (1.226). The thoughts, however progressive, of a 12-year-old boy are not nearly as profound as those of the fully mature man now being tempted by Satan. This is no longer the Son who in *Paradise Lost* seems to be just as concerned with raw power as either Satan or the Father, casting the dispute between the two in remarkably Satanic (or Fatherist) terms:

> Mightie Father, thou thy foes
> Justly hast in derision, and secure
> Laugh'st at thir vain designes and tumults vain,
> Matter to mee of Glory, whom thir hate
> Illustrates, when they see all Regal Power
> Giv'n me to quell thir pride, and in event
> Know whether I be dextrous to subdue
> Thy Rebels, or be found the worst in Heav'n.
> (5.735–42)

This kind of all-or-nothing thought is that of a mere partisan, or a blind ideologue. But the Son is no longer the blustery figure he was before the War in Heaven, declaring in martial tones that he would either be covered in the glory of victory or be revealed through failure as the *worst* in Heaven. Nor is the Son any longer the human child who fantasized physical, even military conquest, though he quickly – if incompletely – rejected the means of force. Now fully mature, the Son reveals an entirely more profound judgment than he has yet displayed in any previous situation. His answer to Satan's earthly appeal emphasizes patience, even suffering, rather than conquest: "All things are best fulfill'd in their due time" and "who best / Can suffer, best can do; best reign, who first / Well hath obey'd; just trial e'er I merit / My exaltation without change or end" (3.182, 194–7). At this point, the Son has made it quite clear what he thinks of the conquests to which Satan would urge him (the "Duty to free / Thy Country from her Heathen servitude"), and to which the Father would urge him ("Winning by Conquest what the first man lost"), by flatly rejecting the idea of external conquest: "They err who count it glorious to subdue / By Conquest" (3.71–2).

Satan's failure here should come as no surprise to any reader who has been attentive to the Son's earlier summation of the real nature of power, authority, and reign. The Son speaks a different language from that spoken by both Satan and the Father, for whom the above-mentioned things are externals, things to be wielded over others. The position the Son expresses is quite the opposite: at the end of Book 2, he rejects the external model of government that "o'er the body only reigns, / And oft by force, which to a generous mind / So reigning can be no sincere delight" (478–80). Instead of this kind of external, public reign, the Son chooses the internal, private government of truth: "to guide nations in the way of truth / By saving doctrine, and from error lead / To know, and knowing worship God aright, / Is yet more Kingly, this attracts the Soul, / Governs the inner man, the nobler part" (2.473–7). For the Son, power, authority, and reign are *internal* and to be exercised, not over others, but over oneself.

The Son's greatest expressions of contempt are reserved for those who do not wield such control over themselves: the "captive Tribes … / Who wrought their own captivity" (3.414–15) by falling into "Idolatries" (3.418), and the Roman people, "That people victor once, now vile and base, / Deservedly made vassal, who once just, / Frugal, and mild, and temperate, conquer'd well, / But govern ill the Nations under yoke" (4.132–5). In each case, the Son is describing a people who have become slaves *internally*, and have projected that slavishness *externally* onto their orientation toward the world.

In the case of the Israelites, the Son dismisses any notion that he is on Earth to liberate them. If they are to be liberated, they must liberate themselves:

> Should I of these the liberty regard,
> Who freed, as to their ancient Patrimony,
> Unhumbl'd, unrepentant, unreform'd,
> Headlong would follow, and to thir Gods perhaps
> Of *Bethel* and of *Dan*? No, let them serve
> Thir enemies, who serve Idols with God.
> (3.427–32)

In the case of the Romans, the Son is even more severe in his judgment: "What wise and valiant man would seek to free / These thus degenerate, by themselves enslav'd, / Or could of inward slaves make outward free?" (4.143–5). In Milton's well-known argument from *The Tenure of Kings and Magistrates*, the internal serves as the base and root cause of the external; as a result, slavish people beget tyrannical regimes: "being slaves within doors, no wonder that they strive so much to have the public State conformably govern'd to the inward vitious rule by which they govern themselves" (*CPW* 3:190). The Israelites and the Romans, who once were free inwardly – the Israelites through "worship[ping] God aright," and the Romans through being "Frugal, and mild, and temperate" and having "conquer'd well" *themselves* – are now slaves internally, and thus slaves externally: Israel as an occupied territory, and the Romans, once citizens of a Republic, now merely vassals of a vast empire. The Son is not on Earth as a savior for either Jews or Gentiles. He is not here to *save* anyone; instead, he is here to show them – if they have eyes to see – how to save themselves.

III

So far, each temptation has been a call to focus on things in themselves, while each rejection of temptation has been grounded in a call to look past, even through, these things, back toward the inner sense of divine similitude, the divine as the origin and ground of all. The famous temptation – and rejection – of knowledge makes most sense when viewed in this context. Since Satan sees the Son as being "otherwise inclin'd / Than to a worldly Crown, addicted more / To contemplation and profound dispute" (4.212–14), his final temptation is at once his most powerful and profound – knowledge, study, wisdom, the very things to which Milton had given his life, and had praised as early as the gorgeous lines of "Il Penseroso":

> Or let my Lamp at midnight hour,
> Be seen in some high lonely Tow'r,
> Where I may oft outwatch the *Bear*,
> With thrice great *Hermes*, or unsphere
> The spirit of *Plato* to unfold
> What Worlds, or what vast Regions hold
> The immortal mind that hath forsook
> Her mansion in this fleshly nook[.]
> (85–90)

Milton's own love letter to knowledge, "Il Penseroso" should be remembered while reading the exchanges between Satan and the Son when Satan extols the virtues of "the Olive Grove of *Academe*, / *Plato's* retirement" (4.244–5), and "Blind *Melesigenes* thence *Homer* call'd" (4.259). The poet who had once begged his own father not to "persist […] in [his] contempt for the sacred Muses" (*Nec tu perge, precor, sacras contemnere Musas* – "Ad Patrem" 56), and who had gone on to claim that such contempt was a mere pretense, "You may pretend to hate the delicate Muses, but I do not believe in your hatred" (*Tu tamen ut simules teneras odisse Camenas, / Non odisse reor* – ["Ad Patrem" 67–8]), is not writing the Son's response to Satan to portray a man with contempt for the Muses of philosophy and poetry. Far from it – the Son's abiding familiarity with both shines through in the very scenes in which he is ostensibly rejecting both. Though the intellectual achievements of the Greek and Roman worlds are characterized by the Son as "false, or little else but dreams, / Conjectures, fancies, built on nothing firm" (4.291–2), the Son goes on to deliver a concise account of the very thinkers and schools of thought he has just critiqued. The Son's characterizations of Socrates, "The first and wisest of them all [who] profess'd / … that he nothing knew" (4.293–4), and Plato, who "to fabling fell and smooth conceits" (4.295) strike – in a familiar and knowing manner – at the very heart of the mental labors upon which Milton has spent the bulk of his life and energy: the search for knowledge, and the ability to present that knowledge in high literary form.

But Milton is not rejecting himself, his studies, his work here. Rather, he is having the Son, through the expression of what seems a radical, even shocking point of view, emphasize the kind of knowledge that is like the "light through which we ripen" of the *Gospel of Philip*.[19] It is through this light, this inner awareness, this *gnosis*, that the seeker can reach the highest good, an awareness of an already existing connection to the true God, and the knowledge that "the kingdom of the Father" referred to in the *Gospel of Thomas* is to be found within. In Milton's case, through the Son, the desire is analogous: to be able to reach the highest good, expressed in this case as an internal realization of divine similitude, one must have the strength to be able to leave behind all that one loves most in the world, about existence itself, which in Milton's case is no other than the knowledge, poetry, and beauty he has spent his entire life pursuing, mastering, and powerfully expressing. This is the core meaning of the poignant phrase from Sonnet 19, "God doth not need / Either man's work or his own gifts" (9–10). No work or gifts or talents can bring humankind to the divine. The one thing, ultimately the *only* thing needed (not desired, not appreciated, not loved, but *needed*) is "Light from above, from the fountain of light" (4.289). This "Light from above" is *gnosis*, the knowledge that reveals, the teacher that teaches the all-important lesson of divine similitude, and it can only be accessed from within, which is the crucial point of the scene in the desert where the Son realizes what he must do, and how he must do it:

> [the] Son tracing the Desert wild,
> Sole, but with holiest Meditations fed,
> Into himself descended, and at once
> All his great work to come before him set;
> How to begin, how to accomplish best
> His end of being on Earth, and mission high[.]
> (2.109–14)

The desert is the ideal location for a withdrawal from the world – from external values and stimuli – that facilitates the kind of internality essential to realizing one's connection to the divine. It is here where the Son realizes "how to accomplish best" his mission, here away from even the extremely private life he has been leading up to this point, away from the expectations of Mary, who believes that he will "By matchless Deeds express [his] matchless Sire" (1.233), away from the expectations of his followers, who are "missing him thir joy so lately found" (2.9), and above all, away from the expectations of the Father, for whom the Son's mission is first and foremost an extension of the Father's own ongoing contest with Satan, as he envisions the Son "Winning by Conquest what the first man lost / By fallacy surpris'd" (1.154–5). But the "Light from above," or the "light through which we ripen" of the *Gospel of Philip*, is not to be found in any of these clamoring voices with their urgent, even imperious demands. This light makes no demands of any kind; rather, it merely shows the Son who and what he is. Self-knowledge becomes divine knowledge. It is this light that allows the Son to read "The Law and Prophets" and find "of whom they spake / I am" (1.260, 262–3).

The Son's most truly "matchless" deed is his choice to focus, not on the world without, but on the world within; to focus, not on externals – food, wealth, power, knowledge, and even divinity conceived of as an external force – but on internals – the quiet, but firm assurance of divine similitude. In himself, and through himself – as he realizes when he "with holiest Meditations fed, / Into himself descended" (2.110–11) – is the only place and the only way that the "inner man, the nobler part" (2.477) can be accessed, that part of each man which is connected to, even comprised by, the "Spirit of Truth" the "inward Oracle" (1.462–3). The Son's conquest is achieved in the realization that for humankind, indeed, for all Creation, the divine is only to be found by searching within, by heeding the promptings of "the Spirit, which is *internal, and the individual possession of each man*" (*De Doctrina Christiana*, CPW 6:587; emphasis added). It is this realization that gives his final response to Satan its tremendous power.

IV

This final scene between Satan and the Son has been the subject of much argument. One common position suggests the Son does not fully realize his identity in the poem; he does not know, until he formulates his rejection of the final temptation, who he really is, and even after becoming aware of his identity he is merely declaring his faith in God – *a God that he is not*. In contrast to this, it has been argued that the Son is fully aware of who he is, and is openly declaring his divine status.[20] As he refuses the final temptation of Satan, the Son says: "Also it is written, / Tempt not the Lord thy God" (4.560–1). What exactly does the Son mean by this? Are readers to assume that the Son is merely refuting Satan, countering Satan's quotation of Psalm 91:11–12 by quoting Deuteronomy 6:16 back at him? Is the Son merely declaring his faith in God, or is the Son declaring that he actually *is* God?

More radical than either of these alternatives is a third, which I believe to be the underlying reason for Satan's "amazement" (4.562). When the Son, referred to here as the man Jesus, says "Tempt not the Lord thy God" (4.561), he has a threefold meaning: (1) *do not tempt me* – I am God; (2) *do not tempt anyone* – all creatures, sharing in the divine as their origin, are also God; and (3) *do not tempt yourself* – you, even you, Satan, are included in points 1 and 2. [21] All temptation is ultimately *self-temptation*. Thus, Satan was "Self-tempted, self-deprav'd" (*Paradise Lost* 3.130), in that he – though not by "[his] own suggestion" (3.129) as the Father claims – did not simply refuse to indulge the feelings being played upon by the Father in the coronation scene of 5.600–15. Satan could have ignored that external provocation, moved past his fixation with finding meaning in rank and power within the confines of a rigid hierarchical system, and focused instead on an inner awareness of divine similitude. Satan's failure ever to realize this, ever to understand who – and what – he has been all along is what truly amazes, not the realization that he cannot successfully tempt this man (or this God). What has Satan smitten with amazement is the profound depth of his misunderstanding and miscalculation about his own nature and the origin of all things. For Satan, the crushing irony is that he was right in characterizing the Father as a usurper, someone claiming solely for himself rights that belonged to all, but that he was tragically wrong about the way he confronted the situation. The Father, in this scenario, is no more or less "God" than are any of the angels, "fallen" or "unfallen," or Adam and Eve, or Satan, or the Son. In his rebellion, Satan had hit upon an essential truth, but he had understood that truth in precisely the wrong way, emphasizing the external rather than the internal, and difference rather than similitude.

In making his radical claim, the Son redefines all of the expectations that have been laid upon him, most notably altering the meaning of what he refers to as "My everlasting Kingdom" (3.199). Mary, Satan, and the Father all seem to envision this kingdom as an earthly or heavenly variant on the political and military kingdom over which the conqueror David reigned. But it is *not* that kind of kingdom. The Son's kingdom is, as Donald Swanson and John Mulryan have argued, "a spiritual kingdom that is neither accompanied by eschatological signs nor located in space ... The inner or spiritual nature of the kingdom might easily have been inferred from the parable of the seed growing secretly or from Luke xvii, 21b: 'for behold, the kingdom of God is within you.'"[22] *The kingdom of God is within you* – in some sense, everyone who attains what Milton elsewhere calls "the mind of Christ" (*CPW* 6:583) has what the Son calls "The Authority which I deriv'd from Heaven" (1.289). This authority is an internal authority, the "double scripture," especially the "internal scripture of the Holy Spirit" that Milton describes in *De Doctrina Christiana* (*CPW* 6:587). He who has "the spirit, who guides truth" (*CPW* 6:583) has an authority that "No visible church ... let alone any magistrate, has the right" (*CPW* 6:584) to gainsay or oppose. The Son in *Paradise Regained* powerfully illustrates what John Shawcross has called "Milton's essential belief," that "[w]orth does not lie in the external, in works for a public arena, in negation and prohibition, nor in a mere following of example, no matter how blest the example might be, if the inner being has not been enlightened."[23]

As the Son returns "unobserv'd / Home to his Mother's house private" (4.638–9), he has accomplished the regaining of Paradise, making of *Paradise Lost* and *Paradise Regained* a complete cycle. Where Adam and Eve move away from, the Son moves in return to, the divine source. *But that source is not the Father.* The divine source is the "Spirit of Truth," the "inward Oracle" (1.462–3), which the Son is at pains to tell Satan will replace the latter's oracles ("henceforth Oracles are ceast" [1.456]). The Son's focus therefore, is on how best to hear, understand, and obey the promptings of the "Spirit of Truth" the "inward Oracle" (1.462–3). In mastering this, the Son, existing in this time and place as the human male Jesus, realizes within himself the strength easily to withstand the all-too-transparent temptations of Satan, but he also realizes that the divine is to be found within, not without, that "Tempt not the Lord thy God" is an admonition, not against tempting a God (mis)conceived and (mis)understood as an external figure, but against *self*-temptation. In regaining Paradise, Jesus neither regains Eden, nor does he shed a drop of sacrificial blood. Such externals are – at best – mere symbols, but at worst – and more typically – active and dangerous distractions from the one basic truth. God is not to be found in the forms, images, and rituals of the world, nor even in the most fervently held ideas and images of God the world has to offer, but is only to be found by looking and listening within. The essential Gnostic insight is also the essential Miltonic insight: "the kingdom is inside of you".

NOTES

1. C. S. Lewis, *A Preface to "Paradise Lost"* [1942] reprint (London: Oxford University Press, 1961), p. 130.
2. Dennis Danielson, *Milton's Good God: A Study in Literary Theodicy* (Cambridge University Press, 1982), p. ix.
3. Even William Empson falls into this category, arguing that Milton "is struggling to make his God appear less wicked, as he tells us he will at the start." William Empson, *Milton's God* (London: Chatto & Windus, 1961), p. 11.
4. David Loewenstein, *Representing Revolution in Milton and His Contemporaries: Religion, Politics, and Polemics in Radical Puritanism* (Cambridge University Press, 2001), pp. 266, 257.
5. Ibid., p. 260.
6. George Fox, *To the Ministers, Teachers, and Priests (So Called, and so Stileing your Selves) in Barbadoes* (London, 1672), sig. 12r.
7. Michael Bryson, *The Tyranny of Heaven: Milton's Rejection of God as King* (Newark: University of Delaware Press, 2004), p. 11; Regina Schwartz, *Remembering and Repeating: On Milton's Theology and Poetics* (University of Chicago Press, 1993), p. 8.
8. John Rumrich, "Milton's God and the Matter of Chaos," *PMLA* 110, 5 (1995), 1035–6.
9. Elaine Pagels, *The Gnostic Gospels* (New York: Random House, 1979), pp. xix.
10. James M. Robinson (ed.), *The Gospel of Thomas*, Thomas O. Lambdin (trans.), in *The Nag Hammadi Library* (San Francisco: Harper San Francisco, 1990), pp. 124–38, saying 108.
11. Ibid. Saying 113.
12. *The Gospel of Philip*, *The Nag Hammadi Library*, pp. 139–60, 61:35.
13. Ibid. 79:25–30.
14. *The Gospel of Thomas*, Saying 3.
15. Andrew Philip Smith, *The Gnostics: History, Tradition, Scriptures, Influence.* (London: Watkins Publishing, 2008), pp. 3–4.
16. All references to Milton's poetry other than *Paradise Lost* will be to Merritt Hughes (ed.), *John Milton: Complete Poems and Major Prose* (New York: Odyssey Press, 1957).
17. All of Satan's temptations are, as Stanley Fish has observed, "allied in their inferiority to an inner word and an inward kingdom." Stanley Fish, "Inaction and Silence," in Joseph A. Wittreich (ed.), *Calm of Mind; Tercentenary Essays on "Paradise Lost" and "Samson Agonistes"* (Cleveland: Press of Case Western Reserve University, 1971), p. 41.
18. See ch. 5 of *The Tyranny of Heaven*, and John Shawcross, *"Paradise Regain'd": Worthy T'Have Not Remain'd So Long Unsung* (Pittsburgh: Duquesne University Press, 1988), p. 1.
19. *The Gospel of Philip*, Wesley W. Isenberg (trans.), in *The Nag Hammadi Library*, 79:25–30.

20 John Shawcross argues that the Son "knows he is the Son of God, despite the unintelligible readings of some critics who have tried to hinge the poem on that question" (Shawcross, "*Paradise Regain'd*," 39). See Lewalski's summary of the controversy over this matter in *Milton's Brief Epic: The Genre, Meaning, and Art of "Paradise Regained"* (Providence: Brown University Press, 1966), pp. 135–8.
21 Milton's account of creation as *ex Deo* (out of God) rather than *ex nihilo* (out of nothing) in both *De Doctrina Christiana* (ch. 7 of Book 1), and *Paradise Lost* (7.168–9) supports the Son's meaning here. If all things (especially all living things) are of God, then all things share in the divine nature, and all things are – in that sense – God.
22 Donald Swanson and John Mulryan, "The Son's Presumed Contempt for Learning in *Paradise Regained*: A Biblical and Patristic Resolution," *Milton Studies* 27 (1991), 250.
23 Shawcross, "*Paradise Regain'd*," p. 76.

CHAPTER 6

Discontents with the drama of regeneration

Elizabeth Sauer

> Poetry often is written to expand th[e] horizon of expectation.
> Wittreich, *Interpreting "Samson Agonistes"* (1986)

"I do not know who invented" the term, William Empson confesses, and it is far from an indictment of Christianity at large, but "'Neo-Christian' seems the right way to describe those recent literary critics, some of whom believe in Christianity and some not, who interpret any literary work they admire by finding in it a supposed Christian tradition."[1] The "supposed Christian tradition" is one of the hermeneutic lenses through which literary works have been read into conformity or coherence, and one of the paradigms applied in resolving uncertainties in Milton's works. Empson and Christopher Hill – both of whom John P. Rumrich names as opponents of a unifying imperative Milton scholarship – credited C. S. Lewis with leading the charge to "'annex Milton' on behalf of orthodoxy."[2] Milton's poetry best lends itself, Lewis had decided, to readings by those who can be counted among Milton's fit (traditional Christian) readers. Lewis himself is a case in point: "I should warn the reader," cautions Lewis, "that I myself am a Christian, and [believe] that ... the atheist reader must 'try to feel as if he believed' ... But for the student of Milton my Christianity is an advantage. What would you not give to have a real, live Epicurean at your elbow while reading Lucretius?"[3] In an essay on "Milton and the Cult of Conformity," Joseph H. Summers tellingly remarked on the critical practice of reading literature into conformity by "reduc[ing] an admired figure to [the critic's] own image."[4] Lewis's influential scholarship reinforced the identification of Milton with moral and Christian orthodoxy, a practice also complemented by the methodological prudence of the New Critics in particular. Lewis became a most formidable contestant for other key Miltonists like Empson in scholarly controversies on Milton's theodicy, Christianity, and poetics.[5] Upon entering the debate from outside the discipline, Marxist historian Christopher Hill cast Milton as "a radical

Protestant heretic" in opposition to the revisionist movement in British historiography and the religious conservatism he discerned in Milton studies. For Hill, the works of Milton's right and left hands testified to Milton's dissenting position. Having cloaked Milton in Marxian ideology, Hill catalogued the evidence for Milton's heterodoxy in the writings of his left and right hands, and concluded, Milton "cannot reasonably be claimed as 'orthodox.'"[6]

In the past half century, controversies over Milton's theology and concomitant poetics have anything but subsided, as the essays in this volume, specifically in Part I, amply demonstrate.[7] In this case study, I focus on *Samson Agonistes*, a poem whose reception history has regularly been underwritten by the neo-Christian interpretations and regenerationist readings that resolve complications in the poem, especially in the final act. Having determined that "Milton's message seems clear," "neo-Christians," Hill ascertained, interpret the poem in support of a particular agenda, "the regeneration of Samson."[8] Judgments on Samson's death "as a proto-martyr's definitive act"[9] "improv[e] the fit of *Samson Agonistes* with Christian orthodoxy and, in the process, diminish its enquiring spirit, its interrogative element," Joseph A. Wittreich attested in *Shifting Contexts*.[10] While neo-Christian readings by their alignment with conservatism and their predilection for conclusiveness are invariably regenerationist, not all Christocentric or regenerationist interpretations conform neatly to the model of the neo-Christian criticism that Empson, Rumrich, Hill, and Wittreich have described. Examples of the latter are numerous and make up the mainstay of the present essay,[11] which, while largely concentrating on recent criticism on *Samson Agonistes*, troubles both neo-Christian and regenerationist readings. Notable here is the transgressive characterization of Dalila as it accentuates the contested nature of Samson's heroism in a poem that "offers debate, not certainty,"[12] specifically by resisting conformity to neo-Christian readings.

I

As with poetry at large, the significances of Milton's poems are plural and never wholly contained by any singular statement or individual voice. "[R]ippling with interpreters, rife with interpretations," Milton's 1671 volume in particular "is a provocation to mental fight and a perpetual prompting to spiritual adventure."[13] The relationship between the works juxtaposed in the companion volume is itself vexed and the joint publication complicates the reading of both poems. Peter C. Herman recently asked: "If at 'the end of *Paradise Regained*, obedience is *reasoned, internal*, and given to *oneself*' [as Bryson contends], then what happens when one's inner promptings tell one to commit mass murder? And if divinity is internalized, then how does one know that it is God, and not Satan, or even one's own madness, speaking?"[14] The indefinable inner promptings that intrigue Milton call to mind the elusiveness that Stanley Fish ascribes to antinomian impulses: because "the roadway of obedience" is for the antinomian "an internal one not available to external confirmation or disconfirmation, the taking of any path is fraught with the danger that it may be the path of self-aggrandizement rather than the path of faith."[15] The contested forms of heroic action that *Samson Agonistes* arguably exhibits, justify its characterization as a most unsettling work, one that presents "more interpretive dilemmas than any of Milton's other major works," one also designated by Jason P. Rosenblatt as "Milton's strangest major poem … with fault lines among [Hebrew, Greek, and Christian] traditions exposed."[16]

By examining some of the ways the poem opens up "interpretive dilemmas," my investigation further disables efforts at reading *Samson Agonistes* into coherence, a practice supported by neo-Christian but also by some Pauline, (negative) typological, and de-Judaized analyses. Much ink has been spilled in countering the open-endedness of a poem in which, as Louis Schwartz discerns, the questions and "answers Milton suggests … seem to run counter to the Milton that emerges from his other major works. This feeling of discontinuity has led some critics to argue with tremendous moral and scholarly energy that this is not what he meant at all."[17] The case of *Samson Agonistes* presented here considers the significance of the extra-biblical episode of Dalila's defense as it informs the interpretation of the poem's controversial last act. Dalila's central encounter with Samson in the dramatic poem is inserted in a narrative based on the over-determined Book of Judges, and situated at the heart of a poem judged to have none. In the *Rambler*, Samuel Johnson, a Tory, authoritatively and influentially declared that Milton's tragedy "must be allowed to want a middle, since nothing passes between the first act and the last, that either hastens or delays the death of Samson."[18] Yet what happens in the middle does drive interpretations of Samson's final performance. In their "Introduction to *Samson Agonistes*," William Kerrigan, Rumrich, and Fallon located "the revival of Samson's fighting spirit," or Samson *agonistes*, at the heart of the drama. Samson's character revelation, explain the editors, "is the main burden of the middle of the play, [and] does in fact motivate or at least render comprehensible the tragic climax."[19] The middle of the dramatic poem also challenges what Johnson alleged was a structural and temporal compression of Milton's Greek tragedy by accommodating a competing and intersecting performance, that featuring Dalila. In a provocative politicized reading of literary form, Achinstein has suggested that Johnson's erasure of the "notorious missing middle" radicalizes the text by putting greater emphasis on its conclusion. Yet neither Achinstein in her essay on Samson and nonconformity, nor Feisal Mohamed, who offers an equally brilliant reading of the poem as sharpening and politicizing the practice of literary interpretation, discusses the role of Dalila and the anti-orientalizing perspective of her defense.[20]

The dominant critical tendency to undervalue Dalila's significance in the dramatic poem and the common practice of citing the portrait as evidence of Milton's misogyny has obscured the ways that *Samson Agonistes* invites readerly engagement in the discovery of competing viewpoints resistant to consensus. The representation of Dalila is one of the problems in a poem whose subject is the art and ethics of interpretation, the overriding action of the tragedy.[21] As David Gay also later reaffirms, "*Samson Agonistes* is largely about the act of interpretation," and, he fittingly adds, about the "anxiety for coherence and continuity" expressed by its built-in interpreters.[22]

William Empson aligns the deliberate, purposeful "moral generosity" that he discerns in *Paradise Lost* with Milton's "mak[ing] out a strong case for Delilah" in *Samson Agonistes*.[23] Yet since the Romantic era (see Chapter 1 of this volume), critics attentive to the fault lines in Milton tended to concentrate on the presence of powerful others in *Paradise Lost*. Some fifty years ago, A. J. A. Waldock wrote that since Milton's "really deep interests could not find outlet in [*Paradise Lost*] in the right way they might find outlet in the wrong way … Satan is there, Satan gives him scope. And the result is that the balance is somewhat disturbed; pressures are set up that are at times disquieting, that seem to threaten more than once, indeed, the equilibrium of the poem."[24] "Any number of people have defended the Devil, in their various ways," Empson acknowledges, but then adds, "I do not know that anyone has defended Delilah" whose case he labels "a pushover."[25] Dalila's role in *Samson Agonistes* is more diminutive than Satan's in the epic, but there may be both poetic and extra-poetic reasons for the underplaying of Dalila as a worthy combatant for the champion Samson: there is possibly more at stake in *Samson Agonistes* than *Paradise Lost*, especially, as suggested above, if the "notorious missing middle" forces a re-evaluation of the catastrophe, from an anti-orientalist perspective, in what has been designated in a post-9/11 era as a disturbingly "fundamentalist poem."[26] To acknowledge the compelling, potent nature of Dalila, as Samson himself does in rehearsing his tragedy, is in the context of the interpretive experience of the poem to mark her as "an agent of change within the action of the text itself, a boundary-crossing presence that defies ideological intractability."[27] As discussed here, Dalila's apologia in particular further unsettles a performance and a text plagued by problems of closure. John Shawcross credits Dalila with broaching the key question about "whose nation is right, whose god is true god?" This essay develops Shawcross's insight, while complicating his thesis on the "consistencies of belief" that distinguish Milton's thinking and that validate the proposition that God inevitably delivers those who, like Jesus, keep their faith or who, like Samson, undergo renovation.[28]

The centrally located episode of Samson's encounter with Dalila was traditionally read as a variation on the autobiographical and biographical narrative of the journey from sin to redemption, in which Dalila, the "cause of Samson's fall," according to Heather Asals, also plays the part of "the agent of his regeneration." For Samuel Hornsby, however, Dalila is guilty of insincerity, and within a Christian context, Dalila's penance is equivalent with repentance and thus no process of renewal is possible.[29] Laurie P. Morrow likewise denounces Dalila's "habitual politicking ... [that] serves only as a hindrance to her spiritual development" and commends the spiritual renewal of Samson, who models the sinner's righteous pursuit for redemption. In 1998, Achsah Guibbory explained that Milton's decision to make Dalila Samson's wife "not only emphasizes the strength of Samson's former attachment to the idolatry she represents. It allows Milton to evoke the radical reformist position, at the center of his earlier divorce tracts and now pointedly appropriate in the Restoration, that the good Christian must permanently separate from all idolatry."[30] Similarly, the Christocentric analysis of *Samson Agonistes*, with which Guibbory's recent and admirable *Christian Identity, Jews, and Israel in Seventeenth-Century England* concludes, argues that the Hebrew Samson must move "beyond the law to become a Christian." Such a conversion demands resistance to the temptations to which he is subject, including that of the seductive Dalila, in a Christianized drama that, according to Guibbory, links "bondage, the law, and women."[31]

The regularly cited link between Dalila and the Law[32] tends to overshadow evidence that the poem yields of Dalila's agency. While Dalila eventually, though consciously, succumbs to Philistine compulsion, the character displays masculine resolve to fend off the authorities, which is reflected as well in the "muscular masculine style" of verse she appropriates:[33] "Hear what assaults I had, what snares besides, / What sieges girt me round, ere I consented; / Which might have awed the best-resolved of men, / The constantest, to have yielded without blame."[34] She re-enacts and testifies to the psychological, intellectual, and ethical battle in which she, like the combatant Samson,[35] "combated ... with hard contést" before consciously permitting the values of "grave authority," "Virtue," "truth," and "duty" to prevail:

> Only my love of thee held long debate,
> And combated in silence all these reasons
> With hard contést: at length that grounded maxim,
> So rife and celebrated in the mouths
> Of wisest men, that to the public good
> Private respects must yield, with grave authority
> Took full possession of me and prevailed;
> Virtue, as I thought, truth, duty, so enjoining.
> (863–70)

Contradicting the victim testimony that Dalila's shifting defense also inscribes, is the shrewd and strategic use of legalisms in her speech, expressed in internally balanced verses that communicate a deliberate assent to the authoritative dictum "to the public good / Private respects must yield" (867–8). In *Paradise Lost,* which ties the "great Argument" (*PL* 1.24) directly to free-will theology, prelapsarian Eve is won over more readily by one tempter than Dalila in *Samson Agonistes* is by her nation's magistrates, princes, and the extra-biblical priest. Though false rhetoric is a significant factor in the falls of both, Eve succumbs to self-serving appetite, whereas an alleged sacrifice of "private respects" to "public good" motivates Dalila.

In defiance of Samson's divorce and dismissal of her, Dalila rescripts her story from the perspective of a Philistine patriot and martyr, whose deeds will be commemorated throughout Philistia:

> in my country where I most desire,
> In Ekron, Gaza, Asdod, and in Gath,
> I shall be named among the famousest
> Of women, sung at solemn festivals,
> Living and dead recorded, who to save
> Her country from a fierce destroyer, chose
> Above the faith of wedlock-bands; my tomb
> With odors visited and annual flowers:
> Not less renowned than in Mount Ephraim
> Jael, who with inhospitable guile
> Smote Sisera sleeping through the temples nailed.

> Nor shall I count it heinous to enjoy
> The public marks of honor and reward
> Conferred upon me for the piety
> Which to my country I was judged to have shown.
> (980–94)

Dalila's speech at large, whose tone has also been described as "noble" and "Heroick,"[36] does resist the condensation of Delilah's representation in the Judges' story and the coherence of the historical memory communicated in the biblical narrative. "The Coherence of Politics and the Politics of Coherence," Mieke Bal's opening chapter in *Death and Dissymmetry*, discusses the interpretive practices and history to which the Book of Judges was subject. In scholarly and popular contexts, narratives of this biblical book commonly display a "principle of coherence ... which readers desire much more than texts exhibit."[37] The link between Bal's feminist inquiry and Milton's extra-biblical poem is the politics and interrogation of reading into coherence, a practice in which neo-Christian criticism is complicit.

In a classical tragedy on a Hebrew hero in which the Philistines are dislocated and vilified, the memory and monument Dalila constructs for herself only serve to heighten the Greek irony. "It is her infamy that will be imparted to the ages, since her story is to be told by Hebrews, not by Philistines," Gordon Teskey states in a reminder that history is written by the victors in their native tongue.[38] One might also note, however, that Samson himself earlier acknowledges the documentation of his history by non-Jews (he laments that his transgression is a "sin / That Gentiles in their Parables condemn" [499–500]). In Dalila's case, she is conscious of the reception history of her story and, moreover, creates a space for a self-styled eulogy (*elogium* "tomb inscription").[39] In the process, she establishes links between herself and celebrated biblical women who surrender "private respects": as wives and patriots, Judith, Jael, and even Delilah assumed public functions and performed controversial feats of heroism.[40] The salience of the prosodic "Smote Sisera sleeping," with its alliteration and elision ("Smote Sis'ra sleeping"), helps cement the identification of Dalila with the Hebrew, Jael, "her present prototype" of female heroism.[41] Etched into Samson's and the nation's historical memory, Dalila's speech helps convert *Samson Agonistes* into a mirror reflecting different sides of the conflict and of national commitment. Dalila's defense ultimately participates in a process, albeit inconsistently enacted throughout the tragedy, of de-orientalizing, whereby the position of the orientalized other is foregrounded.

In *De Doctrina*, Milton lists Jael among the numerous examples of biblical figures guilty of righteous or magnanimous deeds of falsehood. Through an act of "inhospitable guile," Milton states, Jael "enticed Sisera to his death when he sought refuge with her, Judges iv. 18, 19, though he was God's enemy rather than hers" (*CPW* 6:746). Milton's catalog of heroes complicit in dutiful deceit includes a parenthetical allusion to the Junius-Tremellius Latin bible's gloss on Judges 4:20, which sanctions Jael's act: "dissimulavit enim, sed sine mendacio, & pia fraude intercepit Jahel hostem Domini: quam rem Spiritus sanctus probat, infra 5.24" (*CPW* 6:764n.18). Just as Milton distinguishes "pious fraud" and "falsehood" from the "old [theological] definition" of falsehood in *De Doctrina* (*CPW* 6:746), so in *Samson Agonistes* does he invite nuanced comparisons of Dalila's and Samson's acts of dissimulation.

The central space Milton allows for the speech in a poem once judged by Aristotelian standards to lack a middle, challenges the reader of the tragedy to confront alternative models of motivation, piety (loyalty to one's nation) (955, 993), and standards of judgment that will, furthermore, not be invalidated but rather bifurcated, even trifurcated in the recollection of the final performance in the "fifth act" of the poem. By situating Samson in proximity to Dalila, *Samson Agonistes* will ultimately reveal its discontents with regenerationist readings. Reviving Empson's critique of neo-Christian criticism and his bold characterization of Delilah/Dalila in support of her contention that "Milton gives his strongest arguments to Samson's opponent," Victoria Kahn points out that the poem develops similarities between the two tragic characters. Further, "it is not Milton's habit to have similarities erase differences," but rather to invite the reader's discrimination.[42] A comparison between Dalila's apologia and Samson's final performance does not delegitimize or blot out the former, but rather exposes a complementarity by way of the contested interpretive history generated by the latter, thus troubling the poem's conformity to a definitive reading.

II

As Milton's portrayal of Dalila repositions the character in relation to the received biblical and literary traditions, so does the poetic rendering of Samson's performance rescript the Judges' account thereof and its Christianized reinvention. This is no mean feat. The Christianizing agenda of the commentators on the Judges account is deeply influential. F. Michael Krouse, Joseph A. Wittreich, and most recently, R. W. Serjeantson uncovered an array of early modern religious, moral, didactic, philosophic, and nationalist interpretations of the story of Judges,[43] many of which are mediated through Paul's Epistle to the Hebrews 11, where Samson is consigned to sainthood.[44] Milton deviates from the Pauline reading of Samson and that of early modern commentaries on Judges by not preparing the way for the christening of Samson. Whereas Paul omits any discussion of Israel's own ingratitude toward its deliverers, the subject is for Milton a recurrent theme. Milton uses the tragic character to illustrate the elect nation's failings, the Israelites being, like their deliverer himself, deprived of "strenuous liberty" "by their vices" (271, 269), thus defaulting on the chosen status they once enjoyed. In response to the history of Israel's betrayal of Gideon (Judges 6–8) and Jephthah (Judges 11–12) (*Samson Agonistes* 277–89), Samson declares, "add me to the roll" (290), anticipating Dalila's own connection between her controversially patriotic feats and those of Jael from the Book of Judges.

In the denouement, Samson prepares the script for what will be a much-contested heroic performance, first by announcing to the Officer who summons him, "of me expect to hear / Nothing dishonorable, impure, unworthy / Our God, our Law, my nation, or myself" (1423–5), what Achinstein calls the "spheres of moral obligation."[45] "I am an Ebrew, therefore tell them / Our Law forbids at their religious rites / My presence" (1319–21), the Nazarite, Samson asserts; and later: "A Nazarite in place abominable / … / … how vile, contemptible, ridiculous / What act more execrably unclean, profane?" (1359–62). "It has scarcely been noticed that Samson's athletic performance at the Dagonalia contradicts his commitment to do nothing unworthy or dishonorable there," points out Burns.[46] *Pace* Burns, the problem has long plagued Miltonists, who have consequently turned to Christian models for explanations: remarking that the Philistine Temple is off limits to Jews, Samuel Stollman explains Samson's attendance at the Dagonalia as part of the "Christianization of Samson's character," which entails a "de-judaization of Samson, or, as we have labelled this treatment of the Old Testament, an Hebraization."[47] Joan S. Bennett offers a different explanation by turning to antinomianism, stating that revisionist critics who charge Samson with breaking moral and religious laws, fail to appreciate the "antinomian nature of Milton's belief in Christian liberty."[48] In both cases, however, the interpretation and settling of Samson's motives are part of the persistent critical endeavor to read the poem into conformity with Christian thought. Establishing the connection between "Divine impulsion" and the "rousing motions" (422, 1383), Barbara Lewalski concludes that, "Like Jesus going out to the desert in *Paradise Regained*, Samson senses that he is under God's direction."[49] However, "[n]ot every rousing motion is from God," Jane Melbourne counters, and then explains that the rousing motions in *Paradise Regained* issue from Satan and constitute temptations that the Son must resist.[50] For Bennett, for whom "Samson serves as a model for the regenerate Christian" in her Pauline reading of *Samson Agonistes* as antinomian, the motions in *Samson Agonistes* are "divine inspiration, to be sure."[51] Burns christens Samson by rendering his "newfound antinomianism" synonymous with "his proleptic Christian liberty, [which] frees him to suffer indignity."[52] Likewise insisting on a Christianized reading, the analysis of *Samson Agonistes* with which Guibbory's *Christian Identity* concludes, maintains that Milton "presents the story from a distinctly Pauline perspective."[53]

Samson Agonistes, however, does not invite the christening of Samson and disturbs neo-Christian and regenerationist readings of the motives behind Samson's liberating murderous feat. The omission of the biblical Samson's prayer in Milton's tragedy (perhaps in accordance with Josephus's account) is among the curiosities in the internally issued report on the final performance, the motivation for which is rendered more ambiguous by the description of Samson "as one who prayed, / Or some great matter in his mind revolved" (1637–8). The contested oath, "of my own accord" (1643), further destabilizes efforts to decode the catastrophe, which thereby directs attention at how "witnesses respond to events."[54] Before hearing the report on the catastrophe, Manoa and the Chorus participate in staccato and rapidly paced questioning and speculation (1508–40), which, however, is not settled by the *nuntius*, who, at several removes from the site of the catastrophe, fails to offer a definitive account thereof. The final scene gives way to the reactions of the Danites to Samson's act of destruction and self-massacre. Fish discerns that the Danites strive to "make their interpretation cohere" by inventing details that remain "uncorroborated."[55] Indeed, according to the interpreters, Samson is self-destructive (1585), is "tangled in the fold / Of dire necessity" (1665–6), acts willfully (1709–12), and is divinely directed (1751–2). At the same time, however, the Chorus and Manoa thrust heroism upon Samson and thus impose closure on the final act.[56] But the reader is not restored to "calm[ness] of mind" (1758). "Even the most believing readers, with the most traditional approach to Samson's heroism and regeneration" will not experience catharsis at the end of the poem, leaving "a strikingly open-eyed vision,"[57] but also one through which readers confront their blindness. Regenerationist interpretations give way to the elusive motives for Samson's final act – an act that leaves the various truths in play.[58]

Like Dalila's counter-narrative – the indelible defense of her pious works – competing interpretations or the presence of powerful others constitute a mockery of true tragedy, a mockery that can be construed as nothing less than impious. The tragedy of September 11 is among the "shifting contexts" in which *Samson Agonistes* has been interpreted, and which, now over a decade later, continues to leave its scars on the interpretive history of the poem, even in criticism that resists the presentist predilection to connect seventeenth-century radicalism with contemporary radical religion and its violent counterparts.[59] Ever since John Carey, in his *Times Literary Supplement* article, argued for the parallel between Samson's final act of destruction and the events of September 11, the topic of Samson and terrorism has generated a range of critical responses that extend the controversy over the nature and significance of the final performance well "beyond the fifth Act." As the best "illustration of how complexly Milton's poetry enfolds a nuanced political vision,"[60] *Samson Agonistes* imagines a range of possible identities for Samson from terrorist to liberation fighter, identities that have come to the fore in Carey's response to Fish's characterization of the indeterminate motives of the tragic hero that ultimately invalidate regenerationist readings. Instead, decides Fish, "The only wisdom to be carried away from the play is that there is no wisdom to be carried away, and that we are alone, like Samson, and like the children of Israel, of whom it is said in the last verse of Judges: 'every man did that which was right in his own eyes.'" Samson's desire to conform to the divine will establishes the indisputable rightness of his action. "*No other standard for evaluating it exists.*"[61] Fish's reading is disturbing for various reasons, not the least of which is the lack of standards within or outside of the poem for judging the action. His insistence that Samson can be judged only by Samson's own criteria even strikes Carey as "monstrous – a license for any fanatic to commit atrocity ... [so that w]hen the Sept. 11 attacks occurred, they seemed a 'devilish implementation' of Fish's arguments."[62]

"September 11 has changed *Samson Agonistes*," as Carey, Fish, and Wittreich, among others,[63] have in very different ways have argued. Feisal Mohamed, whose work has been at the forefront of scholarship that interrogates (Western) practices that dissociate Milton from terrorism, in part by encouraging regenerationist readings that distance Samson from his violent final act, claims that September 11 changed nothing insofar as critics persist in perpetuating "a discourse that has employed global terrorism to solidify its own power."[64] But in making a case for the higher stakes of literary criticism, which possesses the potential to destabilize "real world implications,"[65] and for the necessity of confronting Western prejudices and exposing orientalist tendencies, Mohamed is certainly heightening the intensity and politics of the act of reading. Critical practice *cries up* the coexistence of multiple truths and mirrors the different sides of the conflict, despite or alongside resistance to such heretical possibilities and the pressure of neo-Christian and traditional Western readings. Rather than settling on a specific interpretation, the poem, a study in incongruities, develops its identity through the interplay and contestation among its different perspectives and its contentious self-consciously built-in reception history. *Samson Agonistes* ultimately invites confrontation with and exploration of the creative dynamics and "brotherly dissimilitudes" (*Areopagitica, CPW* 2:555) engendered by the ways poetry "expand[s] th[e] horizon of expectation,"[66] raising questions and playing different answers off each other.

NOTES

1 William Empson, *Milton's God* (London: Chatto and Windus, 1965), pp. 230, 229.
2 John P. Rumrich, *Milton Unbound: Controversy and Reinterpretation* (Cambridge University Press, 1996), p. 1; Christopher Hill, *Milton and the English Revolution* (New York: Viking, 1978), p. 3. Hill's characterization informed the work of various distinguished Miltonists, including Sharon Achinstein, David Loewenstein, and Rumrich, who, like Hill, emphasize Milton's interconnected religious and political "heterodoxy" (Hill, *Milton*, p. 3). See Sharon Achinstein, "*Samson Agonistes* and the Drama of Dissent," *Milton Studies* 33 (1996), 133–58; Sharon Achinstein, *Literature and Dissent in Milton's England* (Cambridge University Press, 2003); David Loewenstein, *Representing Revolution in Milton and his Contemporaries* (Cambridge University Press, 2001); John Rumrich, "Radical Heterodoxy and Heresy," in Thomas N. Corns (ed.), *A Companion to Milton* (Oxford: Blackwell, 2001), pp. 141–56.
3 C. S. Lewis, *A Preface to "Paradise Lost"* [1942] (London: Oxford University Press, 1963), p. 65.
4 Joseph H. Summers, "Milton and the Cult of Conformity," in Alan Rudrum (ed.), *Milton: Modern Judgements* (London: Macmillan, 1968), p. 30.
5 William Empson, *Milton's God*, pp. 9, 18–19, *passim*. On the invented Milton, see John P. Rumrich, "Uninventing Milton," *Modern Philology* 87, 3 (1990), 249–65; Rumrich, *Milton Unbound*, pp. 1–23.
6 Hill, *Milton and the English Revolution*, p. 3.
7 On Milton's poetics and positions on theology and ecclesiological issues, compare Michael Lieb, *Theological Milton: Deity, Discourse and Heresy in the Miltonic Canon* (Pittsburgh: Duquesne University Press, 2006) to Ken Simpson, *Spiritual Architecture and "Paradise Regained": Milton's Literary Ecclesiology* (Newark: University of Delaware Press, 2007), Phillip Donnelly,

Milton's Scriptural Reasoning: Narrative and Protestant Toleration (Cambridge University Press, 2009), and Dennis Danielson, *Milton's Good God: A Study in Literary Theodicy* (Cambridge University Press, 1982, 2009).
8 Hill, *Milton and the English Revolution*, p. 442.
9 Dennis Kezar reviews the regenerationist–skeptical/revisionist debate in Milton studies in his prize-winning essay, "Samson's Death by Theater and Milton's Art of Dying," *English Literary History* 66 (1999), 327–8 n.11, reprinted in *Guilty Creatures: Renaissance Poetry and the Ethics of Authorship* (Oxford University Press, 2001), pp. 139–71. For the most recent neo-Christian, regenerationist reading of *Samson Agonistes*, see Tobias Gregory, who insists that "Milton wanted readers to see his hero as a hero" ("The Political Messages of *Samson Agonistes*," *Studies in English Literature* 50, 1 [2010], 181).
10 Joseph A. Wittreich, *Shifting Contexts: Reinterpreting "Samson Agonistes"* (Pittsburgh: Duquesne University Press, 2002), p. xiii.
11 See also Dayton Haskin's *Milton's Burden of Interpretation* (University of Pennsylvania Press, 1994), which resists settling on a regenerationist or revisionist reading of the tragedy, while keeping both in play. Cf. Albert C. Labriola's discriminating, regenerationist argument that distinguishes between Samson's "intimate impulse" and his "rousing motions" from God: Albert C. Labriola, "Divine Urgency as a Motive for Conduct in *Samson Agonistes*," *Philological Quarterly* 50, 1 (1971), 99–107.
12 David Norbrook, "The True Republican: Putting the Politics Back into Milton," *Times Literary Supplement* (February 2, 1996), p. 5.
13 Joseph A. Wittreich, *Why Milton Matters: A New Preface to His Writings* (New York: Palgrave Macmillan, 2006), pp. xiv, 166.
14 Peter C. Herman, "Review of Michael Bryson, *The Tyranny of Heaven: Milton's Rejection of God as King*," *Early Modern Literary Studies* 10, 1 (2004), 8.9.
15 Stanley Fish, *How Milton Works* (Cambridge, MA: Harvard University Press, 2001), pp. 5–6. See also Stanley Fish, "'There is Nothing He Cannot Ask': Milton, Liberalism and Terrorism," in Michael Lieb and Albert C. Labriola (eds.), *Milton in the Age of Fish* (Pittsburgh: Duquesne University Press, 2006), p. 252.
16 Louis Schwartz, "The Nightmare of History: *Samson Agonistes*," in Angelica Duran (ed.), *A Concise Companion to Milton* (Oxford: Blackwell, 2006), p. 199. Rosenblatt (ed.), *Milton's Selected Poetry and Prose* (New York: W. W. Norton, 2011), p. 154. See also Stephen M. Fallon, *Milton's Peculiar Grace: Self-Representation and Authority* (Ithaca: Cornell University Press, 2007), p. 251.
17 Schwartz, "The Nightmare," p. 206.
18 Samuel Johnson, *Rambler* 139 [July 16, 1751], in W. J. Bate and Albrecht B. Strauss (eds.), *The Complete Prose Works of Samuel Johnson*, 16 vols. (New Haven: Yale University Press, 1969), vol. IV, p. 376. Suggestively, the poem's middle line is "[I] unbosom'd all my secrets to thee" (879).
19 "Introduction to *Samson Agonistes*," in William Kerrigan, John Rumrich, and Stephen M. Fallon (eds.), *The Complete Poetry and Essential Prose of John Milton* (New York: Random House, 2007), p. 702.

20 Achinstein, "*Samson Agonistes* and the Drama of Dissent," 135. For Mohamed, see notes 62 and 64 below.
21 On this point, also see John B. Mason, "Multiple Perspectives in *Samson Agonistes*: Critical Attitudes toward Dalila," *Milton Studies* 10 (1977), 32, and Rumrich's discussion of the "excluded middle," in relation to Milton's project of theodicy and as a site for the now virtually indistinguishable Samson and Dalila. Rumrich, "Samson and the Excluded Middle," in Mark R. Kelley and Joseph A. Wittreich (eds.), *Altering Eyes: New Perspectives on "Samson Agonistes"* (Newark: University of Delaware Press, 2002), pp. 307–32.
22 David Gay, "'Honied Words': Wisdom and Recognition in *Samson Agonistes*," *Milton Studies* 29 (1993), 53.
23 Empson, *Milton's God*, p. 210.
24 A. J. A. Waldock, *"Paradise Lost" and its Critics* (Cambridge University Press, 1964), 24.
25 Empson, *Milton's God*, p. 211.
26 Balachandra Rajan, "Samson hath quit himself / Like Samson," *Milton Quarterly* 41 (2007), 2.
27 Susannah B. Mintz, *Threshold Poetics: Milton and Intersubjectivity* (Newark: University of Delaware Press, 2003), p. 205.
28 John Shawcross, *The Uncertain World of "Samson Agonistes"* (Cambridge: D. S. Brewer, 2001), pp. 70, 138–45, 141.
29 Cf. John Ulreich's reading of Dalila's sincerity in "'Incident to All Our Sex': The Tragedy of Dalila," in Julia Walker (ed.), *Milton and the Idea of Woman* (Urbana: University of Illinois Press, 1988), pp. 185–210. Heather Asals, "In Defense of Dalila: *Samson Agonistes* and the Reformation Theology of the Word," *Journal of English and Germanic Philology* 74 (1975), 183–94, esp. 183; Samuel Hornsby, "Penance of the Hyaena," *Philological Quarterly* 57 (1978), 353–8.
30 Laurie P. Morrow, "The 'Meet and Happy Conversation': Dalila's Role in *Samson Agonistes*," *Milton Quarterly* 17, 2 (1983), 41; Achsah Guibbory, *Ceremony and Community from Herbert to Milton: Literature, Religion, and Cultural Conflict in Seventeenth-Century England* (Cambridge University Press, 1998), p. 223.
31 Achsah Guibbory, *Christian Identity, Jews, and Israel in Seventeenth-Century England* (Oxford University Press, 2010), pp. 286, 288.
32 Besides Guibbory, see Fish, who states that Dalila is led by "some abstract formula for behavior (like the Law)" (Fish, *How Milton Works*, p. 427). Barbara K. Lewalski makes similar claims about the Hebrew law in "Milton and Idolatry," *Studies in English Literature* 43, 1 (2003), 226.
33 Janel Mueller, "Just Measures: Versification in *Samson Agonistes*," *Milton Studies* 33 (1996), 72. Notably Mueller's meticulous prosodic analysis exhibits the "damning connotations of the prosody with respect to Dalila" (70). Dalila does approach Samson with "doubting feet" (*Samson Agonistes* 732).
34 John Milton, *Samson Agonistes*, in Jason P. Rosenblatt (ed.), *Milton's Selected Poetry and Prose*, ll. 845–8. All quotations from *Samson Agonistes* are from Rosenblatt's edition and cited parenthetically by line number.

35 Rosenblatt notes that "agonistes" is the Greek term for "combatant or contestant in the games," as well as "actor" and "God's champion": Rosenblatt (ed.), *Samson Agonistes*, p. 156 n.1.
36 Empson, *Milton's God*, p. 221; Paula Loscocco, "'Not Less Renown'd Than Jael': Heroic Chastity in *Samson Agonistes*," *Milton Studies* 40 (2001), 188.
37 Mieke Bal, *Death and Dissymmetry: The Politics of Coherence in the Book of Judges* (University of Chicago Press, 1988), pp. 10, 11. On Bal's counter-reading of Judges and its applicability to *Samson Agonistes*, see Hope Parisi, "Discourse and Danger: Women's Heroism in the Bible and Dalila's Self-Defense," in Charles W. Durham and Kristin Pruitt McColgan (eds.), *Spokesperson Milton: Voices in Contemporary Criticism* (London: Associated University Presses, 1994), pp. 264–5.
38 Gordon Teskey, *Delirious Milton: The Fate of the Poet in Modernity* (Cambridge, MA: Harvard University Press, 2006), p. 192.
39 Sharon Achinstein's clever counter-reading of Dalila's relationship to the poem's dominant biblical historical tradition postulates that Milton's ingenious presentation of a "bid for feminist heroism is consistent and plausible" (*Literature and Dissent*, p. 50). Cf. Thomas Kranidas, who negotiates between Empson's and Don Cameron Allen's opposing characterizations of Dalila: Thomas Krandidas, "Dalila's Role in *Samson Agonistes*," *Studies in English Literature* 6, 1 (1966), 125–37.
40 Cf. Norman T. Burns, who acknowledges the potency of Dalila's speech – "it is characteristic of Milton to give strong arguments to his unsympathetic characters" – but concludes that no discerning reader will fail to distinguish Dalila's treachery from Jael's righteous deed of divinely sanctioned violence. Norman T. Burns, "'Then Stood up Phineas': Milton's Antinomianism and Samson's," *Milton Studies* 33 (1996), 34–5. See also David Loewenstein, *Representing Revolution in Milton and His Contemporaries* (Cambridge University Press, 2001), p. 274, and "Interpreting Dalila: *Samson Agonistes* and the Politics of Servility," in Peter C. Herman (ed.), *Approaches to Teaching Milton's Shorter Poetry and Prose* (New York: MLA, 2007), p. 198.
41 The remarks on the phrase are indebted to Mueller's "Just Measures," 73.
42 Victoria Kahn, "Disappointed Nationalism: Milton in the Context of Seventeenth-Century Debates about the Nation-State," in David Loewenstein and Paul Stevens (eds.), *Early Modern Nationalism and Milton's England* (University of Toronto Press, 2008), pp. 264, 265.
43 Michael Krouse, *Milton's Samson and the Christian Tradition* (Princeton University Press, 1949); Joseph A. Wittreich, *Interpreting "Samson Agonistes"* (Princeton University Press, 1986); R. W. Serjeantson, "*Samson Agonistes* and 'Single Rebellion,'" in Nicholas McDowell and Nigel Smith (eds.), *Oxford Handbook of Milton* (Oxford University Press, 2009), pp. 613–31.
44 On Samson's sainthood in the early modern era, see Krouse, *Milton's Samson*, p. 74, and Derek Wood, *Exiled from Light: Divine Law, Morality, and Violence in Milton's "Samson Agonistes"* (University of Toronto Press, 2001), p. 85.

45 Achinstein, *Literature and Dissent*, p. 143.
46 Burns, "'Then Stood up Phineas,'" 41.
47 Samuel S. Stollman, "Milton's Understanding of the 'Hebraic' in *Samson Agonistes*," *Studies in Philology* 69, 3 (1972), 337, 346.
48 Joan S. Bennett, *Reviving Liberty: Radical Christian Humanism in Milton's Great Poems* (Cambridge, MA: Harvard University Press, 1989), p. 96.
49 Lewalski, "Milton and Idolatry," 229.
50 Melbourne, "The Bible and *Samson Agonistes*," *Studies in English Literature* 36 (1996), 124. George F. Butler's remarks support the skeptical reading: "Milton carefully questions whether every 'rousing motion' felt by Samson is an instance of divine inspiration, and whether true inspiration may be determined." George F. Butler, "Donne's *Biathanatos* and *Samson Agonistes*," *Milton Studies* 34 (1997), 212.
51 Bennett, *Reviving Liberty*, pp. 120, 139; William Kerrigan reiterates the connection. "The Irrational Coherence of *Samson Agonistes*," *Milton Studies* 22 (1986), 218, 223. Cf. Fish, *How Milton Works*, p. 419.
52 Burns, "'Then Stood up Phineas,'" 42. Samson, claims Blair Worden, is comparable to the saints who exhibited "an antinomian streak": "Milton, *Samson Agonistes*, and the Restoration," in Gerald MacLean (ed.), *Culture and Society in the Stuart Restoration: Literature, Drama, History* (Cambridge University Press, 1995), p. 132.
53 Guibbory, *Christian Identity*, p. 286. Empson followed his chapter on "Delilah" in *Milton's God* with a chapter on "Christianity" (ch. 7), in which he exposed the neo-Christian bias, outlined at the beginning of this essay. Rosenblatt presents an alternative critique of neo-Christian and Christian readings of the poem in his learned rebuttal to the (negative) typological, Pauline, antinomian, and Christian traditions, in the context of which *Samson Agonistes* and more specifically, the concept of the Law, have regularly been read. (Rosenblatt, *Renaissance England's Chief Rabbi: John Selden* (Oxford University Press, 2006), pp. 93–111).
54 Butler, "Donne's *Biathanatos*," 212.
55 See Stanley Fish's splendid essay, "Spectacle and Evidence in *Samson Agonistes*," *Critical Inquiry* 15 (1989), 569. Cf. Rosenblatt, *Renaissance England's Chief Rabbi*, p. 110. Reprinted in *How Milton Works*, 432–73, Fish's reading of Milton's dramatic poem tends, as Michael Lieb observes, to undermine much of the argument of Fish's book. Michael Lieb, "Returning the Gorgon Medusa's Gaze: Terror and Annihilation in Milton," in Albert C. Labriola and Michael Lieb (eds.), *Milton in the Age of Fish* (Pittsburgh: Duquesne University Press, 2006), pp. 229–42.
56 See Wittreich, *Interpreting "Samson Agonistes*," p. 121, Parisi, "Discourse and Danger," p. 265. See also David Gay, "'Honied Words,'" 53.
57 Schwartz, "The Nightmare," p. 202.
58 On this point, see Stephen B. Dobranski, *Milton, Authorship, and the Book Trade* (Cambridge University Press, 1999), p. 56.

59 David Loewenstein, "*Samson Agonistes* and the Culture of Religious Terror," in Albert C. Labriola and Michael Lieb (eds.), *Milton in the Age of Fish* (Pittsburgh: Duquesne University Press, 2006), pp. 203–28.
60 Wittreich, *Why Milton Matters*, p. 139.
61 Fish, *How Milton Works*, pp. 473, 426.
62 John Carey, "A Work in Praise of Terrorism? September 11 and *Samson Agonistes*," *Times Literary Supplement* (September 6, 2002), 15. Carey does not do justice to the uncertainty Fish introduces in his analysis of *Samson Agonistes* in *How Milton Works*. See Feisal G. Mohamed, "Confronting Religious Violence: Milton's *Samson Agonistes*," *PMLA* 120, 2 (March 2005), 327–40; see also Paul Stevens, "Intolerance and the Virtues of Sacred Vehemence," in Sharon Achinstein and Elizabeth Sauer (eds.), *Milton and Toleration* (Oxford University Press, 2007), pp. 243–67.
63 Carey, "A Work in Praise of Terrorism?" 16. See also Sharon Achinstein, "Cloudless Thunder: Milton in History," *Milton Studies* 48 (2008), 1–12.
64 Feisal Mohamed, "Reading *Samson* in the New American Century," *Milton Studies* 46 (2007), 157, 158.
65 Ibid., 161. Achinstein, who locates Samson in the context of Restoration nonconformity rather than the history of Judges and Judaism, concluded earlier that Milton doesn't completely renounce violence, and that violence is tied up with redemption in the 1671 volume (*Literature and Dissent*, p. 152).
66 Wittreich, *Interpreting "Samson Agonistes,"* p. 24.

PART II
Critical receptions

CHAPTER 7

Against fescues and ferulas: personal affront and the path to individual liberty in Milton's early prose

Christopher D'Addario

In 1645, before lapsing into a four-year, perhaps sullen and disappointed, prose silence, Milton had a few final shots for his anonymous adversary who had dared challenge, in print, his opinion on divorce. In the penultimate paragraph of the vituperative *Colasterion* (1645), he dismisses once more the author of *An Answer to a Book, Intituled, The Doctrine and Discipline of Divorce*, tiredly expressing his disdain for his lowly opponent and wishing for a more worthy foe to debate:

> And if hee have such an ambition to know no better who are his mates [...] if in this penury of Soul hee can bee possible to have the lustiness to think of fame, let him but send mee how hee calls himself, and I may chance not fail to endorse him on the backside of posterity, not a *golden*, but a brazen Asse. Since my fate extorts from mee a talent of sport, which I had thought to hide in a napkin, hee shall bee my *Batrachomuomachia*, my *Bavius*, my *Calandrino*, the common adagy of ignorance and overweening. Nay perhaps, as the provocation may bee, I may bee driv'n to curle up this gliding prose into a rough *Sotadic*, that shall rime him into such a condition, as instead of judging good Books to bee burnt by the executioner, hee shall be readier to be his own hangman. Thus much to this Nuisance. (*CPW* 2:757)

The abrupt dismissal of his opponent at the close of this passage is typically sharp Miltonic polemic: a contemptuously short and simple closure to the lengthy, learned, and angry periods that immediately precede it. But the ease and shortness of his farewell to his adversary also points up, by contrast, the fact that Milton had dignified this low-born and unlearned "Servingman" with a detailed response and put this response into print. Indeed, one has to wonder, in the event of another answer from his opponent, whether "thus much" would have been enough. We might also wonder whether Milton's subsequent silence was merely because of his increasing anger and isolation over what he saw to be the backtracking of Parliament and the Presbyterian party. Might it also have been occasioned by having no one to admonish and asperse after there was no answer to the challenge that he issued at the end of *Colasterion*?

The passage from *Colasterion* finds Milton at his most biting, although it is not entirely unrepresentative of much of the tone of Milton's early prose, a fact that recent scholars have increasingly emphasized.[1] What is perhaps more interesting about this parting salvo, however, is the familiar language that creeps into the middle of his attack, as Milton reveals his attitudes toward the "manner of writing" that he has undertaken here, the "sport" of satire and controversy. Because of the sniping from his adversary, Milton laments that "fate extorts from mee a talent of sport, which I had thought to hide in a napkin." Milton's contemptuous dismissal of his opponent is predicated, as it often is in his prose, upon a denigration of the very medium within which he is working, the "cool element of prose," to borrow from the most famous statement of his lofty ambitions to transcend controversial writing. And yet, we also have the evocation of another touchstone of Miltonic thought, the parable of the talents, which takes on a more rustic, proverbial form here. Certainly its rougher contours seem indicative of the more general mixture of high, rhetorical flights and low, coarse invective everywhere in the early prose. But the appearance of this parable also indicates Milton's admission that polemic and satire are natural to him, indeed his God-given gifts that he has been called to use. Even though Milton might feel that the occasion has extorted this talent from his unwilling hand, the passage can stand as a useful corrective to the more romantic readings of Sonnet 19 that assume that Milton viewed his career as a pamphleteer solely as a waste of his unmistakably poetic genius. In fact, here and elsewhere in the early prose, Milton accepts that his mind naturally takes rather to controversy and harsh dispute. In *An Apology Against a Pamphlet* (1642), Milton admits just as much to an imagined, more urbane interlocuter who has accused him of being too rough, noting that his genius leads him often to what he calls here a "sanctifi'd bitterness" (*CPW* 1:901): "whosoever would but use his eare to listen, might heare the voice of his guiding *Genius* ever before him, calling and as it were pointing to that way which is his part to follow" (*CPW* 1:904). While we might also be hesitant to follow the rougher, often crude, tone of the voice of Milton's genius, the early prose provides ample evidence of it.

The pamphlets that Milton wrote between the years 1642 and 1645 consistently show us a mind motivated, even inspired, by denunciations, both those he issues, as well as those upon his own writings or person. It is worth remarking that the majority of pamphlets that Milton wrote and published during this period were responses to written or unwritten attacks on either his allies or himself. Both the full title to his final antiprelatical tract, *An Apology against a Pamphlet Call'd A Modest Confutation of the Animadversions upon the Remonstrant against Smectymnuus*, as well as the speed with which Milton produced some of this prose, attest to an author with an inexhaustible appetite for public debate and controversy. Moreover, although Milton invariably claimed the logical high ground in his arguments, he often descended into irrational invective and namecalling. In his prose, Milton often argues powerfully and compellingly for the free use of human reason.[2] However, the repeated moments of invective that appear remind us that Milton's high rhetoric of liberty was often matched with occasional, inconsistent and often unfair lines of argument. While a few critics have recognized this descent previously, I argue that the vituperation in Milton's early prose was not necessarily out of a distaste for rational argument and a preference for metaphoric, poetic discourse, but rather due to the frequency with which Milton felt himself personally oppugned and responded in kind.[3] The zeal for polemic, even personal attack, was hardly unique to Milton in the 1640s.[4] However, Milton clearly took to this form, consistently transforming this polemic into personal affront and, concomitantly, personal excoriation of his opponents. Again and again, Milton draws inspiration from imagining his enemies arrayed against him as he enters public debate. The exact contours of these imaginings, which I will outline in this essay, can provide new insights into the importance of private habits and practices to Milton's public rhetoric.

Perhaps more importantly, this antagonistic inspiration also raises questions about, and illustrates underlying faultlines in, Milton's theories on individual liberty, theories that invariably become compromised once faced with the actual practices, such as reading and writing, of others. Since especially the late 1980s and the concerted construction of a radical Milton by Christopher Hill, Joan Bennett, and Michael Wilding among others, Milton has been predominantly portrayed as a writer whose commitment to liberty, be it religious, domestic, or political, was unyielding and based on a similarly intransigent support for the free use of right reason.[5] So, Christopher Hill argues that during the ferment of the early years of the Revolution, Milton came to recognize and advocate "a conception of Christian liberty which started from the absolute integrity of the individual conscience," while Joan Bennett places Milton alongside Richard Hooker as spokesmen for the "same deeply rational Christian liberty."[6] Political and intellectual historians, most recently Blair Worden and Quentin Skinner, have also emphasized the centrality of reason to Milton's theories on individual liberty.[7] Now, I do not wish to deny the existence of a radical Milton; his opinions on Scriptural exegesis, companionate marriage and toleration of dissenting opinion even by 1643–4 were far from customary. However, what I do wish to question is the general acceptance in these analyses of Milton as a wholehearted supporter of individual liberty, one who, at least until 1660, consistently and firmly believed in the unfettered use and efficacy of human reason. In fact, throughout the early prose, Milton repeatedly depicts himself as isolated, his opinions on Christian liberty treated derisively by the majority of his readers. It is this isolation that Milton deemed typical for the scattered friends of truth. In his writing of 1643–4 especially, Milton persistently misdoubts his readers' abilities, passionately attacking their refusal to accept what Milton so plainly sees before them. The jeremiadic tendencies of the early prose, which have largely gone unrecognized by advocates of Milton as consistent defender of liberty, become clearer in 1649 in *Eikonoklastes* and again in 1660 in *The Readie and Easie Way*, when Milton seems to accept fully the inability of the English people generally to fulfill God's call to revolution. However, as we shall see, the latter moments of disappointment were not unique, but rather inhere in Milton's earliest thoughts on liberty and right reason. Indeed, throughout the revolutionary writing, we can see an individual whose opinions are marked more by a repeated tendency to lose faith at key moments, a desire, even, to abandon the "people" and to take up a more comforting, antagonistic pose even as he inconsistently but forcefully argues for their liberty. Once we consider the extent to which personal animus, indeed even passion and antagonism, drive Milton's political theories, we find in the early prose a writer whose conception of individual liberty is far from unified, coherent or sustainable.

Throughout much of the early prose, Milton consistently associated writing style with public actions as well as private virtue; for Milton the polemicist, one's writing stood as evidence of one's personal morality.[8] The extensive and famous self-defense in *An Apology* then seems an inevitable result of his philosophy concerning private habits, a defense both occasioned by his enemies' direct response to this philosophy, and logically necessary to his own claims to truth. As I noted above, it is in *An Apology* that Milton defends his rough invective by noting that he is merely following his natural genius. Earlier in the same pamphlet, in order to provide religious precedent for his style, Milton argues that God purposefully imbued different men with different tempers in order to appeal to as many hearers and readers as possible. So, "The Baptist we know was a strict man remarkable for austerity and set order of life" and, thus, in his teachings appealed to this sort. Similarly, "[s]ome also were indu'd with a staid moderation, and soundnesse of argument to teach and convince the rationall and sober-minded; yet not therefore that to be thought the only expedient course of teaching" (*CPW* 1: 900). In this passage, as well as in his attacks on the Confuter and the defenses of his personal habits, Milton assumes that an individual's way of life is fully figured in his style.[9] At least at this point in his prose career, Milton seems more confident that readers would easily discern his true self in his writings rather than in his public actions, actions which had already been tainted by the misrepresentations of Hall and the Confuter, even after they could provide no evidence of an immoral private life.

With so much of one's personality invested in one's writing, it is no wonder that Milton so consistently and vividly imagined his adversaries and himself privately reading, preparing, and writing as part of their participation in the public world of print. The stridency and detail of the personal invective of these private scenes show Milton working in the Marprelatian tradition, a tradition that had been revived in the early 1640s through reprints and imitations. The lively language and sharp aspersions in these tracts marked a renewed interest in the private foibles of political adversaries and the public airing of such foibles.[10] Milton's "genius" in particular seemed attracted to constructing vibrant pictures of his opponents in solitude. Throughout *Animadversions* and *An Apology*, Milton's satire is at his sharpest, his imagination most invigorated, when he begins to describe Hall or the Confuter in the privacy of an imagined home, or as he constructs their personalities from their writing. For example, toward the end of *Animadversions*, Milton belittles Hall's obsession with Milton's audacity: "A man would thinke you had eaten over liberally of *Esaus* red porrage, and from thence dreame continually of blushing; or, perhaps, to heighten your fancy in writing, are wont to sit in your Doctors scarlet, which through your eyes infecting your pregnant imaginative with a red suffusion, begets a continuall thought of blushing" (*CPW* 1: 725). While Milton is toying with Hall's sense of propriety here, his picture of the inquisitive licenser in *Areopagitica* troubles him more deeply: "He who but of late cry'd down the sole ordination of every novice Batchelor of Art, and deny'd sole jurisdiction over the simplest Parishioner, shall now at home in his privat chair assume both these over worthiest and excellentest books and ablest authors that write them" (*CPW* 2:540). Alongside these peeks into private studies, we also have assumptions about private morality and behaviors from an author's style and even choice of title.[11] We may, not unfairly, use Milton's charge against the Confuter in *An Apology* to describe his own methods in the early prose: "[He] could not let a private word passe, but he must make all this blaze of it" (*CPW* 1:914).

As for Milton's self-perception, when he envisioned himself or his allies in the defense of truth, he increasingly assumed the existence of a sea of foes ready to cry down their efforts.[12] By the time we get to the *Doctrine and Discipline of Divorce*, even the first edition, Milton tends to assume that his tract will be received negatively, depicting it as a call to truth that will be ignored or vilified by vulgar readers:

> This only is desir'd of them who are minded to judge hardly of thus maintaining, that they would be still and heare all out, nor think it equall to answer deliberate reason with sudden heat and noise; remembring this, that many truths now of reverend esteem and credit, had their birth and beginning once from singular and private thoughts; while the most of men were otherwise possest; and had the fate at first to be generally exploded and exclaim'd on by many violent opposers; yet I may erre perhaps in soothing my selfe that this present truth reviv'd will deserve to be not ungently receiv'd on all hands. (CPW 2:240–1)

This passage is fascinating for its movement from the beginning appeal for a fair hearing and reasoned debate to, what was for Milton, the harsh clamor of the public print market. This slippage from the hope for a reasonable audience to a resignation that most, plagued by a blind adherence to custom, would fall prey to false opinions is representative of Milton's thoughts on the reception of his work. In *Eikonoklastes*, Milton begins his response to the King's enormously popular *Eikon Basilike* by noting, at first, that he is merely trying to remind his misled readers of "the truth of what they themselves know to be heer [in the *Eikon Basilike*] misaffirm'd" (*CPW* 3:338). However, shortly after this confidence he admits more pessimistically that "it might have seem'd in vaine to write at all; considering the envy and almost infinite prejudice likely to be stirr'd up among the Common sort" (*CPW* 3:339). By the time we get to *The Readie and Easie Way*, written as the failure of the "good old cause" was imminent, the rhetoric of reasoned debate is starkly incongruent next to the jeremiadic excoriations of the debased virtue of his countrymen. In the early prose, Milton was perhaps more hopeful, and yet there persists an underlying acceptance that his pamphlets will be received ungently, that a crowd of "violent opposers" await them. As a result, throughout the divorce tracts and *Areopagitica*, truth itself is most often rejected and denounced for error when it first appears. So, in the Preface to the second edition of *The Doctrine and Discipline*, Milton laments that truth "never comes into the world, but like a Bastard, to the ignominy of him that brought her forth" (*CPW* 2:225). The focus on the ignominy of the truth-bearer emphasizes that Milton's complaint over truth's hard reception is directly linked to his own treatment in the pulpits and printstalls of London; shortly before this passage, Milton describes himself as the "sole advocate of a discount'nanc't truth" (*CPW* 2:224). As much as he took the outcry against truth personally, he also more generally portrayed the majority as historically desiring or advocating the wrong path. In *The Doctrine and Discipline of Divorce*, Milton praises above all other leaders the two "matchless generals," Themistocles and Fabius Maximus, who "had the fortitude at home against the rashnes and the clamours of their own Captains and confederates to withstand the doing or permitting of what they could not approve in the duty of their great command" (*CPW* 2:315). The lofty encomium, and his general stance against what he saw to be the "rashnes" of majority opinion, surely derives from Milton's wholehearted and lifelong rejection of custom and received opinion. But this intransigent rejection of custom holds such prominence in Milton's thought precisely because of its presumed power over most people and, as evidenced from his worries about his work's reception, over most of his audience as well.

In presupposing a harsh reception for his writing and imagining himself solitarily defending truth, Milton evinces a vibrantly spatial imagination throughout his work on domestic liberty. In *Areopagitica* particularly, people, books and ideas "speed and post" over the world, or else remain confined and bound by licensers and oppressors: from truth-seekers who "scout into the regions of sin and falsity," to the banned books which stand imprisoned in darkness waiting to "passe the ferry backward into light" to minds "that can wander beyond all limit and satiety" because of God's permission. Recently, Adrian Johns has perceptively identified in John Goodwin's writings of the same years a similar tendency to use "place-based metaphors to describe the roles of reason in faith." In what Johns calls experiments "with the geography of faith," Goodwin sought to transform traditional conceptions of parish that were necessarily associated with a particular physical location by reconceiving his radical congregation as an "essentially placeless church."[13] In *Areopagitica*, we might see Milton, who in his adult life never clearly participated in a specific organized church, contributing to the same devaluation of place.[14] By conceiving of truth as scattered, collaged and often heterodox, Milton disassociates that truth from any single church (part of his defense of sects and schism in *Areopagitica*) as well as from any particular geographic location associated with that church. Considered alongside his distinct visions of readers and writers in their private studies in this pamphlet and others, we can begin to recognize a Miltonic "geography of faith" that privileges individual practice over communal abstractions. Or, to put it another way, Milton shifted the search for spiritual truth away from place to space, away from physical location to various loci where spiritual truth (or error) resided.[15] More broadly, this shift signifies the centrality of practice, of particular and individual acts of writing, reading, exercising, and eating for example, to Milton's theories on truth, human reason, and elective virtue.[16] In one of the more striking juxtapositions in the early prose, Milton defends his morning activities in *An Apology*, noting that he generally turns to exercise "to render lightsome, cleare, and not lumpish obedience to the minde, to the cause of religion, and our Countries liberty, when it shall require firme hearts in sound bodies to stand and cover their stations, rather then to see the ruine of our Protestation, and the inforcement of a slavish life" (*CPW* 1:885–6). The relationship between physical health and moral fortitude expressed here, and repeated metaphorically throughout *Areopagitica*, is remarkable for its fluidity, for its assumption that the exercise of individuals can help the Parliamentary cause, not only because it will produce a stronger soldier, but also because its practice will result in a more vigorous and labile intellect capable of discerning and defending true religion and liberty. However, the physical and moral virtue depicted above, or else in *Of Education*, remained imagined ideals not yet attained by most, ideals that often reminded Milton that many ended up like the "tavern-hunting" bishops, or those misguided readers who mistook his own calls for true reformation. Because of such a focus on the practice of virtue, that is, Milton seemed inevitably to turn to the reality of vice and error that he saw around him even as he formulated his more hopeful and theoretical stances on the efficacy of human reason, and especially as his increasingly radical opinions on divorce and heresy were derided and denounced.

It is not surprising, then, that for Milton those who seek truth must invariably journey far and into darkness and danger to find its scattered limbs. The friends of truth, including, of course, Milton himself, are few, often lonely and inveterate explorers, surrounded by oppression and derision. Without a doubt, Milton is drawing on the prophetic tradition in constructing such a picture of truth's friends; his sense of separation must also have been exacerbated by the domestic turmoil of his first marriage.[17] Yet the divorce tracts are by no means the first, nor the last, writings in which Milton vividly imagines himself among the enemy. We have the "foedissima turba" [the most detestable band] that surrounds him in "Ad Patrem"; the "owls and cuckoos, asses, apes and dogs" in his sonnet on the reception of *Tetrachordon*; the "troubled sea of noises and harsh disputes" that arise around him in *The Reason of Church Government*; and, of course, the poet writing in "darkness and with dangers compast round" in *Paradise Lost*. He often expects the worst from his readers, chafing at those who, inferior in judgment, mistrust and suspect the deliberative author. The consistency of these imaginings demonstrates not only Milton's most enduring perception of himself, but also, I would suggest, a writer who draws inspiration from isolation, from antagonism and criticism, and from affront at the unfair reception of his work. While he may emphasize the importance of Christian rationality to the free man, as most commentators have noted, he often seems more comfortable denying the very possibility of such reason in his audience.

In light of such self-representation, it might be useful to reconsider Milton's oft-discussed choice to come forth in support of divorce due to incompatibility at a moment when no one was discussing this issue. To be sure, much of Milton's motivation came from his recent separation from Mary Powell, as Annabel Patterson and Stephen Fallon have wonderfully elucidated.[18] But we might also consider, alongside the failure in confidence that this separation entailed, Milton's growing dissatisfaction with the Presbyterian party and the recently convened Westminster Assembly. With its move to a national church and compulsive uniformity, the Assembly surely seemed the wrong direction to Milton, who even in 1643, had begun to move toward some heretical opinions, as well as religious toleration.[19] The summer of 1643 and after can be seen as another one of those Miltonic moments of crisis in which he is vigorously seeking to understand God's role in what seems to be a turning aside from the path to true reformation. In the context of such growing disappointment, Milton's willful assertion of his own idiosyncratic interpretation of Scripture, indeed the choice of subject matter itself, is intriguing.[20] As he was losing faith in Presbyterian reform, Milton prominently and repeatedly advocates a heretical opinion on divorce, unabashedly reinterprets Christ's injunctions (justified with a radical theory of Scriptural exegesis) and substantially reorients his audience's definitions of heresy in *Areopagitica*. The move looks forward to a similar moment of crisis for Milton in early 1660. Then, as well, he would knowingly adhere to an unpopular opinion in *The Readie and Easie Way*, an act of studied resistance in which he stubbornly clings to the rhetoric of republicanism even as the Good Old Cause had already crumbled about him. To call the second edition of *The Readie and Easie Way* "urgent optimism," as William Riley Parker has, seems misguided in light of the facts of the situation, as Milton surely knew them, in April 1660.[21] Instead, we should consider that Milton understood that the return of Charles Stuart was nearly inevitable, that the tide of public opinion had turned inexorably, and that his adherence to the language of reasoned proposal stood out as idiosyncratic and willful.

The rhetorical position that Milton takes up in these two moments is representative of what seems an instinctive turn away from his readers, a swift loss of faith in their abilities that Milton seems ready to accept or even expect. So, at another of these moments, in 1649 after the success of the *Eikon Basilike*, Milton also angrily dismisses the majority of the English nation as possessing a "besotted and degenerate baseness of spirit" (*CPW* 3:344), while establishing himself as part of the small minority who argue for the truth: "Certainly, if ignorance and perversness will needs be national and universal, then they who adhere to wisdom and to truth, are not therfore to be blam'd, for beeing so few as to seem a sect or faction" (*CPW* 3:348). In 1649, as well as in 1643 and 1660, Milton must have expected dismissal from many of his readers, despite his appeals to the clear light of human reason; his often impatient cajoling of his audience in the divorce tracts, *Eikonoklastes* and *The Readie and Easie Way* assumes just such anger. In 1643, with his coming forth unexpectedly arguing for divorce due to incompatibility, we can feel Milton settling in to a familiar position; in the Preface to the second edition of *The Doctrine and Discipline*, he considers himself a solitary and heroic defender of an unpopular truth: "a high enterprise Lords and Commons, a high enterprise and a hard, and such as every seventh Son of a seventh Son does not venture on. Nor have I amidst the clamor of so much envie and impertience, whether to appeal, but to the concourse of so much piety and wisdome heer assembl'd" (*CPW* 2:224).

This last passage is one of Milton's more remarkable assertions of unique timeliness and prophetic calling; yet, we should not forget that these sentences are addressed confidently and directly to Parliament and the Westminster Assembly and these bodies' "piety and wisdom," even as he imagines the "clamor" that accompanies his writing. Indeed, of his tracts on domestic liberty, Milton addressed all but the first edition of *The Doctrine and Discipline* and *Colasterion* directly to Parliament. These addresses are hortatory, calling Parliament and the nation onward to the remote realms of Milton's truth, where most could not follow. At least in 1643–4, he was still tentatively hopeful that Parliament would not shout him down as his common readers would. That he was serious in his direct address to Parliament, might even have thought that his radical arguments would transform members' opinions, is suggested by the fact that Parliament and England generally assumed a similar position in Milton's imagination as the author himself. So, in one of his most vivid depictions of the ever-present enemies of truth, it is the English nation that heroically rises against the world's noisy distrust of heavenly discovery:

> Methinks I see in my mind a noble and puissant Nation rousing herself like a strong man after sleep, and shaking her invincible locks: Methinks I see her as an Eagle muing her mighty youth, and kindling her undazl'd eyes at the full midday beam; purging and unscaling her long abused sight at the fountain it self of heav'nly radiance; while the whole noise of timorous and flocking birds, with those also that love the twilight, flutter about, amaz'd at what she means, and in their envious gabble would prognosticat a year of sects and schisms. (*CPW* 2:557–8)

The power of this passage comes not only from the dynamically hopeful vision of the nation as Samson and the eagle, but also from the vividly contemptuous image of the "flocking birds" which misdoubt English intellect and capacity for change. We have the familiar Miltonic opposition between the friends of Osiris and those who tore his body to pieces; however, this time, the solitary individual has been subsumed into a national community that, as a whole, fights in truth's cause.

However, the subsumption of the besieged individual, of Milton, into a heroic community is not always so beautifully successful. In the early prose, Milton's willful assertion of idiosyncratic truths (and the isolation that this assertion entails) stands alongside his hopes that the English nation, and Parliament specifically, would come to its senses about divorce and pre-publication licensing. Yet, we can already see hints of where Milton's sense of individuality and of affront at those readers who misunderstand him will eventually lead him in *Eikonoklastes* and later in *The Readie and Easie Way*. Admittedly, *Eikonoklastes* ends on a note of reserved hope that at least some, deceived by "ignorance without malice, or some error, less then fatal," will recover and recognize the profound sins of Charles (*CPW* 3:601). However, the pamphlet generally is suffused with a tremendous bitterness toward "the Image-doting rabble" and even in 1649, Milton is illiberally arguing for the "strength and supremacie of Justice" over truth and that we should "soon perceave that Truth resignes all her outward strength to Justice" (*CPW* 3:585). Eleven years later, in *The Readie and Easie Way*, Milton prophetically chastises the "perverse inhabitants" of England for falling prey to the "deluge of this epidemic madness" and troublingly argues that the "less" number can compel the greater to liberty, if necessary (*CPW* 7:463). In both of these later pamphlets Milton's rhetoric and argument inconsistently oscillate between the reasonableness of his argument, be it his interpretation of the King's book or his republican proposals, and the angry acknowledgment that the English people were tragically submitting to their own enslavement.

This inconsistency, far from deriving solely from the swiftly changing realities of the weeks after the King's execution or the early months of 1660, however, is endemic to his thoughts on individual liberty and human reason, and can already be seen in the earlier tracts of the 1640s. Recent work on Milton as political theorist has substantially complicated the older, Whiggish picture of Milton as unwavering supporter of the people's rights and liberties, both civil and political.[22] Instead, we have an author who in the revolutionary prose develops his theories on liberty in reaction to the immediate occasion, and who never formulated a coherent constitutional model to replace monarchy until *The Readie and Easie Way*. To be sure, Milton at times situates himself among the more radical political reformers, particularly in *The Tenure of Kings and Magistrates*. There, Milton draws on natural rights theories to argue for the inalienable rights of the people and the concomitant ability to revoke power from a tyrannous monarch.[23] However, Milton's argument in *The Tenure* seems an amalgam of various political perspectives, which should remind us that English republican theories were being constructed haphazardly and unevenly, even after 1649, and that many English "republicans" did not clearly advocate for universal or full-fledged liberties for even the "people," loosely defined. Indeed, as Blair Worden has clarified, Milton persistently questioned the ability of his countrymen to govern themselves appropriately, and never clearly sought equality or political liberty for more than the educated and virtuous.[24]

Although the story of "that grand Whig Milton" has taken on water, most intellectual historians have continued to emphasize the importance of right reason to Milton's theories on liberty. Most recently, in a pair of lectures on "Milton as a Theorist of Liberty," Quentin Skinner has argued that Milton made a fundamental distinction between masters and slaves in his conception of liberty, identifying those who were governed by reason, instead of passion, as those who possessed self-mastery and thus the capability to distinguish between liberty and license.[25] And yet, this neo-Platonic view of Milton seems far too comforting, particularly considering the passion that I have shown animating much of Milton's early writings in the years that he began to formulate these theories. This passion, reinforced by the cultivation of a sense of personal affront, underlies Milton's vision of an unsympathetic audience that was adverse to his novel and independent opinions. What is important to recognize is that these unwelcome opinions are the very theories that defend the exercise of liberty and that embody the use of right reason rather than an unthinking acceptance of the tyranny of custom. Again and again in *The Doctrine and Discipline of Divorce* and *Areopagitica*, Milton laments the human tendency to welcome servitude; toward the close of *The Doctrine and Discipline*, echoing the opening sentences of the tract, Milton decries our inability to see the charity in God's law permitting divorce: "While we literally superstitious through customary faintnes of heart, not venturing to peirce with our free thoughts into the full latitude of nature and religion, abandon our selvs to serv under the tyranny of usurpt opinions" (*CPW* 2:343). Even as Milton outlines the Christian liberty allowed under God's law, a liberty which should be clear to the light of human reason, he admits the inability of most to embrace, reasonably, this liberty.

Thus, while Skinner's characterization of Milton as *theorist* seems accurate, his too limited focus on Milton's abstract theories, and the attendant emphasis on Milton's belief in human reason, obscures the inconsistencies that arise as Milton attempts to imagine the actual practice of liberty. The discrepancy between Milton's idealistic advocacy of civil liberties and his pessimistic acceptance of mistaken practice cannot be ignored in the early prose and, in fact, provides much of the rhetorical energy for almost all of Milton's defenses of liberty. That is, the vehemence with which Milton argues against prelacy, permanent marriage, pre-publication licensing, or monarchy is often driven by his anger over the majority's inability to see their own freedom, the extent to which they are unworthy of liberty. More significantly, Milton's dim view of human practice encourages a view of liberty that is easily restricted to those few worthy of such freedom and might even explain the surprising consistency with which Milton delimits these freedoms to those that think as he does.

The inconsistencies generated by the discrepancy between theory and practice become clearest in the tracts on domestic liberty in Milton's depictions of the practice of reading. As suggested by the phrase "literally superstitious" in the passage from *The Doctrine and Discipline* above, Milton viewed the free and reasoned interpretation of all texts, including Scripture, as central to his theories on Christian and civil liberty. In *The Doctrine and Discipline*, Milton very clearly associates elective virtue with the employment of the "full latitude of nature and religion" in the reading of Christ's words and opposes this latitude to the "letter-bound servility of the Canon Doctors" (*CPW* 2:342). Similarly, in *Areopagitica*, he consistently advocates the right of the private individual to read and "know aright" and argues for unfettered access to heretical and idle pamphlets since, "to all men such books are not temptations, nor vanities; but usefull drugs and materialls wherewith to temper and compose effective and strong med'cins, which mans life cannot want" (*CPW* 2:521). These moments demonstrate the full reach of Milton's theoretical embrace of the liberty to read. However, Milton's mind, as I have suggested above, also tended to the particulars of action; and when he turned to the practices of readers, he mostly emphasized their inability to read aright, their misprision due to the unfortunate influence of blind custom. Notably, after the whole-hearted support for the usefulness of books to "all men," Milton immediately qualifies himself, noting that "[t]he rest, as children and childish men, who have not the art to qualifie and prepare these working minerails, well may be exhorted to forbear, but hinder'd forcibly they cannot be" (*CPW* 2:521). While Milton does not embrace state control at this point in his thinking, he does seemingly recoil when faced with the consequences of such all-encompassing support for the freedom to read. For someone so used to envisioning his audience mistaking his arguments and misguidedly denouncing his opinions, indeed, for someone who used these denunciations as inspiration for the high work he saw himself performing, Milton inevitably thought most of his readers incapable of exercising correctly the civil liberties he so vehemently defended.

I have argued that personal animus inspired much of Milton's writing in the early 1640s and that affront should be seen as an important psychological force present in the writings where Miton developed his theories on elective virtue and human reason. In *Areopagitica*, for example, Milton draws a picture of the diligent author, unmistakable in its self-referentiality, as he argues for the right to publish his opinions:

When a man writes to the world, he summons up all his reason and deliberation to assist him; he searches, meditats, is industrious, and likely consults and conferrs with his judicious friends; after all which done he takes himself to be inform'd in what he writes, as well as any that writ before him; if in this the most consummat act of his fidelity and ripenesse, no years, no industry, no former proof of his abilities can bring him to that state of maturity, as not to be still mistrusted and suspected, unlesse he carry all his considerat diligence, all his midnight watchings, and expence of *Palladian* oyl, to the hasty view of an unleasur'd licencer, perhaps much his younger, perhaps far his inferiour in judgment, perhaps one who never knew the labour of book-writing ... it cannot be but a dishonor and derogation to the author, to the book, to the priviledge and dignity of Learning. (*CPW* 2:532)

That these lively visions arise out of anger at the treatment of his own divorce tracts is to state the obvious. Yet, a theory of liberty derived in part from personal animus and a more general distrust of his readers' ability to recognize truth has the worm of its own spoiling within it. Some of this assumption of misunderstanding can be explained by a general disdain for the commonality from many revolutionaries and republicans in the 1640s and 1650s, a belief that the learned elite must instill republican virtues in the many. However, for an author so driven by occasion, response, and personal antagonism, so inspired by assumed misunderstanding and misreading, Milton's distrust of the majority of his readers seems more than a classical predilection for an educated meritocracy. As Milton consistently envisioned his opinions shouted down, he just as consistently saw the majority led astray by custom and lack of understanding. His cultivation of an antagonistic relationship with his assumed audience can be seen to have contributed to his faltering faith in human reason. The contradictory notions of individual liberty and general ignorance that are central to Milton's thinking in 1643–5 would always lead to a theory of liberty necessarily inchoate and unstable in the mind of the author. After all, Milton did accept the role of licenser in 1649 and, in 1660, he would chastise this same "noble and puissant nation" in the jeremiadic portions of *The Readie and Easie Way* for "choosing their captain back to Egypt," even as he willfully clung to the rhetoric (but not the belief) of reasoned republicanism. In April 1660, England had ended up, perhaps, where he believed it would all along.

NOTES

1 See Thomas Kranidas, *Milton and the Rhetoric of Zeal* (Pittsburgh: Duquesne University Press, 2005); Thomas Corns, *Uncloistered Virtue: English Political Literature, 1640–1660* (Oxford University Press, 1992), esp. pp. 18–53; and Lana Cable, *Carnal Rhetoric: Milton's Iconoclasm and the Poetics of Desire* (Durham: Duke University Press, 1995), pp. 55–89.
2 See especially Joan S. Bennett, *Reviving Liberty: Radical Christian Humanism in Milton's Great Poems* (Cambridge, MA: Harvard University Press, 1989), pp. 6–32.
3 See Joan Webber's account of the early prose as a spiritual autobiography written in literary terms in *The Eloquent "I": Style and Self in Seventeenth-Century Prose* (Madison: University of Wisconsin Press, 1968), p. 216 and Cable, *Carnal Rhetoric*, pp. 52–89.
4 Sharon Achinstein, *Milton and the Revolutionary Reader* (Princeton University Press, 1994), pp. 27–70; and David Norbrook, *Writing the English Republic: Poetry, Rhetoric and Politics, 1627–1660* (Cambridge University Press, 1999), pp. 93–139.
5 Christopher Hill's *Milton and the English Revolution* (London: Penguin, 1977), esp. pp. 93–162, laid the groundwork for this reconception. See also Joan S.

Bennett, *Reviving Liberty* and Michael Wilding, *Dragon's Teeth: Literature and the English Revolution* (Oxford University Press, 1987); and Stevie Davies's *Images of Kingship in "Paradise Lost": Milton's Politics and Christian Liberty* (Columbia, MO: University of Missouri Press, 1983), pp. 9–50.

6 Hill, *Milton and the English Revolution*, p. 154 and Bennett, *Reviving Liberty*, p. 7. Although Hill acknowledges some limits to Milton's liberty, he maintains that they were due to Milton's pragmatic recognition that the full scope of his "true" opinions on liberty would not be accepted by the English people of the 1640s (see pp. 155–7).

7 Blair Worden, "Marchamont Nedham and the Beginnings of English Republicanism, 1649–1656," in David Wooton (ed.), *Republicanism, Liberty and Commercial Society, 1649–1776* (Stanford University Press, 1994), pp. 45–81; Blair Worden, "English Republicanism," in Mark Goldie and J. H. Burns (eds.), *The Cambridge History of Political Thought, 1450–1700* (Cambridge University Press, 1995), pp. 449–76; Quentin Skinner recently argued for the overriding importance of a Roman conception of right reason to Milton's theories on liberty in "Milton as Theorist of Liberty," plenary lecture given at the Ninth International Milton Symposium, London, 2008.

8 See Thomas Kranidas, "'Decorum' and the style of Milton's antiprelatical tracts," in *Seventeenth-Century Prose: Modern Essays in Criticism* (Oxford University Press, 1971), pp. 475–88.

9 Reuben Sanchez also notes that Milton believes that "the author cannot be separated from his text," *Persona and Decorum in Milton's Prose* (Newark: Fairleigh Dickinson University Press, 1997), p. 45.

10 See James Egan, "Milton and the Marprelate Tradition," *Milton Studies* 8 (1975), 103–21 for Milton's use of the Marprelate tradition in *Animadversions* and *Colasterion*; see as well Kranidas, *Milton and the Rhetoric of Zeal*, pp. 21–3 and Nigel Smith, *Literature and Revolution in England, 1640–1660* (New Haven: Yale University Press, 1994), pp. 297–304.

11 The latter comes in *An Apology* (*CPW* 1:877).

12 Stephen Fallon also notes that Milton often creates a fictional, antagonistic audience in his prose tracts in "The Metaphysics of Milton's Divorce Tracts," in David Loewenstein and James Grantham Turner (eds.), *Politics, Poetics and Hermeneutics in Milton's Prose* (Cambridge University Press, 1990), p. 73.

13 Adrian Johns, "Coleman Street," *Huntington Library Quarterly* 71 (2008), 40–2. Michael Walzer, in *The Revolution of the Saints: A Study in the Origins of Radical Politics* (Cambridge, MA: Harvard University Press, 1965), argues more broadly for the creation of a godly community of the saints after the Marian exile that transcended physical spaces, pp. 114–37.

14 Although, as Nigel Smith reminds us, Milton's conception of truth was far more worldly and Erastian than the sectarians, see "*Areopagitica*: Voicing Contexts, 1643–5," in Lowenstein and Turner (eds.), *Politics, Poetics and Hermeneutics*, pp. 105–6.

15 See Michel de Certeau's discussion of "place" and "space" in *The Practice of Everyday Life*, trans. Stephen Rendell (Berkeley: University of California Press, 1984), pp. 117–18.

16 In *Milton's Places of Hope: Spiritual and Political Connections of Hope with Land* (Aldershot: Ashgate Press, 2006), Mary C. Fenton outlines in detail the centrality of place-based metaphors to Milton's notions of hope (p. 33).
17 William Kerrigan, *The Prophetic Milton* (Charlottesville: University of Virginia Press, 1974) details the Protestant prophetic tradition and Milton's use of this tradition in his own self-representations in both the prose and late poetry.
18 Annabel Patterson, "No meer amatorious novel?" in Lowenstein and Turner (eds.), *Politics, Poetics and Hermeneutics in Milton's Prose*, pp. 85–103 and Stephen M. Fallon, *Milton's Peculiar Grace: Self-Representation and Authority* (Ithaca: Cornell University Press, 2007), pp. 110–46.
19 Thomas Corns, "Milton's antiprelatical tracts and the marginality of doctrine," in *Milton and Heresy*, pp. 39–49 and David Loewenstein, "Toleration and the Specter of Heresy in Milton's England," in Sharon Achinstein and Elizabeth Sauer (eds.), *Milton and Toleration* (Oxford University Press, 2007), pp. 45–72.
20 See Stanley Fish, "Wanting a Supplement: the Question of Interpretation in Milton's Early Prose," in Lowenstein and Turner (eds.), *Politics, Poetics and Hermeneutics in Milton's Prose*, pp. 54–9; Lana Cable, *Carnal Rhetoric*, pp. 92–5; David Loewenstein, "Toleration and the Specter," pp. 66–9.
21 William Riley Parker, *Milton: a Biography*, 2nd edn. (Oxford: Clarendon Press, 1996), p. 543.
22 See, particularly, the essays by Worden in n. 7 above; Martin Dzelzainis, "Milton's Classical Republicanism," in David Armitage, Armand Himy, and Quentin Skinner (eds.), *Milton and Republicanism* (Cambridge University Press, 1995), pp. 3–24; Thomas Corns, "Milton and the Characteristics of a Free Commonwealth," in *Milton and Republicanism*, pp. 25–42.
23 For an overview, see Richard Tuck, *Natural Rights Theories: Their Origin and Development* (Cambridge University Press, 1979), pp. 143–56.
24 Milton, in his increasingly firm belief in the necessity of education for the corrupt populace, could easily have been influenced by the defeatist attitudes of the Italian republican theorists of the sixteenth century as their hopes were dashed by political realities; see Quentin Skinner, *The Foundations of Modern Political Thought*, 2 vols. (Cambridge University Press, 1978), vol. 1, pp. 168–86.
25 Quentin Skinner, "Milton as a Theorist of Liberty." See also Worden, "English Republicanism," p. 456.

CHAPTER 8

Disruptive partners: Milton and seventeenth-century women writers

Shannon Miller

This essay argues that John Milton and *Paradise Lost* were embroiled in a century-long dialogue about gender that positions his epic alongside writers in the early seventeenth-century "anti-feminist" debate (Rachel Speght and Ester Sowernam), women poets from the early and late seventeenth century (Aemilia Lanyer and Mary Chudleigh), and a major female political and educational theorist (Mary Astell). Surrounded by women writers who engage narratives of the Fall, issues of gendered culpability, and even representations of Christ's Passion and redemption, Milton's *Paradise Lost* internalizes lines of inquiry posed by early seventeenth-century texts authored by women. This essay focuses mainly on how the works of Speght and Sowernam are explored through *Paradise Lost* and then further interrogated and reworked in the writings of Mary Astell. In their early seventeenth-century responses to Joseph Swetnam's *The Arraignment of Lewd ... Women* (1615), Ester Sowernam in *Ester Hath Hanged Haman* (1617) and then Rachel Speght in her "Dreame" vision poem within *Mortalities Memorandum* (1621) offer a portrait of a solitary Eve in search of knowledge who disrupts the implications of the Fall story. Aspects of their complex portraits exploring the "esse" of women and its consequences for considering women's relationship to knowledge become sedimented into Milton's portrait of Eve in *Paradise Lost*, only to be reworked in Mary Astell's 1694 *A Serious Proposal*. What in Speght and Sowernam begins as a negotiation of women's sense of "esse" or self in portraits of the first woman becomes interrogated through Milton's Eve to become a full-blown articulation of women's "self-knowledge" in Astell's argument for female education.

I am suggesting a mode of analyzing textual influence in which the refraction of an earlier ideological or conceptual problem – here culpability for the Fall and the gendered hierarchy it establishes – can resonate through a century of texts. A second and complementary dialogue, presented in a much more compressed form, will help to illustrate this method. There, I will examine the status of looking and its relation to redemption and the Fall in Lanyer, Milton, and Chudleigh. The biblical tradition of Eve's visual access to the tree of knowledge – Eve "saw that the tree was good" – and the ocularly inflected result – Adam and Eve's eyes are "opened" at the Fall – prompt all three texts to interrogate the relationship between falling and seeing.[1] As a coda to this essay, then, the *Viewing Eve* section illustrates this method through the possibilities posed by Eve looking and others looking onto Eve. Lanyer's 1611 *Salve Deus Rex Judaeorum* explores the relationship between redemption and visuality, suggesting that acts of looking – often in the hands of Eve-like figures – are redeemable. A complex layering of the meanings – sacred and profane – of viewing is equally embedded into Milton's *Paradise Lost*. Specific scenes and passages in *Paradise Lost* will then serve as sources for Mary Chudleigh's 1703 poem, "Song of the Three Children Paraphras'd." Responding to possibilities in the "fallen" form of the visual, Chudleigh, as Milton before her, and Lanyer before him, reworks the promise, and dangers, of redemptive gazing.[2]

The conversation that I observe between and within all of these texts repositions the recently emerged "canon" of writings by seventeenth-century women as fully engaged with Milton's epic. But it equally illuminates the ideological construction(s) in and richness of *Paradise Lost*. Interrogating earlier strategies for negotiating the significance of the Fall, of gender, and the implications for knowledge, Milton injects these concepts into, and modifies them in, *Paradise Lost*. Redeployed by Milton, they are then repurposed by writers like Astell and Chudleigh; modified traces of earlier seventeenth-century debates consequently serve these later writers' needs. While Astell and Chudleigh explicitly deploy elements of Milton's Genesis epic for their own purposes, earlier women such as Speght and Lanyer engage – and in many case re-direct – discussions about gender that infuse the early seventeenth-century English anti-feminist debate. Elsewhere, I have argued for their influence on *Paradise Lost*: the internal evidence of early seventeenth-century writers such as Speght, Sowernam, and Lanyer influencing Milton is quite strong. A series of tropes – for example, a disputing and solitary Eve – appear in these texts and become prominent motifs within *Paradise Lost*. Further, generic and linguistic parallels – such as Milton's and Lanyer's innovations in Passion poem conventions and suggestive phrasing linking *Salve* and *Paradise Lost* – provide a very different view of the literary and cultural influences shaping Milton's text.[3] We do not, of course, have a "smoking gun" proving this influence, such as Milton's annotations on Speght's defenses or alongside Lanyer's verses. We know Speght's and Sowernam's works were available in

St. Paul's churchyard, near Milton's childhood home and school. Yet the presence of these texts in Milton's library isn't necessary to consider larger cultural discourses on the representation of Eve and the Garden, and on the implications for gendered culpability in Speght and Sowernam that profoundly shape Milton's poem.

"SOLE EVE, ASSOCIATE SOLE": PORTRAYING THE FIRST WOMAN FROM LANYER TO ASTELL

As critics such as John Ulreich and Kari McBride, Alinda Sumers, Catherine Gimelli Martin, and myself have now begun to suggest explicitly, the seventeenth-century *querelle des femmes* appears internalized within *Paradise Lost*; Milton negotiates the elements of gender hierarchy and authority that resonated through the Fall narrative in the hands of writers such Speght and Sowernam.[4] The very "apologies" offered about women's behavior in these texts become variously internalized in Milton's narrative of the Fall, especially in Eve's own "Apologie" of her behavior in Book 9 which "Came Prologue" to her ensuing debate, or "contest," with Adam (9.854; 1189). In sharp distinction to other modes of defending women in a usually male-authored genre, Speght's and Sowernam's texts describe a figure for the female defender entering into a prelapsarian garden space. Since to write in the anti-feminist tradition was necessarily to occupy the distinctly gendered positions maintained by the genre itself, Speght and Sowernam adapt this necessity to their advantage.[5] In both Speght's somewhat later 1621 poem "A Dreame" and Sowernam's 1617 prose defense, the narrator takes on an identity just like Eve by providing a defense of women: they become "disputing Eves" in their rejection of the genre's condemnation of women.

This entrance into the garden space within their defenses allows Speght and Sowernam to prove woman's elevated character through "her" alignment with Eden. As these defenses work to define women's "esse" or essential nature, they deploy an argument supporting women originally introduced by Agrippa: that woman was created in the garden and thus is made of more refined material than man. Both Speght and Sowernam draw on this definition of Eve to stress a connection between the first woman and the garden whose essential nature she literally embodies. The "first and principall *esse*, or being" that grounds women's "temper" and "inclination" is the Garden itself, which, in Sowernam's and Speght's tracts, will be re-entered by a woman fulfilling the biblical identity occupied by Eve.[6] Sowernam states "that woman neither can or may degenerate in her disposition from that naturall inclination of the place, in which she was first framed, she is a Paradician, that is, a delightfull creature, borne in so delightfull a country" (B3v.). While Sowernam will acknowledge the Fall, Eve is defined – and elevated above Adam – by the Garden. There is a "naturall inclination" of women toward the Paradisical, argues Sowernam, that Milton could be seen as engaging in the close and emotional connection he establishes between Eve and (in the Agrippean view) her birthplace: "Must I thus leave thee Paradise? thus leave / Thee native Soile …" (11.269–70).[7] Sowernam expands on this premise, offering women, through her defense, access back into this place that characterizes women's identity: she has "*entred into the Garden of Paradice, and there haue gathered the choysest flowers which that Garden may affoord, and those I offer to you*" (A4r.).

Sowernam establishes this in part locational, in part psychic, identity or "esse" for women on which Speght will substantially elaborate in her verse exploration of women (re)-entering a prelapsarian-styled Garden. Her defense of women becomes inextricably tied to the acquisition of forms of knowledge in the poem "A Dreame," thus expanding upon certain conventions about educated and virtuous women within the antifeminist tradition. Now, the Eve-like narrator's acquisition of a kind of self-knowledge will join Sowernam's granting of a Paradisian "esse." These traits, described by Sowernam, will be enacted by Speght. Here, a reflective Eve asks basic questions about the self, illustrating aspects of her essence: "Upon a sodeyne, as I gazing stood, / *Thought* came to me, and ask't me of my state, / Inquiring **what I was**, and what I would."[8] Sowernam's solitary Eve entering the garden becomes Speght's Eve-like figure in search of self-knowledge.

This elaboration of the strategy of defending women in these two tracts reappears in one of the most important portraits of Eve's "esse" in *Paradise Lost*: Milton's Book 4 account of Eve's creation as Eve asks or muses upon parallel questions: "That day I oft remember, when from sleep / I first awak't, and found my self repos'd / Under a shade on flours, much wondring where / And **what I was**, whence thither brought, and how" (4.449–52; bold emphasis added). Eve, as Speght's narrator, asks a series of metaphysical questions – who am I, where am I, and why – that aligns Milton's Eve with these seventeenth-century portraits of women's "esse." That innovations by Sowerman and Speght become sedimented into the body of Milton's poems is supported by comparison with Milton's other analogues. In other early seventeenth-century Fall narratives, Eve's portrait is much less complex, largely because of her almost immediate fall. Grotius's 1601 play *Adamus Exul*, for example, allows little time to explore Eve's "inclinations," as she is exposed to the Serpent at her second appearance. Complex motivation is similarly erased within Serafino Della Salandra's 1647 poem *Adamo Caduto*; Salandra's Eve's almost fetishistic fascination with the apple precludes any development of her as a character.[9]

Contrastingly, Sowernam's and Speght's defenses of Eve exploring her "esse" imprint onto Milton's representation of our first mother as he explores similar strands of her character. In the Sowernam account, Eve is represented as solitary in her gathering of the Garden's *"choysest flowers,"* an impulse developing into a necessarily solitary acquisition of knowledge in Speght. As a result, one might even call one of Eve's "inclinations" solitariness. In Sowernam's narrative of entering back into the Garden to find the "esse" of Eve, she is alone, with no complementary Adam to be found. Speght's redeemed Eve stand-in is more purposefully alone, both for Eve's and for Speght's purposes. In her search for knowledge, this Eve supplants Adam as she acquires knowlege that can redeem women; at the end of the poem, the male anti-feminist Joseph Swetnam is defeated by Speght/Eve's acquisition of knowledge: "I saw a full fed Beast, … / And with a *Mouzel* sought to binde his chaps" (241, 246). Redeemed by knowledge, Eve can avoid the fall into gendered subjection that Swetnam's text delineates, while Speght can engage – and defeat – her antagonist through this same acquisition of knowledge.

The details of this search for knowledge, one acquired to define and defend the self in an incipient form of "self-knowledge," are set into a highly resonant conversation with Milton's text. Milton's Adam "found not what me thought I wanted still" (8.355) when looking at the animals and concludes, "In solitude / What happiness, who can enjoy alone" (8.364–5). Speght's Eve stand-in occupies the same narrative position, but registers a very different emotion: "My griefe, quoth I, is called *Ignorance*" (43). In "A Dreame," solitude is never articulated as a problem specifically *because* of her search for knowledge. Eve even understands her condition by comparing herself with the animals: it is "*Ignorance*" that "makes me differ little from a brute: / For animals are led by natures lore" (44–5). This Eve-like figure's meditation on the Garden's animals clarifies her need to escape ignorance, but it prompts no thoughts about a mate. Thus, if Milton's Adam asks the question, "how can I be solitary?," Speght's Eve-figure asks, "how do I differentiate myself from the animals in order to have knowledge?" Companionship is consequently supplanted by her search for (self)-knowledge.

Milton's Eve appears to share this inclination, recorded by both Adam's dismay about her actions and God's corrections of her. Adam – and I might suggest the poem itself – perceives and fears the traits of a solitary, often knowledge-seeking Eve, whom we have seen re-enter the Garden in Speght's and Sowernam's tracts. Eve's narcissism in Book 4 has been well discussed by critics, but even once she is told that the image she has seen "is thy self," she inclines away from Adam when led to him: "yet methought less faire, /…Then that smooth watry image" and "back I turnd" (468, 478–80). She only "yield[s]" to become Adam's "other half" when her hand is "Seisd" (488–9). Thus, Adam isn't completely wrong in Book 8 when he states that "she seems / And in her self compleat" (547–8); she's illustrated just such an "esse" since her creation. This doubleness of Eve, meant to be Adam's helpmate and yet with an inclination to be "sole," is accurately, if unknowingly, described by Adam. This "compleat"ness that Adam identifies in Eve distances her from his desire for companionship, which had prompted him to ask for a mate in order to not be "sole." She turns away from him in Book 4, wanders away during Books 5 and 6, and specifically asks to be excused in Book 9, a choice leading to her search for what could be described as self(ish) knowledge.

The poem records this tension between God's and Adam's impulse that it is not good for man to be alone and Eve's inclination to be "sole." While Sowernam and Speght define Eve's "esse" to engage specific aspects of the anti-feminist debate, Milton reuses this character trait to explore contradictions within Eve. This doubled identity layered into the text re-emerges in Adam's description of her as "Sole *Eve*, Associate sole" (9.227). This beautifully compressed line positions the contradictory inclination in Eve to be "Sole" against Adam's insistence that she was to be, in the words of Book 4, his "Sole partner and sole part of all these joyes" (4.411). She is in fact both: in inclination "Sole," at times "alone," and yet formed to be Adam's only "Associate."

This impulse to solitariness, one linked by Speght to the possibility for knowledge acquisition, is also internalized into Eve's Book 5 dream. Though in the dream Eve initially responds to a "call" she believes to be Adam's, she wanders solitary, but also toward knowledge (48): "And on, methought, *alone* I pass'd through ways / That brought me on a sudden to the Tree / Of interdicted *Knowledge*" (5.50–2; emphasis added). Here, Speght's account seems more actively disputed: Adam is right (in God's eyes) to argue for a mate. Further, Eve's inclination not to join with Adam, and her status as "alone" in the dream, associate her with Satan. Such inclinations of Eve toward knowledge establish another rich intertextual parallel between Speght's portrait of an Eve-like figure in "A Dreame" and Milton's portrait of Eve in her Book 5 dream and her subsequent Book 9 fall. The Book 5 dream, unique in accounts of the Fall, offers a vision that plants the seeds of Eve's fall through the temptation of knowledge. With its night-time situation of the dream and focus on visual access to the fruit, Milton's evocative sequence actively interrogates the possibilities offered by Speght's "A Dreame." Both of these dreams occur at night: "Then did *Morpheus* close my drowsie eyes" (7), states Speght, who in her "mentall quiet sleepe" is "entertaining a nocturnall guest" that "did my minde and sense possesse" (15–17).[10] Some "high power," also identified as "of supernall power" (35, 19), brings her to the prelapsarian Garden space in which the dream takes place: "At the appoyntment of supernall power, / By instrumentall meanes me thought I came / Into a place most pleasant to the eye" (19–21). Alinda Sumers has noted a further generic link between *Paradise Lost* and Speght's dream vision: the manner in which Eve acquires information. The dream vision in *Mortalities Memorandum* recalls Eve's dream-like acquisition of knowledge in Book 12[11] – "For God is also in sleep, and Dreams advise" (611) – though it simultaneously recalls the Satanically inspired dream in Book 5.

This generic alignment to the experiences of Milton's Eve, whose mind is also "possesse'd" by a "supernall power," shows the complexity produced by such layering or sedimenting of Sowernam's and Speght's Garden narrative in Milton's poem. The result, as any exposure of diffuse layered material, is distinctly not one of homogeneity: Eve's "Sole" "esse" resists her identity as "Associate sole." In Milton's poem, the effect is the unresolvability of Eve's character. The kinds of questions posed by Sowernam's and Speght's exploration of woman's, and Eve's, "esse" in their contributions to the *querelle* cannot be banished by *Paradise Lost*. Certainly, Milton's portrait of Eve is in tension with Speght's version of women's acquisition of knowledge: in Speght's "A Dreame," the Eve-like and solitary narrator searches for and "Desire[s]" a "plant" within the garden of knowledge that resonates with "the Fruit / Of that Forbidden Tree" (182, 174; *PL*, 1.1–2). The very status of this portrait of an Eve pursuing knowledge in Speght is countered by, but also challenged by, the questions that Eve poses throughout *Paradise Lost*, from the purpose of the stars to the organization of work in Book 9. In "A Dreame," the narrator's "avarice" for knowledge is "lawfull," her "covet[ing]" of knowledge praised (231, 232). In *Paradise Lost*, Milton's introduction of a diabolic dream sequence, unique in accounts of the Fall, suggestively positions the poem as a response to Eve-like figures acquiring knowledge within defenses such Speght's.

And yet Eve's knowledge remains in suggestive and, in light of prevailing misogyny in the period, even subversive traces. She is declared "capable ... / Of what was high," even if this skill is presented in a double negative: "Yet went she not, as not ... or not" (8.48–50). She's aligned with "solv[ing] high dispute," if "With conjugal Caresses" (8.55–6). While she herself states that "to know no more / Is womans happiest knowledge and her praise," this self-declared limitation frames her subsequent subversive question: "wherefore all night long shine these" stars if no one is watching (4.637–8, 657). Milton's poem seems to offer an account of her "esse" which suggests some ability. And in what may produce the most problematic of responses by the reader – one that could well be prompted by the traces of a "Sole" Eve that inhabited Speght's and Sowernam's tracts – we have Eve's question about female solitude: "Was I to have never parted from thy side?" (9.1153). The orthodox answer is no. But the question appears posed, possibly even positioned into Milton's text, by the tracts authored by Sowernam and Speght.

By positively representing knowledge acquisition, Speght's "Dreame" produces a solitary Eve who defines a woman's "esse." By offering an "esse," Speght and Sowernam were countering the relational and necessarily secondary definition of womanhood upon which this anti-feminist tradition rested: instead of women coming from, and being understood through, men, there is an individualized "esse" to be defined. Such challenges to the tradition, while muted and shaded, are scattered throughout Milton's poem. Drawing upon the "esse" of Eve, her "disputing" identity, her search for knowledge, *Paradise Lost* unearths the portrait of an earlier seventeenth-century Eve that resonates through the 1667 poem. The "nocturnall guest" in Speght's poem will become Satan, who "Squat[s] like a Toad, close at the eare of *Eve*; / Assaying by his Devilish art to reach / The Organs of her Fancie, and with them forge / Illusions as he list ..." (4.800–3). But whispering into Milton's ear were tracts, like those of Speght and Sowernam, containing a knowledge-seeking, post-lapsarian, redemptive image of Eve.[12]

These remnants in Milton's poem are most fully illuminated by Mary Astell's *A Serious Proposal*. This educational, proto-feminist tract proposes a female seminary to train women in self-knowledge, the very trait I argue she uncovers in traces of *Paradise Lost*. Astell's awareness of Milton's poem is indisputable: she famously derided Milton because "not *Milton* himself wou'd cry up Liberty to poor *Female Slaves*, or plead for the Lawfulness of Resisting a Private Tyranny."[13] Astell's description of the Garden throughout *A Serious Proposal* further substantiates her engagement with Milton's poem. Thick with references to the Garden of Eden, the imagery specifically invokes Milton's *Paradise Lost*. J. David Macey, Jr. effectively argues that Astell appropriates "the pastoral rhetoric of *Paradise Lost*" and links Astell's account of Eve with Milton's characterization of her as Eden's "fairest unsupported Flour" (9.432). He documents Astell's geographic placement of her garden on a "steep savage Hill," specifically recalling *Paradise Lost* (4.172).[14]

Additionally, *A Serious Proposal* repurposes the language of woman's "esse," the role of education, and the relationship between knowledge and the Fall that Milton extracted from earlier anti-feminist tracts. Astell's plan for female education and consequent acquisition of knowledge by Eve-like women invokes Speght's and Sowernam's Edenic accounts: these women will specifically *not* fall as a result of their engagement with knowledge in a garden space. Milton's poem serves as a prompt for Astell to retheorize the "esse" of women, the terms of their "solitariness," and its implications: the "self-knowledge" tentatively explored in Speght is nervously negotiated in the extended treatment of Eve in Milton's *Paradise Lost*. Astell's richly contradictory portrait of Eve, knowledge, and the dangers of temptation allows her to fashion education as an escape from the Fall itself.

As we see within Speght and Sowernam, the garden is made accessible to redeemed or, in the case of Astell, redeemable Eves. "Happy Retreat! which will be the introducing you into such a *Paradise* as your Mother *Eve* forfeited":[15] here, Astell welcomes women back into the lost garden, much as Sowernam claims that she has "*entred into the Garden of Paradice, and there haue gathered the choysest flowers*" (A4r.). Describing this space of educative retirement as "Paradise" throughout the text, Astell provides education and the acquisition of knowledge to women once they have "gain'd an entrance into Paradise themselves" (p. 38).

As in earlier tracts, this new generation of Eves will be "redeemed" when they re-enter this now educative garden space; the "*choysest flowers*" will provide women with knowledge which forstalls any threat of falling. The site of the "*Monastery*" quickly becomes transformed into the very Edenic space in which Eve, and within Speght and Sowernam later Eves, walked (p. 18). "[T]hese delicious Gardens" of learning will allow women access to the knowledge from which they have been blocked (pp. 19–20): "Men," Astell asserts, "will resent it, to have their enclosure broke down, and Women invited to tast of that Tree of Knowledge they have so long unjustly *monopoliz'd*" (p. 24). For in this garden of redeemed Eves, "[h]ere are no Serpents to deceive you" (19).

But the "delicious Gardens" and "blissful recess" where women find themselves produce a turn away from society, in particular male society (pp. 20, 18). Woman's *"Religious Retirement"* is described as a space of retreat, and as such portrays the productive impulse to solitude characterizing Speght's and Sowernam's tracts (p. 18). The connection Speght suggested between solitude and the acquisition of knowlege is then oriented in Milton's poem toward the threat of temptation and the Fall itself. What Astell perceives in Milton is this darker conclusion to which she then responds. These women will acquire their education through solitude: "[D]ead to the world," as a redeemed Eve, she "devotes her self entirely to the Contemplation and Fruition of her Beloved" (p. 20). But this "devot[ion]" to the "Beloved" is not to any Adam: he is ejected from this Edenic space as woman's contemplation becomes her own, with a focus solely onto God. Astell's account of a woman's education offers us the very "sole," "solitary" woman far from the community of men haunting *Paradise Lost*. Rather than tracing an earlier version of this trope from Speght's text, likely unavailable in 1694, Astell's tract appears a reaction to a more orthodox treatment of women and education she located in Milton's political theory and poetry. In her reaction to Milton's portrait of the Garden, she responds to its orthodoxy while gaining ammunition from embedded opportunities for recalling a "sole" Eve searching for knowledge. Such traces exist, of course, in Milton's contradictory "Sole *Eve*, Associate sole" (9.227), whom Adam both desires and fears.

Astell seems particularly drawn to respond to a number of Milton's representations of Eve's "sole" inclinations. In the Book 4 Creation account, Eve's desire to remain alone after viewing her reflection is represented in a negative and, as so many critics have commented, narcissistic light. This mirroring of the self produces an external image which Eve must be taught to reject. The consequence is a lesson to denigrate herself as only an outside: "from that time [I] see / How beauty is excelld by manly grace / And wisdom, which alone is truly fair" (4.489–91).[16] Astell re-engages the motif of reflection, image, and its relation to the gendered hierarchy that Milton's Eve voices. Astell's very garden space, one which makes education available for women, transforms the central mirror image in Eve's creation to allow for an alternative kind of "reflection," one moving inside: "Your *Glass* will not do you half so much service as a serious *reflection* on your own Minds" (p. 6; emphasis added). Astell thus overtly reverses a focus onto Eve's "outside," while drawing women to focus on their internal abilities.

Eve's threatening inclination toward solitude, as recorded in Milton, now becomes the central characteristic of Astell's Eves. The marked difference is that their solitude, registered by their withdrawal from the world and the community of men, becomes an internal retreat. Their withdrawal is to "the calm and secret Plaudit of her own Mind" (p. 13). Astell's treatise thus fuses the imagery of a reclaimed Edenic space, making knowledge accessible through a mental solitary state resulting in self-knowledge. As Astell offers women the "leisure to tast those delights which arise from a Reflection on it self," she transforms the "*Glass*" of women's vanity into "serious *reflection* on your own Minds" (pp. 29, 6). Self-knowledge, the concept floated in Speght, then ambivalently explored in Milton, now becomes the primary mechanism for, and result of, education. As women now "receive the *Ideas* which such a Reflection conveys," the narcissistic image of a "sole" Eve aware of herself is transformed into genuine self-reflection (p. 29). Transforming the narcissistic appeal that characterizes Milton's Book 4 pond scene into a lesson of reflection onto "wisdom, which alone is truly fair" (4.491), Astell rewrites the potential for a self-knowing Eve coyly emerging in *Paradise Lost*.

Astell's offer of educative possibilities through a "Retirement" from all society depends upon, and helps make visible, the "sole" Eve haunting *Paradise Lost*. Astell expands her educative uses of solitude in *A Serious Proposal* to a larger socio-political argument for solitude within *Reflections on Marriage*: many women should remain "sole" or unmarried. Uncoupling Adam's certainty that "In solitude / What happiness" and God's assertion that "I ... / Knew it not good for Man to be alone" (8.364–5, 444–5) from the purpose of women, Astell's garden develops a "Happiness" only achievable through one's solitary "reflection" (pp. 23, 6). Her tracts consequently record the anxiety in Milton that seems, at least in part, a function of the image of the "sole," and even emergently self-reflective, Eve gestured at in Speght and Sowernam. The dangers, but also the possibilities, of a solitary Eve are unearthed by Astell as she engages and rewrites this seventeenth-century story of the Fall and consequent gender relations.

VIEWING EVE: OCULAR POWER AND REDEMPTION IN LANYER, MILTON, AND CHUDLEIGH

As we have seen with the issues of women's education and the "esse" of Eve, other texts from throughout the seventeenth century – Lanyer's 1611 passion poem, Milton's 1667 epic, and Chudleigh's platonically inflected 1703 poem – return to similar issues of gender hierarchy, now exploring the duality of visuality's association with (forbidden) knowledge and its possible redemptive power. Milton will explore the visual power accorded to Eve as both the subject and object of gazing as he reconsiders how looking operates in his narrative of the Fall. In a suggestive parallel move, Lanyer redistributes redemptive power to (gendered) gazers and objects of the gaze through an Eve-substitute in her text. In both *Salve* and *Paradise Lost*, the poets explore the triangulated relationship between visual acts, the Fall, and salvation. Lanyer considers the work that a "look" can accomplish in a poem marked by transformative visuality, a theme that Milton engages and interrogates in *Paradise Lost*. Theologically redemptive in *Salve*, theologically unstable in Milton, in Chudleigh's hands acts of gazing, now borrowed directly from *Paradise Lost*, allow her to transcend the very limits of gender through a spiritualized form of looking embedded into the language and philosophy of her poem. All three poets thus explore the culturally overdetermined constellation of the Fall, the redemptive power of the Passion, and the bridge between fallen and saved spiritual states provided by acts of viewing.

My goal throughout this essay has been to consider how texts are drawn to similar questions about the gendering of salvation and thus can be seen in a productive conversation. No one would dispute the influence that Milton's *Paradise Lost* has on a later poem by Mary Chudleigh. In part, the very gendered assumptions about hierarchy undergirding these texts substantiate the argument that a major male poet would be a source for a minor female poet. Yet this same interpretive frame of gendered hierarchy deforms the suggestion that Lanyer's *Salve* – a poem exploring issues similar to Milton's *Paradise Lost* as well as to his earlier failed attempt at a passion poem – could have influenced a future canonical writer. Nonetheless, extensive textual links between the poems are supported by possible avenues through which Milton could have gained access to Lanyer's poem, which appeared in two editions in 1611. For example, Alinda Sumers has suggested a possible transmission path through Henry Lawes, who was acquainted with members of Lanyer's family of court musicians.[17]

Yet the prominence and significance of gazing in Aemilia Lanyer's *Salve* are another reason to place it in conversation with Milton's epic.[18] Calling upon a specified female readership to "view" both *Salve* and the event of the Crucifixion at its heart, the ocular dominates this poem about looking onto the body of Christ.[19] Specifically, while working within the conventions of the sanctifying visual possibilities of the Passion, Lanyer's poem offers a transactional character to the visual act. She invites her (female) readers to view Christ's body, an act that redeems them. But in the course of her poem, she theorizes further on power acquired not only by the act of looking, but by the act of being gazed upon. The mechanism of this gaze, frequently in the poem represented through the image of reflection, begins the process of extending the power of the gaze into the visual interaction of the Countess and Christ and then to all women. The Countess herself, allowed back into the Edenic garden in "The Description of Cooke-ham," is explicitly linked to a pre-fallen Eve in Lanyer's poem. Her visual involvement with Christ in the body of Lanyer's passion poem will extend this redeemed identity to other women. When "behold[ing]" Christ, a process of "reflecting" back onto first the Countess and then to all women is initiated (25, 26). The Countess's act of gazing, which had first sanctified herself, now extends beyond this singular visual exchange: "thou (deere Ladie) by his speciall grace, / In these his creatures dost behold his face" (31–2). "His blessed beams on all" are subsequently cast onto those on whom he now gazes (27). As a result of the Countess's looking, others of Christ's "creatures" will be marked by the sanctification of Christ: his "face" and virtue will be observable in them because of the Countess's "reflect[ed]" gaze (32, 26). As Lanyer extends the power of looking onto Christ from a single viewer, the Countess, to women as a category, Lanyer's poem makes act(s) of looking a process enabling spiritual enlightenment. The closing lines of the poem enact a profoundly reconfigured vision of the gaze: "I must commend / You that appear so faire in all mens sight" (1836–7). Now all "men" – not just the Savior – will view the "faire[ness]" of Lanyer's female patron, as her viewing has prompted her salvific position at the center of "all mens sight."

One of the most suggestive connections between Lanyer's and Milton's negotiation of the gaze occurs in redemptive acts of looking. Eve is actively in the poem's sights as *Paradise Lost* theorizes gazing and the power derived from and through it. In fact, Eve is the site of, as well as the initiator of, a theory offered in the poem about acts of looking that recalls Lanyer's text: to be gazed upon is a form of power. Used and abused by Satan, "gazing" is explored through the poem, ultimately redefining the matrix of the Fall, looking, and the possibilities of redemption. Book 4, which houses our introduction to Adam and Eve through the gaze of Satan and the reader, begins this meditation. Here, Eve asks about the night, querying why the stars shine if no human can observe them: "But wherfore all night long shine these, for whom / This glorious sight, when sleep hath shut all eyes?" (4.657–8). The mechanism of looking and the acquisition of knowlege are interwoven in Eve's question, as they will be throughout the poem. Here, though, she is also posing a more metaphysical question. She defines being looked at, being the object of someone's gaze, as a necessary aspect of existence: why would something be if it were not to be observed? Put another way, Eve appears to conjecture "I am seen, therefore I am." While lacking the importance of Descartes's expression of cognitive authority, this link between being and seeing signals in Milton's poem a transition to acknowledging the power of being seen.

And in Book 9, Eve, as object of the gaze, will have the power to pause the movement toward (fallen) human history, establishing a parallel between Lanyer's and Milton's treatment of gazing and gender. Lanyer suggests that women gain redemptive power through being gazed upon: the Countess "appeare[s] so faire in all mens sight" (1837). We see this very moment in *Paradise Lost*. Just as Eve's view of the Tree of Knowledge positions us on the edge of the original sin, Satan's gaze onto Eve makes him "Stupidly good" (9.465). His stupefied state suspends the poem's movement toward the Fall itself. At this moment, Milton considers the same matrix of viewing, power, and gender embedded into Lanyer's *Salve*. For, at the heart of both of these explorations of looking is the status of women's souls. In *Salve*, we see a "reconsider[ation of] the implications for women of seeing and being seen by men" through which Lanyer rewrites the Fall narrative.[20] Most significantly, the very mechanism of gazing in the poem constitutes Lanyer's strategy for defending Eve, the Countess, and all women. In Milton, these moments of gazing are positioned at exactly the moment of temptation and the Fall, the events necessitating defenses within the anti-feminist tradition.

Milton is equally intrigued by this matrix of gazing and salvation. Ultimately casting the link between gazing and Eve as Satanic, Milton's conclusions about the redemptive power of gazing are not those of Lanyer. Nonetheless, through his portrait of Eve and the effects of her gazing and being gazed upon, Milton records traces of gendered visual power offered within *Salve*. Unable to suppress the power of multiple forms of gazing, this exploration of gender and acts of gazing resonates through *Paradise Lost*.

While Milton's exploration of Eve's and Satan's gazing intervenes only into the Fall, Mary Chudleigh's (re)turn to Milton's poem in her "Song of the Three Children Paraphras'd" becomes a Cambridge Platonist-inspired mini-epic depicting multiple falls and redemption. Repurposing Milton's own negotiation of the strategies that Lanyer had explored in 1611, while echoing *Paradise Lost*'s emphasis on viewing, Chudleigh extends the matrix of the Fall, the crucifixion, and redemption for all souls initiated by Lanyer. What Lanyer so clearly sketched out in *Salve*, and what Milton refracts through his text, is the power of looking, gazing, and viewing. Possibly discerning traces of the earlier matrix that Lanyer had exploited, Chudleigh reconfigures the acts of, and meaning of, "gazing" as she produces an account of a purely spiritual existence in "Song." Chudleigh discerns possibilities for exploring, and exploding, gender categories within Milton's *Paradise Lost*. Chudleigh can now realize the ultimate leveling of such categories in her philosophical narrative of redeemed souls and the effects of transformative gazing.

The language of "gazing," a prominent motif in *Paradise Lost*, is repeatedly invoked and will in fact gesture to an even more extreme version of the redemption linked to viewing in Lanyer. In Chudleigh's account of the Fall itself, the event is presented in highly visual terms:

> Prove but obedient, and your Bliss shall be
> As lasting as my own Eternity.
> He spoke; they listen'd to the joyful Sound,
> Then cast their ravish'd Eyes around,
> Where e'er they gaz'd, they some new Wonder found.
> Ah! thoughtless Pair! how soon were you undone![21]

This compressed Fall scene actually is a rewriting, even a redeeming, of a *Paradise Lost* sequence. Satan's first view of Eden deployed a similar constellation of words emphasizing the act of viewing. Satan first acquires a "prospect" from the Tree of Life, while "Beneath him with *new wonder* now he views / To all delight of human sense expos'd" (4.200, 205–6; emphasis added). The visual emphasis in Chudleigh, where the Edenic couple with "ravish'd Eyes ... gaz'd" onto the Garden, is the same perspective offered to Satan in *Paradise Lost*, who "Saw" the couple, and is "still in gaze" as Book 4 continues (286, 356). Chudleigh repeatedly transforms scenes, much more "fallen" in Milton's poem, through acts of gazing: a number of Milton's primary Satan scenes are thus reoriented toward salvation, such as when she positions the Passion and our promised redemption right after the Fall, or when she translates the same scene into an alternate spiritual plane. And throughout these rewritten scenes, a matrix of words – "view"; "survey"; "prospect"; "wonder" – resonates through parallel passages in Milton's and Chudleigh's poems, highlighting the power of the gaze and its ability to enable acts of redemption within "Song."

Most explicit is Chudleigh's treatment of Christ's passion, positioned at the center of the poem. Language used by Lanyer but ultimately unredeemable in Milton becomes reworked into the very transformative, reflective acts of viewing that marked *Salve*. In Chudleigh's crucifixion scene, redemption is achieved through the act of looking onto Christ that characterized Lanyer's poem. As "They gaz'd on the transporting Sight, / He his Blessing to them gave; / And then before their wond'ring Eyes ... re-assum'd his Regal State" (1215–19). Viewing, specifically here "gazing," spiritually elevates the observer: the "gaze" onto the "Sight" of Christ earns the viewer a "Blessing." The act of gazing thus becomes transformed, and transformative, as in the closing verses of the poem: "At once their Pleasure, and their fear they shew'd, / And with fixt Eyes the dazling Wonders view'd" (2007–8). In Chudleigh's redeployment of this language of visuality, it is precisely because of such "fixt Eyes" that "num'rous Gazers" can access the Divine "Wonders" of God (2004).

In Chudleigh's hands, the repurposing of this language in Milton saves the visual act itself: "gazing" can be a redeeming act, while in Milton the word is only ever used to describe demonic or demonically inspired acts.[22] Simultaneously, Chudleigh redeploys visual language to allow for the salvation of Christian souls, especially those of women. Gazing and fixing on the wrong object become aligned with Eve's act of falling in *Paradise Lost*: in Book 9, once Eve "Fixt on the Fruit [upon which] she gaz'd" (9.735), the previous moment of redemptive possibility embedded in looking at the stars and being looked on by Satan become swallowed by the Fall. Chudleigh's poem turns to this constellation of words to offer redemption for all by de-emphasizing the distinctions gender creates. While Chudleigh "fixes" our "gaze" onto salvation, she undoes the fixation onto gendered culpability.

In transforming the language of consumptive vision, that which marks Milton's use of "gaze," into the salvific vision of "gazing" in Chudleigh, "Song" unifies fallen and unfallen, male and female, into a "they" marking spiritual fusion. While Lanyer will treat women's and men's perspectives onto the Passion differentially, as women "see" Christ and men don't, Chudleigh creates a fused "they" that experience the Fall in unison. This is her most significant rewriting of Milton: "*they*" "cast *their* ravish'd Eyes around / Where e'er *they* gaz'd, *they* some new Wonder found" (986–8; emphasis added); the "Pair" are "thoughtless," but their actions are in concert (989). While remapping linguistic patterns from *Paradise Lost* to redeem acts of viewing and gazing, Chudleigh redeems the female part of the "Pair" by erasing gender distinctions. Once in her Platonic schema, all souls "Ascend" and all material differences are erased. The opening lines of the poem provide a portrait of a de-gendered soul offered a vision of the entire universe:

> Ascend my Soul, and in a speedy Flight
> Haste to the Regions of eternal Light;
> Look all around, each dazling Wonder view,
> And thy Acquaintance with past Joys renew.
> Thro' all th'AEthereal Plain extend thy Sight,
> On ev'ry pleasing Object gaze.
>
> (1–6)

Acts of viewing, and in particular the word "gazing" linked solely to Satan and acts of falling in Milton's poem, are redeployed as all souls are given this redemptive possibility to "gaze" in Chudleigh's "Song."

The varied meanings of "gazing" begin with Lanyer's exploration of a redemptive union with Christ, evolve into the vexed relationship between the Fall, knowledge, and visuality in Milton, and are finally reconciled in Chudleigh's Platonic scheme of gazing and redemption. While Milton engaged the implications of according power to the gazer as well as to the one who is gazed upon, thus disrupting any simply gendered identification of s/he who controls the gaze, Chudleigh erases the distinctions of gendered viewing. Chudleigh could be seen as completing the work that Lanyer began in *Salve*, possibilities within acts of looking that Milton took up in his Fall narrative. The Miltonic distinctions in gender, probably more rigid than in Lanyer, provided Chudleigh an opportunity to profoundly rewrite her story of Creation, Fall(s), and redemption, accomplishing this through tropes of visuality inflected through Milton. Milton's explorations into visuality thus offered a rich field, linguistic and theological, into which Chudleigh could enter.

Such textual repurposing through early, mid-, and late seventeenth-century writings maps an alternative set of conclusions about Milton by partnering his epic with this range of seventeenth-century writings. While this conversation may rewrite our sense of who Milton was reading and engaging, this partnering also suggests a different kind of Milton, a different vision of *Paradise Lost*. As Astell and Chudleigh turn to *Paradise Lost* in the late seventeenth and early eighteenth centuries, they expose for us the very instabilities – over the representation of Eve and meaning of gender in the act of acquiring knowledge and redemption – embedded into the poem. Their own writings' engagement with *Paradise Lost* illustrates the conflicting possibilities within Milton's poem for a knowledgeable Eve and the gendering of culpability within the Fall. In repurposing earlier interrogations of these issues within *Paradise Lost*, these writers highlight the highly productive, and ultimately slippery, questions that we pose to *Paradise Lost*, and that the poem continues to pose to us.

NOTES

1 Revised King James Bible, Genesis 3:6; 3:7.
2 My discussion of female-authored texts engaging *Paradise Lost* extends Joseph A. Wittreich's argument in *Feminist Milton* substantially (Ithaca, NY: Cornell University Press, 1987).
3 See chs. 1 and 2 of my book *Engendering the Fall: John Milton and Seventeenth-Century Women Writers* (Philadelphia: University of Pennsylvania Press, 2008).
4 Kari McBride and John Ulreich, "'Eves Apologie': Agrippa, Lanyer, and Milton," in C. Durham and K. Pruitt (eds.), *"All and All": Unity, Diversity, and the Miltonic Perspective* (Selinsgrove, PA: Susquehanna University Press, 1999); Alinda Sumers, "Milton's Mat(t)erology: *Paradise Lost* and the Seventeenth-Century *Querelle des Femmes*," *Milton Quarterly* 38 (2004), 200–25; Miller, *Engendering* (2008); Catherine Gimelli Martin (ed.), *Milton and Gender* (Cambridge University Press, 2004).
5 "Sowernam"'s actual gender is under dispute, but the female gendering of the subject enacts this identification with Eve.
6 Ester Sowernam, *Ester Hath Hang'd Haman* (London, 1617), B3v.
7 See McBride and Ulreich on Agrippa's influence on *Paradise Lost*.
8 Rachel Speght, "A Dreame," in Barbara Lewalski (ed.), *The Polemics and Poems of Rachel Speght* (Oxford University Press, 1996), pp. 25–7; bold emphasis added.
9 Diane McColley argues that Milton "assigns more dignity to Eve than was usual" in the analogues, but certainly does not remove all negative traditions from the poem. Diane McColley, *Milton's Eve* (Urbana: University of Illinois Press, 1983), p. 35.
10 Also see Josephine Roberts, "Diabolic Dreamscape in Lanyer and Milton," in Susanne Woods and Margaret P. Hannay (eds.), *Teaching Tudor and Stuart Women Writers* (New York: Modern Language Association, 2000), pp. 299–302.
11 Sumers, "Mat(t)erology," 208.
12 Also see Desma Polydorou's "Gender and Spiritual Equality in Marriage: A Dialogic Reading of Rachel Speght and John Milton," *Milton Quarterly* 35, 1 (2001), 22–32.
13 Mary Astell, *Astell: Political Writings*, Patricia Springborg (ed.) (Cambridge University Press, 1996), pp. 46–7.
14 J. David Macey, Jr., "Eden Revisited: Re-Visions of the Garden in Astell's *Serious Proposal*, Scott's *Millenium Hall*, and Graffigny's *Lettres d'une péruvienne*," *Eighteenth-Century Fiction* 9, 2 (1997), 161–82, 165, 166.
15 Mary Astell, *A Serious Proposal to the Ladies*, Patricia Springborg (ed.) (London: Pickering and Chatto, 1997), p. 19.
16 For the priority given to male interiority versus women as an "outside," see Christina Froula's "When Eve Reads Milton: Undoing the Canonical Economy," *Critical Inquiry* 10, 2 (1983), 321–47.
17 Presentation copies might have existed within the Cumberland household, and the possible performance of *Comus* at the fourth earl's Skipton Castle

provides another possible link between the two poets. See Martin Butler's "A Provincial Masque of *Comus*, 1636," *Renaissance Drama* 17 (1986), 149–74.
18 For discussion of viewing in the poem, see Erica Longfellow, "Ecce Homo: The Spectacle of Christ's Passion in *Salve Deus Rex Judaeorum*," in *Women and Religious Writing in Early Modern England* (Cambridge University Press, 2004), pp. 59–91; Lynette McGrath, "Metaphoric Subversions: Feasts and Mirrors in Amelia Lanier's *Salve Deus Rex Judaeorum*," *LIT* 3 (1991), 101–13; and Suzanne Trill, "Reflected Desire: The Erotics of the Gaze in Aemilia Lanyer's *Salve Deus Rex Judaeorum*," in Claire McManus (ed.), *Women and Culture at the Courts of the Stuart Queens* (London: Palgrave Macmillan, 2003), pp. 167–92.
19 Aemilia Lanyer, "To the Queenes Most Excellent Majestie," in Susanne Woods (ed.), *Poems of Aemilia Lanyer* (Oxford University Press, 1993), p. 3.
20 Longfellow, "Spectacle," p. 75.
21 Mary Chudleigh, "Song of the Three Children Paraphras'd," in Margaret Ezell (ed.), *The Poems and Prose of Mary, Lady Chudleigh* (Oxford University Press, 1993).
22 In Eve's dream, for example, Satan "gaz'd" on the Tree as he repeatedly gazes on Adam and Eve throughout the poem (5.57).

CHAPTER 9

Eve and the ironic theodicy of the New Milton Criticism

Thomas Festa

By attending to the history of reception, new Milton critics may find supports but also challenges for their own intuitions and experiences. This has been one of the founding concepts of recent revisionist criticism, and for my purposes in this essay, it is best illustrated by the thesis and findings of Joseph A. Wittreich's *Feminist Milton*.[1] As Wittreich shows, early women readers, in particular of the last quarter of the eighteenth century and the pre-Victorian nineteenth century, read Milton as a source of liberation, and mined proof-texts from his works, especially *Paradise Lost*, in order to counter the patriarchal tradition of biblical misogyny, all the while crediting Milton with the exposure of an unjust moral code of repression that many of his eighteenth-century male readers and editors, most notably Thomas Newton, attributed to the poet himself.[2] "Newton aimed," as Marcus Walsh says, "to justify the poetic ways of Milton to eighteenth-century men."[3] Thus these male editors and readers produced the orthodox and masculinist Milton of tradition, which has ironically become the figure reproduced by some feminist reactions against Milton from the 1970s on. Although the epic's representation of sexuality is, in my reading, marked by contradiction, I share the view, eloquently expressed by James Grantham Turner, that Milton's "poem sees when he is seen least wise."[4] This essay joins with Wittreich to provide a minority report on the reception of Milton's epic, with an eye toward the prospect such a report opens on critical practice today, its limitations and perhaps unrealized possibilities.

By its nature, the study of reception argues for the enduring importance of history, in its full particularity, as a component of interpretation – not just as an engine that sets the consensus in motion, but also as an enabling vehicle for future work that dissents from majority positions. How else to approach the crises and cruxes of interpretation but by, in *Areopagitica*'s terms, trying all things? To speak of a consensus of opinion when discussing Milton criticism is perilously to beg the question of exemplarity: to what extent is one view of Milton's Eve more extraordinary or more common than another?[5] It is doubtless true that reception history has a way of unearthing preconditions of interpretation that lie at the very foundations of the readings built at specific moments. Given the multiplicity of interpenetrating receptions of her character over the thousands of years of biblical interpretation, opinions about Eve that are exceptional merit close attention as well as more conventional ones. Regardless of whether this approach corresponds to a consensus among critics in our own time, there are two immediate benefits to reading critical representations of Milton's Eve against the historical grain, each of which corresponds to a main section of my essay.

In the first part, I investigate early responses to Eve's narration of her birth in order to show how early critics' assumptions about gender difference determine their evaluation of, and response to, the episode in Book 4 of *Paradise Lost*. This establishes the premises we will see staunchly resisted in an idiosyncratic allegorization of the passage by fideist writers who reject any simple moralizing of the text. In this appropriation, the episode illuminates a conceptual shift concerning the nature of the imagination and the role of self-reflection in the creation of literary art. By the mid-eighteenth-century, the concept of creativity had taken on new attributes as the nature of belief in the psychology of creation had begun to change, and it became possible to regard Milton's Eve as a figure of a new form of poetic self-consciousness. This reception I situate within a brief intellectual history of the imagination.

The second part of my essay examines the scene in Book 10 in which Eve becomes contrite before Adam as a way of registering readers' imaginative compassion in ethical trial. Through the pathos of the scene, Milton shows how the imaginative sympathies that arise from calamity may have unexpected contours and filiations. As fallen suppliant, Eve becomes a figure for the suffering of the saints and the abjection of the chosen seed. Analyzing Adam's response to Eve, alongside the traditions of response from misogynist editors and critics, I show that the passage emerges as a key to a larger, structural aspect of the poem. Thus I argue that Milton in *Paradise Lost* undermines the "great Argument" of orthodoxy through the more nuanced "local argument" of dissent.[6] The "local argument" of dissent aligns *Paradise Lost* ironically with "Patience and Heroic Martyrdom" (9.32), the argument deemed less heroic, and with narrative rather than deductively imposed assertions of dogmatic triumphalism.

EVE'S CREATION

In her first speech in the epic, Eve describes her initial perceptions of life. Why does she recollect this now? Why does she recall her birth at precisely this moment? Just as Adam, in his first speech (4.411–39), reveals, to eavesdropping Satan, the injunction against eating of the tree, so Eve imparts the story of her belated creation, in each case providing a prolepsis of, or perhaps supplying a motive for, the method of the Satanic spectator's temptation in Book 9. Eve's narration commences with a non sequitur, "That day I oft remember, when from sleep / I first awak't, and found my self repos'd" (4.449–50), as if to suggest that she has been alive for some time ("oft" seems a stretch otherwise), and the remembrance of her birth gives her something to tell:

> As I bent down to look, just opposite,
> A Shape within the watry gleam appeard
> Bending to look on me, I started back,
> It started back, but pleas'd I soon returnd,
> Pleas'd it returnd as soon with answering looks
> Of sympathie and love; there I had fixt
> Mine eyes till now, and pin'd with vain desire,
> Had not a voice thus warnd me, What thou seest,
> What there thou seest fair Creature is thy self,
> With thee it came and goes: but follow me,
> And I will bring thee where no shadow staies
> Thy coming, and thy soft imbraces, hee
> Whose image thou art, him thou shalt enjoy
> Inseparablie thine, to him shalt beare
> Multitudes like thy self, and thence be call'd
> Mother of human Race[.]
> (4.460–75)

In rhetoric as in imagery, these lines replicate the confusion of identity at its origin, for Eve, and then God, through her ventriloquism, employs figures of speech that double – particularly the trope anadiplosis, or the repetition of a phrase from the end of one line at the start of the next. Thus in "I started back, / It started back" and "pleas'd I soon returnd, / Pleas'd it returnd," the aural effect reproduces the visual field as a kind of sonic mirroring. In a manner that seems intended for consolation and ease, the warning voice of God repeats the figure with "What thou seest, / What there thou seest fair Creature is thy self." Like the assonance, alliteration, and prosonomasia spread across the description of the "murmuring waters" in a lake, "That to the fringed Bank with *Myrtle crownd*, /

Her chrystal mirror holds" (4.260, 4.262–3; emphasis added), the sonorous verse echoes the optical illusion. Similar poetic and rhetorical effects register wonder at beauty, especially in the descriptive speeches of Eve in Book 4, as, for example, in the repetitions that occur in her invention of the love song, "Sweet is the breath of morn [...] / [...] is sweet" (4.641–56).[7]

This conspicuous property could, however, be seen as confirming a negative and culpable self-regard on her part, as the allusion to Ovid in the episode has indicated to some. And so the further question arises: is Eve narcissistic in a pejorative sense that implicates women more generally, a notion given its questionably authoritative expression for modern readers in Freud's essay of 1914?[8] Throughout the representation of Eve in *Paradise Lost*, readers have found negative indications of Milton's views on women, so much so that it has become a critical commonplace to unite her "narcissistic" tendencies with the corrective measure of her prelapsarian submissiveness: "God is thy Law, thou mine," says Eve, "to know no more / Is womans happiest knowledge and her praise" (4.637–8). The poet echoes the phrase later (4.776–7), as Satan approaches the sleeping pair (soon to squat at Eve's ear like a toad), which accentuates the narrator's longing for an apocalyptic "warning voice" that could intervene and prevent the action (4.1). Eve's rehearsal of "womans happiest knowledge" tempts us to compare her sense of injured merit before and after her fall, her feeling of having been denied "intellectual food" and not having been made "more equal" than she was (9.768, 823).

The presumption that her complaint lacks legitimacy has had a twofold effect. First, misogynist readers have blamed her ambition instead of God's plan, which invariably leads to the conclusion that she is a satanic agent, or that her desire for agency is by its nature satanic. For some patriarchal interpreters, the very presence of a will in Eve suggests a willfulness in women more generally that must be curbed. Commenting on Adam's accusatory lines, "Thus it shall befall / Him who to worth in Women overtrusting / Lets her will rule" (9.1182–4), James Paterson extrapolates from the verses: "Here, an excellent Caution, how to rule a Wife."[9] In the first variorum edition of the poem, directly beneath the lines in which Eve eats the fruit, Thomas Newton approvingly quotes Robert Thyer's opinion that Eve possessed "those little defects in her intellectual faculties before the fall, which were sufficiently compensated by her outward charms, and were rather softnings than blemishes in her character," thereby revealing an intention of Milton's to ridicule women:

It has been remark'd that our poet in this work seems to court the favor of his female readers very much, yet I cannot help thinking, but that in this place he

Eve and the ironic theodicy of the New Milton Criticism 179

intended a satirical as well as a moral hint to the ladies, in making one of Eve's first thoughts after her fatal lapse to be, how to get the superiority and mast'ry over her husband.[10]

The second effect of this presumption (that Eve's complaint is illegitimate) results, with a gloomy predictability, from the first: feminist readers have blamed Milton for placing Eve in this situation and for essentializing the attributes of gender in his representation of her. This criticism seems more aptly directed at the allusion to Eve's story of the reflecting pool in *The Rape of the Lock* – where Pope pours scorn on Belinda's worship of her own image in the mirror on her dressing table – than its source in *Paradise Lost*:

> A heav'nly Image in the Glass appears,
> To that she bends, to that her Eyes she rears;
> Th'inferior Priestess, at her Altar's side,
> Trembling, begins the sacred Rites of Pride.[11]

Nonetheless, understandably, the depiction of Eve's "perfect beauty" and her demure submission to Adam's lawful authority provokes Mary Wollstonecraft's allegorization of *Paradise Lost* 4.634–8, where the thrust of her commentary exposes what she deems to be Milton's concealed "arguments" about gender: "These are exactly the arguments that I have used to children; but I have added, your reason is now gaining strength, and, till it arrives at some degree of maturity, you must look up to me for advice – then you ought to *think*, and only rely on God."[12] Wollstonecraft represents Milton as infantilizing women in his depiction of Eve, an injustice motivated by Milton's need to reject his own sensuality, which he projects onto her throughout the epic.[13]

What, then, are the ramifications of this charge of narcissism against the first woman, particularly for critics who dispute the reification of gender identity that an essentialist reading of Eve's creation would affirm? This, as John Guillory has shown, has become to a certain extent an unavoidable question asked of Milton's Eve, which has at least as much to do with the intractability of certain psychoanalytic categories in our culture's imagination as it has to do with the text of Milton's epic.[14] Readers today may approach the episode of Eve's birth with a Lacanian or Freudian bias, but the idea that Milton out-Ovids Ovid has been around in the criticism since at least the first commentary on the epic by Patrick Hume, who notes that:

Milton has improved the Fable of *Ovid*, by representing *Eve* like a She *Narcissus* admiring her self; and has made it much more probable, that a Person who had never seen any thing like her self, should be in love with her own faint reflected Resemblance, than that a Man acquainted with the World and himself, should be undone by so dull a Dotage.[15]

Milton's improvements on Ovid, according to Hume, derive from his misogyny; the modern poet tells the more likely tale of "a She *Narcissus*," as the greater plausibility of Eve's circumstances unites with Hume's assumption about the psychology of the sexes. His use of "a Person" to refer to the self-admirer might seem to suggest that her youth is the key to Milton's revision of Ovid, instead of her gender. The shift from a "Person … like her self" to "a Man acquainted with the World," however, reasserts the note of condescension by implying congruence between gender difference and the attribution of inexperience. Although Eve exhibited "all the Charming Ornaments of which her Sex was capable," Hume comments elsewhere, "In the Mind, and its inward Powers and Perfections, Women are generally inferior to Men …"[16] Praised for his creative imitation, Milton, too, shows himself to be "a Man acquainted with the World and himself." But Milton's self-knowledge does not register, in this conception, as fatuous self-regard. Experience tells us, Hume implies, that an inexperienced woman makes a "more probable" Narcissus than a worldly man. Later male commentators narcissistically concurred. The author of a letter to *The Spectator*, quoted at length in a meandering essay on a motto from Ovid, refers to "the hidden Moral" in Addison's observations on Book 4 of *Paradise Lost*, and smugly asks, "whether there may not also be some Moral couched under that Place in the same Book where the Poet lets us know, that the first Woman immediately after her Creation, ran to a Looking-glass [?]"[17] Thomas Newton adds that Milton's account "is much more probable and natural, as well as more delicate and beautiful, than the famous story of Narcissus in Ovid, from whom our author manifestly took the hint"; Milton "expressly imitated some passages" from Book 3 of the *Metamorphoses*, "but has avoided all his puerilities without losing any of his beauties."[18] Milton's psychoanalytic insight yields and even impels his departure from his ancient source and therefore may be adduced as evidence of poetic acumen replacing immature innocence about the ways of the world.

Divergence from the models of antiquity frequently figured in the defense of the creative imagination during the Restoration and eighteenth century, particularly in critics who praised self-reflection as a productive and legitimate source of invention.[19] As the model for "invention" began its glacial shift from the rhetorical conception of *inventio* to the modern psychogenetic principle of artistic creation, the question of originality as the sign of genius in poetic composition came to seem paramount. There was a tendency among intellectuals, in the century that followed Milton's, to value self-reflection and even self-consciousness highly, and this correlated gradually with a more pliable attitude toward the authority of classical literary sources. Clear evidence of this drift may be found in the study by Thomas Warton the Younger, Professor of Poetry at Oxford and subsequently Poet Laureate, *Observations on the Fairy Queen of Spenser*, which defends Spenser's imaginative originality and justifies his "Use and Abuse of antient History and Mythology" as a proper attribute of the poet's "native force of invention."[20] Although Warton is best known to Miltonists for the annotations in his edition of Milton's minor poems (1785, 1791), his scattered remarks in the commentary on Spenser are valuable too for the light they shed on changing attitudes toward the primacy of the classics as models for emulation. In his wonderfully rambling way, Warton descants on "Spenser's Imitations of Himself," but not before digressing on Milton's imitations of his own early poetry and prose in his great poetical works. Warton emphatically claims that "Milton's peculiar genius for describing DIVINE things, which shines with so distinguished a lustre in the *Paradise Lost*, discovered itself in his most early productions."[21] Milton's unique ability to represent "DIVINE things" comes from a genius that "discovered itself" – a phrase suggesting at once the solipsistic autonomy of self-knowledge and the revelation of a generative force in the intellect.

These remarks were timely, for the 1740s and 1750s witnessed a strong "fideist reaction" to the empiricism and descriptivism of the dominant Augustan literary culture. Of course, both sides of this debate over poetics in the middle decades of the eighteenth century found ample support for their views in *Paradise Lost*.[22] But Milton's Eve drew profoundly sympathetic attention from those on the side of fideism, particularly the poet Edward Young, remembered today chiefly as the author of *Night Thoughts* (1742–5), and his friend and publisher, the novelist Samuel Richardson. It is well known that Richardson read the epic carefully. "If one may judge by frequency of quotations," as his modern biographers estimate, "the earlier poetic work with which he was most familiar was *Paradise Lost*. He at least knew well the sections on the relations between Adam and Eve."[23] Richardson's knowledge of the poem exemplified the tastes of a great variety of readers in his time.[24]

For such readers, Milton's depiction of Eve's birth had positive and even liberating significance while carrying none of the stigma we have seen associated with the episode in the early commentary tradition. In his once influential but now mostly forgotten *Conjectures on Original Composition* (1759), written as a familiar letter to Richardson and with some collaboration by him, Young reframes Eve's story of her birth from *Paradise Lost* as an allegory for the emergence of genius. Focusing our attention on the theoretical possibilities of the meaning of Eve's life, Young's *Conjectures* suggest the metamorphic potential of critical self-consciousness to unbind the episode from traditional, misogynistic interpretations of the kind proposed by Hume's note on the passage. Looking forward to conceptions of subjectivity that reached maturity in the philosophy of Kant, and locating the driving force of sentimental genius in the narration of the first woman, Young further uncovers an antithetical reading of Milton for which I would argue the text of the epic makes copious provision.[25]

This interpretation of Eve's birth story should not be understood as opposing the flow of Milton's allusion to the tale from the *Metamorphoses*, but ought rather to be seen as a consequence of the profundity of Milton's engagement with Ovid.[26] Response to Milton's Eve may resonate with Milton's reception of Ovid in the epic, so that, from the perspective of anyone reading *Paradise Lost* today, the dynamics of reception work to unfix the boundaries of the "text" being interpreted through the episode.[27] Until recently, the critical vocabulary employed in the study of allusion has tended to "suggest an inequality of the two texts in question," even to the point of giving "the impression that the earlier text possesses an admirable creative plenitude, while the later text is secondary not just in time but in value – derivative, unoriginal."[28] A similar fallacy, as Northrop Frye observed, underlies the habit of attaching the term "creative" to writing in the genres of poetry and fiction while relegating expository and critical writing to a "secondary" status.[29] Undoing the linear logic inherent in the traditional study of intertextuality may therefore allow readers to explore the radiant creativity that surrounds a text such as *Paradise Lost* when it is seen as the point of convergence for reception. For just as the epic interprets and reshapes the Ovidian text it echoes, so later readers such as Young create original interpretive possibilities by allegorizing Milton.

Young's appropriation of the passage from Book 4 of *Paradise Lost* occurs at a crucial juncture in his argument. A person "may possess dormant, unsuspected abilities, till awakened by loud calls." This awakening to consciousness is an author's discovery of his or her own genius, a process that takes shape in a series of richly allegorical moments in Young's exuberant prose:

Few authors of distinction but have experienced something of this nature, at the first beamings of their yet unsuspected Genius on their hitherto dark Composition: The writer starts at it, as at a lucid Meteor in the night; is much surprized; can scarce believe it true. During his happy confusion, it may be said to him, as to *Eve* at the Lake,

> What there thou seest, fair creature! is thyself.
> MILT.

Genius, in this view, is like a dear Friend in our company under disguise; who, while we are lamenting his absence, drops his mask, striking us, at once, with equal surprize and joy. This sensation, which I speak of in a writer, might favour, and so promote, the fable of poetic Inspiration: A Poet of a strong imagination, and stronger vanity, on feeling it, might naturally enough realize the world's mere compliment, and think himself truly inspired. Which is not improbable; for Enthusiasts of all kinds do no less.[30]

In Young's allegory, Eve stands for the writer's "happy confusion" at the sudden appearance of genius, while the voice of God represents what "may be said to him" by that stranger within because of critical self-consciousness.

This allegory of self-reflection contrasts with Young's vivid diminution of narcissistic vanity: "Wit, indeed, however brilliant, should not be permitted to gaze self-enamour'd on its useless Charms, in that Fountain of Fame (if so I may call the Press,) if Beauty is all that it has to boast." In this metamorphosis of Wit into Genius, the emblem and action are the same; sacrifice differentiates the two, not only in style, but also in substance. The sentence continues: "… like the first *Brutus*, [Wit] should sacrifice its most darling Offspring to the sacred interests of Virtue, and real Service of mankind."[31] Young holds classical virtue, sacrifice of offspring, and virtuous service to "the *Public Good*" in opposition to the negative double of Eve at the lake – the Narcissus wit at the press.

As Young's use of the passage makes clear, Eve's story is to an important extent her own creation, always received within a framework of narration, and told from a particular character's perspective in the epic. And of course, the first act of this story's reception – Adam's separate narration of Eve's birth to Raphael – likewise occurs within the narrative structure of the epic, thereby engendering a further reflection upon the relationship between representations, perspective, and desire.[32] Yet Eve's tale of her origin is her creation in another sense as well, for her narration establishes the conditions through which readers of the epic may understand the particular plight and opportunity of the first woman as a productive if enigmatic rebus of the human psyche. The charge that an appropriation like Young's is anachronistic and misleading has less relevance once it is acknowledged that all interpretation is a reception, situated within its own historical space and influenced by the history of receptions. "A 'text'... is never just 'itself,' appeals to that reified entity being mere rhetorical flag-waving[,]" as Charles Martindale colorfully puts it; "rather it is something that a reader reads, differently."[33] No doubt Young's allegorical retelling will remain, for some, a far-fetched adoption of Milton's text, though the commentary traditions applied by Fulgentius or Bernardus Sylvestris to the *Aeneid*, by Giacopo Mazzoni or Dante to the *Divina Commedia*, or by Tasso to the *Gerusalemme liberata* or Spenser to *The Faerie Queene* could hardly be thought less liberal in their application of kindred interpretive strategies. While Young's reading neither conclusively validates nor invalidates the episode from *Paradise Lost* for a contemporary reader, it has the effect of resuscitating the representation of Eve as itself a representation, of demonstrating how productive and liberating such an interpretation has been in literary history, and, consequently, of opening the field of contemporary interpretation to include more extensive aesthetic and even moral imperatives than might be possible without it.

EVE'S CONTRITION

The creation of Eve brings into being a distinct perspective, one that is often presumed to lie outside the epic's masculinist affective range and that criticism of the poem has, with notable exceptions such as we have seen, rejected or employed as a vehicle to dismiss women as secondary, unoriginal, an afterthought.[34] In this, then, Eve's creation is not unlike the "secondary" status afforded the allusive intertext – the text that draws on a precursor like Ovid or Milton and thereby gains creative momentum from its self-conscious interpretation. The twinned logic of priority, the way temporal precedence becomes hierarchical favor, applies mutually to poem and person in the ledger of custom. And yet, "as both daughter and mother, rebellious child and matrix of salvation," John Rumrich writes, Eve "is the human site for a world of sometimes irreconcilable symbolic associations signifying the *poesis* of creation."[35] The connection between maternity and poetic making was, if the evidence of one of the poet's early biographers may be trusted, Milton's own: "hee waking early ... had commonly a good Stock of Verses ready against his Amanuensis came; which if it happend to bee later than ordinary, hee would complain, Saying *hee wanted to bee milkd*."[36]

Early readers of *Paradise Lost* commonly brought insights gleaned from biography together with a sense of the poem's ethical import. Many readers confronted with the scene in which Eve supplicates Adam have located the promise of salvation in her actions, if not the salvaging of her agency, from this moment forward. To such readers she commences humanity's regenerative turn toward contrition and self-sacrifice by means of her humility. In Eve's speech to Adam, according to Joseph Summers, "we hear the fullest human expression of the will to redemptive love" that the poem offers.[37] Nowhere is her "lowliness Majestic" (8.42) more apparent than in the speech with which Eve responds to Adam's abusive and misogynistic rant against her:

> Forsake me not thus, *Adam*, witness Heav'n
> What love sincere, and reverence in my heart
> I beare thee, and unweeting have offended,
> Unhappilie deceav'd; thy suppliant
> I beg, and clasp thy knees; bereave me not,
> Whereon I live, thy gentle looks, thy aid,
> Thy counsel in this uttermost distress,
> My onely strength and stay: forlorn of thee,
> Whither shall I betake me, where subsist?
> While yet we live, scarse one short hour perhaps,
> Between us two let there be peace, both joyning,
> As joyn'd in injuries, one enmitie
> Against a Foe by doom express assign'd us,
> That cruel Serpent[.]
> (10.914–27)

How is one to measure the affective potential of this moment, particularly as a harbinger of women's unequal suffering in the wake of the curse, against the flat declaration of patriarchal critics such as Samuel Johnson that, "Both before and after the Fall the superiority of Adam is diligently sustained"?[38] It is undoubtedly true that, as C. S. Lewis put it, "royalty is less apparent in Eve" than her husband, but this is no reason to conclude as Lewis does that she is therefore, according to Milton, "in fact Adam's inferior."[39] Due consideration of Milton's politics would suggest the opposite. Eve's repetition of "Mee mee onely" (10.936), her offer of herself as sacrifice, does not satisfy certain critics as legitimately selfless, or anything other than misled. Despite her repetition of the Son's offering (3.236), itself repeated by Adam to himself (10.832), Eve is again charged with becoming a solipsistic Narcissus, instead of an imaginative echo of pious humility. Her text is again relegated to a secondary order of importance owing to Adam's priority. The notion that Eve is attempting to act as redeemer, Alastair Fowler contends in his note on the passage, "is untenable in view of her proposal of suicide."[40] He then approvingly sums up the idea that "Eve is disobedient, self-destructive, and emulous in despair, although less egoistic than Adam" (which last concession might be thought to undo a great deal of the attack in the first three adjectives). Brandishing his superior intellect, Adam, claims Fowler, "controls her irrational excess," while "Eve imitates everything in Adam's soliloquy."[41] As when early readers responded haughtily to Eve's tale of her birth, moralizing commentary here demotes her moving speech to a secondary status through the accusation that it is narcissistically emulative and somehow inauthentic.

Yet Adam is moved to relent, and in fact Eve has enabled him to recall the promise within the curse, that her seed will crush the serpent's head. She calls for peace between herself and Adam so they may be "joyn'd" together "Against a Foe by doom express assign'd us" (10.925, 926). Despite her subsequent equivocation and the possibility of reading her suggestions of abstinence and suicide when their conversation proceeds as an attempt to evade punishment, this irenic strain in her speech seems to me to set the couple (and thus humanity) on the path to salvation, and therefore to make Adam's hermeneutic recollection less extraordinary than some critics have contended.[42] The affective center of the poem has shifted, and its ethical calculus has forever changed.[43]

Reading the episode biographically, eighteenth-century critics argued that Milton modeled the scene on the experience of his first wife's return from Oxfordshire following their separation during the First Civil War. Jonathan Richardson paints the picture thus:

he was at a Friend's house upon a Visit; his Wife surpriz'd him; she came into the Room and all in Tears flung her Self at his Feet. at first he seem'd Inexorable, but the Submission of a few Minutes drove away the Provocations of So Long a Crime. He Melted, Receiv'd her, and was Reconcil'd; Probably not only mov'd by Good Nature, and his Unextinguish'd Former Love, but as not at Liberty Now in Conscience, as when She seem'd Irreclaimable. a Like Scene between *Adam* and *Eve* in *Parad. Lost.* X. 937. seems to have been Copy'd from This.[44]

In a kind of "novelization" of the scene of reconciliation between Milton and Mary Powell, Richardson's narrative culls corroborating details from the poem. Eve's "Tears that ceas'd not flowing" (10.910) become Mary Powell's countenance "all in Tears," etc. Characteristically extending this line of interpretation of the poem, Newton quotes Thyer's opinion: "that reader must have a very sour and unfriendly turn of mind, whose heart does not *relent* with Adam's, and melt into a sympathizing commiseration towards the mother of mankind."[45] Male readers, Thyer and Newton propose, should have Adam's reaction, and their hearts, like his, ought to relent toward her after her speech.

Our sympathy for Eve may or may not bear the authenticating mark of the author's own identification with his creation. A further biographical fact may supply an important clue. In the period just before the composition of the epic, the blind poet adopted a personal motto resonant with Eve's humility.[46] In the autograph books of two foreign luminaries in 1652 and 1656, Milton dictated, and in the earlier case affixed his signature to, a Greek phrase meaning "I am perfected in weakness." Milton's Greek alludes to St. Paul's paradoxical report that the Lord told him, "my strength is made perfect in weaknes" (2 Cor. 12:9), but with a difference.[47] Not merely his strength, but the whole of his being, attains perfection in his weakness. To accomplish this shift of emphasis, Milton borrows the passive form of the first person indicative Greek verb from Jesus in Luke 13:32 (*teleioumai*: I am perfected, matured, or finished). Considering such ends, Eve's final speech – which is in fact the last speech the epic records – concludes by humbly recollecting the prophecy, "By mee the Promis'd Seed shall all restore" (12.623). Milton ties together what might too casually be dismissed as the "secondary" effects that comprise salvation at the poem's end.

One limitation that has beset treatments of Milton's theodicy may be seen with greater clarity in relation to Eve than any other character, and it unites the concern I have just been exploring with the attempt to "justifie the wayes of God to men."[48] It might be understood as an outgrowth of the problem of evil, and it may be termed *the problem of good*. Such a reconstruction of the traditional problem addressed by theodicy is no mere inversion, but instead an effort to take into account the alienness of the good and the reality of our loves.[49] By virtue of Eve's recognition of her own limitations, even before the Fall, I would argue that Eve indicates a line of critique and questioning that – whether consciously or not does not ultimately matter – Milton's epic makes available in the face of Adam's egoistic "rejoicing" at the providential scheme (see 12.475ff.). It almost goes without saying that Michael sharply rebukes Adam's imperceptive celebration and reminds him that he should not praise himself for being the feeble cause of a divine effect. This reminds us: it is not only that the power of critical self-reflection imitates the divinely creative imagination. But the intention underlying self-sacrifice, so essential to Young's differentiation between narcissistic wit and reflexive genius, further shows love to be an imaginative and, in Christian ethics, divine, recognition of another, and it is this difference that separates Eve's humility from Adam's pride after the Fall.

How, then, does assertion of God's providence relate to justification of his ways to men – and to women? Must coherence finally elude such a project? A finding of incoherence always runs the risk of revealing the limitations of the interpreter more starkly than those of the text or author. But the plight of Eve, humble and Christ-like in her abjection before Adam, radically realigns the issue by putting our imaginative sympathy to the test. Modern criticism of *Paradise Lost* has run up against the problem, nowhere more potently for the interpretation of Milton's Eve than in Diane Kelsey McColley's celebrated monograph. Central to McColley's apology for Milton's Eve is an argument that has a direct bearing on theodicy: McColley insists that to criticize unfallen Eve, or the conditions into which she was born, is to criticize God's providence.[50] What if our critique reverses the polarity of McColley's defense? What if, accepting her logic as irrefutable, we view the epic from outside and resist the positing of God's providence as perfect, at least at its most ostensible level – the level on which the "great Argument" intrudes upon the poetry? Let us assume, instead, that Eve has a just grievance against God for the specific limitations imposed upon her and the unfair situations into which she is placed, and suppose therefore that her perception is linked to a reasonable critique of God's providence, at least as it is usually understood. What if Milton has found an indirect way, through Eve, to expose the unethical impetus toward theodicy – to reveal, in her discomfort and ours, the ultimate immorality of rationalizing the suffering of others, including Christ, as a way to secure consolation for the evil that occurs? Just as Eve with telling wisdom walks away when Adam enters on "studious thoughts abstruse" (8.40), so her character sees feelingly beyond the limitations of Adam's (and the narrator's) reading of providential ends that seems so forgetful of sacrificial means. To adapt Milton's motto, it is as if Adam reads "I am perfected," and it is left to Eve to add "in weakness." I think here of a radical possibility suggested in Jonathan Lear's classic essay on "Katharsis": what if tragedy allows us to consider and even experience the overturning of our ordinary emotional states, just as skepticism forces us to reconsider our settled beliefs by interrogating their premises, from without?[51] Building on Jonathan Lear's remark about the unsettling and even revolutionary emotional implications of *katharsis*, I would argue that Milton's Eve exposes a conventional emotional response to suffering for what it is.

CONCLUSION: IRONIC THEODICY

"It will be best to start right and not let the record get confused," mused Mark Twain in "Eve's Diary," for some instinct tells me that these details are going to be important to the historian some day. For I feel like an experiment, I feel exactly like an experiment, it would be impossible for a person to feel more like an experiment than I do, and so I am coming to feel convinced that that is what I *am* – an experiment; just an experiment, and nothing more.[52]

Twain creates irony from the intersection of gender and genre, nicely casting back an anachronistic glance at a genre deeply encoded for modern readers, as he knows, with indications of subjectivity. These signals of subjective experience run throughout the text's rhetoric and its diction, its "instinct," its "I feel" and "I am coming to feel," its emphasis on Eve's inward conviction as much as on her proleptic awareness of her future prosecution according to the verdict of patriarchal history. In her self-consciousness, Twain's Eve *knows* she is a fictional "experiment," and she understands, or intuits, her own hermeneutic stance according to the patriarchal traditions within which she has been inscribed by "the historian" well enough to claim a narrative authentically her own. Her subjective authority inheres in her ability, that is, to narrate her experience, to be the author of so canny and prescient a "diary." If Twain's Eve represents ironic subjectivity by displaying a self-conscious character and becoming a narrator in her own right, she is also one whose subjectivity resides in her instinctual awareness that the record of her actions will be determined by "the historian" retrospectively. To engender this satiric friction, Twain's perspective, like the other vantages on Milton's Eve we have seen, indeed like Milton's reception of the traditions of representation he reshapes to create the character in his epic, is entirely dependent upon the retrospective glance it casts back.

Twain's ironic deflection of misogynist narrative expectations thus recasts the central questions of this chapter: what is the status of Eve's claim to authority within the hierarchies of the epic, and how does her freedom or determination – in a word, her agency – disclose the authority of narrative relative to doctrine? How does the eighteenth-century reception of Milton's Eve, which is inclusive of critical narratives poised against a tradition of doctrinaire and orthodox misogyny also attributed to Milton, allow a different view on the changing fate of the imagination, but even more, on the sympathies of Milton criticism?

This essay has looked to a time when Milton criticism was new and found the lineaments (in that reflecting pool) of a new Milton criticism. By the time of Hume's *Annotations* of 1695 – which was not only the first full-length commentary on Milton, but also the first lengthy commentary on a work of English literature and one of the first "on the text of a modern vernacular author"[53] – the dynamic was already in place. Readers, critics, and editors had begun to contest that tradition even as it took shape. The creation of a triumphal narrative, the emergence of the first English classic, initiated varied and powerful resistance. Yet even this contestation was, for many, true to the spirit of Milton's writing. If, as Hegel put it, "The philosophy of history rightly understood takes the rank of a Théodicée" – or, in R. G. Collingwood's blunt formulation, "history is the only possible theodicy" – then a new Milton criticism must work to resist the casual acceptance and occlusion of suffering and sacrifice that a "great Argument" in narrative form entails.[54] As a figure of dissent and a representation of the pathos of self-conscious reason at odds with circumstance, Milton's Eve fatefully beckons her progeny.

NOTES

1 Joseph A. Wittreich, *Feminist Milton* (Ithaca: Cornell University Press, 1987).
2 Similarly, Shannon Miller, "Serpentine Eve: Milton and the Seventeenth-Century Debate Over Women," *Milton Quarterly* 42 (2008), 44–68, has persuasively demonstrated the relevance of contemporary "anti-feminist" debates to Milton's depiction of Eve. See also her contribution to this volume, ch. 8.
3 Marcus Walsh, *Shakespeare, Milton, and Eighteenth-Century Literary Editing: The Beginnings of Interpretative Scholarship* (Cambridge University Press, 1997), pp. 94–110 (at p. 99).
4 James Grantham Turner, *One Flesh: Paradisal Marriage and Sexual Relations in the Age of Milton* (Oxford: Clarendon Press, 1987), p. 285. Turner, of course, echoes *Paradise Lost*, 8.578, where Raphael says this of Eve.
5 See Catherine Gimelli Martin (ed.), *Milton and Gender* (Cambridge University Press, 2004), for a sophisticated, yet representative, collection of essays employing the historical and theoretical advances of the latest feminist work.
6 For an account of "Milton's literal proximity to Dissent" in his residences during the composition of his great poems, and for a careful consideration of the meaning of the term "dissent" in the epic and in its historical context, see Sharon Achinstein, *Literature and Dissent in Milton's England* (Cambridge University Press, 2003), pp. 116–24.
7 See Barbara K. Lewalski, *Paradise Lost and the Rhetoric of Literary Forms* (Princeton University Press, 1985), p. 187.
8 Sigmund Freud, "On Narcissism: An Introduction," in James Strachey (trans.), *Standard Edition of the Complete Psychological Works of Sigmund Freud*, 24 vols. (London: Hogarth Press, 1953–64), vol. XIV, pp. 69–102.
9 James Paterson, *A Complete Commentary, with Etymological, Explanatory, Critical, and Classical Notes on Milton's Paradise Lost* (London, 1744), p. 406.
10 Thomas Newton (ed.), *Paradise Lost*, 2 vols. (London, 1749), vol. II, pp. 182–3.

11 Alexander Pope, *The Rape of the Lock* (1714), 1.125–8, in John Butt (ed.), *Poems* (New Haven: Yale University Press, 1963), p. 222.
12 Mary Wollstonecraft, *A Vindication of the Rights of Women* (1792), Miriam Brody (ed.), rev. edn. (Harmondsworth: Penguin, 2004), p. 30.
13 See Ana M. Acosta, *Reading Genesis in the Long Eighteenth Century: From Milton to Mary Shelley* (Aldershot: Ashgate, 2006), pp. 134–9.
14 John Guillory, "Milton, Narcissism, Gender: On the Genealogy of Male Self-Esteem," in Christopher Kendrick (ed.), *Critical Essays on John Milton* (New York: G. K. Hall & Co., 1995), pp. 194–233.
15 Patrick Hume, *Annotations on Milton's Paradise Lost* (London, 1695), p. 150.
16 Ibid., pp. 146, 239.
17 Eustace Budgell, letter to *The Spectator*, no. 325 (March 13, 1712), Donald F. Bond (ed.), 5 vols. [1965] (reprint Oxford: Clarendon Press, 1987), vol. III, p. 191.
18 Newton (ed.), *Paradise Lost*, vol. I, p. 264.
19 See Douglas Lane Patey, "Ancients and Moderns," in H. B. Nisbet and Claude Rawson (eds.), *The Cambridge History of Literary Criticism: Volume IV: The Eighteenth Century* (Cambridge University Press, 1997), pp. 32–71.
20 Thomas Warton, *Observations on the Fairy Queen of Spenser*, 2nd edn., 2 vols. (London, 1762), vol. I, p. 66.
21 Ibid., vol. II, p. 32; the digression on Milton runs from vol. II, pp. 22–33; the section on Spenser's self-imitation from vol. II, pp. 36–70.
22 Blanford Parker, *The Triumph of Augustan Poetics: English Literary Culture from Butler to Johnson* (Cambridge University Press, 1998), ch. 6.
23 T. C. Duncan Eaves and Ben D. Kimpel, *Samuel Richardson: A Biography* (Oxford: Clarendon Press, 1971), p. 573.
24 See Naomi Tadmor, "'In the even my wife read to me': Women, Reading and Household Life in the Eighteenth Century," in James Raven, Helen Small, and Naomi Tadmor (eds.), *The Practice and Representation of Reading in England* (Cambridge University Press, 1996), pp. 162–74, esp. p. 168.
25 See Matthew Wickman, "Imitating Eve Imitating Echo Imitating Originality: The Critical Reverberations of Sentimental Genius in the *Conjectures on Original Composition*," *English Literary History* 65 (1998), 904–5.
26 Maggie Kilgour, "'Thy perfect image viewing': Poetic Creation and Ovid's Narcissus in *Paradise Lost*," *Studies in Philology* 102 (2005), 307–39, esp. 307, 312, 331, 334; Richard J. DuRocher, *Milton and Ovid* (Ithaca: Cornell University Press, 1985), pp. 86–93.
27 See Craig Kallendorf, "Allusion as Reception," in Charles Martindale and Richard F. Thomas (eds.), *Classics and the Uses of Reception* (Oxford: Blackwell, 2006), pp. 67–79.
28 Gregory Machacek, "Allusion," *PMLA* 122, 2 (2007), 522–36, at 524–5.
29 Northrop Frye, *Spiritus Mundi: Essays on Literature, Myth, and Society* [1976] (Richmond Hill, ON: Fitzhenry and Whiteside, 1991), pp. 24, 105.
30 Edward Young, *Conjectures on Original Composition* (London, 1759), pp. 50–1.

31 Ibid., p. 4.
32 See Karen L. Edwards, "Resisting Representation: All about Milton's 'Eve,'" *Exemplaria* 9 (1997), 231–53.
33 Charles Martindale, "Introduction: Thinking Through Reception," in Martindale and Thomas (eds.), *Classics and the Uses of Reception*, p. 3.
34 Largely due to his preference of the Yahwist account of staggered creation instead of the Priestly account of simultaneous birth of the sexes in Genesis, this is the commonplace view attributed to Milton himself, "English literature's paradigmatic patriarch," according to Mary Nyquist, "The Genesis of Gendered Subjectivity in the Divorce Tracts and *Paradise Lost*," in Mary Nyquist and Margaret W. Ferguson (eds.), *Re-membering Milton: Essays on the Texts and Traditions* (New York: Methuen, 1987), pp. 99–127 (at p. 101).
35 John P. Rumrich, *Milton Unbound: Controversy and Reinterpretation* (Cambridge University Press, 1996), p. 117.
36 This is from the life now generally attributed to Cyriack Skinner, but attributed to Milton's nephew John Phillips by Helen Darbishire in her edition of *The Early Lives of Milton* (London: Constable, 1932), p. 33.
37 Joseph Summers, *The Muse's Method: An Introduction to "Paradise Lost"* (Cambridge, MA: Harvard University Press, 1962), pp. 176–85 (at p. 183).
38 Samuel Johnson, *Lives of the English Poets*, George Birkbeck Hill (ed.), 3 vols. (Oxford: Clarendon Press, 1905), vol. I, p. 174. For the impact of Milton's own experience of women's suffering on the creation of the epic, see Louis Schwartz, *Milton and Maternal Mortality* (Cambridge University Press, 2009), pp. 232–60.
39 C. S. Lewis, *A Preface to "Paradise Lost"* (London: Oxford University Press, 1942), p. 116.
40 Alastair Fowler (ed.), *Paradise Lost*, 2nd edn. (London: Longman, 1998), p. 589.
41 Ibid., p. 590.
42 Richard Strier, "Milton against Humility," in Claire McEachern and Deborah Shuger (eds.), *Religion and Culture in the English Renaissance* (Cambridge University Press, 1997), pp. 272–3.
43 See Turner, *One Flesh*, pp. 296, 298, 306.
44 Jonathan Richardson, father and son, *The Life of John Milton, and a Discourse on Paradise Lost* (1734), in Darbishire (ed.), *Early Lives*, pp. 258–9.
45 Newton (ed.), *Paradise Lost*, vol. II, p. 289.
46 Turner, *One Flesh*, p. 307; W. R. Parker, *Milton: A Biography*, 2nd edn., Gordon Campbell (ed.), 2 vols. (Oxford: Clarendon Press, 1996), vol. I, p. 389.
47 For the Greek of Milton's motto, see F. A. Patterson et al. (eds.), *The Works of John Milton*, 18 vols. (New York: Columbia University Press, 1931–8), vol. XVIII, p. 271; and see further the commentary in Parker, *Milton*, vol. II, pp. 988, 1219, 1238. The biblical verse in English is quoted from Gordon Campbell (ed.), *The Holy Bible: King James Version, 1611 Text* (Oxford University Press, 2010). Later in this paragraph, I transliterate the Greek of the New Testament

from E. Nestle, K. Aland, B. Aland et al. (eds.), *Novum Testamentum Graece*, 27th edn. (Stuttgart: Deutsche Bibelgesellschaft, 2006).

48 The standard, traditional account of Milton and theodicy is that of Dennis Danielson, *Milton's Good God: A Study in Literary Theodicy* (Cambridge University Press, 1982). The issue and its difficulties for the orthodox and monistic views of Milton's epic have been explored lately by Richard Strier (see ch. 1 in this volume) and Annabel Patterson, "Milton and the Problems of Evil: A Preemptive Modernism?" in Charles W. Durham and Kristin A. Pruitt (eds.), *Uncircumscribed Mind: Reading Milton Deeply* (Selinsgrove: Susquehanna University Press, 2008), pp. 25–43.

49 See Charles T. Matthewes, *Evil and the Augustinian Tradition* (Cambridge University Press, 2001), esp. pp. 15–46.

50 Diane Kelsey McColley, *Milton's Eve* (Urbana: University of Illinois Press, 1983), pp. 2, 23, 27, 63, 69, 100, 102, 218.

51 Jonathan Lear, "Katharsis," in Amélie O. Rorty (ed.), *Essays on Aristotle's Poetics* (Princeton University Press, 1992), p. 333.

52 Mark Twain, "Eve's Diary: Translated from the Original," *Harper's Monthly*, December 1905, 25.

53 Walsh, *Shakespeare, Milton, and Eighteenth-Century Literary Editing*, p. 57.

54 *The Logic of Hegel: Translated from the Encyclopaedia of the Philosophical Sciences*, § 147, William Wallace (trans.), 2nd edn. (Oxford, 1892), p. 269; R. G. Collingwood, *The Idea of History*, rev. edn. (1946; Oxford University Press, 1994), p. 400.

CHAPTER 10

Man and thinker: Denis Saurat, and the old new Milton criticism

Jeffrey Shoulson

Counting among its participants some of the central figures in English letters, including T. S. Eliot, F. R. Leavis, C. S. Lewis, and William Empson, the lively mid-twentieth-century dispute known as the Milton Controversy represents a fascinating chapter in the emergence of the discipline of academic literary criticism. My intention here is not to rehearse that dispute in any great detail.[1] My primary subject is a book that preceded the Milton Controversy, which began in earnest with the publication of Leavis's 1933 essay, "Milton's Verse."[2] I argue that Denis Saurat's 1925 landmark study, *Milton: Man and Thinker*, was the underlying trigger for the Milton Controversy in the wake of which it has been largely consigned to its role as an aberrant curiosity.[3] For the last fifty years, Saurat's work has been remembered – if it is remembered at all – for its claims concerning Milton's debt to Jewish mysticism.[4] In an effort to correct this widespread misapprehension, I shall argue that Saurat's book played a central role in the formulation of many of the key features of the academic study of Milton's writings, prompting the development of an *old* new Milton criticism long before its insights, albeit not identified with Saurat, began to receive renewed attention in the New Milton Criticism the present volume seeks to delineate. In my recovery of this critical genealogy, one that restores Saurat and many of his early readers – William Empson being perhaps the most prominent among them – to their proper places in the history of Milton studies, I shall also have occasion to reconsider what has become something of a truism in accounts of trends in Milton studies, that is, the apparent absence of any explicit influence or imprint of what generically gets called "theory." Critical theory, in all its diverse and often conflicting avatars, has come to represent the destabilizing of literary signification; similarly, Saurat's work anticipates the New Milton Criticism's arguments with interpretive orthodoxies. Yet Saurat is also largely responsible for the stubborn, and seemingly un-theoretical, presence of the author Milton – Man and Thinker – in virtually all efforts to render his writings meaningful, whether they be neo-Christian or heterodoxical. By making Saurat's influence more visible, I will suggest how we might better understand the characteristically idiosyncratic presence – and erasure – of theoretical approaches to the reading of Milton's writings.

Asked to pronounce on the fate of the school of Derrida, the eminently quotable Stanley Fish once replied, "Deconstruction is dead in the same way that Freudianism is dead. It is everywhere."[5] Spoken like a true Milton scholar, Fish's statement reminds us that we are all the products of a post-lapsarian world, though here the Fall is into theoretical knowledge and not knowledge of Good and Evil, *per se*. One faces a similar challenge – an epistemological blind spot – in identifying the importance of Saurat's contributions to, and lasting presence within, Milton studies. We can best understand Saurat's contributions by recalling the view of Milton held by the Victorian literary critical world prior to his intervention, encapsulated in the famous characterization of *Paradise Lost* by Walter Raleigh as "a monument to dead ideas."[6] Assuming a general distaste for the severe Puritanism and anti-Royalism with which Milton was inevitably associated, Raleigh celebrated what he saw as the "magic of [Milton's] style" while dismissing the relevance of his thought. Critics writing about Milton in the late nineteenth and early twentieth centuries had everything to say about Milton's language, his prosody, his imagery, and little to say (certainly of an affirming nature) about his biography, his theology, or his politics.

When Saurat published his extensive and thorough argument for the importance of throwing "on the poems the light which comes from a study of [Milton's] abstract ideas," and "inversely, [how] many gaps in the thought are filled in by the poetry" (p. xiv), he was therefore making a set of claims that were by no means fully accepted at that time. It is true that in 1919, a year before Saurat had published the French version of his analysis, James Holly Hanford had made his important case for reading Milton as heir to the European Renaissance in his "Milton and the Return to Humanism." Hanford had also favorably reviewed Saurat's *Milton: Man and Thinker*, calling it "certainly the best that has been written on the intellectual fabric of Milton's work." Similarly, in his appendix to *Milton: Man and Thinker*, Saurat called Hanford's 1919 essay, "A manifesto of the new conception of Milton ... Very important," and described Hanford's 1921 essay, "The Chronology of Milton's Private Studies," as "the most scholarly and useful instrument of work in Miltonic research; indispensable to a proper study of Milton."[7] Yet, though they shared the same insistence on the importance of intellectual and cultural contextualization for the proper study of Milton, and though they expressed enthusiasm for each other's work, Hanford and Saurat *differed* in the essential conclusions they drew from this historicizing. In his essay on Milton and Humanism, Hanford had asserted that "Milton's true kinship is not with Bunyan or Baxter, nor yet altogether with Cromwell and the heroes of the battle for religious and political liberty, but with those men of the older day, whose spiritual aspirations were united with the human passion for truth and beauty…"[8] Hanford's was a Milton of high humanist culture, largely detached from the complex political and religious issues of his day. Indeed, Hanford's characterization ought to be regarded as an effort to frame his claims about Milton's intellectual seriousness in terms recognizable and sympathetic to an audience still under the sway of the Arnoldian notion of "sweetness and light." Hanford credited the assumption behind Raleigh's half-praise of Milton, i.e., that *all* poetry's value depends largely on its relevance, while asserting that the ideas in Milton's writings were not dead at all, indeed, they played a vital role in the transmission of the humanist ethos from the Renaissance to the modern era. Saurat's conclusions put Milton in different company, among the most radical religious and political writers of the seventeenth century, staunch republicans and independents, mystics, Millenarians, Fifth monarchists, Mortalists, and Levellers – men like Robert Fludd, John Bradshaw, Henry Vane, Richard Overton, and John Lilburne.

When Saurat's book first appeared it was met with high acclaim. Critics took issue with this or that specific argument or bit of evidence, but it was universally acknowledged to constitute a watershed moment in the field.[9] Edwin Greenlaw, to cite only one highly regarded example, began his acerbic and critical review by saying, "M. Saurat has given us a book that must be taken into account by every serious student of Milton." Joan Bennett, in her review of the book when it was reissued two decades later, remarked, "Many of those who read Professor Saurat's book twenty years ago and reread it now will find that an approach to *Paradise Lost* which then seemed startling, and even over-intellectual, has now become natural to them, and that their enjoyment of the poem has consequently grown richer and fuller." Readers recognized the radically new approach to Milton that Saurat had proposed, one that made it essential to read Milton in dialogue with his own cultural, intellectual, and political milieu, and just as important, in dialogue with himself throughout his extensive and diverse career as a writer. Though it had been discovered in the Old State Paper Office at Whitehall in 1823, a full century before the publication of Saurat's book, Milton's theological treatise, *De Doctrina*

Christiana, was still largely regarded as an obscure curiosity with little relevance to his poetry. Saurat was the first scholar to make extensive use of the *De Doctrina* in a systematic reading of Milton's poetry and prose.[10] Indeed, the argumentative method of Saurat's book, with its massive quotations from Milton's poetry and prose introduced or followed, in some cases, by remarkably little comment, strikingly resembles Milton's construction of the *De Doctrina* out of extensive, sometimes dizzyingly interwoven, scriptural citations as though these were self-evidently in support of his often heterodoxical views.[11] Both Milton and Saurat make their cases through the sheer weight of quotation and surprising juxtapositions as much as through extensive discursive arguments. It is difficult not to hear Saurat reading a bit of his own revisionary project into Milton when he writes, "Running through the whole of the *De Doctrina* – and in this it is still a poet's work – there is the fierce joy of the iconoclast, a well-nigh juvenile jubilation, under the stiff sentences and accumulated texts, in the destruction of orthodox ideas, in the ardor of turning on the theologians the tables of their own definitions" (pp. 113–14). Saurat's resituating of Milton among the more radical political and religious writers was recognized as a major shift and his proposal of Robert Fludd, Richard Overton, and the Jewish Kabbalah as sources for some of Milton's most innovative thinking was regarded as a genuine challenge to the more orthodox and sanitized Milton of previous generations.[12] Most important, Saurat's early readers understood how essential the synthesis of these new approaches was to Saurat's recovery of Milton as a man, a poet, and an intellect of great moment. The very fact that *Milton: Man and Thinker* was reissued in 1944 serves as evidence of its importance and also – more subtly, perhaps – a clue to its subsequent disappearance. And here I return to the Milton Controversy.

T. S. Eliot's attack on Milton's stature came in two salvos that serve as bookends to the 1944 reissuing of Saurat's volume, the first in 1936 and the second in an address to the British Academy in 1947. In both essays, it becomes eminently clear that the Milton to whom Eliot objected was, *precisely*, the Milton of Saurat's *Milton: Man and Thinker*: "As a man," Eliot writes, Milton "is antipathetic. Either from the moralist's point of view, or from the theologian's point of view, or from the psychologist's point of view, or from that of the political philosopher, or judging by the ordinary standards of likeableness in human beings, Milton is unsatisfactory." As if deliberately ticking off the table of contents from Saurat's recovery of a Milton beyond the verse, Eliot enumerates the very elements of Milton's thought (recall that the title of Saurat's French version was the overtly

Pascalian *La Pensée de Milton*) to which the French critic attributed such value and centrality. Whereas Saurat had insisted on the complex unity of Milton as poet and thinker, Eliot's reply left no doubt about his reaction: "There seems to me to be a division, in Milton, between the philosopher or theologian and the poet."[13] Eliot's 1947 "retraction" was no less explicit – if somewhat less combative – in acknowledging "an antipathy toward Milton the man" and drawing a clear connection between that antipathy and the radical Milton established by Saurat. "Of no other poet," writes Eliot, "is it so difficult to consider the poetry simply as poetry, without our theological and political dispositions, conscious and unconscious, inherited or acquired, making an unlawful entry … Professor Saurat has produced evidence to show that Milton's theology was highly eccentric, and as scandalous to Protestants as to Catholics – that he was, in fact, a sort of Christadelphian, and perhaps not a very orthodox Christadelphian at that …"[14] Eliot cites Saurat in order to bracket his prejudices. But the very anxiety about "unlawful entry" reveals Eliot's predilections. As Carl Freedman has observed, Eliot's ideological biases and reactionary politics are in evidence in so much of his argument that no such bracketing is possible.[15] Eliot's target is Saurat's Milton.

The same can be said for F. R. Leavis's hostility to Milton. In his two attacks – which also appeared before and after the 1944 reissuing of *Milton: Man and Thinker* – Leavis's strategy was to dismiss Milton's poetry specifically because Milton is "disastrously single-minded and simpleminded" and because he suffers from a "defect of intelligence [which] is a defect of imagination." Fully aware of Saurat's grand claims for Milton's sophisticated and complex thought, the only way Leavis could assure his reader that "Milton's dislodgment … after his two centuries of predominance, was effected with remarkably little fuss" was flatly to deny the very central argument of Saurat's study.[16] The attack on Saurat's Milton – that is, a Milton who can only be understood within the expansive intellectual, cultural, and religious context in which Saurat had first placed him – became more explicit in Leavis's second foray into the controversy, where he insists that Milton "hasn't the kind of energy of mind needed for sustained analytic and discursive thinking. That is why," he concludes, "the ardours and ingenuities of the scholars who interpret *Paradise Lost* in terms of a supposed consistency of theological intention are so absurd, and why it is so deplorable that literary students should be required to take that kind of thing seriously, believe that it has anything to do with intelligent literary criticism, and devote any large part of their time to the solemn study of Milton's 'thought'."[17] The central tenets of the emerging

New Criticism – close readings of the text itself, to the exclusion of extra-textual factors – are obvious in such an assertion.

The two mid-century defenders of Milton, C. S. Lewis and William Empson, came at the matter from diametrically opposed perspectives and yet at the heart of both their arguments lay the Milton re-fashioned by Saurat. Lewis's *Preface to Paradise Lost*, which was published just two years before the reissue of *Milton: Man and Thinker*, offered a sustained analysis of Milton's theology, ethics, and ideas about sexuality, one that was prompted – according to Lewis's own account – by an encounter with Saurat. Though he comes to very different conclusions about Milton's status as an orthodox or heterodox writer, Lewis acknowledges that his "debt to Professor Saurat is not the less. It was from him that I first learned to look for answers at all, or indeed to suspect that they were worth finding. He has made most criticism of Milton before his time look somewhat childish or dilettante; and even those of us who disagree with him are, in one sense, of his school." Resisting the argument implicit in Eliot's attacks, Lewis defends the importance of Milton's work beyond what it can or cannot offer later generations of poets.

Empson's debt to Saurat is, on the one hand more thorough, and on the other, less explicit. Like Lewis – and thus, like Saurat – Empson takes seriously the complex intellectual apparatus that is part of the warp and woof of Milton's writings. Unlike Lewis, and following Saurat far more closely, Empson explores – and clearly values – the very radical nature of Milton's theories of divine sexuality and republicanism, placing them within the context of heterodox Christian practices and theologians of Milton's own time. As striking and unsettling as Empson's claims about the wickedness of Christianity's God and Milton's intense ambivalence toward that God may have been, they find their direct precursors in statements like the following, from Saurat's detailed discussion about the theological and narrative inconsistencies in *Paradise Lost*: "Poets in particular need myths ... [And] poets are always sorry when they cannot believe in their fictions. Therefore Milton believed through his poetical needs and his high need of sincerity, whereas intellectually he was very near to not believing. He insists with pride – and a certain amount of bad faith, so mixed are human motives – on the fact that his myths are truth whereas the ancients' were false" (p. 207). If late Victorians like Raleigh had no patience for, or interest in, the "bad ideas" in Milton's poem, Saurat and Empson sought to interrogate the content of those ideas and to correlate them far more closely with the merits of the epic.

Sixty years before the New Milton Criticism, antagonists in the Milton Controversy were engaged in a debate about a prevenient novelty in Milton studies. In his spirited response to Lewis's work on *Paradise Lost*, E. E. Stoll, lamented that "in Milton the intrusion of irrelevant learning has come about only of late, by the hand of scholars, especially the 'New Miltonians,' as they call themselves, not poets or critics."[18] The distinction between "scholars," on the one hand, and "poets or critics," on the other, speaks volumes, reflecting Stoll's sympathies with the Leavis–Eliot camp. It is also clearly a rueful acknowledgment of the influence of Saurat's scholarship. A. S. P. Woodhouse's review of Saurat's book when it was reissued in 1944 took Stoll to task for his dismissive homogenization of this scholarship: "on any definition, the new Miltonians are a varied group, ... their cumulative learning is very impressive, ... by their variety and learning they furnish (usually good-tempered) correction one to another, ... in fact Milton criticism is in a far more vigorous and healthy state than it has ever been before." For Woodhouse, the health and vigor of Milton studies, the exciting and diverse work produced by the "New Miltonians," were all thanks to Saurat's book, "the most influential book on Milton written in the twentieth century. There is no Miltonian who would deny it that title, and perhaps hardly one who would not utter a caveat against its preconceptions and many of its findings."[19] If, as it has been suggested elsewhere in this volume, the New Milton Criticism has been inspired, at least in part, by a neo-Empsonian revival, it is also clear, I think, just how important Saurat was to Empson – and hence to the current critical moment. Indeed, I would suggest further that the provocative arguments made in the last several years by scholars like Victoria Silver and Michael Bryson concerning the absolute discontinuity between Milton's imaginative representations of God and the "true" God who is necessarily unrepresentable are themselves anticipated in Saurat's identification in Milton's writings of "the only feeling that may yet move God with regard to the efforts directed against him, or even those that aim at knowledge of him, ... a feeling of irony: the irony of intelligent Fate looking on at the vain struggles of beings submitted to inevitable law" (p. 229).[20]

Despite the enormous importance of Saurat's work to the terms of the dispute, when we look for Saurat's legacy in the waning years of the Milton Controversy, we find mostly a critical diminishment of his contributions. In the wake of such a lively dispute, it was only a matter of time before the field of Milton studies would undergo a series of metacritical assessments. The mid-1950s saw at least two such appraisals and, though they both mention Saurat, their characterizations are striking for what they include and what they omit. In 1951, James Thorpe published his influential anthology of four centuries of Milton criticism, offering, by way of introduction, a summary of the trends in Milton studies from the writer's death in 1674 to the mid-twentieth century. In his account of Saurat's contribution (the anthology includes an excerpt from *Milton: Man and Thinker*), though Thorpe does acknowledge the importance of Saurat's organization of Milton's thought as "a considerable contribution," he condemns the work by suggesting that Saurat – and another Continental critic, S. B. Liljegren – have made Milton into a "lawless criminal or physical freak" or, what's worse, a "rationalistic anti-theologian."[21] Thorpe's full approval is saved for the Anglo-American school of Tillyard, Grierson, Bush, Williams, and Lewis, those whom Empson would disdainfully describe as the "neo-Christian" critics, but whom Thorpe sees as recovering Milton for the "Christian humanism" he so clearly values. Then, in 1955, Robert Adams published his *Milton and the Modern Critics*, which has left its indelibly negative mark on Saurat's legacy. Relegating the treatment of Saurat's work to his chapter on "Milton's Readings," Adams effectively reduces Saurat's contributions to his proposition that Milton derived his ontology from the Jewish Kabbalah. Ignoring 320 out of its 340 pages, Adams assigns *Milton: Man and Thinker* to the shelf of naïve, mistaken curiosities for the twenty pages that had come under attack by subsequent scholars of Jewish writings. Without giving so much as a sentence of notice to the significance of Saurat's larger arguments, Adams condescendingly observes, "Unfortunately for M. Saurat's theory, since *Milton: Man and Thinker* was published, the *Zohar* has been translated into English. It reveals itself as a tangled, confused, elaborate mass of mumbo jumbo."[22] Adams's pigeon-holing of Saurat as a failed Hebraist has had remarkable staying power. It may account for Empson's silence in acknowledging his debt to Saurat in his *Milton's God*, which appeared five years after Adams's book. By simultaneously narrowing Saurat's claims to the discredited notion of Kabbalistic influence and describing those texts with the stunningly unselfconscious, xenophobic epithet "mumbo jumbo," Adams sets the terms for Saurat's disappearance. It subsequently follows this admittedly crude outline: Saurat's association with Jewish learning becomes axiomatic and thus serves the cause of his removal from the canon of (mostly neo-Christian) Milton critics. But Saurat is also the critic primarily responsible for the introduction of a complex philosophical analysis of Milton. When Saurat's Jewish esotericism is dismissed, his philosophical and theoretical approaches to Milton go into hiding.[23]

And here, at last, do we come to my final point about the fitful and uneven fortunes of Saurat's work in the history of Milton criticism. Reviewing the trajectory of Milton studies in this way asks us to revisit the surprisingly common assertion that the field of Milton criticism has been relatively untouched by the advent of critical theory. In a recent version of that assertion, Peter Herman writes, "unlike the shifts in other areas of early modern studies ... the development of a new paradigm in Milton studies owes very little to the direct influence of post-structuralism, feminism, or New Historicism ... [T]he New Milton Criticism uses a conservative hermeneutics in the service of a destabilizing ideology."[24] By recovering the formative influence of Denis Saurat's *Milton: Man and Thinker* on older new paradigms, I think we can begin to see that such an account of the absence of theory is a misrecognition of its latency and invisibility. What Eliot, Leavis, and subsequent generations of both neo-Christian and liberal critics objected to in Saurat was, precisely, the way Milton studies could lend itself *too readily* to the destabilizing complexities of philosophy and (though never named as such) critical theory, that is, how alien and non-English Milton would become when read through the lens of Continental philosophy or Jewish mysticism. The Frenchness – the alterity, the non-Englishness – of Saurat's work was prejudicially remarked upon at its initial reception, when a reviewer of *Milton: Man and Thinker* observed,

> Though France is probably the country where the standards of literary criticism stand highest, ... it is curious that French 'universitarians' who devote themselves to the study of foreign literatures should be so consistently uniform in their complete absence of understanding for the really literary values of alien literatures. French scholars have produced works of great value on the lives of foreign writers, and on the history of ideas in foreign countries, but their critical judgment will be almost invariably found wanting. M. Denis Saurat is no exception to the rule, but he wisely evades this shortcoming by refusing, in his new book on Milton, to discuss Milton as a poet. (Mirsky, 548)

It will be recalled that one of T. S. Eliot's key criticisms of Milton's style was that Milton wrote English in a "foreign idiom." Saurat was quite explicit in his efforts to show how the originality of Milton's thought could most readily be understood by adopting "the abstract plans of nineteenth-century metaphysics" (p. 111). Such abstractions and metaphysical analyses quickly came to be seen as a sign of Milton's foreignness, especially as they were reduced by Saurat's detractors to the "tangled, confused ... mumbo jumbo" of Jewish mysticism.

If Saurat's work marked a watershed moment in the study of Milton in the first half of the twentieth century, it is no small irony that the publication of *Surprised by Sin: The Reader in "Paradise Lost"* marks another watershed moment nearly a half century later. Whereas Saurat's work was by then exclusively remembered for its linking of Milton's writings to esoteric Jewish texts, the work of Stanley Fish, a Jewish critic effectively reconfirming the Christian dogmatism of Milton's poem, depended on the deployment of an emerging strain of hermeneutics, considerably more esoteric than the close-reading techniques of the New Critics.[25] Both Annabel Patterson and John Rumrich have remarked on the paradox of *Surprised by Sin*, which enlists an interpretive method that has the potential to be highly destabilizing in the service of a traditional, normative Protestant reading of *Paradise Lost*.[26] The paradox is even more suggestive than either acknowledge, however. Fish's book appeared at a time when Milton's stature had been diminished considerably as a result of two converging critical strains. On the one hand, there was the Leavis–Eliot school, about which I have said much already, which took Milton's poetry to task for not conforming to the modernist, New Critical aesthetic, not to mention a reactionary politics it sought to promote. On the other hand, critical discussions by Empson and, before him, by A. J. A. Waldock, judged *Paradise Lost* a failure (albeit a courageous one) in terms of the categories of psychological coherence and ethical consistency far more appropriate to the novel.[27] As Jonathan Freedman has shown, the poetical–historical narrative that emerged out of Eliot's essays on Milton and blossomed in the New Criticism positioned Milton's influence almost exclusively in negative relation to the desired, stable canon of taste and value, as a "dissociation of sensibility, a sundering of thought and feeling." In dismissing Milton, critics reached for a national and metaphysical coherence built on ideas like "organic unity" that had direct ties (structural as much as theological) to High Church Episcopalianism and Anglo-Catholicism.[28] In an impressive act of critical *chutzpah*, Fish located a different kind of coherence by showing how the techniques of close reading reveal the manner in which meaning emerges, not in the poem itself, but in the experience of the reader of Milton's poem, even as he brilliantly argued that the reader's response became the basis upon which the poem confirmed its orthodox Protestant theology.[29] If the New Criticism required of readers that they bracket the notion of intention when reading a poem, Fish's sophisticated hermeneutics enlisted close rhetorical analysis of the sort practiced by the New Critics to recenter authorial intention and locate it in the reader's response. The shift is apparent in the subtitles of the two books that mark these watershed moments. In them we see the movement from a study concerned with the "man and thinker" behind the poem to the "reader in *Paradise Lost*."

Yet, when theory does constitute an explicit feature of analyses of Milton's work over the last several decades, it is a theory notably marked by Saurat's project of fashioning a man and thinker whose relevance to the meaning of the poem stands firm. I haven't the space necessary to adduce enough examples to give this assertion the full support it deserves but, for the sake of argument, I shall take the instance of deconstruction – since its methods are most clearly at odds with an author-centered criticism – to probe the claim further. There have, in fact, been a few efforts to enlist the insights of Derrida, et al., in the service of an analysis of Milton's writings, most notably two book-length studies published in the 1980s, R. A. Shoaf's *Milton, Poet of Duality* and Herman Rapaport's *Milton and the Post-Modern*. It is true that unlike, say, the field of Romanticism, where deconstructionist analysis was *de rigueur* for nearly a decade, and despite the many useful insights offered by Shoaf, Rapaport, and those others who attempted to apply Derridean interpretation to Milton, a survey of the criticism, book- and article-length, published during the heyday of that theoretical model shows nothing like the dominance it held elsewhere. This absence may seem especially surprising given the literary–historical associations between the canonical figures of High Romanticism who so often served as the occasions for the writings of the Yale School – Wordsworth, Coleridge, Shelley, Keats – and Milton. Yet even, for example, in Shoaf's subtle rhetorical and post-structuralist readings, the question of intentionality, the function of the author, has a way of resurfacing. "[S]igns in *Paradise Lost*," writes Shoaf, "are to be considered instruments, in some measure contingent on the intentionality of their user or maker." Shoaf thus acknowledges somewhat sheepishly that to deconstruct Milton's text "would necessarily be to transgress his intention."[30] Imagine coming across such an admission in a Derridean discussion of a Shakespearean soliloquy or a Donne lyric. It simply wouldn't happen because the concern about intentionality lost its force in other aspects of literary study in ways that it never did in the study of Milton's writings. Or take Herman Rapaport's justification of the use of a deconstructive hermeneutic in his analysis of Milton:

> Milton's perspective on metaphysics is compatible … with that of the poststructuralists, particularly with that of Derrida … I do not allow just any other English poet to occupy the kind of critical arena that I accord to Milton … [O]ne cannot simply take any English poet and turn the poststructuralist critical machine loose on him or her in good faith … For us Milton will be considered a special case, particularly since he is such a monumental figure, ranking in my estimation with Hegel and Marx.[31]

The very reason it might be appropriate to apply such a radical methodology to the study of Milton, Rapaport suggests, is because Milton so authorizes it! And the reason such an authorization exists, for Rapaport, is because the author under examination is Milton, *man and thinker*, a writer whose metaphysics are as weighty as those of Hegel and Marx. Behind such a bold assertion stands the Milton whom Saurat fashioned.

Unlike other areas of literary study, even of periods and texts that are more or less contemporaneous with Milton, the world of Milton criticism has been – and stubbornly continues to be – characterized by the importance given to what Foucault has called the "author function"[32] and the persistence of intentionality as a key to interpretation. While the New Critical notion of the intentional fallacy[33] and Barthes's pronouncement on the death of the author[34] have gone a long way to dislodging the author function in much literary criticism of the last half century, those key critical concepts have not had nearly the same impact on Milton studies. Compare Milton studies with Shakespeare studies, the Milton Society of America with the Shakespeare Association of America (SAA).[35] Look at the conferences and panels of these two important scholarly groups. At MLA, at the International Milton Symposia, at the biennial Murfreesboro conference, every paper offered deals directly with Milton. That might not seem especially astonishing, and yet while the majority of papers offered at the SAA address some Shakespearean text or history of staging and/or reception, a significant minority deal with texts that are not in and of themselves about Shakespeare's writings. Shakespeare studies have, in many ways, become synonymous with early modern studies or Renaissance studies. The New Historicism, which made its first impact in the study of Shakespeare, converted that field into a far more interdisciplinary study of culture, politics, and society, where Shakespeare's plays served as a rich resource of information and a fertile testing ground for new theories. Christopher Kendrick writes of the "wonderment and irritation" non-specialists must feel "at the naïve intentionalism of Miltonists, at the extent to which readings of Milton's poems are deemed appropriate or out-of-court depending on their accordance with 'what Milton meant.'"[36] It is precisely because of the persistence of the author, Milton, however he is understood, that those newer critical methodologies that so often are associated with the dislodgement of the author function – whether it be deconstruction, feminism, New Historicism, or post-colonial studies – have seemed to have a more difficult time gaining any explicit foothold in Milton studies.

As the New Milton Criticism pushes past the Christian orthodoxy Fish and his followers have located in Milton's writing through their deployment of the rhetorical techniques of the New Critical and post-structuralist criticism, it is returning to the *old* new Milton criticism initiated in the first quarter of the twentieth century. A brief survey of even a few of Saurat's more audacious claims reveals both just how new and prescient *Milton: Man and Thinker* was and, with the recovered capacity to recognize Saurat's legacy, the extent to which these insights are indeed informed by various theoretical perspectives. Let's compare some statements from Saurat's book with what I take to be a key text in the formulation and expression of the New Milton Criticism, Stephen Dobranski and John Rumrich's important collection, *Milton and Heresy*.[37] In the Introduction, Dobranski and Rumrich summarize the shared premise that unites the individual essays in their volume as a view of "Milton as poet, thinker, and public servant [who] shunned reliance on set beliefs …"[38] One could do far worse than such a statement as a summary of Saurat's key conclusions.

Saurat observes that as early as in Milton's anti-prelatical tracts, he finds "one of the chief tendencies of his philosophy, one that will lead him to Arianism, and further: the notion that God is boundless, without form, and incomprehensible" (p. 34) and that Milton's Arianism is "an important part of his ontology" (p. 117). Rumrich's essay in the *Milton and Heresy* collection argues that "the import of Milton's monistic ontology should figure into any comparison with … dualistic subordinationism," and that "Milton's Arianism is consistent with his political ideology and view of apocalyptic history."[39] Janel Mueller's fine essay, "Milton on Heresy," amounts to an extended and erudite commentary on Saurat's insistence that even in his Presbyterian phase, "Milton is already an apostle of toleration; his heart leans toward 'sects and schisms …'" (p. 42) and that "neither blasphemies nor heresies much frighten him" (p. 95). Though he never uses the term now currently in vogue, Saurat is especially interested in Milton's monism and its centrality not only to his ontology, but also to his cosmology, psychology, religion, and politics. He writes, "the body is a part of God, matter is a part of the Divinity … Milton was driven to pantheism by his pride and chastity: his body was holy in his eyes; his body will be of the substance of God; matter will be of the substance of God" (p. 46), thereby adumbrating William Kerrigan's useful contribution to the Dobranski and Rumrich collection, "Milton's Kisses," which makes explicit the interanimation of ontological, sexual, and generic discourses in Milton's writings. Stephen Fallon's essay in the *Milton and*

Heresy volume, "'Elect above the rest': Theology as Self-Representation in Milton" was anticipated by Saurat's extensive consideration of Milton's life circumstances as not only having inspired his writings, but also having informed his Arminian theology, his idiosyncratic views on marriage, and the very vocational stance he assumes in virtually everything he wrote – Saurat, by the way, was the first critic to have made a sustained case for Milton (the epic narrator/poet) being the hero of *Paradise Lost*.

Or, to cite an even more recent and pertinent example, I could quote Saurat's wonderful encapsulation of the epic as "an attempt to give a precise answer to a metaphysical question which arises both from personal anguish and universal suffering. It is a voice singing of mankind at a loss to understand its repeated failures in its struggle against Fate" (p. 104), as precursor to Peter Herman's fascinating account of the uncertainties inscribed by the Restoration Miltonic "Or."[40]

As Christopher Kendrick has observed, a partial way of accounting for the apparently unremarkable impact of literary theory on Milton studies is to point out that Milton's thought and poetry has long been understood in a far more philosophical sense than many of his immediate predecessors or contemporaries.[41] The infiltration of Continental philosophy into Milton criticism was accomplished long before it became the vogue in Romanticism or Shakespeare studies. We have, I would suggest, Denis Saurat to thank for the *early* influence of philosophical thought on Milton studies. If that theoretical quality remains hidden, it is because it has been misrecognized by virtue of its un-theoretical attachment to the "man and thinker" behind the writings. And if Saurat's theoretical influence has been suppressed, it has been because it was so threatening to a nativism – sometime explicit, often latent – characteristic of so many accounts of the history of the field.

NOTES

1 For a polemical account of the controversy, see Carl Freedman's essay, "How to Do Things with Milton: A Study in the Politics of Literary Criticism," in Christopher Kendrick (ed.), *Critical Essays on John Milton* (New York: G. K. Hill & Co., 1995), pp. 19–44. For an earlier attempt at assessing the controversy (no less ideological, though less self-consciously so), see Paul J. Alpers, "The Milton Controversy," in Reuben A. Brower (ed.), *Twentieth-Century Literature in Retrospect*, Harvard English Studies 2, (1971), 269–98.
2 F. R. Leavis, "Milton's Verse," *Scrutiny* 2 (1933), 123–36. Reprinted in F. R. Leavis, *Revaluation: Tradition and Development in English Poetry* (London: Chatto and Windus, 1936), pp. 42–67.

3 Denis Saurat, *Milton: Man and Thinker* (New York: The Dial Press, 1925), reissued by AMS Press, 1975. All references to Saurat's book will be given as parenthetical page numbers in the body of the essay.
4 I include myself in this category. See Jeffrey S. Shoulson, *Milton and the Rabbis: Hebraism, Hellenism, and Christianity* (New York: Columbia University Press, 2001), pp. 2–3 and notes.
5 Quoted in Mitchell Stephens, "Jacques Derrida and Deconstruction," *The New York Times Magazine*, January 23, 1994.
6 Walter Raleigh, *Milton* (London: Edward Arnold & Co., 1900).
7 James Holly Hanford reviewed *La Pensée de Milton* in *Studies of Philology* 18 (1921), 375 and *Milton: Man and Thinker* in *Modern Language Notes* 41 (1926), 55–9. Hanford's 1921 essay, "The Chronology of Milton's Private Studies" appeared in *PMLA* 36 (1921), 251–314.
8 James Holly Hanford, "Milton and the Return to Humanism," *Studies in Philology* 16 (1919), reprinted in James Thorpe (ed.), *Milton Criticism: Selections from Four Centuries* (London: Routledge & Kegan Paul Ltd., 1951), pp. 143–68.
9 The French version of Saurat's work, *La Pensée de Milton*, had been reviewed positively when it first appeared, though it was known by a smaller readership. The English *Milton: Man and Thinker* garnered a much larger readership and was reviewed more widely. The reviews included: George Saintsbury, *The Nation & the Athenæum* 37 (1925), 178; S. B. Liljegren, *Beiblatt zur Anglia* 36 (1925), 274–6; Raymond D. Haven, *Saturday Review of Literature* 2 (1925), 276; D. S. Mirsky, *London Mercury* 12 (1925), 547–9; Edwin Greenlaw, *Journal of English and Germanic Philology* 25 (1925), 437–43; Émile Legouis, *Revue Anglo-Americaine* 3 (1926), 254–5; H. J. C. Grierson, *Modern Language Review* 21 (1926), 440–2; and T. V. Smith, *Studies in Philology* 23 (1926), 184–8. When the book was reissued in 1944 it received a number of further reviews, again mostly positive, including: E. M. Forster, *La France Libre* 8 (1944), 449–50; unsigned review, *Times Literary Supplement*, September 16, 1944, 451; Charles Williams, *The Spectator* 172 (1944), 154; Joan Bennett, *New Statesman and Nation* 28 n. s. (1944), 156–7; and A. S. P. Woodhouse, *University of Toronto Quarterly* 15 (1946), 200–5.
10 Maurice Kelley's seminal work on Milton's epic in relation to his theological treatise, *This Great Argument: A Study of "De Doctrina Christiana" as a Gloss upon "Paradise Lost"* (Princeton University Press, 1941), appeared a full sixteen years after the publication of *Milton: Man and Thinker*. In it, Kelley directly challenges many of Saurat's assertions concerning the systematic nature of Milton's theology and philosophy. Yet it is clear that Kelley's conceptualization of his own project, which reads Milton's work against itself, owes a crucial debt to Saurat's own formulation of this approach.
11 For a convincing discussion of how the treatise's assemblage of biblical citations constitutes an exchange of authority, a "politics" of citation, see Regina Schwartz, "Citation, Authority, and *De Doctrina Christiana*," in David Loewenstein and James Grantham Turner (eds.), *Politics, Poetics,*

and Hermeneutics in Milton's Prose (Cambridge University Press, 1990), pp. 227–40.
12 Saurat's ascription of esotericism to Milton was preceded by Margaret Lewis Bailey's study, *Milton and Jakob Boehme: A Study of German Mysticism in Seventeenth-Century England* (New York: Oxford University Press, 1914), which is notably absent from Saurat's work. Far more speculative, even, than *Milton: Man and Thinker*, Bailey's volume does make the important argument that Milton's humanism was inextricably bound up with his interest in Hebraica.
13 T. S. Eliot, "Milton," *Essays in Studies* of The English Association (Oxford University Press, 1936), reprinted as "Milton I" in *On Poetry and Poets* (New York: Farrar, Straus, & Giroux, 1969), pp. 156 and 163.
14 T. S. Eliot, "Milton II," *On Poetry and Poets*, p. 168, originally delivered to the British Academy in 1947.
15 Carl Freedman, "How to Do Things with Milton," 31. Annabel Patterson has addressed Eliot's partial acknowledgment of his own political consciousness in his delineation of a New Critical reading practice that "attend[s] to poetry for the poetry's sake." She notes the confluence of the more reactionary views taken by Johnson, Coleridge, and Eliot, with the seemingly more radical views of Milton's writings by Marxists like Christopher Hill and Fredric Jameson. See Annabel Patterson, *Reading Between the Lines* (Madison: University of Wisconsin Press, 1993), pp. 244–51.
16 F. R. Leavis, "Milton's Verse," pp. 58 and 42.
17 F. R. Leavis, *The Common Pursuit* (New York: George W. Stewart, 1952), p. 23.
18 E. E. Stoll, "Give the Devil his Due: A Reply to Mr. Lewis," *The Review of English Studies* 20 (1944), 115.
19 A. S. P. Woodhouse, Review Essay, *University of Toronto Quarterly* 15 (1946), 200–1.
20 Victoria Silver, *Imperfect Sense: The Predicament of Milton's Irony* (Princeton University Press, 2001), and Michael Bryson, *The Tyranny of Heaven: Milton's Rejection of God as King* (Newark: University of Delaware Press, 2004).
21 James Thorpe, "Introduction: A Brief History of Milton Criticism," *Milton Criticism*, pp. 16–17. Thorpe's influence can be seen in something as late as William Kolbrener's otherwise quite perceptive analysis of the polarizing habits of Milton studies. Accepting Thorpe's characterization of Saurat as part of the same movement to secularize Milton as Hanford, Kolbrener, quoting Thorpe, writes, "Denis Saurat saw [bourgeois liberty and rationalist monism] dovetail in Milton; Milton was for him a 'rationalist anti-theologian.' … Re-fashioned as a 'rationalist' and 'humanist,' Hanford and Saurat together tried to 'strip Milton of all elements of Puritanism.'" See William Kolbrener, *Milton's Warring Angels: A Study of Critical Engagements* (Cambridge University Press, 1997), p. 109.
22 Robert Martin Adams, *Milton and the Modern Critics* (Ithaca: Cornell University Press, 1955), p. 140.

23 Matthew Biberman offers a provocative account of Eliot's impact on Milton studies, linking it directly to his anti-Semitic aesthetics. See Matthew Biberman, *Masculinity, Anti-Semitism, and Early Modern English Literature: From the Satanic to the Effeminate Jew* (London: Ashgate, 2004). While I agree with much of Biberman's analysis, I part ways with him by arguing that Milton's apparent "Jewishness" created the conditions under which explicitly theoretical analyses of his writings were less likely to emerge.

24 Peter C. Herman, "Paradigms Lost, Paradigms Found: The New Milton Criticism," *Literature Compass* 2 (2005), 14–15. For parallel observations about earlier phases of Milton criticism, see Annabel Patterson's Introduction to *John Milton, Longman Critical Reader* (London: Longman, 1992), pp. 2–3, and William Kerrigan, "Seventeenth-Century Studies," in Stephen Greenblatt and Giles Gunn (eds.), *Redrawing the Boundaries: The Transformation of English and American Literary Studies* (New York: MLA Press, 1992), pp. 73–7.

25 Stanley Fish has touched upon the significance of the influx of critics of Jewish origin into the field of Milton studies, proposing that such Jewish critics were able to take a more objective view of matters that were of great theological concern to critics who assumed a Christian perspective. See his "Transmuting the Lump: *Paradise Lost*, 1942–1979," *Doing What Comes Naturally: Change, Rhetoric, and the Practice of Theory in Literary and Legal Studies* (Durham: Duke University Press, 1989), pp. 247–93. This same topic has more recently been taken up by Matthew Biberman in *Masculinity, Anti-Semitism, and Early Modern English Literature* and in "T. S. Eliot, Anti-Semitism, and the Milton Controversy," pp. 105–27, in Douglas A. Brooks (ed.), *Milton and the Jews* (Cambridge University Press, 2008). See also Brooks's helpful introduction to his volume.

26 Patterson, *John Milton*, p. 6; John Rumrich, *Milton Unbound: Controversy and Reinterpretation* (Cambridge University Press, 1996), p. 4.

27 See, for example, A. J. A. Waldock, *Paradise Lost and its Critics* (Cambridge University Press, 1947), p. 56, where Waldock wrings his hands over Adam's decision about whether to eat of the fruit offered to him by Eve or not.

28 Jonathan Freedman, *The Temple of Culture: Assimilation and Anti-Semitism in Literary Anglo-America* (Oxford University Press, 1999), pp. 177–8. In another forthcoming essay, I argue that the reassertion of Milton's centrality to English literary history by numerous Jewish critics ought to be read also as a recovery of the Hebrew Bible as a text whose meaning should not exclusively depend upon its typological refashioning as the Old Testament.

29 Fish frames his critical intervention as a systematic defense of Milton's poem against the attacks of the preceding decades of "anti-Miltonism," which he attributes not only to Leavis and Eliot, but also to Empson and Waldock. See *Surprised by Sin: The Reader in "Paradise Lost"* [1967] (Berkeley: University of California Press, 1971), p. 2 n.

30 R. A. Shoaf, *Milton, Poet of Duality: A Study of Semiosis in the Poetry and Prose*, 2nd edn. (Gainesville: University of Florida Press, 1993), pp. 28 and 57.

31 Herman Rapaport, *Milton and the Postmodern* (Lincoln: University of Nebraska Press, 1983), pp. 19–21.

32 Michel Foucault, "What is an Author?" Donald F. Bouchard and Sherry Simon (trans.), *Language, Counter-Memory, Practice* (Ithaca: Cornell University Press, 1977), pp. 124–7.
33 W. K. Wimsatt, Jr. and Monroe C. Beardsley, *The Verbal Icon: Studies in the Meaning of Poetry* (Lexington: University of Kentucky Press, 1954).
34 Roland Barthes, "The Death of the Author," in *Image-Music-Text*, Stephen Heath (trans.) (New York: The Noonday Press, 1977), pp. 142–8.
35 The Shakespeare–Milton contrast has recently received new attention in Nigel Smith, *Is Milton Better than Shakespeare?* (Cambridge: Harvard University Press, 2008). Significantly, Smith's efforts at recovering Milton's relevance for a contemporary American audience hinge upon the content of Milton's thought far more than on the aesthetics of his poetry.
36 Christopher Kendrick, "By Way of Introduction: Bentley, Lauder, and Miltonic Identifications," in Kendrick (ed.), *Critical Essays*, p. 1.
37 Stephen B. Dobranski and John P. Rumrich (eds.), *Milton and Heresy* (Cambridge University Press, 1998).
38 Stephen B. Dobranski and John P. Rumrich, "Introduction: Heretical Milton," in Dobranski and Rumrich (eds.), *Milton and Heresy*, p. 12.
39 John P. Rumrich, "Milton's Arianism: Why it Matters," in Dobranski and Rumrich (eds.), *Milton and Heresy*, pp. 83 and 89.
40 Peter C. Herman, "*Paradise Lost*, the Miltonic 'Or,' and the Poetics of Incertitude," *SEL: Studies in English Literature, 1500–1900* 43 (2003), 181–211.
41 Christopher Kendrick (*Critical Essays*, p. 10) lists Masson, Saurat, Hanford, Woodhouse, Tillyard, and Barker as having initiated the "old historicist" approach to Milton, favorably comparing it to the old historical approaches to Shakespeare studies.

CHAPTER 11

The poverty of context: Cambridge School History and the New Milton Criticism

William Kolbrener

My title, "The poverty of context," with its implication that Cambridge School History, informed by the methodology of Quentin Skinner, has not been salutary for Milton studies is certainly hard to fully justify. In the past generation, some of the most important critical work on Milton has relied upon Skinnerian method – in particular, the emphasis on the recovery of discursive contexts to elicit intentions, as well as the performative force of those utterances in the contexts in which they are made.[1] Sharon Achinstein's *Milton and the Revolutionary Reader* of 1994, for example, builds, as she writes in her Introduction, upon "Skinner's emphasis on the recovery of the text's position within the framework of its own system of communication."[2] Nigel Smith, in the Introduction to *Literature and Revolution in England* of the same year, though not citing Skinner, explicitly invokes the performative nature of "speech acts," that is, the action entailed by a text in the context in which it was uttered.[3] David Norbrook's *Writing the English Republic* (1999) describes itself as explicitly following the Skinnerian model – as "concerned with the links between language and action" and "the kinds of 'illocutionary act[s]' the author was performing," as well as how he was "intervening in a contemporary context of debate."[4] That Skinner was the only historian featured as a plenary speaker at the 2008 International Milton Symposium in London, and that a version of the lecture which he delivered was featured in the *London Review of Books* (released to overlap with the symposium) testifies to Skinner's stature and influence among contemporary Miltonists.[5] But perhaps more than that, Colin Burrow's recent review of Blair Worden's *Literature and Politics in Cromwellian England*, which focuses on Milton, Marvell, and Marchamont Nedham, demonstrates Skinner's pervasive influence among scholars of seventeenth-century literature in England. To Burrow, Worden's book exemplifies the "New Model Criticism" which "subjects literary works to more and more intensive contextualization," affirming that "poems are acts or events, or testaments to political positioning," that require "highly specialised contextual labours."[6] The unnamed presence behind the reading of Milton and his contemporaries, emphasizing the centrality of contexts and texts as performative acts, is of course none other than Skinner. To be sure, Milton scholarship has become more rigorous and disciplined because of Skinner's attention to contexts, but the subordination of Miltonic intention to singular contexts – very often political – has sometimes simplified the work of both the political thinker and poet.

Skinner's method – emerging from the twin strands of Austinian language philosophy and the historical traditions of Collingwood and Butterfield – always emphasizes the importance of reconstructing authorial intentions. Writing in 1972 against Wimsatt's New Critical rejection of intention, Skinner fashioned a method that would shift emphasis "off the idea of the text as an autonomous object" toward an understanding of the text which would take into account what he would call "intentionalist action."[7] Skinner, rejecting New Critical principles, would turn to the "idea of the text as an object linked to its creator, and thus on to the discussion of what its creator may have been doing in creating it." Skinner thus not only emphasizes intention, but also Austin's "central insight" about the performative nature of language, distilled in the Wittgensteinian insight that, as Skinner quotes him, "words are also deeds." This is to say, Skinner's intentionalism does not entail a focus on the text in itself, but on rather what he terms, following Austin, the "particular force with which a given utterance … may have been issued on a particular occasion." Skinner thus invokes discursive contexts – or Wittgensteinian "language games" – as a means for reconstructing the intentions of particular texts, or, as Skinner following Austin would have them, texts as performative utterances. Although acknowledging that it is impossible "to step into the shoes of past agents," and "still less into their minds," Skinner nonetheless still holds out the hope of the recovery of the "intentions with which their utterances were issued, and hence what they meant by them."[8] New Critics of an earlier generation often turned to Romantic poets; Skinner whose work in political theory made major contributions to the study of Hobbes was a natural fit to Milton studies, not least because of Milton's commitment to commonwealth and political discourse.

Yet as much as the works that have been influenced by Skinner cited above have helped to re-shape our sense of Milton, the insistence on the elaboration of discourses may not be fully adequate to Milton's works, for they rarely yield the kind of singular intention promised by Skinnerian methodology and his focus on the performative intervention of utterances within particular contexts. The notion that authors perform "this or that move," and that their intentions "must be conventional … in upholding some particular position in argument" becomes problematic in relation to Milton's manifest complexity.[9] Indeed, Milton seems to have, not only in his poetry but in his political prose as well, produced a species of what Skinner defines as "abnormal forms of discourse," in which an author's utterances are not so easily reducible to the demands of a particular context. In the terms that inform the "New Milton Criticism," Cambridge History seems to advocate a conception of univocal certainty not in line with the focus on fault lines and uncertainty characterizing much of current critical debate. If, as Thomas Corns suggests, there is a "plurality of Miltonic ideologies," then the Skinnerian insistence on the clarity of intention within a specific context will certainly produce an impoverished conception of Milton.[10]

The emphasis on contexts may in some sense have emerged as a result of changing disciplinary priorities, and the increased emphasis over the past two decades on Milton's prose works, and his politics, testified to by, among other things, the publication in 1995 of the volume co-edited by Skinner, *Milton and Republicanism*. But even Milton's political discourses are only with difficulty reduced simply to the contexts in which they were written. Keith Stavely, in 1975, argued that if Milton's political tracts "were the only surviving documents of the English Revolution, we would know little about it as a major political event."[11] In Stavely's reading it is hard to read Miltonic argument as entailing simply a rhetorical choice or "move" in the Skinnerian sense, for Milton's habit of mind sometimes appears to refuse the conventional restraints of polemic, or simple or certain political and philosophical positions.

True, Skinner has shown us, in relationship to manifold political discourses, the extent to which discourses matter – and that canonical literary and philosophical figures do not write within an ethereal ahistorical canon, but are in fact in conversation with their contemporaries in the specific discourses available to them. But what sometimes gets lost in bringing Skinnerian insights about intellectual history into Milton studies is the difference between political and literary discourses: Hobbes, on whom Skinner has written so authoritatively, marks the beginning of a modern Western philosophical tradition, to which Skinner in some sense himself is an heir, in which contradictions are rejected as a function of *incoherence*. So Skinner laments the way in which contradictory utterances come only to thwart the historian's task. Since the "primary aim" of the historian "is to use our ancestors' utterances as a guide to the identification of their beliefs," if "they display no concern for consistency," if "they are willing ... both to affirm and deny the truth of some particular proposition, then we can never hope to say what they believe about that proposition at all."[12] To hold up this set of criteria to the Milton of the political prose may be problematic, but even more problematic in relationship to his poetic or theological utterances. The historian's desire for this kind of singular consistency has produced a Milton who may be easily assimilated within specific political traditions, but has been less successful in eliciting the Milton who nurtures paradox and ambivalence.[13]

I focus here on the ostensible "contradictions" of Miltonic theological positions, his metaphysical assumptions, and the ways as well in which they dovetail with the parallel political positions to which Milton's complex thought has sometimes been assimilated. Rachel Trubowitz has recently called attention to Milton's shifting and contradictory perspectives on mind–body, spirit/matter. Stephen Fallon (who situates his own work in the "hypothetical thousand volume Intellectual History" imagined by Skinner) finds Milton's monist materialism through placing Milton among the philosophers (for example, Hobbes and the Cambridge Platonists). John Rogers has also compellingly shown that the animist vitalism of *Paradise Lost* emerges from the same milieu that nurtured the works of Gabriel Harvey and Francis Glisson. By contrast, Trubowitz goes against the grain of what she perceives to be the current critical consensus in eliciting dualism residual in Milton's works. Similarly, Victoria Silver, strongly contesting the monist Milton (which she also attributes to Rogers and Fallon), elaborates the frameworks of Reform theology which helps to reveal a Milton always emphasizing the incongruity – dualist separation – between spirit and matter.[14]

According to the evidentiary criteria of Skinner's empiricist model, both the monist and dualist Milton are compelling, thus either demonstrating the inadequacy of the Cambridge conception of context in Milton studies, the uncertainty of Milton, or both. Yet, perhaps there is another approach which would begin with the question of whether the alternative to the Miltonic poet of "certainty" is really the Milton of "conflict, ambivalence and open-endedness."[15] That is, perhaps Milton as poet of indeterminacy is as similarly incomplete a construct as that of Milton the poet of certitude. For just as it is possible to say that the Derridian conception of *différance* is still locked in the Platonic binary of all or nothing, philosophy or sophistry, "full presence" or "erasure," so perhaps, we might affirm, is a Milton criticism focused on "uncertainty" simply providing an equally partial counter-image to the Milton of "certainty."

To elaborate this point further, I'd like to return to the question of metaphysics – Milton's ostensible monism or dualism – and how Milton's contested cosmology is implicated in the history of his reception as recounted in Peter Herman's "Paradigms Lost, Paradigms Found." In Herman's account, it was first Dryden, then Marvell who "sanitized" those Miltonic texts which "challenge orthodoxy." Later, as Nicholas von Maltzahn points out, the 1688 and 1695 editions of the epic were instrumental in the establishment of Milton "the national poet," whose epic would be safely read in years to come with other "Sunday-Books."[16] As Herman argues, the desire to rescue Milton for "religious orthodoxy" was pursued most aggressively (and sometimes, one assumes, with tongue firmly in cheek) by Richard Bentley who, in his 1732 edition of the epic, excised those ostensibly interpolated passages of *Paradise Lost* that marred the poet's orthodoxy – attributing them alternatively to the printer, Milton's daughter, or to a meddlesome "Editor."[17]

Bentley, however, did not propose his version of the "certain" or "orthodox" Milton in a vacuum. His own intervention to rescue Milton, informed by a Newtonian cosmology in which spirit and matter were indisputably separate, was itself a polemical reaction to an antecedent Milton – not that of Dryden, nor that of Marvell, but the Milton of John Toland. Though elusive to us, Toland was, however, sufficiently well-known among his contemporaries. Leibniz found him "odious"; Locke wanted to disassociate himself from the views expressed in Toland's *Christianity Not Mysterious*. Parliament shared Locke's disdain for this work, and proclaimed it deserving of burning by the public hangman.[18] But in the yet-unwritten history of the Enlightenment in England, Toland's works would occupy a pre-eminent position, and in those works, the presence of Milton is central. Against the version of Milton forwarded in the editions of the late seventeenth century, Toland reminded readers of Milton's not so orthodox past, reprinting Milton's complete prose in 1698, with his *Life of Milton* serving as a preface. In his *Amyntor*, published in the following year, Toland answers charges of his own ostensible political heresies (and the accusations were manifold), by pointing to Milton as his explicit antecedent and source. While there were those who looked at the Milton of *Amyntor* account as Toland's "own Creation," Toland went to great pains to assert the veracity of his account, providing as he claims, an "exact History" of Milton's "Books and Opinions."[19]

Toland not only pursued a radical political agenda based, as he himself claimed, on Milton's "excellent Volumes" on "Civil, Religious, and Domestic Liberty," but that political agenda was based on an equally radical cosmology.[20] This is to affirm John Rogers's sense of the confluence between metaphysics and politics, or what Margaret C. Jacob describes as the "intimate" relationship between "the world natural" and "the moral and social relations prevailing or desired in the 'world politick.'"[21] Toland may have "derogated the Majesty of Kings, the holy Liturgy, and the Church"; he also advocated a radical conception of the priority of a unified and spiritualized matter, the metaphysical perspective that underpinned his equally radical politics. While Toland, as George Sensabaugh writes, was celebrating the Milton who "look'd upon true and absolute Freedom" as "the Greatest Happiness of this Life," he was also trying to prove that "Motion is essential to matter … and that Matter neither ever was nor ever can be a sluggish, dead, and inactive Lump."[22] As Yirmiyahu Yovel writes, the belief that man is "the unique source of ethical value and political authority" (prevalent in the work of Toland) usually came with a corresponding metaphysical belief in "the immanence of spirit."[23] So recent attempts to see Milton as a radical monist are in consonance with Toland's vision of Milton as a radical republican and metaphysical monist.

To understand fully the force of Bentley's attempts to provide a version of *Paradise Lost* suitable for orthodoxy, it's necessary first to describe the context for Bentley's edition. For Bentley's polemical appropriation of Milton comes in response to Toland's precedent appropriations of the poet, as well as his engagement with another figure, Isaac Newton. This complex set of interactions between the renowned classicist Bentley, the radical politician Toland, and the epic poet – with Newton in the middle – provides a better means for understanding the construction of the "orthodox Milton."

Bentley corresponded with Newton in the 1690s, and his inaugural set of Boyle lectures, named after the founder of the Royal Society, employed the Newtonian scientific rendering of the cosmos as a support for Bentley's particular conceptions of theological orthodoxy. Toland's mappings of the cosmos began, however, as Jacob has suggested, with Giordano Bruno.[24] While Newton had provided an image of the universe suitable for the hierarchies of latitudinarian orthodoxy, Toland found in Bruno an altogether different cosmos, hearkening back to an occult world of alchemy. Bruno's cosmological works, shaped, at least in their inception, by the influence of Copernicus, inveighed against the "pitiful fancy of the figure of the Spheres" – the set of concentric rings that was thought to circumscribe the globe in the older Ptolemaic mapping of the universe. The "Circles" or the "imaginary nine moveable Spheres" were merely the means by which "Gentlemen Astrologers" and "Philosophers" might "imprison" their "brains" – like "so many parrots in their cages, hopping and dancing from one perch to another, yet always turning and winding within the same wires."[25] Against the restrictions imposed by the Ptolemaic universe, Toland following Bruno, not only places "the Sun in the Center of the Planets," but goes on to suggest that like the Earth, there are "other innumerable Earths, making their Revolutions in stated Times, according to their respective Distances about their own Suns."[26]

For Toland, the Copernican de-centering of the earth, and the positing of an "infinite field" with its various inhabitants, not only challenged cosmological hierarchies, but sublunary ones as well (*AJB* 344). Instead of the stratified relation of elements (and spheres) related by the poets, Toland argues that what had been conceived of as independent elements are in fact interdependent. There are no hierarchical and separate spheres, as in the Ptolemaic vision, codified in what Lovejoy called "the great chain of being," but rather "Men, Birds, Beasts, Trees, Plants, Fishes, Worms, Insects, Stones, Metals, and a thousand other differences" which all "depend in a Link on one another." For "their Matter … is mutually resolv'd into each other." Indeed, Toland argued that "Earth, and Water, and Air, and Fire, are not only closely blended and united, but likewise interchangeably transform'd in a perpetual Revolution; Earth becoming Water, Water Air, Air Æther, and so back again in Mixtures without End or Number" (*LS* 187–8). Undoing the stratified world of the poets, Toland's Brunoian cosmos was marked by fluidity and continuity. Toland's attacks were directed both back toward the older "fancies" of the poets, as well as forward to the newest scientific conceptions. As Jacob argues, Toland not only assailed the cosmos of Ptolemy, but his primary target was the one to whom he referred sarcastically as "the greatest Man in the world," the author of the *Principia* and the *Opticks*, Isaac Newton himself (*LS* 182).

Newton had posited a universe composed of "absolute space," where "bodies remain at rest until moved, or retain their motion depending on the degree of force initially applied."[27] In this view, inert matter or bodies would remain at rest until moved by a force from without. What Newton described as the "void" was that intermediate medium through which an external divine force (God) could act on inert matter. Bentley, in his Boyle lectures, employed Newtonian assumptions about the relation between spirit and matter in order to attack a newly revived materialism of the 1690s. "But first, these faculties of sensation and perception are not inherent in matter," Bentley wrote. "[I]f it were so," he continues, "what monstrous absurdities would follow! every stock and stone would be a percipient and rational creature."[28] It was the Newtonian conception of the divine which allowed for the motion of matter without making spirit immanent in matter. Newtonian physics thus provided a scientific justification for a not only theological, but political orthodoxy which sought to keep spirit and matter separate while allowing in ways – that most always remained unarticulated – for their interaction.

In the *General Scholium* to the second edition of the *Principia*, as well as in the queries added to the *Optics*, Newton provides an elaboration of the relationship between spirit and matter, answering to the concerns of the newly consolidated latitudinarian Church. In the former text, Newton described space as a divine "sensorium" or "sensory," in which God perceives and comprehends all things. Things move and are known, Newton explains, "within His boundless uniform sensorium."[29] Like the "pineal gland" for Descartes, Newton's "sensorium" functions as a means of mapping the divine and the material without allowing them to overlap. Dodging between the equally dangerous and heretical poles of mechanical and pantheistic materialism (the former most usually associated with Spinoza, the latter with Hobbes), the constitution of space as "sensorium" – the space in which "through his omnipresence everything is present to him" – God could at once be present to the world, without, however, being identical to it.[30] Investing the material world with spirit had dangerous theological and political consequences: Toland himself was not hesitant about drawing out the republican political ramifications of his version of Spinozan materialism. Bentley's defense of the Newtonian void was a means of mapping a universe suitably ordered and hierarchical – with, as Jacob writes, "the God of Newton comfortably in control."[31]

When Toland takes on the "greatest of men," he focuses his attention on Newton's elaboration of the void. The "Opinion of a Void" or "sensorium," Toland explains, is simply "erroneous," the consequence of two primary errors: (1) making matter "naturally inactive," and (2) "thinking [matter] divided into real Parts every way independent of one another" (*LS* 172–3). Addressing the latter point, Toland asserts that "there's but one sort of Matter in the Universe; and if it be infinitely extended, it can have no absolute Parts independent of one another" (*LS* 174). Infinitely extended, there are no independent or discrete parts: fire, air, water, and earth form a continuum, rather than constituting different elements. "Mathematicians" (like Newton), who "cou'd not otherwise account for the Generation of Motion in Matter" were forced, Toland argues, to imagine a Space distinct from Matter as the intermediate place through which God would act on inactive matter. Toland himself, however, affirms that there could be no "absolute Space distinct from Matter," and further, that the Newtonian necessity of the void emerged from a fundamental misunderstanding of the nature of matter itself (*LS* 182).

Where Newtonians had argued that matter is inactive, Toland builds his own cosmological edifice upon the assumption that matter is essentially active. There is no need "to help it to motion," Toland writes, by the Newtonian "Invention" of the void (*LS* 181–2); for motion is intrinsic to matter. One does not need, therefore, the introduction of "absolute Space" or a "void," since matter moves autonomously, and requires neither a divine agent nor a medium through which that agent would work (*LS* 222). Rather, as Toland affirms in his *Pantheisticon*, enthusiastically citing his beloved ancient pantheists, "*the Universe … is infinite both in Extension and Virtue, but one, in the Continuation of the Whole*": "*Intelligent also by an eminent Reason*," and "*always in Motion*," Toland's matter is thus both autonomous and self-moving (*P* 15).

Toland's cosmology permits the mobility of matter, as well as a different kind of mobility for man. "Infinite matter," he writes, "is the real Space and Place, as well as the real Subject of its own particular Portions and Modification" (*LS* 188). The natural outcome of material mobility and agency is the proclamation that "it is no harder thing to fly from hence up into Heaven, than to fly from Heaven again to the Earth" (*AJB* 343). The vitalist monism that underwrites the "one Sort of Matter" in Toland's Universe allows for an upward mobility for the Creation (*LS* 174). What follows, as Toland draws out the politics implicit in his metaphysical assumptions, is that man is "deliver'd from the vain anxiety and foolish care of desiring to enjoy that good afar off" which may be possessed "so near at hand, and even at home" (*AJB* 343). Whatever goods Heaven may promise, are already near at hand, "at home." Indeed, the "internal Energy, Autokinesy, or essential Action of all Matter" leads upwards to the heavens, but more generally points to an equality between worldly and heavenly space, where this world need not be transcended for another better one (*LS* 193). In Toland's mappings of space, the place of matter (the world) is itself celebrated, or, in the alternate, but complementary version, the de-centered heavens (which continue to occupy an ambiguous space in Toland's cosmos) are constituent parts of a continuous and materialized cosmos. "[N]othing is more certain," writes Toland, "than that every material Thing is all Things, and that all Things are but one" (*LS* 192). As Toland in his *Pantheisticon* intones: "All Things in the World are one, / And one is All in All Things" (*P* 70).

As the late John Shawcross has written, Toland's "view of religion," not to mention his cosmology, were after 1698, "usually transferred uncritically to Milton."[32] It was not by accident that Toland was dubbed by one of his contemporaries, "Milton junior"; indeed, the *Life of Milton* and later *Amyntor* served the purpose of creating a radical image of the poet, modeling Milton in Toland's own image.[33] Herman is right to argue that the "assumptions governing a very great deal of Milton criticism in the twentieth and twenty first centuries" echo those of Bentley (as well as other eighteenth-century critics) who attempted to promote an image of Milton suitable for orthodoxy.[34] Yet one might also argue that there is an equally powerful version of Milton, the vitalist and radically political Milton, the *monist* Milton, having its origin in the Milton promulgated by Toland.[35] Indeed, a clear trajectory can be traced between Toland's materialist monism and the animist Milton forwarded by recent critics. To be sure, Toland's metaphysics echo (and one could argue, stake out as an antecedent) Book 3 of *Paradise Lost* where God is anticipated to become one day "All in all" (3.341). In this context, Toland's materialist vitalism, his own "all in all," anchored in his conception of "one Sort of Matter in the Universe," appears to have its origin in the conception of the cosmos articulated by Raphael in Book 5 of *Paradise Lost*:

> O *Adam*, one Almightie is, from whom
> All things proceed, and up to him return,
> If not deprav'd from good, created all
> Such to perfection, one first matter all,
> Indu'd with various forms, various degrees
> Of substance, and in things that live, of life;
> But more refin'd, more spiritous, and pure,
> As neerer to him plac't or neerer tending
> Each in thir several active Sphears assignd,
> Till body up to spirit work, in bounds
> Proportiond to each kind. So from the root
> Springs lighter the green stalk, from thence the leaves
> More aerie, last the bright consummate floure
> Spirits odorous breathes: flours and thir fruit
> Mans nourishment, by gradual scale sublim'd
> To vital Spirits aspire, to animal,
> To intellectual, give both life and sense.
> (5.469–85)

In Milton's cosmic vision, matter and spirit are on a continuum, much as Toland would argue, and the "one first matter all" tending toward refinement into spirit. Similarly, the cosmic mobility – between flies and

Heaven so important to Toland's metaphysics and politics – appears to have an antecedent in the Miltonic vision in which "All things proceed" to God and are eventually "by gradual scale sublim'd."

In this framework, Bentley's *Paradise Lost*, then, is not merely an attempt to rescue Milton for orthodoxy. As J. G. A Pocock argues, there are many kinds of orthodoxy; Bentley's *Paradise Lost* rescues Milton for latitudinarian orthodoxy, and more particularly, from the association with the politics and metaphysics of his radical contemporaries – for which Toland's work itself became emblematic.[36] Toland appropriated Milton and attacked Newton. Bentley's "Emendations" to *Paradise Lost* not only represent an implicit attack on the world view founded by Toland and other radicals, but also represented a continuation of the project begun in the Boyle Lectures – a defense of the world view represented by Newton (and the political orthodoxies it upheld). When Bentley in the Boyle Lectures mocked the assumption that sensation and perception are inherent in matter, he undoubtedly had the radical metaphysics which Toland helped to articulate in his sights.[37] Bentley's *Paradise Lost* provides a polemical version of Milton as a response to an equally polemical antecedent, and in so doing instates (or re-instates as Bentley would have it) the Newtonian cosmology more appropriate to the poem.

Bentley was on the lookout for heresy, and he can thus be counted upon to object to any hint of monism in the epic. To the suggestion that spiritual entities require physical sustenance, that, more simply put, angels eat, Bentley snarls: "If the Devils want *feeding*, our Author made poor Provision for them in his Second Book; where they have nothing to eat but *Hell-fire*."[38] But the most "vulgar misprint" in the whole poem, Bentley writes, is where in Book 7, Milton anticipates the time when "Earth be chang'd to Heav'n, & Heav'n to Earth, / One Kingdom, Joy and Union without End" (7.160–1). For Bentley, the assumption of the continuity between spiritual and divine, so much part of the world view – both political and metaphysical – of Toland could not reflect the author's true intentions: "I scarce know two viler Misprints in the whole poem." "Surely," he continues, "it's little advantage for *Heaven, to be chang'd* to Earth," rather, "the Author gave it: *And earth be* CHAIN'D *to Heav'n and Heav'n to Earth*."[39] In Bentley's reading, earth does not change to Heaven, as in Toland's rendering of Miltonic cosmology. Not continuous, but contiguous, spirit and matter were separable, and thus Bentley made Milton safe for the Newtonian cosmos, where heaven and earth remained independent, separated by the newly fashioned Newtonian void.[40] Where Toland's metaphysics everywhere asserts continuity – there is "no Space void, nor a last Barrier" – Bentley was sure to instate a clear barrier in his universe between spirit and matter; so Newton's "absolute space" finds a place in *Paradise Lost* (*P* 19).

Does this mean that the "real" Milton, reflected in the works of Toland, was occluded by the orthodox creation of Bentley's works? Both yes, and no. For the cosmology of *Paradise Lost* approximates neither Bentley's dualism nor Toland's monism; neither set of discursive contexts are adequate to the task of understanding Milton, by themselves. Milton's monism, if one can speak of it, is persistently qualified. In the Creation represented in Book 7, all the elements of the Creation seem to overflow with their own autonomous energies: the egg "bursting with kindly rupture" (419); "[t]he Libbard, and the Tyger, as the Moale / Rising" (467–8); the "swift Stag" with its "branching head" (469–70) – all combine to suggest that the teeming "fertile Woomb" (454) is an independent agent of its own creation. The image of the "Main Ocean" fermenting "the great Mother" – the "Embryon," earth – already "[s]atiate with genial moisture" to "conceave" strengthens the sense of creation as both independent and autonomous (277, 281–2). Seeming to drift into a metaphysical Manichaeism, the "torrent rapture," hasting "with glad precipitance" flows with "Serpent errour wandring" (299, 291, 302). But the monist account of an inspirited self-generating matter is finally balanced by the simple account of the "Earth / God made" (335–6). These two competing narrative perspectives – one gesturing toward monism, the other dualism – are manifest in the rendering of the divine fiat: "Boundless the Deep, because I am who fill / Infinitude, nor vacuous the space. / Though I uncircumscrib'd my self retire" (168–70). Milton's God is simultaneously present in his Creation, filling infinitude, though he is paradoxically, "uncircumscrib'd," and retired. In Milton's complex representation, there is no "vacuous" space (as in Bentley's emendation), nor is God to be identified with his Creation, for He withholds his presence: "I … put *not* forth my goodness" (170–1; emphasis added). These lines confound simple monist or dualist readings. The epic as a whole, however, as Balachandra Rajan writes, resorts to both monist and dualist perspectives to provide competing – though not necessarily contradictory – "translations" of "the greatest of all events.[41]

The complexity of Milton's metaphysics is present even in Book 5, the ontological centerpiece of the evidence for what John Guillory calls Milton's "ideological monism."[42] Even here, the process by which "substance" is "refin'd" and by "gradual scale … sublim'd" has no immediate relevance to Adam and Eve. They are told rather to enjoy their "fill what happiness this happie state / Can comprehend, incapable of more"

(5.503–5). Which is to say, the "all in all" – the full identity between spirit and matter which Toland attributes to *this* world – Milton attributes only to a post-history when "[t]he World shall burn, and from her ashes spring / New Heav'n and Earth" (3.334–5). Similarly, even as Milton affirms the possibility of the return to "one first matter all," he asserts "proportion" and "degree." Thomas Newton's 1749 edition of the poem notes in this passage what he calls Milton's "mistaken metaphysics." "The notion of matter refining into spirit," Newton writes, "is by no means observing the *bounds proportion'd to each kind*." Not only does Milton, as Newton writes, evidence "false notions in philosophy," but he seems to contradict himself.[43] Newton's eighteenth-century sensibility could not entertain the possibility that Milton's metaphysics defied the more simple dichotomies of Enlightenment thought. Though sensitive to a textual crux in the poem, Newton's Enlightenment prejudices kick in – the resistance to poetic paradox shared by some critics today – and he calls Milton's account contradictory. But to Milton himself, body may "up to spirit work" – to fulfill his conception of the end of days of "all in all" – but in the "meanwhile" (the Miltonic shorthand for time as we experience it), the parts of the Creation are "plac't," in "their several active Sphears assignd."

It's not only Milton's earlier editors who sense the ambiguity of Milton's verse. Even the most articulate expositors of Milton's monistic tendencies, Fallon and Rogers, admit Milton's qualification of the full monist contiguity between creator and created. Fallon notes that the metaphysics of "emanation" is qualified by the stratified great chain of being; while Rogers acknowledges the lack of a "full homogenous saturation of all matter with spirit" (attributing it to Milton's "political resignation" during the post-Restoration period).[44] To be sure, the passage undoubtedly manifests the monist tendency in Milton's thought, but the assertion of continuity between spirit and matter, creator and created, is qualified by powerful dualist undercurrents. Though there is the possibility of "continuity," as Milton writes in the wholly different context of the *Areopagitica*, things can be "but contiguous in this world."[45] Bentley, however, could not suffer the ambivalences of *Paradise Lost*: the seeming conviction that Milton's great epic had been infected by the metaphysics of contemporary radicals pushes him, as Herman argues, to provide a version of the epic safe for orthodoxy. Thus, in the interest of his own polemical agenda, Bentley had opposed his dualist and orthodox version of Milton against the radical and heretical, but no less partial, version of Milton forwarded by Toland. Driven by the interests of party and the categories of philosophy (which existed in a post-Enlightenment world, but not for Milton), both

Bentley *and* Toland are emblematic of a critical tradition which has created conceptions of the poet which are one-sided.

The complexity of Milton's work may demonstrate the need to complicate Skinner's model, which emphasizes tracing "the relations between an utterance" and the wider "linguistic context" for that utterance.[46] Indeed, the methodological emphasis upon the recovery of contexts has recently come under attack for its potentially reductive tendencies. Christopher Lane, for example, asserting the irreducibility of texts to contexts, has proclaimed what he calls, the "poverty of context"; while Peter Burke, situating himself within the Cambridge School, has nonetheless elaborated "the price to be paid" by an uncritical use of the term.[47] Burke, in the event, emphasizes not "context," but rather, "contexts in the plural." For, he writes, what looks like "'the' context for an idea, object, statement, or event generally turns out to be more than 'a' context."[48] Milton becomes a model subject for a historiographical inquiry on the lines which Burke elaborates, one which emphasizes not so much *the* context, but rather the diverse (and sometimes competing) *contexts* for his work. It is not, then, that there are a plurality of Miltonic ideologies as Corns writes, but that a complex Miltonic corpus lends itself to a plurality of appropriations. This is certainly not to return to the unsituated ahistoricism of the New Criticism, but a call for a New Milton Criticism informed and enacting a more complex Skinnerian method, soliciting – not rejecting – Miltonic paradox. In this reading, Cambridge School Methodology remains impoverished only insofar as it focuses on a singular context, and not *contexts*.

Pocock, in a corrective to the early methodology of the Cambridge School, emphasized "patterns of polyvalence."[49] Following Pocock, in the 1988 *Meaning and Context* volume, Skinner, citing Kuhn, acknowledges that "whenever we report our beliefs, we inevitably employ some classificatory scheme with the result that none of these different schemes" can "ever be uncontentiously employed to report undisputable facts." Though Skinner does not deny that "that there are undisputable facts to be reported,"[50] he does acknowledge, opening up the way for a diversity of approaches, that different "schemes" come to reveal different aspects of the world.[51] Skinner is even more explicit about the reciprocal relationship between subjective and objective constraints in interpretation when he claims, in the same volume, that historians "inevitably approach the past in the light of contemporary paradigms and presuppositions, the influence of which may easily serve to mislead us at every turn." Skinner's insistence upon the role of "contemporary paradigms and presuppositions" may have been implicit in his earlier work; the acknowledgment of that role in the response to his critics shows Skinner demonstrating an awareness – indeed incorporating – others' criticism of his own methodology. Further, with his *Reason and Rhetoric in the Philosophy of Hobbes* of 1996, Skinner turned, for his understanding of *Leviathan*, not only to the engagement controversy, the local context (which he invoked in an essay of 1972), but to ancient theorists of rhetoric as well. Similarly, in the essay on Milton for the *London Review*, Skinner turns his attention not only to Milton's contemporaries, but also to Roman historians, Livy, Sallust, and Tacitus – evidencing a taste for the complexity entailed by considering contexts in the plural.[52]

From this perspective, the New Milton Criticism will, following Rogers, turn to Harvey and Glisson (Milton's vitalist predecessors) as well as, following Silver, Luther and Calvin (the sources of his dualism) – which all equally elicit truths about Milton's metaphysics. Skinnerian contextualism would then lead to Gadamerian historiography and reception history, and to the mis-readings (or partial readings) of both Toland and Bentley. Such an approach will, I suspect, not reveal a Milton mired in contradictions, but a Milton who argues through paradoxes that confound the oversimplified categories of party politics and Enlightenment philosophy. This manifestation of the New Milton Criticism may rescue Milton from impoverished versions of Burrow's "New Model Criticism," where Miltonic texts are merely mined for their "sedimentary layers of topicality," and *Paradise Lost* transformed "into little more than superior belated newsbook."[53] Milton's works may be – indeed should be – elaborated through reference to pamphlet wars and political contexts, but they cannot be reduced, as they sometimes are, to such categories. Skinner has taught Miltonists the importance of the disciplinary rigors of the historian; though Miltonists should remain committed to a set of texts – not only poetic but political as well – which show the extent to which some models from intellectual history are inadequate. However, the Cambridge emphasis on contexts in the plural, becoming a kind of Geertzian "thick description," will render a Milton not reduced into polemical caricature or philosophical simplicity, but rather reveal the complex intentions of a figure who continues to confound our expectations.

NOTES

1 For Skinner's engagement with J. L. Austin, see Quentin Skinner, "'Social Meaning' and the Explanation of Social Action," in James Tully (ed.), *Meaning and Context: Quentin Skinner and his Critics* (Princeton University Press, 1988), pp. 79–96.

2 Sharon Achinstein, *Milton and the Revolutionary Reader* (Princeton University Press, 1994), p. 6.
3 Nigel Smith, *Literature and Revolution in England, 1640–1660* (New Haven: Yale University Press, 1994), p. 3. In the following year, the essays published in *Milton and Republicanism*, co-edited by Quentin Skinner with David Armitage and Armand Himy (Cambridge University Press, 1995), almost all show evidence of Skinner's method and influence.
4 David Norbrook, *Writing the English Republic: Poetry, Rhetoric and Politics, 1620–1667* (Cambridge University Press, 1999), p. 10.
5 For the convention program, see: http://ies.sas.ac.uk/events/conferences/2008/Milton/programme.htm; "What Does it Mean to be a Free Person: Quentin Skinner on Milton," *London Review of Books* (May 22, 2008), 16–18.
6 Colin Burrow, "New Model Criticism," *London Review of Books* (June 19, 2008), 25.
7 See Tully (ed.), *Meaning and Context*, esp. pp. 70–2, and pp. 233–4.
8 Ibid., pp. 260, 279. Skinner's critique of Wimsatt may seem, at this point, both dated and irrelevant. For his confrontation with a triumvirate of more contemporary figures (Barthes, Foucault, and Derrida), see pp. 272–81.
9 Ibid., p. 77.
10 Thomas Corns, "'Some rousing motions': The Plurality of Miltonic Ideology," in Thomas Healy and Jonathan Sawday (eds.), *Literature and the Civil War* (Cambridge University Press, 1990), p. 140.
11 Keith Stavely, *The Politics of Milton's Prose Style* (New Haven: Yale University Press, 1975), p. 112.
12 Tully (ed.), *Meaning and Context*, p. 77.
13 Of course, Milton criticism is itself a varied enterprise: and the desire for Miltonic consistency not local to Skinnerians. So while Stanley Fish extrapolates from "troublesome contradictions" to the "one true interpretation of *Paradise Lost*" through his theological assumptions, it's Skinnerians who have tended to reduce Milton to clear and singular positions through importing the methods of Cambridge intellectual history. Stanley Fish, *Surprised by Sin* (New York: St. Martin's Press, 1967), pp. 37, 272.
14 Rachel Trubowitz, "Body Politics in *Paradise Lost*," *PMLA* 122, 2 (2006), 388–404; Victoria Silver, *Imperfect Sense* (Princeton University Press, 2001). Stephen Fallon, *Milton Among the Philosophers: Poetry and Materialism in Seventeenth Century England* (Ithaca, NY: Cornell University Press, 1991), p. 16; John Rogers, *The Matter of Revolution: Science, Poetry and Politics in the Age of Milton* (Ithaca, NY: Cornell University Press, 1996).
15 Peter C. Herman, "Paradigms Lost, Paradigms Found: The New Milton Criticism," *Literature Compass* 2 (2005), 13. Stanley Fish, *How Milton Works* (Cambridge, MA: Harvard University Press, 2001), p. 14.
16 Nicholas von Maltzahn, "Wood, Allam, and the Oxford Milton," *Milton Studies* 32 (1994), 169.
17 Richard Bentley (ed.), *Milton's Paradise Lost* (London, 1732). For accounts of Bentley's edition, see Robert Bourdette, "A Sense of the Sacred: Richard

Bentley's Reading of *Paradise Lost*," *Milton Studies* 24 (1988), 73–106, and my *Milton's Warring Angels* (Cambridge University Press, 1997), pp. 107–32.
18 Leslie Stephen and Sidney Lee (eds.), *Dictionary of National Biography* (Oxford University Press, 1917), vol. XIX, pp. 918–19.
19 John Toland, *Amyntor or, A Defence of Milton's Life* (London, 1699), pp. 5–7.
20 John Toland (ed.), *A Complete Collection of the Historical, Political and Miscellaneous Works of John Milton* (Amsterdam, 1698), p. 5.
21 Rogers, *The Matter of Revolution*, pp. 1–16; Margaret C. Jacob, *Newtonians and the English Revolution 1689–1720* (New York: Routledge, 1990), p. 24.
22 George Sensabaugh, *That Grand Whig, Milton* (Stanford University Press, 1952), p. 192; John Toland, *Letters to Serena* (London, 1704), c3 (cited within as *LS*).
23 Yirmiyahu Yovel, *Spinoza and Other Heretics: The Adventures of Immanence* (Princeton University Press, 1989), p. ix.
24 Margaret C. Jacob, "Toland and the Newtonian Ideology," *Journal of the Warburg and Courtauld Institutes* 32 (1969), 307–31. For the suggestion that Toland's sources were ancient (Anaxagoras) and not early modern, see Jeffrey R. Wigelsworth, "A pre-Socratic source for John Toland's *Pantheisticon*," *History of European Ideas* 34 (2008), 61–5.
25 John Toland, "An Account of Jordano Bruno's Book Of the Infinite Universe and Innumerable Worlds," in *A Collection of Several Pieces of Mr. John Toland* (London, 1726), 1.346 (cited within as *AJB*).
26 John Toland, *Pantheisticon* (London, 1751), p. 34 (cited within as *P*).
27 Jacob, "Toland and the Newtonian Ideology," 16.
28 Richard Bentley, *The Works of Richard Bentley*, Alexander Dyce (ed.) (New York: AMS Press, 1966), pp. 1, 35.
29 H. S. Thayer (ed.), *Newton's Philosophy of Nature* (New York: Hafner Publishing Company, 1953), pp. 43, 177.
30 The Cambridge Platonists most famously tried to mediate that void with their own poetic invention, that of the "plastic power." Thus Ralph Cudworth wrote in his compendious *True Intellectual System* that the "plastick nature" prints "its Stamps and Signatures every where throughout the World; so that God ... will not only be the Beginning and End, but also the Middle of all things." See C. A. Patrides, *The Cambridge Platonists* (Cambridge University Press, 1969), p. 293.
31 Jacob, "Toland and the Newtonian Ideology," 331.
32 John T. Shawcross (ed.), *John Milton, The Critical Heritage: 1732–1801* (London: Routledge, 1972), p. 89.
33 William Baron, *Regicides No Saints Nor Martyrs* (London, 1700), p. 132.
34 Herman, "Paradigms Lost," 10.
35 Victoria Silver, whose account of Milton (Silver, *Imperfect Sense*) emphasizes the insurmountable incommensurability between the creator and the created world, dismisses the "recent currency" of arguments for Milton's "so-called heresies" and "animist materialism," claiming that they, in fact, emerge from the "Brunoian fascination with the occult" (p. 359 n.12).

36 J. G. A. Pocock, "Within the Margins: The Definitions of Orthodoxy," in Roger Lund (ed.), *The Margins of Orthodoxy* (Cambridge University Press, 1995), pp. 33–53.
37 Bentley was also likely thinking of the Locke of the *Essay* who, as John Yolton writes, entertained the notion of "thinking matter" – that God could "add to a system of matter the power of thought." See John Yolton, *Thinking Matter: Materialism in Eighteenth Century Britain* (Minneapolis: University of Minnesota Press, 1983), p. 17.
38 Richard Bentley (ed.), *Milton's Paradise Lost*, p. 162.
39 Ibid., p. 222.
40 The publication of Newton's hermetical and alchemical writings over the past decades raises the tantalizing suggestion that Newtonian metaphysics also manifests a complexity about the relationship between spirit and matter. In an early alchemical treatise, Newton sought the "corporeal spirit," or the "living universal innate spirit of matter." For more on Newton's alchemical writings, see Betty Jo Teeter Dobbs, *The Janus Face of Genius: The Role of Alchemy in Newton's Thought* (Cambridge University Press, 1991), as well as my "Newton in Jerusalem," *Azure* 30 (2007), 27–31.
41 For Rajan, Milton's "philosophical monism" is qualified, "difficult to embody in a poem that relies so heavily on binaries." The monistic and dualistic "voices" of the epic are equally present in "a poem whose orchestration is persistently contrapuntal." See Elizabeth Sauer (ed.), *Milton and the Climates of Reading: Essays by Balachandra Rajan* (Toronto University Press, 2006), pp. 120, 114, 118.
42 John Guillory, *Poetic Authority: Spenser, Milton and Literary History* (New York, Columbia University Press, 1983), p. 149.
43 Thomas Newton (ed.), John Milton, *Paradise Lost*, 2nd edn. (London, 1750), 1.391.
44 Fallon, *Milton Among the Philosophers*, p. 103; Rogers, *Matter of Revolution*, p. 111.
45 Don Wolfe (ed.), *Complete Prose Works of John Milton* (New Haven: Yale University Press, 1959), vol. II, p. 555.
46 Tully (ed.), *Meaning and Context*, p. 272.
47 Christopher Lane, "The Poverty of Context," *PMLA* 118 (2003), 450–69; Peter Burke, "Context in Context," *Common Knowledge* 8, 1 (2002), 174. See also Burke's citation of Alain Boureau, who notes the dangers of circularity in contextual methodology: "Too often the context is implicitly or unconsciously constructed as a function of the explanation it is called on to provide" (p. 172).
48 Burke, "Context," 174. The emphasis of plurality of contexts should not be confused with a Derridean emphasis on the "joyous affirmation" of the free play of language which would render Skinner's project impossible. For Skinner's response to Derridean attacks upon his work, see "'Social Meaning,'" p. 272.
49 J. G. A. Pocock, *Virtue, Commerce and History* (Cambridge University Press, 1985), p. 9; for a notable exception, see Tully (ed.), *Meaning and Context*, p. 338, n.172.

50 Ibid., p. 257. For an earlier acknowledgment of the influence of Kuhn on the Cambridge School, see J. G. A. Pocock, *Virtue, Commerce and History*, pp. 3, 61.
51 Quentin Skinner, *Vision of Politics* (Cambridge University Press, 2002), asserts an unexpected affinity – despite earlier resistance – with the works of Hans Georg Gadamer: Gadamer's arguments, writes Skinner, embody "a salutary reminder about the need to be aware of our inevitable tendency towards pre-judgement and the fitting of evidence into pre-existing patterns of interpretation and explanation" (p. 15).
52 Quentin Skinner, *Reason and Rhetoric in the Philosophy of Hobbes* (Cambridge University Press, 1996); for his essay on the engagement controversy, see "Conquest and Consent: Hobbes and the Engagement Controversy," in G. E. Aylmer (ed.), *The Interregnum: The Quest for Settlement* (London: Palgrave Macmillan, 1972), pp. 79–98.
53 Burrow, "New Model Criticism," 25.

Afterword

Joseph A. Wittreich

> Criticism is about taking sides, ... but not without forgetting there is another side, which we should be thankful for because it makes us better by contest.
>
> Gordon Teskey[1]

John Milton belongs to a special class of writers, and his last poems (especially *Paradise Lost*) belong to a singular category of works, whose grounds, as Louis Menand attests, "have entirely eroded"; and yet, ironically, "we can no longer understand the way things are without taking [such works] into account."[2] If, as Menand writes, their "afterlife is in certain respects more impressive than [their] life," it is because such works, written with the hope that the world will not willingly let them die, cannot (as Menand quips) "be killed."[3] They just will not go away and, often born of controversy, continue to engender controversy. In Milton's case, the argument is over whether Milton is a poet "obedient of submission" or of "subversive mutiny."[4]

If there seem to be two Miltons, in the last poems there also seem to be two different poems circulating at once – poem and counter-poem, "the official one," as Balachandra Rajan would have it, and "the true poem ... overthrow[ing] the establishment exercise."[5] The salient feature of Milton's last poems is their propensity for reconsidering, then revising themselves. As Edward Phillips reports, Milton initially cast *Paradise Lost* as a tragedy, and thereupon turned the poem into an epic in ten, and then twelve books.[6] The poem's unstable genre matches its shifting structure, its moving center, as further demonstrated by Milton's admission on the title page to the poem's second edition (1674) that the text has been "Revised and Augmented" (3). Later issues of the 1667 *Paradise Lost* contain supplementary materials: a printer's note to the reader, the poet's note on why his poem rhymes not, arguments first printed seriatim and, starting in 1674, appended to individual books of the poem. The arguments themselves are in a sometimes asymmetrical relationship with the books they accompany and, on the issue of whether God drives Satan from Heaven or whether Satan hurls himself, contradict each other. Dedicatory poems supplement the second edition of *Paradise Lost*, shifting contexts and issuing competing directives for reading the poem. Within its first five lines, the narrative of losing Paradise is displaced by the story of its recovery. Moreover *Paradise Lost* and *Paradise Regained* offer strikingly different accounts of how Paradise lost will be recovered, whether on the cross or in the desert, whether by God alone, or by God and man working collaboratively. *Samson Agonistes* yields discrepant interpretations, depending on whether one reads the poem separately or together with *Paradise Regained*, "To which [it] is added" – and, in the addition, apparently subordinated. Milton's final poems seem designed to engender uncertainty and incite controversy.

I: THE MILTON CONTROVERSY

As Peter C. Herman and Elizabeth Sauer observe in this volume's Introduction, in one sense we find nothing at all new in the New Milton Criticism. Instead, we are drawn back to the first phase of *Paradise Lost*'s reception history. Here, Milton emerges not as Stanley Fish's "absolutist poet,"[7] but as the vexing poet/polemicist insinuated by the Hobarts, the wily poet/politician of H. L. Benthem, the troubled and troubling theologian of Theodore Haak, Samuel Barrow's poet of hidden truths and mysterious discoveries, the poet of perplexing explanations whom Andrew Marvell sought expediently to closet, the poet – "a new track making" – eventually acknowledged by Thomas Ellwood, and a poet so irksome to some readers (such as John Dryden) that they felt obliged to weed from *Paradise Lost* its annoying contradictions.[8]

In possession of a changing mind, this Milton – a poet of ambivalences, complexities, and uncertainties in conversation not only with his times but with himself – is subverted not from within but from without, initially by a crew of traditionalists who, over time, have morphed into today's court of neoconservatives. Before Joseph Addison and Richard Bentley set about emulating Milton, John Dennis and Daniel Defoe sought to discredit him as an erring theologian, assuming that the function of criticism – *their* Milton criticism at any rate – is correction. Dennis and Defoe, like their successors Bentley and Zachary Pearce, correct not just Milton, but representations of him by John Toland (as William Kolbrener argues), taking their lead from the often misunderstood example of Marvell's dedicatory poem and from the critical initiatives evident in the later published imitations of *Paradise Lost* by Dryden and Lucy Hutchinson.

If Samuel Barrow fixes inordinate attention on Book 6, where he thinks the secrets of Milton's poem are hidden, he does so at the poem's (at Raphael's) prompting: "to thee I have reveal'd / What might have else to human Race bin hid" (6.895–6).[9] Initially "misdoubting his intent" (8), Marvell worried that Milton's poem may contain a revenge fantasy. Marvell thus brakes against rebellious reading with the assurance that, despite appearances, Milton remains faithful to Scripture, not wanting to "ruine … / The sacred Truths" (ll.7–8). By implication, Milton toes the line of Christian orthodoxy even as Marvell also aligns Milton's epic with the subversive tradition of prophecy – "Just Heav'n thee like *Tiresias* … / Rewards with Prophesie thy loss of sight" (ll.43–4) – and, further, hints in the dedicatory poem's final lines ("Thy verse … / In Number, Weight, and Measure, needs not Rhime") (ll.53–4) at Milton's master theme of liberty by alluding to Milton's note (added in 1668) justifying the poem's rhymeless verse: "ancient liberty recover'd to Heroic Poem from the … modern bondage of Rimeing" (p. 10). Marvell's reflections leave the reader bewildered and, accompanied as they are by Milton's own preliminary words to the reader, create the impression that, with poet and reader in compact, *Paradise Lost* will complete itself by poem's end in the mind of its readership, even if that requires Marvell, along with Barrow, to perform complex mediatorial roles.

Marvell's poem, an attempt to inoculate Milton against expected criticism, exemplifies what Annabel Patterson calls "oblique discourse," wherein writers, through strategies of indirection, often in preliminary material, develop the art of not meaning exactly what they say, with Marvell, in this instance according to Patterson, representing Milton as "a Prometheus without recklessness, a sacred pioneer."[10] And Patterson continues: "Marvell and Dryden were each, from different points of view, aware of what Milton was up to," with Dryden later taming the poem that Marvell would save through an act of "protective disingenuity."[11] When Marvell and Dryden are thus yoked together (the two, it should be remembered, walked with Milton in Cromwell's funeral procession), we hear ideological antiphony, much more so than in the pairing of Barrow and Marvell, where we witness something more akin to ideological mobility, each of these poets placing Milton within different interpretive traditions, classical and scriptural, but also together allying Milton with a poetics of disclosure in a poem that promises to "unfould / The secrets of another world, perhaps / Not lawful to reveal" (5.568–70). Poems, which would differently contextualize *Paradise Lost*, also host alternative premises concerning interpretation, and then tease us with one, then another of the interpretive possibilities before we ever cross the threshold into *Paradise Lost* itself. Once there, as Peter C. Herman so masterfully shows, questions prevail and answers proliferate in ways that complicate, even confound, interpretation. In the process, interpretation itself, now resembling (to borrow Herman's words) "a fascinating puzzle," requires adjudication and becomes stubbornly provisional.

Pace Stanley Fish, the prophetic Milton, the subversive Milton, this polysemous and paradoxical poet, is not postmodernism's refashioning of the Milton of Romantic liberalism. Rather, the Romantic's Milton is the *ur* Milton of critical tradition, as well as the Janus-faced poet of Miltonic Romanticism, a compound of Shelley's – and Coleridge's – poets. Shelley's Milton hit then-current orthodoxies with a mighty mental blow, demolishing the most oppressive forms of religion and politics; and his *Paradise Lost* (and one supposes *Paradise Regained*) "contains within itself a philosophical refutation of that system of which, by a strange and natural antithesis, it has been a chief popular support."[12] Coleridge's Milton, despite traces of Arianism and Socinianism in his epics, is faithful to scriptural texts and their venerable truths, borrows his imagery from and founds his theology upon them, and displays judgment and skill, as well as genius, in his biblical adaptations, with the proviso that this "most interesting of the Devil's Biographers" represents Satan and Beelzebub as "different Persons" when "in the Scriptures they are different names of the same Evil Being."[13]

Coleridge's complaint echoes Defoe's earlier one that Milton's Satan is a flat contradiction of the most express declarations of Holy Writ; that his thinking is not always "reconcilable with Scripture, and that the job of Milton's critics," once alerted to such difficulties, is to bring Scripture and poetry into accord. Contradictions are sometimes the erasures of careful reading. Other times they are stubborn features of Milton's texts, usually breeding uncertainties, with Milton sometimes overturning his own uncertainties rather than, as Stephen Fallon proposes, spawning certainties to which he is steadfastly committed.[14]

Like Dryden, both Lucy Hutchinson and Daniel Defoe, the former implicitly, the latter explicitly, defend orthodox Christianity against Milton's supposed sallies against it. Start with Hutchinson. Written before but published after Dryden's *The State of Innocence* (1677), Hutchinson's *Order and Disorder* (1679) nowhere mentions Milton, but repeatedly in the first five cantos tries to free *Paradise Lost* (and perhaps *Paradise Regained*) from "blasphemous inventions" and "human error" – in Hutchinson's words, from "the pernicious and perplexed maze of humane inventions."[15] As Hutchinson explains, she wants to rid the Creation and Fall story of all that is blasphemous and brutish, of the "foolish fancies" and "wild impressions" and "defective Traditions" that are now associated with it.[16] This means that Hutchinson will not countenance Milton's dilations of Scripture, nor his integrations of classical with Christian mythology. Moreover, Hutchinson proves to be an equally resistant reader of Milton when it comes to explaining how the lost Paradise will be recovered.

To Milton's claim that with no middle flight, he will soar beyond the Aonian Mount, Hutchinson responds: "Let not my thoughts beyond their bounds aspire" (1.41), in effect turning Raphael's advice to Adam against Milton himself: "Sollicit not thy thoughts with matters hid ... be lowlie wise" (8.167, 173). Concerning Milton's depiction of Adam pleading for a mate, she proffers: "Whether he begged a mate it is not known" (3.312); and of Milton's celestial battle, she chides: "But circumstances that we cannot know / Of their rebellion and their overthrow / We will not dare t'invent, nor will we take / Guesses" (4.43–6). Hutchinson's version of the Genesis story corrects Milton's at nearly every point of transgression, indicating that some women of Milton's time, even if they gender their own writings with female perspectives and women's concerns, are more in the clutches of patriarchy than Milton ever seems to have been himself. They know that transgressions and contradictions of Scripture signal doubt and produce "*uncertainty*," with Hutchinson then opposing the uncertainties of Milton's epic with her own steadfast commitment to things "true / And only *certain*."[17]

Defoe's attitude toward Milton, however, owes more to Dryden than Hutchinson. As we have recently been reminded (after centuries of forgetting), *The State of Innocence*, "Dryden's best-selling dramatic work during the Restoration," went through ten different editions and then, as Addison's *Spectator* essays on *Paradise Lost* are published, is repeatedly performed at Punch's theater in Covent Garden as a puppet show.[18] Hutchinson and Dryden, performances of Dryden's "Opera" and Addison's *Spectator* papers on *Paradise Lost*, together conspire against powerful counter-forces to produce the Milton of religious orthodoxy. Hence Defoe moves to let religious orthodoxy repeatedly trump Milton's heterodoxies.

Defoe's chief targets are the anachronisms of Milton's referring to saints in Heaven before there were any saints there, and his locating the exaltation of the Son much earlier in time than it occurs – as provocation for the celestial battle rather than as a manifestation of the Resurrection.[19] Moreover, Defoe questions whether there was ever copulation in Paradise, and then complains about Milton's forgetting "most egregiously," and "erroneously," that Beelzebub, Lucifer, Belial, Mammon, etc., are "all names proper and peculiar to *Satan* himself"; and, finally, chastises Milton for such "unpardonable improprieties" as angels dancing in Heaven and devils singing in Hell, not to mention Milton's "strain'd" and "trifling" representation of Pandemonium.[20]

The interpretive straitjacket Dryden, Hutchinson, and Defoe would impose strains against both Milton's poems and their source material. Both epics emerge as a new revelation, a scriptural supplement, accommodating rival hermeneutics, arraying different versions of the Creation, Fall, and Recovery stories, dueling cosmologies, and in *Paradise Regained*, both literalist and figurative readings of the wilderness experience. Each of these poems is in interpretive dialogue both with itself and (after 1671) with one another. Milton's last poems – all of them – are sites of contestation, just as each of them derives from sites of contestation in its scriptural source. In Genesis and the Gospels, in Genesis, Judges, Hebrews and Revelation, stories are at odds with one another and details within them are in conflict with each other, which is only to remind us, in the words of Rosemary Radford Ruether, that "conflict was so naturalized into Christianity that it could be completely identified with the Christian tradition itself."[21]

Understandably, therefore, these same features spill over into Milton's poems, where the voice of the narrator, so often confused with Milton's voice, may not be Milton's voice at all; where the teller and his tale pull oppositely, the one toward determinacy and the other toward indeterminacy of meaning. The narrator's allegations, the narrative's demonstrations are at odds – deliberately so. Thus, we are told in Book 1 of *Paradise Lost*, by the epic narrator, first that Satan's own "Pride / Had cast him out from Heav'n" (1.36–7), then (almost in the same breath) that "Him the Almighty Power / Hurl'd headlong flaming from th' Ethereal Skie" (1.44–5; cf. 2.178–82), these latter verses reinforcing the "The Argument" to Book 1 that "*Satan* ... was by the command of God driven out of Heaven" (p. 11), only to learn later from Raphael that "headlong *themselves* they threw / Down from the verge of Heav'n" (6.864–5; my italics), which, in contradiction to what we are told in the Argument to Book 1, is what the author of the poem, in his Argument to Book 6, also instructs: "they leap down with horrour and confusion into the place of punishment prepar'd for them in the Deep" (p. 149). Fearful of the "red right hand" of God (2.174), Moloch worries that "*One day*" they "*shall* be hurl'd / ... the sport and prey / Of racking whirlwinds" (2.178, 180–2; my italics), while Beelzebub conjectures that God's newly created sons may one day be driven "as we are driven" and "Hurl'd headlong" (2.366, 374) and Sin recalls that "down they fell / Driv'n headlong ... down / Into this Deep"

(2.771–3). Chaos, though, recalling the same event, tells Satan of his host fleeing "not in silence" (2.994) – but noisily, perhaps "bellowing," as does Moloch in 6.362, In any case, the explanation by Chaos better accords with the stipulations in the Argument to Book 6 where, again, with the Son "driving into the midst of his Enemies," the rebellious angels are said to "leap down with horrour and confusion into … the Deep" (p. 149).

The devils offer one account of their expulsion (they are hurled by an angry God from Heaven); the poem's author, in his Arguments, another; and Raphael yet a third; in his version, the Son, in whom "all his Father [is] full exprest" (6.720), "Not [meaning] to destroy" (6.855), "check'd" his rage (6.853), then "Drove them" (6.858) until "headlong themselves they threw / Down … / … to the bottomless pit" (6.864–6). These clashing narratives, exhibited by the poem's author but also mediated by him, are mediated, likewise, by Chaos and, more obliquely perhaps, by the fabled story of Mulciber who "fell / From Heav'n, … thrown by angry *Jove*" – a story "they relate, / Erring" (1.1.740–1, 746–7). Initially, the insights of the author of *Paradise Lost*, together with his poem's narrator, both representatives of fallen consciousness, are pitted against those emerging from the angelic consciousness of Raphael and his narrative, although Raphael himself is by no means a flawless narrator, while the author of the poem is clearly in possession (as was the author of *Lycidas*) of an evolving consciousness. The secret of this poem's narrative, its yield, is graduated insight; and the insight folded into this tear in the text of Milton's poem reinforces its free will theology: that the devils, no less so than man, are responsible for their own Fall. They leap, they hurl themselves, into Hell.

Simply stated, interpretations enforced by the poem's narrative may undermine those enunciated by its narrator – like his insistence that Eve, not Adam, falls deceived by Satan: Eve is "deceiv'd," she alone is "deceiv'd" (1.35), while "he scrupl'd not to eat / … not deceav'd, / But fondly overcome with Femal charm" (9.997–9). Both God and Satan speak as one and say, as Satan does in *Paradise Regained*, that "Adam and his facile consort Eve / Lost Paradise deceived by me" (1.51–2). In God's words from *Paradise Lost*: "Man falls deceiv'd" (3.130). Similarly, in Book 10, Satan says "Man I deceav'd" (10.496); Eve allows the same, that Adam she has "Unhappilie deceav'd" (10.917) – a point with which Adam has already concurred: "Fool'd and beguil'd, by him thou, I by thee" (10.880) and a point he will make again (but in another context) concerning himself: "I was farr deceav'd" (11.783). The only character in the poem not susceptible to deception, as Moloch discerns (2.188–90), and Books 3.682–4 and 10.6–9 make clear, is God himself. Yet the crucial point to be made here is that, nesting in this entire discourse, is a passage from Timothy 2:14 ("and Adam was not deceived, but the woman was deceived and became a transgressor"). Far from confirming the clichés of patriarchy, *Paradise Lost* contravenes them. It roots them out. As founding texts for the myths of modern culture, Milton's epics stand in dialogic, not monologic, relation to hermeneutical traditions and thus are repositories for overlapping, incongruent discourses, as well as sites from which to observe not so much a received myth and dominant ideology as the crevices and contradictions in both.

In addition to the fissures in the story, Milton's narrative regularly curls back upon itself, becoming self-reflexive, and in the process, reflects upon its own reliability and limitations: "thus they relate, / Erring" (1.746–7); "to tell how, if Art could tell" (4.236), "*Hesperian* Fables true, / If true, here only" (4.250–1), until we eventually begin to wonder whether, like God's nature, Milton's art does not at times transgress the boundaries of "Rule or Art" (5.297) and then, in the telling of the celestial battle, wonder just how much correspondence exists between earth and Heaven (5.571–6) and how much knowledge can be gleaned from stories folded so deeply into allegory. Such questioning persists into the next book where we will learn, as Blake later teaches us, that events in time spring forth in a moment, in the pulsation of an artery: "Immediate are the Acts of God … / … but to human ears / Cannot without process of speech be told" (7.176–8). A moment in time, thus anatomized, exfoliates through time in "looping" narratives, as Judith Herz explains, with an often suspect, scrambled chronology; with fissures, gaps, and contradictions fracturing sequence and baffling certainty; in narratives that, never allowing for "a resting place," are "cross-grained, both light and darkness coming in through the cracks."

The New Milton Criticism showcased in this volume would effect another Reformation, this one in literary criticism, and like the Reformation of the sixteenth century, would return us to origins, not now of Christianity but of initial perceptions, earliest understandings of Milton's literary enterprise. It understands full well that, in the first century and a half after its publication, *Paradise Lost*, as it was conventionalized, was subjected to repeated disfigurations: its rhymeless verse was made to rhyme, the poem was turned into a play and its poetry recast as prose. It was interpreted and reinterpreted – *correctively* – through illustration, translation, and imitation and, at the same time, weeded of its contradictions, was bowdlerized, evangelized, catechized, and anthologized, these strategies working in concert to realign Milton's epics with the orthodoxies they flaunted. Hence, the lessons learned from studying Milton's last poems in relation to the Bible and its hermeneutic traditions are strikingly similar to those garnered from reading each poem within the context of literary imitations inspired by it, or within the context of the poems' emerging interpretive traditions. In the simple formulation of Christopher Hill: Milton is "not an orthodox reader"[22] or interpreter of Scripture, his project involving less the reproduction of biblical tales than the re-imagining of their myths in light of current politics and contemporary history.

The most powerful and eloquent spokesperson for those newly bent upon returning Milton to orthodoxy is Stanley Fish, whose mantra is that the critic's job is not to be new but to be right. To get Milton right, the critic must accept, according to Fish, that Milton's is an unchanging mind; that his vision is coherent, harmonious, and unified; that the function of criticism is not to put meaning into play, but to arrest its play – to isolate, determine, and proclaim the meaning, the single meaning, of a text. In a counter move, prizing multi-perspectivism and pluralism, the New Milton Criticism, in the words of Peter C. Herman and Elizabeth Sauer, recognizes "uncertainty as a constituent element of Milton studies" and seizes upon it as an opportunity, rather than an embarrassment. Sauer, in her essay on *Samson Agonistes*, also shows how the New Milton Criticism "disables" conventional readings of this poem with "counter-narratives," which speak to "the coexistence of multiple truths," while mirroring "different sides of the conflict," thus assuring us that in the New Milton Criticism there is something *new*. The New Milton Criticism has its own Blakean mantra: the eye altering alters all.

II: MILTON CRITICISM AT A CROSSROADS

Milton criticism is cumulative, and while it may not repeat itself, it does rhyme. The controversy over Miltonic certainty and the critical attempt at imposing orthodoxy has been in place for centuries now. We see this paradigm at work in the controversy that resurfaced in the 1990s over the authorship of *De Doctrina Christiana* – in the argument that because the radical theology of Milton's treatise clashes with the supposed orthodoxy of his epic poem, he cannot possibly have authored *De Doctrina*.[23] We see it also in the Milton Controversy with its staggering swoop from Denis Saurat to William Empson, with C. S. Lewis and John S. Diekhoff ranged against A. J. A. Waldock and John Peter, with Stanley Fish making a crucial intervention in which he explains – or hopes to explain away – fissures, conflicts, and contradictions in Milton's poetry by subsuming them within strategies of reader entanglement and harassment. An aesthetic resolution masks an ideological problem, providing cover for a traditionalist Milton, and with that, and with the appeasement of Lewis and Diekhoff, controversy abated – abated despite the fact that Fish's theorizing had all the potentiality, still untapped, to root out orthodoxies from Milton's poetry, thus subtending the poet of a New Milton Criticism, especially when Fish's ideas of reader harassment, textual entanglement, and self-consuming artifacts are traced back to a biblical poetics founded upon the Book of Revelation and secured by the poetics of prophecy.

The Milton Controversy, at least in its twentieth-century manifestations, is inaugurated, as Jeffrey Shoulson demonstrates, by Denis Saurat, who amasses many of the narrative and theological inconsistencies of which a subsequent criticism would sanitize the poem, but to which the New Milton Criticism gives renewed attention. Saurat anticipates many of its arguments with critical orthodoxies, while in his conclusions anticipating Christopher Hill by "put[ting] Milton in company ... [with] the most radical religious and political writers of the seventeenth century."[24] Saurat probably let Empson know as well that playing still another card, and thereby exposing ideological conflicts, he could move Milton criticism in a completely different direction. After all, Saurat – and later Waldock, Empson, and Peter – foreground everything that C. S. Lewis would hide in the basement of *Paradise Lost*: unbearable stresses, perplexing ambiguities, nagging inconsistencies, unsettling contradictions, mystifying imperfections; narrative presentation and narrator's commentary pulling oppositely; a language and a style both of which seem more like "a screening haze than a lucid medium"[25] and finally broken, often difficult, sometimes mysterious, narrative sequences with menacing undercurrents. Fissures and contradictions, for Waldock opening upon a chasm into which Milton's poem was splintering, for Empson spilled into a cauldron in which those splinterings began to coalesce. If Milton's God was the chief problem in *Paradise Lost*, the epicenter of its difficulties, cruxes were resolved and obstacles surmounted in the understanding that *Paradise Lost* is a great poem not despite, but because of, Milton's God; because of the theological quagmires and metaphysical bramble bushes He introduces to Milton's poem. Milton's God is thus the emanating center for the fields of conflict and contradiction that provide *Paradise Lost* with its variegated landscape.

Much, of course, has happened since the Milton controversy of the mid-twentieth century. We have lived through the reign and, Fish insists, demise of theory at the very time that the profession of English letters was undergoing a sea-change. The appeal, *let's theorize*, was accompanied by another, *let's diversify*. English programs became umbrellas for the humanities and sometimes social sciences – and thereupon the chief sponsors for interdisciplinary study, at which point the physical sciences joined the mix. The culture wars of our time may imply that theology and poetry, science and religion are at odds, but the lesson to be learned from *Paradise Lost* is that the great fissures, the gaping contradictions are within poems, inside of hermeneutic traditions, internal to scientific discourses. Milton taught Coleridge perhaps, and still needs to teach us: "Nothing can be more absurd than this belief of the necessary opposition of poetry and science. In all great poets the reverse is manifest."[26] In Milton, as Richard Strier remarks, "Genesis and Lucretius happily mix," and in that mix we begin to witness Milton's exhilarating iconoclasm. Citing Angus Fletcher, Jonathan Goldberg is right to remind us that "Galileo is … the only contemporary of Milton's named in *Paradise Lost*," positing with Fletcher "congruence" between Galileo's science and Milton's poetics.[27]

Before searching any further into self-proclaimed examples of the New Milton Criticism, we should look selectively outside of it, long enough to acknowledge that Milton criticism is, almost obsessively so, in the process of rewriting itself. Some obvious examples are Erik Gray's *Milton and the Victorians* (2009), a redoing of James G. Nelson's *The Sublime Puritan* (1963), which cops Nelson's subtitle for its own title; Jonathon Shears's *The Romantic Legacy of "Paradise Lost"* (2009), which revisits both Joseph A. Wittreich's *The Romantics on Milton* (1970) and *Visionary Poetics: Milton's Tradition and His Legacy* (1979), along with Leslie Brisman's *Milton's Poetry of Choice and Its Romantic Heirs* (1973), as well as many intervening books, chief among them Lucy Newlyn's *"Paradise Lost" and the Romantic Reader* (1993); and Feisal G. Mohamed's *In the Anteroom of Divinity: The Reformation of the Angels from Colet to Milton* (2008), as well as Joad Raymond's *Milton's Angels: The Early-Modern Imagination* (2010), both of which rethink Robert West's *Milton and the Angels* (1955). Last, and most interestingly, Joanna Picciotto's *Labors of Innocence in Early Modern England* (2010) is the latest in a long list of titles harking back to Kester Svendsen's *Milton and Science* (1956) and Walter Clyde Curry's *Milton's Ontology, Cosmogony and Physics* (1957) – books in which poetry and science are reconciled but, in the case of Svendsen certainly, in ways that suggest that it is the old science, not the new – surely not Galileo, surely not "conflicting cosmological theories" – which matter to Milton.

The question of contradiction and incertitude has also started to make inroads, as indicated by Michael Lieb's acknowledgment that, "If there are contradictions, then there are contradictions."[28] The same point is augmented, indeed magnified, by Abraham Stoll as he explains the narrative problems, especially in Milton's last poems, most of which derive from Milton's God, his monotheism, and thus from a "fundamental disjunction between the monotheistic God and narrative," wherein "gaps and contradictions ... can be read as the markers of the Bible's monotheistic narrative" that, transplanted into Milton's poems, become defining features of their narrative art.[29] Tensions and contradictions, which are aspects of the stories Milton inherits, as well as of the instruments he deploys in their telling, invigorate (rather than stymie) generic interplay and conflict. Thus, as Balachandra Rajan observes, "*Paradise Lost* presents itself as not only a mixed-genre poem but as a mixed-genre poem of deep generic uncertainty."[30]

These books, without themselves openly subscribing to the tenets of the New Milton Criticism, emerge from a critical climate, which Bryson, Herman, and Sauer have created – not, however, without the assistance of precursors like Harold Bloom, Christopher Hill, Balachandra Rajan, John Shawcross, and Jackie DiSalvo. Indeed, these critics may be said to inhabit the climate, even to contribute to the climate out of which the self-identified New Milton critics are themselves emerging; and they serve as a reminder that it is primarily Milton's poems (rather than the critics' reactions to them) which spark controversy and are sites of contestation for readers. The foundation stone of the New Milton Criticism is the recognition that, in Strier's words, "*Paradise Lost* is a poem deeply divided against itself." If Milton writes in fetters when he writes of God and the Angels, he also writes without them in "the presentation of Eden and of unfallen human life within it." Strier quickly tells us that while his is not another Satanist reading of the poem, it nonetheless shares common ground with the Satanists, as, for example, his insistence that: "[t]he difficult question is not how to think about Satan but how to think about Satan's portrayal of God." From this question tumble forth others: what are we to think about Raphael's portrayal of God, couched in his explanation: "For I that Day was absent ... / ... (such command we had) / To see that none thence issu'd forth a spie, / Or enemie, while God was in his work, / Least hee incenst at such eruption bold, / Destruction with Creation might have mixt" (8.229, 232–6)? This God is not only an overseer of Creation but, potentially, its saboteur. In the attention he gives to the deep divide in *Paradise Lost*, Strier necessarily notices Milton's "anomalous position of admiring the fallen angels." Like Blake, Strier does not get stuck in the first two books of Milton's poem; if anything, he focuses on Book 4, which reportedly Blake and his wife read aloud as they sat nude in their garden.

A New Milton Criticism endows *Paradise Lost* with another center of gravity, as well as changing inflections. Its interest reaches beyond the narrator's voice to narrative voices, and then to the questions of whether some are privileged and, more challengingly, to an assessment of the relative reliability of those often competing voices. Less concerned with mounting a critique of Milton than with examining Milton's critiques, especially of God, the New Milton Criticism, acknowledging that Milton often engages in what John Rogers calls "oblique questioning," gives full attention to Milton's interrogations, both theological and political, even when that means entering upon hitherto forbidden spaces of discourse. In Rogers's words, "Why Milton constantly presses the heretical view that God's decree to create the Son, and in fact all the decrees issued by God, are not necessary acts, but contingent, arbitrary, fundamentally unnecessary acts, is not a question that Milton scholars have attempted to pursue." Yet Rogers also knows that if there is a "radical creaturely freedom" to be found in Milton's thought, it "emerges not in spite of, but because of, the dread phenomenon that Satan labels, provocatively, and on some level justly, the 'Tyranny of Heav'n.'" It is here that Rogers and Bryson and, outside the Herman–Sauer collection, Stuart Curran, lock arms.[31]

Still, the concluding essays in this volume also make us wonder again: just how *new* is the New Milton Criticism, and how viable are its assertions? If the New Milton Criticism finds its forebears not only in Blake and Shelley but, quite powerfully, in Saurat, Empson, and Rajan, it also learns from them to turn its strategies of questioning and critique upon itself. Early on in this volume, Rogers raises the specter that Kolbrener revisits as he frets over "the poet's commitment to, and perhaps even faith in, a paradoxical *certain* form of 'incertitude.'" Kolbrener brings this problem to the fore again when he asks "whether the alternative to the Miltonic poet of 'certainty' is really the Milton of 'conflict, ambivalence, and open-endedness.'" That is, perhaps Milton "as a poet of indeterminacy is as similarly incomplete a construct as that of Milton as the poet of certitude … so perhaps a Milton criticism founded on 'uncertainty' [is] simply providing an equally partial counter-image to the Milton of 'certainty.'"

What Kolbrener calls for is a Milton "not reduced to caricature, or philosophical simplicity," "not a Milton mired in contradictions," but rather one who continues to "confound our expectations." What he gets in response – indeed, the yield of this collection, one hopes – is a criticism newly sensitized to, not smothered by, tensions and conflicts in Milton's poetry. One hopes for a criticism of new opportunities because it will possess a wider circumference, expanded and remapped borders, and a new audacity, and because its altering eyes and refined, as well as re-inflected, voices, will keep modifying the past and how the present perceives it. The New Milton Criticism does not allow us to forget that Milton's last poems are written in a language of uncertainty; that what Joanna Picciotto calls their "deferral of certainty" is the crucial element in an experimental poetics that, making "uncertainty productive, and therefore redemptive," is simultaneously a means of refining insight and of inciting intervention.[32]

Indeed, this New Milton Criticism, whether acknowledged as such or not, is emerging as the dominant mode of discourse in Milton studies. Milton's poetry, as Theo Hobson observes of *Paradise Lost*, is "uniquely critic-proof"[33] in as much as every interpretation, especially of *Paradise Lost*, seems to contain the seeds of its own destruction, and in as much as the last poems collectively press for a shift in mythic paradigms, thereby renewing the myths by which our culture continues to live. *Certainty* has been, but no longer is, "the default assumption" in Milton criticism, which, as Andrew Mattison demonstrates, is increasingly open to "Milton's pluralism," whether in the form of generic ambiguity, riddling contradiction, or interpretive uncertainty, all of which are aspects of a world wherein deception curtails perception, indeed creates a crisis in perception.[34] But, as Christopher D'Addario goes on to show, these strategies are allied with others such as negative prefixes, proliferating "or's," a litany of "seems," semantic confusions, and scrambled syntax so as to create through "linguistic uncertainties" a "poetics of negation and option," where the options themselves are typically "uncertain and "unresolved."[35]

"Miltonic uncertainty" (to use David Ainsworth's phrase)[36] has become a recurring theme in Milton studies, with Milton's own stories from *Areopagitica* of building God's temple, but not without "brotherly dissimilitudes" (*CPW* 2:555); of truth scattered, then recovered, but never completely so "till her Masters second comming" (*CPW* 2:549–50); of truth "in a perpetual progression" until it "sicken[s] into a muddy pool of conformity and tradition" (*CPW* 2:543) – these stories in concert underscore the perversions of truth in the fallen world, as well as its provisionary status. Moreover, such perversions infect Scripture, which, itself tainted by "superstitions and traditions," cannot, as *Paradise Lost* attests, "but by the Spirit [be] understood" (12.512, 514). Milton's own acknowledgment of scrambled chronology in the Hebrew Bible and of textual corruption in the Christian Bible, together with his insistence upon the gradual emergence of truth, and upon ongoing revelation in *De Doctrina Christiana* (*CPW* 6:589–90) further ballast his assertions concerning the contingency of truth, its uncertainty, and also its provisionary nature owing to interpretive tangles, blurred vision, and flawed perceptions, all of which are the burdens of interpretation in the fallen world.

The New Milton Criticism means to blaze the way for a criticism alert to fault lines, awaiting controversy, and refitting Milton to a twenty-first-century mind that is finally less taken with certainties, or uncertainties, than with the productive jostling of both – their potentiality for enlarging the mind by confounding its expectations and for advancing learning by eliminating some still large perceptual gaps in our understanding.

The New Milton Criticism also gives us Milton as a global figure, a cultural icon, a person of world importance, who, if hidden away by some, is now unmasked by others, especially within the popular culture, and who, as now revealed by those with a new story to tell, was a friend, not an enemy, of the theater, interested in its role in revolution, as Nigel Smith insists, and providing us not with redactions of Scripture, but with new revelations. If his last poems are Christian, they are also poems that, from an orthodox point of view, as Smith acknowledges, are "heretical and full of forbidden knowledge, through and through."[37] Here, once again, we are shocked into the recognition that poets sometimes deliver messages at odds with those with which they are credited. As Herman Melville reminds us of a doubting Milton, of Milton as "an Infidel," he also alerts us to a poetry full of "many profound atheistical hits"; of a poetry "Put into Satan's mouth, but spoken with John Milton's tongue," in ways that convey "strong controversial meaning." Thus, Milton's is a poetry with what Melville calls "a twist"[38] – a poetry in which, increasingly, answers come in the form of questions. It is also a poetry in which, as has been said of Abraham Lincoln, Milton's personal mythology becomes "our national mythology … calling us to our destiny."[39] The New Milton Criticism is presenting its Milton on a vaster canvas and weaving him into huger conversations – literary, critical, theoretical, historical, cultural, and global. So doing, it is moving Milton studies to a new location, making for it a new future, and allowing it to dwell in new possibilities. With this gathering of essays, a *new* criticism beckons Miltonists, especially the newest generation of them, to ride its wave, albeit with the intention of making new ones.

NOTES

1. Gordon Teskey, "Recent Studies in the English Renaissance," *Studies in English Literature 1500–1900* 50 (2010), 244.
2. Louis Menand, "Introduction" to Sigmund Freud, *Civilization and Its Discontents*, James Strachey (trans.) (New York: W. W. Norton, 2005), p. 9.
3. Ibid.
4. Richard Corum, "In White Ink: *Paradise Lost* and Milton's Idea of Women," in Julia Walker (ed.), *Milton and the Idea of Women* (Urbana: University of Illinois Press, 1988), p. 142.
5. Balachandra Rajan, *The Form of the Unfinished: English Poetics from Spenser to Pound* (Princeton University Press, 1985), p. 106.
6. Edward Phillips, "The Life of Milton," in Merritt Y. Hughes (ed.), *John Milton: Complete Poems and Major Prose* (New York: Odyssey Press, 1957), p. 1034.
7. Stanley Fish, *How Milton Works* (Cambridge, MA: Harvard University Press, 2001), p. 5.
8. See Joseph A. Wittreich, *Why Milton Matters: A New Preface to His Writings* (New York: Palgrave Macmillan, 2006), pp. 118–21 (for Hobart), p. 126 (for Benthem and Haak), pp. 72–3, 81, 124–31 (for Barrow and Marvell), p. 122 (for Ellwood), and p. 82 (for Dryden and Thomas Brown).
9. The dedicatory poems by Samuel Barrow and Andrew Marvell are cited from the Lewalski edition of *Paradise Lost*. Citations of other poems are from John Carey (ed.), *John Milton: Complete Shorter Poems*, 2nd rev. edn. (London and New York: Longman, 2007).
10. Annabel Patterson, *Censorship and Interpretation: The Conditions of Writing and Reading in Early Modern England* (Madison: University of Wisconsin Press, 1984), p. 15; Annabel Patterson, *Early Modern Liberalism* (Cambridge University Press, 1997), p. 59.
11. Annabel Patterson, *Reading Between the Lines* (Madison: University of Wisconsin Press, 1993), p. 241.
12. Percy Bysshe Shelley, in Joseph A. Wittreich (ed.), *The Romantics on Milton: Formal Essays and Critical Asides* (Cleveland: Press of Case Western Reserve University, 1970), p. 537.
13. Samuel Taylor Coleridge, in Wittreich (ed.), *The Romantics on Milton*, pp. 157, 161, 211.
14. Stephen M. Fallon, "Certain My Resolution: Contradiction Versus Uncertainty in Milton," The Ninth International Milton Symposium, University of London, July 11, 2008.
15. See Sir Allen Apsley (now attributed to Lucy Hutchinson), *Order and Disorder: Or, the World Made and Undone. Being Meditations Upon the Creation and the Fall; As It is Recorded in the Beginning of Genesis* (London: printed by Margaret White for Henry Mortlock, 1679), unpaginated Preface. Hereafter, the "Apsley" volume will be identified as Hutchinson. On this attribution, see especially David Norbrook, "John Milton, Lucy Hutchinson and the Republican Biblical Epic," in Mark R. Kelley, Michael Lieb, and

John T. Shawcross (eds.), *Milton and the Grounds of Contention* (Pittsburgh: Duquesne University Press, 2003), pp. 37–63.
16 Hutchinson, *Order and Disorder*, unpaginated Preface.
17 Ibid. Hutchinson's words, my emphasis, and 13 (again my emphasis).
18 I am indebted to Peter C. Herman for directing me to Elizabeth Bobo, "Advertising in *The Spectator* and the Early Eighteenth-Century Promotion of *Paradise Lost*." For the Advertisement, see *The Spectator*, no. 302 (Friday, February 15, 1712).
19 R. Michael Bowerman, "Headnote," in Irving N. Rothman and R. Michael Bowerman (eds.), Daniel Defoe, *The Political History of the Devil* [1726], (New York: AMS Press, 2003), p. xxvii, and Defoe, *The Political History of the Devil*, p. 28.
20 Bowerman, "Headnote," p. lxii, and Defoe, *Political History*, p. 35 (cf. p. 33 and Bowerman, p. lix), pp. 54, 13, 23, 28, 35 (cf. Bowerman, p. lix, p. 33).
21 Rosemary Radford Ruether, *Gregory of Nazianzus: Rhetor and Philosopher* (Oxford: Clarendon Press, 1969), p. 174.
22 Christopher Hill, *The English Bible and the Seventeenth-Century Revolution* (London: Allen Lane, and New York: Penguin, 1993), p. 373.
23 William B. Hunter, *Visitation Unimplor'd: Milton and the Authorship of "De Doctrina Christiana"* (Pittsburgh: Duquesne University Press, 1998).
24 Cf. Christopher Hill, *Milton and the English Revolution* (New York: Viking Press, 1977); and Christopher Hill, *The Experience of Defeat: Milton and Some Contemporaries* (New York: Viking Press, 1984).
25 John Peter, *A Critique of "Paradise Lost"* [1960]; reprint (New York: Columbia University Press, and London: Longmans, 1962), p. 164.
26 Coleridge, in Wittreich (ed.), *The Romantics on Milton*, p. 276.
27 Jonathan Goldberg, *The Seeds of Things: Theorizing Sexuality and Materiality in Renaissance Representations* (New York: Fordham University Press, 2009), p. 193. Cf. Angus Fletcher, *Time, Space, and Motion in the Age of Shakespeare* (Cambridge, MA: Harvard University Press, 2007), pp. 30–51.
28 Michael Lieb, *Theological Milton: Deity, Discourse and Heresy in the Miltonic Canon* (Pittsburgh: Duquesne University Press, 2006), p. 123.
29 Abraham Stoll, *Milton and Monotheism* (Pittsburgh: Duquesne University Press, 2009), pp. 14, 15.
30 Balachandra Rajan, *The Form of the Unfinished: English Poetics from Spenser to Pound* (Princeton University Press, 1985), p. 118.
31 In this volume, see Rogers, pp. 82, 68–84, and Bryson, pp. 102–19; but see also Michael Bryson, *The Tyranny of Heaven: Milton's Rejection of God as King* (Newark: University of Delaware Press, 2004); and Stuart Curran, "God," in Nicholas McDowell and Nigel Smith (eds.), *The Oxford Handbook to Milton* (Oxford University Press, 2009), pp. 648–57.
32 Joanna Picciotto, *Labors of Innocence in Early Modern England* (Cambridge, MA: Harvard University Press, 2011), pp. 439, 462, but also pp. 497, 499. On Milton's language of uncertainty, see ibid., p. 545.

33 Theo Hobson, *Milton's Vision: The Birth of Christian Liberty* (London: Continuum, 2008), p. 52.
34 Andrew Mattison, *Milton's Uncertain Eden: Understanding Place in "Paradise Lost"* (New York: Routledge, 2009), pp. 6, 15, but see also pp. 3, 7, 10, 79, 90, 141, 157.
35 Christopher D'Addario, *Exile and Journey in Seventeenth-Century Literature* (Cambridge University Press, 2007), p. 122.
36 David Ainsworth, *Milton and the Spiritual Reader: Reading and Religion in Seventeenth-Century England* (New York and London: Routledge, 2008), p. 6.
37 Nigel Smith, *Is Milton Better Than Shakespeare?* (Cambridge, MA: Harvard University Press, 2008), p. 167; see also p. 166; and on "the role of theater during a revolution," p. 94.
38 See Herman Melville's annotations, in Robin Grey (ed.), *Melville and Milton: An Edition and Analysis of Melville's Annotations to Milton* (Pittsburgh: Duquesne University Press, 2004), pp. 121, 158, 173, 187.
39 See Mario M. Cuomo, *Why Lincoln Matters: Today More Than Ever* (New York: Harcourt, 2004), p. 12.

Index

Achinstein, Sharon, 20n45, 20n42, 21n52, 123, 134n39, 190n6, 212
"Ad Patrem," 113, 146
Adams, Robert, 201
Addison, Joseph, 48n45, 232, 235
Aeneid, 39
Agamben, Giorgio, 98
Agrippa, Cornelius, 158
Ainsworth, David, 244
Allen, Michael J., 61
Alpers, Paul J., 207n1
Ames, William, 79
An Answer to a Book, Intituled, The Doctrine and Discipline of Divorce, 139
An Apology Against a Pamphlet, 140
An Apology for Smectymnuus, 141, 142
Anderson, Judith, 67n46
Animadversions, 143
Anti-Trinitarianism, 26
Areopagitica, 97, 143, 145–6, 147, 149, 151, 152, 175, 224, 244
Arianism, 72, 234
Aristotle, 44, 127
Arius, 80
Arminius, 26, 28
Art of Logic, 29
Asals, Heather, 124
Astell, Mary, 156, 163–6
Athanasius, 72, 82n8
Austin, John L., 213

Bailey, Margaret Lewis, 209n12
Baker, John H., 53
Bakhtin, Mikhail, 9
Bal, Mieke, 126
Barker, Arthur, 10
Barrow, Samuel, 232, 233
Barthes, Roland, 205
Bauman, Michael, 82n5
Bayley v. Merrel, 54
Belsey, Catherine, 10

Bennett, Joan, 128, 141, 196
Benthem, H. L., 232
Bentley, Richard, 6–7, 216, 217, 219, 222–3, 224, 229n37, 232
Bernardus Sylvestris, 184
Biberman, Matthew, 173n2, 210n25
Blake, William, 25, 243
Bloom, Harold, 242
Bobo, Elizabeth, 17–18n16, 247n18
Boesky, Amy, 86, 99n4
Book of Judges, 126, 128
Bourdette, Richard, 227n17
Brisman, Leslie, 241
Bruno, Giordano, 217
Bryson, Michael, 12, 46n21, 68, 69, 70, 76, 99n5, 122, 200, 242
Burke, Peter, 225
Burns, Norman, 128
Burrow, Colin, 212
Bush, George W., 59
Butler, Martin, 174n17
Butterfield v. Forrester, 53

Calvin, Jean, 26, 72
Cambridge School, 212, 214, 215, 225
Carey, John, 130–1
Cassirer, Ernst, 28
Chaplin, Gregory, 98
Charles I, 69
Chudleigh, Mary, 156, 169–72
Cohen, Leonard, 98
Colasterion, 139–40, 148
Coleridge, Samuel, 234
Collingwood, R. G., 190
Comyns, John, 50
Contributory negligence, 50–5
Corns, Thomas N., 11, 214, 225
Cromwell, Oliver, 69
Curry, Walter Clyde, 241

D'Addario, Christopher, 244

Index

Danielson, Dennis, 102, 193n48
Dante, 38, 184
De Doctrina Christiana: see *On Christian Doctrine*
de Molina, Luis, 80, 84n17
Defence of the People of England, 35
Defoe, Daniel, 232, 234, 235–6
Dennis, John, 5, 232
Deuteronomy 6:16, 116
Diekhoff, John S., 239
DiSalvo, Jackie, 242
Dobranski, Stephen B., 20n41, 101n18, 135
Dobranski, Stephen and John Rumrich, 206
Doctrine and Discipline of Divorce, 144, 145, 148, 151
Dryden, John, 232, 233, 234, 235
The State of Innocence, 4–5
Duncan, Joseph E., 42
Dzelzainis, Martin, 83n15

Eikon Basilike, 144, 148
Eikonoklastes, 68, 142, 144, 148, 149
Eliot, T. S., 8, 197–8, 202, 203
Ellwood, Thomas, 232
Empson, William, 5, 6, 7, 8, 25, 30, 47n41, 68, 75, 83n13, 100n9, 120, 121, 123, 127, 135n53, 194, 199, 201, 203, 239, 240, 243
Erasmus, 26
Evans, J. Martin, 9, 12
Eve
  and portrayal by women poets, 158–66

Fallon, M. Stephen, 21n52, 45–6n18, 47n32, 66n44, 147, 206, 215, 224, 234
Ferry, Anne D., 8
Fish, Stanley, 9, 10, 11, 21n52, 102, 118n17, 122, 129, 130, 195, 203, 206, 210n25, 227n13, 232, 234, 239
Fitzherbert, Sir Anthony, 51, 60
Flannagan, Roy, 2
Fleming, James Dougal, 86, 93
Fowler v. Sanders, 54
Fowler, Alastair, 86, 185
Fox, George, 103
Freedman, Carl, 198
Freedman, Jonathan, 203
Freud, Sigmund, 178
Froula, Christine, 173n16
Frye, Northrop, 182
Frye, Roland M., 2
Fulgentius, 184

Gay, David, 123
Gnosticism, 104–5
God
  representation of, 102

Goldberg, Jonathan, 10
Goodwin, John, 145
Gospel of Philip, 105, 114, 115
Gospel of Thomas, 105, 114
Gray, Erika, 241
Greenlaw, Edwin, 196
Gregerson, Linda, 2
Grose, Christopher, 2
Grotius, Hugo, 160
Guibbory, Achsah, 124, 129
Guillory, John, 9, 179, 223

Haak, Theodore, 232
Hampton, Bryan Adams, 2
Hanford, James Holly, 195–6
Harris, James A., 84n19
Hegel, George Wilhelm Friedrich, 190
Herman, Peter C., 12, 46n24, 68, 69–70, 76, 99, 100n10, 121, 202, 207, 216, 224, 234, 242
Herman, Peter C. and Elizabeth Sauer, 232, 239
Herz, Judith, 238
Hill, Christopher, 120, 121, 131n2, 141, 154n6, 239, 240, 242
Hobart, Sir John, 3, 232
Hobbes, Thomas, 81, 219
Hobson, Theo, 244
Hooker, Richard, 141
Hornsby, Samuel, 124
Hoxby, Blair, 86
Hume, Patrick, 179
Hunter, William B., 26
Hutchinson, Lucy, 232, 234–5
Hyppolytus, 103

Iraeneus, 103
"Il Penseroso," 113

Jacob, Margaret C., 217
Jael, 126, 128
Jauss, Hans, 50
Jeremiad, and Milton's early prose, 142
Johns, Adrian, 145
Johnson, Samuel, 185
Josephus, 129
Judges, 127
Judith, 126

Kabbalah
  and John Milton, 197
Kahn, Victoria, 83n16, 127
Kelley, Maurice, 26, 76
Kendrick, Christopher, 205, 207
Kerrigan, William, 3, 206, 210n24
Kezar, Dennis, 132n9

Index

Knoppers, Laura, 20n42
Kolbrener, William, 12, 209n21, 228n17, 232, 243

Lane v. Cotton, 51
Lane, Christopher, 225
Lanyer, Aemilia, 156, 157, 167–8
Lear, Jonathan, 188
Leavis, F. R., 8, 194, 198, 203
Lee, Nathaniel, 4
Leibniz, Gottfried, 216
Lenhof, Kent, 100n15
Leonard, John, 100n14
Lewalski, Barbara, 9, 119n20, 128
Lewis, C. S., 35, 102, 120, 185, 199, 239, 240
Lieb, Michael, 242
Liljegren, S. B., 201
Lincoln, Abraham, 245
Locke, John, 216
Loewenstein, David, 20n42, 103
Longfellow, Erica, 174n18
Lovejoy, A. O., 28
Lovejoy, Arthur, 218
Luke 4:1–13, 108
Luther, Martin, 26, 27
Lycidas, 237

Macey, Jr., J. David, 164
Machiavelli, Niccolo, 81
Marprelate Tracts, 154n10
Martin, Catherine Gimelli, 158, 190n5
Martindale, Charles, 184
Martz, Louis, 9
Marvell, Andrew, 232, 233
  "On *Paradise Lost*," 4–5
Matthew 4:1–11, 108
Mattison, Andrew, 244
Mazzoni, Giacopo, 184
McBride, Kari, 158
McColley, Diane K., 9, 48n43, 188
McColley, Grant, 86
McGrath, Lynne, 174n18
Melbourne, Jane, 129
Melville, Herman, 245
Menand, Louis, 231
Miller, Shannon, 158, 190n2
Milton Controversy, 194, 197–200, 239–40
Milton criticism
  and "author-function," 205
  and "critical idolatry," 102
  and imposition of certainty, 1–11, 232–9
  and "unifying imperative," 8–11, 120
  compared with Shakespeare studies, 205
Milton, John, 187
  and dissatisfaction with Presbyterians, 147
  and first marriage, 146
  and Gnosticism, 103
  and inevitability of Restoration, 147
  and Jael, 127
  and misogyny, 178
  and monism, 221–2
  and sense of isolation, 146
  and "theory of obligation," 77–8
  as poet of ambivalence, 232
  early pamphlets and denunciation, 140
  faultlines in theories of liberty, 141–53
  knowledge of law, 50
  politics of, 77–8
  rationalism, 25–9
  special class of writer, 231
Mitchell v. Allestry, 52
Mitchell, J. Allan, 67n45
Mohamed, Feisal G., 19n36, 60, 123, 130, 131, 241
Mueller, Janel, 206
Mulryan, John, 116

Nag Hammadi, 103
Nelson, James G., 241
neo-Christian Milton Criticism, 120–1, 201, 202
New Criticism, 199, 203, 205, 213, 225
New Historicism, 10, 205
New Milton Criticism, 10, 11–12, 175, 194, 200, 202, 206, 214, 225, 226, 232, 238–9, 240, 242, 245
  and Shakespeare studies, 3
Newlyn, Lucy, 20n45, 241
Newton, Sir Isaac, 217, 218–20
Newton, Thomas, 175, 178, 180, 186, 224
Norbrook, David, 4, 212
Nuttall, A. D., 17n12
Nyquist, Mary, 11, 192n34
Nyquist, Mary and Margaret W. Ferguson, 10, 17n5

Of Education, 146
On Christian Doctrine, 25–9, 37, 72, 76, 77, 79, 102, 104, 117, 127, 197, 239, 245
Overton, Richard, 197
Ovid, 178, 179, 180, 182, 184
Owen, John, 82n9

Parable of the talents, 140
Paradise Lost
  Abdiel, 32–3, 74
  Adam, 80, 92, 158, 160, 161, 166, 177, 183
  Adam and Eve, 42
  Adam, and Raphael, 61–3
  and contradictions, 236–8
  and early women readers, 175
  and elective affinities, 76–82
  and foreknowledge, 91

Paradise Lost (*cont.*)
  and imposition of certainty, 1–11, 232–9
  and liberatory politics, 77
  and "meanwhile," 86–7, 93–7
  and "now," 88–9
  and problem of gender, 157–8
  and problem of narrator, 236
  and problem of temporality, 85–99
  and publishing history, 97
  and science, 241
  and the gaze, 168–9
  and women poets, 156–72
  Angels, collective failure and the Fall, 60
  Belial, 31
  Book 5 and "meanwhile," 91–2
  cosmology, complexity of, 223–4
  Death, 60
  Eden, 41, 85
  Elevation of the Son, 32, 73–4
  Eve, 107, 158, 159, 161–2
  Eve, and contrition, 184
  Eve, early reception of birth story, 177–84
  Eve, response to Adam's misogyny, 185
  Evil, 43
  Gabriel, 60, 88
  God, 5, 25, 35–7, 60, 68, 74, 161, 166, 178, 221, 240, 243
  God and "meanwhile," 89–90
  God, and indifference to Eve, 63–4
  God, and negligent chaining of Satan, 55–7
  God, gives Sin key to Hell, 57–8
  Heaven, and earthly political structure, 81
  Heaven, politics of, 31–4
  Hell, politics of, 31
  Michael, 96
  narrator, 91
  nature, 40–1
  Pilot simile, 1–3
  Plowman simile, 6, 8
  Poetics of Incertitude, 49
  political theology, 68–82
  politics, 29–40
  problem of narrator, 8–9
  Raphael, 34, 38, 91–3, 107, 183, 221
  Raphael, and contribution to the Fall, 60–4
  Raphael, and indifference to Eve, 63–4
  reception history, 232–6
  revisions of, 231
  Satan, 30, 37, 40, 42, 75, 76, 82, 85, 91, 93, 102, 106, 177, 178
  Satan, and escape from chains, 55–7
  Satan, and escape from Hell, 57–8
  Satan, and stairway to Heaven, 58–60
  Sin, 60
  Sin, and key to Hell, 57–8
Sin, narrative of origins, 93
theodicy, 25, 187–90
Uriel, 5, 40, 60, 88
Paradise Regained, 69, 72, 90, 232, 234
  and Gnosticism, 103–17
  and interiority, 115–17
  and Satan's temptations, 108–12
  and Son's rejection of classical learning, 113–15
  and the Son's rejection of temptations, 108–12
  Eve, 107
  Satan, 107
  the Son, 106–17
Parisi, Hope, 134n37
Parker, William Riley, 147
Paterson, James, 178
Patterson, Annabel, 18n24, 147, 193n48, 203, 209n15, 233
Paul, 128, 187
Pearce, Zachary, 6–7, 8, 232
Peter, John, 11, 239, 240
Phillips, Edward, 231
Picciotto, Joanna, 241, 244
Plato, 28, 114
Plotinus, 28
Pocock, J. G. A., 222, 225
Pope, Alexander, 5, 179
Post-structuralism, 10
Powell, Mary, 147, 186
Psalm 91:11–12, 116

Quakers, 103
Qvarnstrom, Gunmar, 86

Rajan, Balachandra, 9, 11, 19n34, 101n19, 223, 229n41, 231, 242, 243
Raleigh, Walter, 195, 199
Rapaport, Herman, 10, 204
Raymond, Joad, 241
Readie and Easie Way to Establish a Free Commonwealth, 97, 142, 144, 147, 148, 149, 153
Reason of Church Government, 105, 146
Reformation Trinitarianism, 72
Revard, Stella P., 46n27, 90
Richardson, Samuel, 181
Ricks, Christopher, 8
Riggs, William, 9
"Right Reason," 78
Rogers, John, 47n38, 215, 217, 224, 226, 243
Rosenblatt, Jason P., 122
Ruether, Rosemay Radford, 236
Rumrich, John P., 11, 26, 104, 120, 121, 184, 203, 206
Rust, George, 28

Index

Salandra, Serafino Della, 160
Samson Agonistes, 232
  and 9/11, 130–1
  and Dalila, revaluation of, 122–7
  and interpretive dilemmas, 121–31
  and neo-Christian readings, 121, 122
  and omission of biblical prayer, 129
  and Philistinian perspective, 125–6
  and terrorism, 123, 130
Sauer, Elizabeth, 229n41, 242
Saurat, Denis, 11, 194–207, 239, 240, 243
  and deconstruction, 204–5
  and Judaism, 201
  and New Milton Criticism, 194
Schwartz, Louis, 122
Schwartz, Regina, 104, 208n11
Sensabaugh, George, 217
Serjeantson, R. W., 127
Servetus, 26
Sewell, George, 5
Shakespeare, William
  Measure for Measure, 3
Shawcross, John T., 21n49, 117, 119n20, 124, 221, 242
Shears, Jonathan, 241
Shelley, Percy Bysshe, 25, 234, 243
Shoaf, R. A., 204
Shoulson, Jeffrey, 12, 208n4, 240
Silver, Victoria, 200, 215, 228n35
Skinner, Cyriac, 184
Skinner, Quentin, 141, 150–1, 154n7, 225–6
  and Milton Studies, 212–15
Smith, Nigel, 1, 20n42, 154n14, 211n35, 212, 245
Socinianism, 76, 234
Socrates, 113
Sonnet 19, 140
Sowernam, Ester, 156, 157, 158–63, 164
Speght, Rachel, 156, 157, 158–63, 164, 165
Spenser, Edmund, 184
Stapleton's Case, 50
Stavely, Keith, 214
Stein, Arnold, 9, 46n25
Stevens, Paul, 1, 11
Stoll, Abraham, 242
Stoll, E. E., 200
Stollman, Samuel, 128
Strier, Richard, 91, 192n42, 193n48, 241, 242
Suarez, Francis, 80, 84n18

Sumers, Alinda, 158, 167
Summers, Joseph, 120, 185
Svendsen, Kester, 241
Swanson, Donald, 116
Swetnam, Joseph, 156

Tasso, 184
Tate, Nahum, 8
Tenure of Kings and Magistrates, 68, 83n15, 105, 112, 150
Terry *v.* White, 53
Teskey, Gordon, 9, 18n27, 98, 126
Tetrachordon, 146
The Passion, 106
Theodicy, 25–9
Thorpe, James, 201
Thyer, Robert, 178, 186
Tillyard, E. M. W., 25
Toland, John, 4, 216–17, 218–23, 224, 232
Trill, Suzanne, 174n18
Trubowitz, Rachel, 215
Turner, James Grantham, 175
Tuve, Rosamond, 18n27
Twain, Mark, 188

Valentinians, 105
von Maltzahn, Nicholas, 216

Waldock, A. J. A., 11, 123, 203, 240
Walsh, Marcus, 175
Warton, Thomas, the Younger, 181
Weaver *v.* Ward, 53, 58
Welch, Anthony, 86, 94
West, Robert, 241
Wilding, Michael, 141
Williams, Bernard, 35, 40, 44
Wimsatt, W. K., 213
Wittgenstein, Ludwig, 213
Wittreich, Joseph A., 5, 9, 11, 19n36, 121, 130, 173n2, 175
Wollstonecraft, Mary, 179
Woodhouse, A. S. P., 10, 200
Worden, Blair, 20n42, 141, 150, 212

Young, Edward, 181
Young, Thomas, 181–4, 187
Yovel, Yirmiyahu, 217

Zively, Sherry Lutz, 86